CUMBRIA LIBRARIES

3 8003 04448 58

D1576589

The Mighty Dead

By the same author

Wetland: Life in the Somerset Levels
Restoration: The Rebuilding of Windsor Castle
Perch Hill: A New Life
Sea Room: An Island Life
When God Spoke English: The Making of the King James Bible
Atlantic Britain
Men of Honour: Trafalgar and the Making of the English Hero
Sissinghurst: An Unfinished History
Arcadia: The Dream of Perfection in Renaissance England
The Gentry: Stories of the English

The Mighty Dead

Why Homer Matters

ADAM NICOLSON

WILLIAM
COLLINS

William Collins
An imprint of HarperCollins*Publishers*
77–85 Fulham Palace Road,
Hammersmith, London W6 8JB
WilliamCollinsBooks.com

Published by William Collins in 2014

Copyright © Adam Nicolson 2014

1

The author asserts the moral right to be identified as the author of this work

A catalogue record for this book is available from the British Library

ISBN 13 978-0-00-733552-7
ISBN 10 0-00-733552-0

Endpaper illustration: Mural from the palace of Nestor at Pylos.
(*Courtesy of the Department of Classics, University of Cincinatti*)

Typeset in Adobe Caslon Pro by Palimpsest Book Production Ltd, Falkirk, Stirlingshire

Printed and bound in Great Britain by Clays Ltd, St Ives plc

All rights reserved. No part of this publication may be reproduced, stored in a retrieval system,
or transmitted, in any form or by any means, electronic, mechanical, photocopying, recording or
otherwise, without the prior permission of the publishers.

This book is sold subject to the condition that it shall not, by way of trade or otherwise, be lent,
re-sold, hired out or otherwise circulated without the publisher's prior consent in any form of
binding or cover other than that in which it is published and without a similar condition
including this condition being imposed on the subsequent purchaser.

FSC™ is a non-profit international organisation established to promote the responsible management of the world's forests. Products carrying the FSC label are independently certified to assure
consumers that they come from forests that are managed to meet the social, economic and
ecological needs of present and future generations, and other controlled sources.

Find out more about HarperCollins and the environment at
www.harpercollins.co.uk/green

For
Sarah Raven
Thomas Nicolson
William Nicolson
Ben Nicolson
Rosie Nicolson
&
Molly Nicolson

Contents

List of Illustrations

COLOUR PLATES

'The Mask of Agamemnon'. *(Universal History Archive/Getty Images)*

Stamnos (vase) depicting Odysseus tied to the mast listening to the songs of the Sirens, c.480 BC, Athens. *(Werner Forman/Universal Images Group/Getty Images)*

Mycenaean funerary stele with relief chariot scene, c.1600 BC. *(Photo by Adam Nicolson)*

Mycenaean gold cup, sixteenth century BC. *(National Archaeological Museum of Athens. DeAgostini/Getty Images)*

Engraving depicting an octopus on a gold cup from Tholos of Dendra, near Midea, sixteenth century BC. *(National Archaeological Museum of Athens. DeAgostini/Getty Images)*

Mycenaean gold butterfly scales from the Shaft Graves, sixteenth century BC. *(National Archaeological Museum of Athens. Photo by Adam Nicolson)*

Attic terracotta lekythos (oil flask), attributed to the Achilles Painter, c.440 BC. *(The Metropolitan Museum of Art. akg-images)*

Mycenaean gold elliptical funeral diadem, from the 'Grave of the Women', sixteenth century BC. *(National Archaeological Museum of Athens. Universal History Archive/UIG via Getty Images)*

A gold death suit for a Mycenaean child, sixteenth century BC. *(National Archaeological Museum of Athens. Photo by Adam Nicolson)*

Damascened daggers made of gold, silver, bronze and niello, from Mycenae and Pylos. *(DEA/G. DAGLI ORTI/De Agostini/Getty Images)*

Writing tablet from the Ulu Burun wreck, c.1325 BC. *(© Institute of Nautical Archaeology)*

The tower of the Acropolis in Tiryns. *(DeAgostini/Getty Images)*

Nestor's cup. *(Museum of Ischia, Italy. © Maria Grazia Casella/Alamy)*

Kantharos (drinking cup) depicting Odysseus and Nausicaa. *(© The Trustees of the British Museum. All rights reserved)*

Extremaduran warrior with shield, sword and mirror. *(Museo Arqueológico Provincial de Badajoz. Photo by Adam Nicolson)*

Stabbed Bronze Age *phalera* (horse harness ornament). *(Wiltshire Museum. Photo by Adam Nicolson)*

Extremaduran warriors with bow, spear, shield, swords, a bubble-handled mirror, what may be a musical instrument and large, man-slaughtering hands. *(Museo Arqueológico Provincial de Badajoz. Photo by Adam Nicolson)*

The Rio Odiel. *(Photo by Adam Nicolson)*

Silver gilt Cypriot bowl, c.725–675 BC. *(© The Metropolitan Museum of Art/Art Resource/Scala, Florence)*

Gold libation bowl, c.625 BC, found at Olympia, 1916. *(Museum of Fine Arts, Boston. Photo by Adam Nicolson)*

Minoan Kamares eggshell ware cup. *(Heraklion Archaeological Museum, Crete. Leemage/UIG via Getty Images)*

Ivory cosmetic case in the form of a duck. *(© The Trustees of the British Museum. All rights reserved. Photo by Adam Nicolson)*

David and Goliath by Michelangelo Merisi da Caravaggio (1571–1610), oil on canvas. *(Museo del Prado. Photo by DeAgostini/Getty Images)*

Mycenaean bronze dagger with an integral hilt and pommel, c.1300–1100 BC *(© The Trustees of the British Museum. All rights reserved)*

Wild pear tree, Ithaca. *(Photo by Adam Nicolson)*

Minoan bath, mid-fourteenth century BC. *(© Carlos Collection of Ancient Art, Emory University)*

Dionysus on a reach, surrounded by dolphins, 530 BC. *(Staatliche Antikensammlung, Munich. Ann Ronan Pictures/Print Collector/Getty Images)*

TEXT ILLUSTRATIONS

Title page: Terracotta plate depicting a poet on his death bed, musing on the past with his lyre above him, c.595–570 BC. *(© The Metropolitan Museum of Art/Art Resource/Scala, Florence)*

The World of the Ancient Greeks

N

BOSNIA-
HERZEGOVINA

SERBIA

ITALY

Adriatic Sea

MACED

Naples

Ischia

APULIA

ALBANIA

CAMPANIA

GREE

Tyrrhenian Sea

EPIRUS

TH

CALABRIA

Ionian Sea

Ithaca

Trapani

O

Sicily

Thapsos

Castelluccio

PELO

Pylos

Mediterranean Sea

0   100   200 miles

0   100   200   300 km

KEY

→   Wind

⋯▸   Current

LIBYA

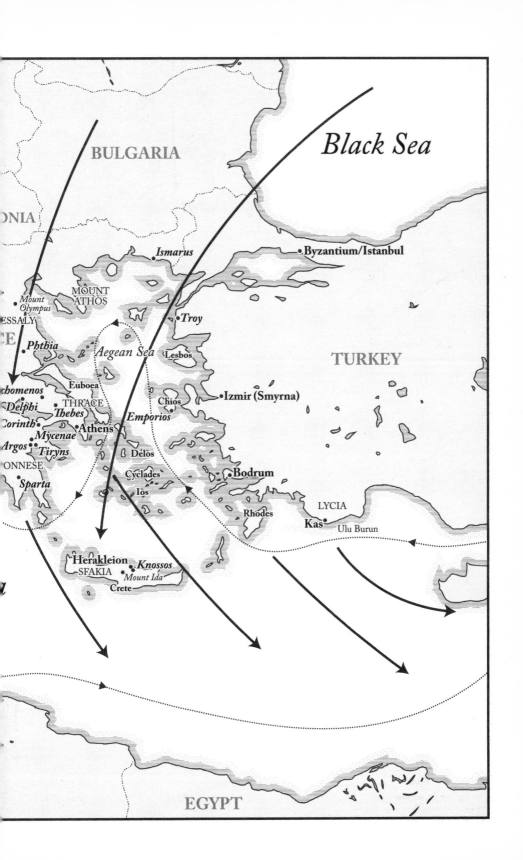

BULGARIA

Black Sea

•Byzantium/Istanbul

•Ismarus

MOUNT
ATHOS

•Troy

Mount
Olympus

ONIA

ESSALY

•Phthia

Aegean Sea

Lesbos

TURKEY

C

chomenos

Euboea

Chios

•Izmir (Smyrna)

•Delphi

THRACE

Emporios

Thebes

Corinth•

•Athens

Mycenae

Delos

Argos••
•Tiryns

ONNESE

Cyclades

•Bodrum

•Sparta

Ios

LYCIA

Rhodes

Kas•
Ulu Burun

^Herakleion
SFAKIA

Knossos

Mount Ida
Crete

The Bronze Age World

N

Faeroes

SWEDEN

Orkney Is.

Baltic
Sea

Stornoway
Hebrides

North Sea

DENMARK

BELAR

Mayo
IRELAND BRITAIN
Llandissilio Oxford Cambridge
Baltimore Cornwall London
Falmouth Wiltshire Kent

County
Durham

Bernstorf

Berlin

Pripiat
marshes

Leipzig

Bohemia

Dniester

Heidelberg

Paris

Stuttgart

Munich

Vienna

HUNGARY

The Carpathians

The Alps

Venice

ROMANIA

Atlantic Ocean

Milan

Florence

TRANSYLVANIA

BOSNIA-
HERZEGOVINA

Danube

Galicia

Massalia

Elba

Tuscany

ITALY

Bijelo Polje

MONTENEGRO

BULGARL

Porto
Madrid
SPAIN
El Pozuelo

Latium

Rome

MACEDONIA

Sardinia

Naples

ALBANIA

GREECE

Badajoz
Extremadura

Sierra de Aracena

Chinflón
Córdoba
Andalusia

Guadalquivir

Aegean
Sea

Athens

Straits of
Gibraltar

Sicily

Ionian Sea

Mycenae

Carthage

Crete

Mediterranean Sea

RUSSIA

The Urals

Sintashta

Moscow

Steppelands

KAZAKHSTAN

agod

RAINE

Dnieper

Donets

Don

Volga

Usatovo

Black Sea

The Caucasus

Caspian Sea

Sinope

Byzantium/Istanbul

y

Armenia

zmir

Hattusa

TURKEY

ANATOLIA

Nineveh

SYRIA

Palmyra

IRAQ

MESOPOTAMIA

Cyprus

Byblos

Sidon

Tyre

Canaan

Euphrates

Tigris

IRAN

Babylon

exandria

Bethlehem

Uruk

Fayum

Socoh

THE NEAR EAST

Ur

Sumer

KUWAIT

St Catherine's Monastery

Hawara

Persian Gulf

EGYPT

Nile

Thebes

Preface

THERE IS A PAIR of linked questions at the heart of this book: where does Homer come from? And why does Homer matter? These ancient poems can be daunting and difficult, but I have no doubt that their account of war and suffering can still speak to us of the role of destiny in life, of cruelty, humanity, its frailty and the pains of existence. That they do is a mystery. Why is it that something conceived in the eastern Mediterranean Bronze Age, maybe four thousand years ago, as foreign as the Dayak, as distant as Vanuatu, can still exert its grip on us? How can we be so intimate with something so far away?

Perhaps it is a mistake to give the answer before the questions are properly asked, but this is complicated country, and an idea of the destination is worth having. Besides, it is a Homeric technique to tell the story before it begins. And so, if you ask why and how the Homeric poems emerged when they did, and why and how Homer can mean so much now, the answer to both questions is the same: because Homer tells us how we became who we are.

That is not the usual modern answer. The current orthodoxy is that the *Iliad* and the *Odyssey* are both products of the eighth century BC, or thereabouts, early Iron Age Greece, a time that has been called the Greek Renaissance. In the preceding half-millennium, Greek civilisation had largely sunk into isolated pockets of poverty. Many of the islands in the Aegean were deserted. One or two had remained rich and kept up links with the Near East, but the great palaces of an earlier Greece had fallen into ruin. But for reasons that have yet to be explained, the eighth century saw a widespread revival. The population of Greece and the islands began to grow. The tempo of life quickened. The art of making bronze, dependent on imported tin, was revived for the first time in four centuries. Colonies, trade, improved ships, gymnasiums, coinage, temples, cities, pan-Hellenic competitions at Olympia (the first, traditionally, in 776 BC), the art of writing, of depicting the human figure on pottery and in the round, the first written law codes, the dating of history, the first tentative moves towards the formation of city-states: every one of these aspects of a renewed civilisation quite suddenly appeared all over the eighth-century Aegean. Homer, in this view, was the product of a new, dynamic, politically inventive and culturally burgeoning moment in Greek history. Homer was the poet of a boom.

I see it differently: my Homer is a thousand years older. His power and poetry derive not from the situation of a few emergent states in the eighth-century Aegean, but from a far bigger and more fundamental historic moment, in the centuries around 2000 BC, when early Greek civilisation crystallised from the fusion of two very different worlds: the semi-nomadic, hero-based culture of the Eurasian steppes to the north and west of the Black Sea, and the sophisticated, authoritarian and literate cities and palaces of the eastern Mediterranean. Greekness – and eventually Europeanness – emerged from the meeting and melding of those worlds. Homer is the trace of that encounter – in war, despair and eventual reconciliation at Troy in the *Iliad*, in flexibility and mutual absorption in the *Odyssey*. Homer's urgency comes from the pain associated with that clash of worlds and his immediacy from the eternal principles at stake: what matters more, the individual or the community, the city or the hero? What is life, something of everlasting value or a transient and hopeless irrelevance?

The idea I have pursued is that the Homeric poems are legends shaped around the arrival of a people – the people who through this very process would grow to be the Greeks – in what became their Mediterranean homeland. The poems are the myths of the origin of Greek consciousness, not as a perfect but as a complex, uneasy thing. As a civilisation, what emerged in Greece was distinct from both the northern steppelands of the Bronze Age and the autocratic bureaucracies of the Near East, and fused qualities of both. Homer is a foundation myth, not of man nor of the natural world, but of the way of thinking by which the Greeks defined themselves, the frame of mind which made them who they were, one which, in many ways, we have inherited. The troubled world described by Homer remains strangely familiar.

This is also a book about epic poetry, and the value of epic in our lives. Epic is not an act of memory, not merely the account of what people are able to recall, since human memory only lasts three generations: we know something of our grandparents, but almost nothing, emotionally, viscerally, of what happened in the generations before them. Nor is it a kind of history, an objective laying out of what occurred in a past to which we have little or no access. Epic, which was invented after memory and before history, occupies a third space in the human desire to connect the present to the past: it is the attempt to extend the qualities of memory over the reach of time embraced by history. Epic's purpose is to make the distant past as immediate to us as our own lives, to make the great stories of long ago beautiful and painful now.

A wonderful depiction of epic itself survives from Mycenaean Greece. In the summer of 1939, the University of Cincinnati archaeologist Carl Blegen, along with a Greek team, began excavating the Mycenaean palace of Pylos, in the south-western Peloponnese. In the great columned room at the centre of the palace, Blegen discovered, in pieces on the floor, where it had been dumped by the fire which brought the Mycenaean world to an end around 1200 BC, a revelatory fresco.

Against a ragged background, perhaps a rough, mountainous horizon, a poet – call him Homer – sits on a luminous, polychromed rock, a nightclub idea of a rock, dressed in a long striped robe with the sleeves of his overshirt coming almost halfway down his bare brown arms. His hair is braided, tendrils of it running down his neck and on to his back. He looks washed. Everything about him is alert, his eye bright and open, his body poised and taut, upright, ready. In his arms he holds a large five-stringed lyre, the fingers of his right hand plucking at those strings, which bend to his touch.

Against the florid red of the wall behind him – the colour of living, not dried blood, the red of life – is the most astonishing part of this image: an enormous, pale bird, the colour of the bard's robe, the feathers of its wings half-delineated in the red that surrounds it, its eye as bright and open as Homer's, its body larger than his, its presence in the room huge and buoyant, nothing insubstantial about it, making its way out into the world, leaving Homer's own static, singing figure behind.

The bird is poetry itself taking wing, so big, so much stronger than little Homer with his hairdo and his fingers on the lyre. It is the bird of eloquence, the 'winged words', *epea pteroenta*, which the Homeric heroes speak to each other, *epea* having the same root as 'epic', *pteroenta* meaning 'feathered': light, mobile, airy, communicative. Meaning and beauty take flight from Homer's song.

It is one of the most extraordinary visualisations of poetry ever created, its life entirely self-sufficient as it makes its way out across that ragged horizon. There is nothing whimsical or misty about it: it has an undeniable other reality in flight in the room. There is a deep paradox here, one that is central to the whole experience of Homer's epics. Nothing is more insubstantial than poetry. It has no body, and yet it persists with its subtleties whole and its sense of the reality of the human heart uneroded while the palace of which this fresco was a part lies under the thick layer of ash from its burning in 1200 BC. Nothing with less substance than epic, nothing more lasting. Homer, in a miracle of transmission from one end of human civilisation to the other, continues to be as alive as anything that has ever lived.

Homer is no wild, gothic figure. He is shown supremely controlled, as organised and calmly present as anything in this civilised place, with its great store rooms, its archive centre and its beautifully dressed and fragrant inhabitants. He is civility itself. By the time this fresco was painted, the Greeks had been able to write for about 250 years, running sophisticated palace-based economies, with record-keeping bureaucracies to organise tax and military service, and to administer complex commercial and quasi-imperial relations across the eastern Mediterranean.

If that is the world in which Homer sang, it is not the world he sang about, which was much older, rougher, more elemental. He sang of the past which the occupants of this palace had left behind. That time gap allows one to see the Homeric poems as I think they should be seen: as the violence and sense of strangeness of about 1800 BC recollected in the tranquillity of about 1300 BC, preserved through the Greek Dark Ages, and written down (if not in a final form) in about 700 BC. Homer reeks of long use. His wisdom, his presiding, god-like presence over the tales he tells, is the product of deep retrospect, not immediate reportage. His poetry embodies the air of incorporated time, as rounded as something that for centuries has rolled back and forth on the stony beaches of Greece. But it is also driven by the demands of grief, a clamouring and desperate anxiety about the nature of existence and the pains of mortality. This is the story of beginnings, and that feeling for trouble is the engine at the heart of it.

This book will make its way back towards that fresco, looking for Homer anywhere he might be found, in my own and many others' reactions to the poems, in life experiences, in archaeology and in the landscapes where the Homeric ghosts can still be heard. It is a passionate pursuit, because these epics are a description, through a particular set of lenses, of what it is like to be alive on earth, its griefs, triumphs, sufferings and glories. These are poems that address life's moments of revelation. Here you will find 'the neon edges of the sea', as Christopher Logue described the waves on the Trojan beach; the horror of existence, where 'Warm'd in the brain the smoking weapon lies', as Pope translated one murder in the *Iliad*; and its transfixing strangeness – the corona-light in the scarcely opened helmet slits of Achilles's owl-like eyes, which Logue saw burning 'like furnace doors ajar'.

In all the walking and thinking this book has given me, no moment remains more lasting in my mind than an evening on a small rocky peninsula near Tolo on the south-eastern coast of the Peloponnese. I had been thinking about George Seferis, the Greek poet and diplomat who won the Nobel Prize in 1963, and who had come here before the Second World War, when archaeologists were discovering that this little stony protuberance into the Aegean was the acropolis of Asinē, a place entirely forgotten, except that it had survived in the *Iliad* as a name, one of the cities from which Greek warriors had set out for the siege at Troy.

The sea in the bay that evening was a mild milk-grey. The puttering of the little diesel-driven fans that keep the air moving through the orchards on a frosty night came from the orange groves inland. The sky promised rain. Sitting by the sea squills and the dry grasses blowing in the wind off the Gulf of Argolis, I read what Seferis had said about our relationship to the past. 'The poem is everywhere,' he wrote. Our own imaginative life

> sometimes travels beside it
> Like a dolphin keeping company for a while
> With a golden sloop in the sunlight,
> then vanishing again.

That glowing, if passing, connection is also what this book is about, the moment when the dolphin is alongside you, unsummoned and as transient, as Seferis also said,

> As the wings of the wind moved by the wind.

ONE

Meeting Homer

ONE EVENING TEN YEARS ago I started to read Homer in English. With an old friend, George Fairhurst, I had just sailed from Falmouth to Baltimore in south-west Ireland, 250 miles across the Celtic Sea. We had set off three days earlier in our wooden ketch, the *Auk*, forty-two feet from stem to stern, a vessel which had felt big enough in Falmouth, not so big out in the Atlantic.

It had been a ruinous journey. A mile or so out from the shelter of Falmouth we realised our instruments were broken, but we had been preparing for too long, were hungry to go, and neither of us felt like turning back. A big storm came through that night, Force 8 gusting 9 to 10, west of Scilly, and we sailed by the stars when it was clear, by the compass in the storm, four hours on, four hours off, for that night, the next day and the following night. The seas at times had been huge, the whole of the bow plunging into them, burying the bowsprit up to its socket, solid water coming over the foredeck and driving back towards the wheel, so that the side-decks were like mill-sluices, running with the Atlantic.

After forty hours we arrived. George's face looked as if he had been in a fight, flushed and bruised, his eyes sunk and hollow in it. We dropped anchor in the middle of Baltimore harbour, its still water reflecting the quayside lights, only our small wake disturbing them, and I slept for sixteen hours straight. Now, the following evening, I was lying in my bunk, the *Auk* tied up alongside the Irish quay, with the *Odyssey*, translated by the great American poet-scholar Robert Fagles, in my hand.

I had never understood Homer as a boy. At school it was taught to us in Greek, as if the poems were written in maths. The master drew the symbols on the green blackboard and we ferreted out the sense line by line, picking bones from fish. The archaic nature of Homer's vocabulary, the pattern of long and short syllables in the verse, the remote and uninteresting nature of the gods, like someone else's lunchtime account of a dream from the night before: what was that to any of us? Where was the life in it? How could this remoteness compare to the urgent realities of our own lives, our own lusts and anxieties?

The difficulty and strangeness of the Greek was little more than a prison of obscurity to me, happily abandoned once the exam was done. Homer stayed irrelevant.

Now I had Fagles's words in front of me. Half idly, I had brought his translation of the *Odyssey* with me on the *Auk*, as something I thought I might look at on my own sailing journey in the North Atlantic. But as I read, a man in the middle of his life, I suddenly saw that this was not a poem about *then* and *there*, but *now* and *here*. The poem describes the inner geography of those who hear it. Every aspect of it is grand metaphor. Odysseus is not sailing on the Mediterranean but through the fears and desires of a man's life. The gods are not distant creators but elements within us: their careless pitilessness, their flaky and transient interests, their indifference, their casual selfishness, their deceit, their earth-shaking footfalls.

I read Fagles that evening, and on again as we sailed up the west coast of Ireland. I began to see Homer as a guide to life, even as a kind of scripture. The sea in the *Odyssey* was out to kill you – at one point Hermes, the presiding genius of Odysseus's life, says, 'Who would want to cross the unspeakable vastness of the sea? There are not even any cities there' – but hidden within it were all kinds of delicious islands, filled with undreamt-of delights, lovely girls and beautiful fruits, beautiful landscapes where you didn't have to work, dream lands, each in their different way seducing and threatening the man who chanced on them. But every one was bad for him. Calypso, a goddess, unbelievably beautiful, makes him sleep with her night after night, for seven years; Circe feeds him delicious dinners for a whole year, until finally one of his men asks him what he thinks he is doing. If he goes on like this, none of them will ever see their homes again. And is that what he wants?

In part I saw the *Odyssey* as the story of a man who was sailing through his own death: the sea is deathly, the islands are deathly, he visits Hades at the very centre of the poem and he is thought dead by the people who love him at home, a pile of white bones rotting on some distant shore. He longs for life and yet he cannot find it. When he hears stories told of his own past, he cannot bear it, wraps his head in his 'sea-blue' cloak and weeps for everything he has lost.

It was Odysseus I really fell in love with that summer as we sailed north to the Hebrides, Orkney and the Faroes: the many-wayed, flickering, crafty man, 'the man of twists and turns' as Fagles calls him, translating the Greek word *polytropos*, the man driven off course, the man who suffered many pains, the man who was heartsick on the open sea. His life itself was a twisting, and maybe, I thought, that was his destiny: he could never emerge into the plain calm of a resolution. The islands in his journey were his own failings. Home, Ithaca, was the longed-for moment when his own failings would at last be overcome. Odysseus's muddle was his beauty.

He is no victim. He suffers but he does not buckle. His virtue is his elasticity, his rubber vigour. If he is pushed, he bends, but he bends back, and that half-giving strength was to me a beautiful model for a man. He was all navigation, subtlety, invention, dodging the rocks, story-telling, cheating and survival. He can be resolute, fierce and destructive when need be, and clever, funny and loving when need be. There is no need to choose between these qualities; Odysseus makes them all available.

Like Shakespeare and the Bible, we all know his stories in advance, but there was one in particular which struck me that summer sailing on the *Auk*. We had left the Arans late the evening before, and George had taken her all night up the dark of the Galway coast. We changed at dawn, and in that early morning, with a cup of tea in my hand at the wheel, and the sun rising over the Irish mainland, I took her on north, heading for the Inishkeas and the corner of County Mayo, before turning there and making for Scotland.

The wind was a big easterly, coming in gusts over the Mayo hills, the sun white and heatless. George, and my son Ben who had joined us, were asleep below. There were shearwaters cruising the swells beside us, black, liquid, effortless birds, like the sea turned aerial, and a fulmar now and then hung in the slot between the headsail and the main, flying with us on the current of air. The *Auk* surged on the wind that morning, heeling out into the Atlantic, churning her way north, horse-like in her strength. I don't know when I have felt so happy.

Steering across the swells, holding the wheel against them as they came through, releasing it as they fell away, I propped the great Robert Fagles translation of the *Odyssey* against the compass binnacle, tying it open with a bungee cord in the wind, and absorbed his words. That morning I read the story of the Sirens. Just as we do, Odysseus knew he would be exposed to the songs which the strange, birdlike creatures sang to mariners and with which they lured passing ships on to the shore, wrecking them there and then leaving the men to linger until they died.* The only way Odysseus could get past the Sirens was to cut up a round cake of beeswax, knead it in his hands, softening the wax in the heat of the sun, and then press plugs of it into the ears of the sailors. Once they were deafened, he had himself lashed to the mainmast, so that any desire he might have to steer towards the delicious honeyed voices could have no effect on his men. Only if he were powerless could he listen to them singing from their meadow, as Robert Fagles translated it, 'starred with flowers'.

That meadow of death is the most desirable place any man could imagine. It is yet another island into which a man might long to sink and die. A dead calm falls on the sea. The men brail up the sail and then sit to their oars. The Sirens, just within shouting distance of the ship, taunt Odysseus as he passes. They can give him wisdom if he will come to them and listen. If he will let them, they will make him understand. They press on him the comfort and beauty of what they have to offer. They sing to him and Odysseus longs for them, his heart *throbbing* for them, as Fagles says, and with his eyebrows gestures to the crew to set him free. But the crew won't respond. Deaf to all persuasion, they bind him tighter and row the ship through and past.

---

* Homer's Sirens do not devour men. It was later Greeks who thought they ate their victims.

Odysseus, bound to the mast of his ship, its mainsail brailed up, resists the seduction of the Sirens' song. From a stamnos, or storage jar, made in Athens in about 480 BC but exported to the Etruscan city of Vulci, on the Mediterranean shore sixty miles north of Rome, where it was excavated in the nineteenth century. It is now in the British Museum, which bought it in 1848 from its collector, one of Napoleon's daughters-in-law.

Never is Homer more rapid. Like Odysseus's 'sea-swift' ship, the whole scene sweeps past in forty lines. Rarely can something so brief have spread its ripples so wide. But the point is this: the song the Sirens sing is not any old crooning seduction tune. It is the story of the *Iliad* itself.

> We know all the pains that the Greeks and Trojans once endured
> On the spreading plain of Troy when the gods willed it so –
> All that comes to pass on the fertile earth, we know it all.

The Sirens sing the song of the heroic past. That is the meadow of death. They want to draw Odysseus in with tempting stories of what he once was. And Odysseus, after his years of suffering and journeying, of frustration in the beautiful arms of Calypso, whose name means 'the hidden one', the goddess of oblivion, longs to return to the active world, the world of simplicity and straightforwardness he had known at Troy. The Sirens are wise to that: they know the longing in his heart. The prospect of clear-cut heroism summons him and he struggles to escape his bindings. But his men, like the poem itself, know better, and they tie him tighter to his ship. They won't be wrecked on the illusions of nostalgia, on the longing for that heroised, antique world, because, as the *Odyssey* knows, to live well in the world, nostalgia must be resisted: you must stay with your ship, stay tied to the present, remain mobile, keep adjusting the rig, work with the swells, watch for a wind-shift, watch as the boom swings over, engage, in other words, with the muddle and duplicity and difficulty of life. Don't be tempted into the lovely simplicities that the heroic past seems to offer. That is what Homer, and the Sirens and Robert Fagles all said to me that day.

I can still see the sunlight coming sheening off the backs of the swells that morning, as they made their way past and under me, combed and slicked with the sea-froth running down them, every swell the memory of storms in the Atlantic far to the west, steepening to the east and then ruining themselves ashore. The *Auk* sailed north with the shearwaters and the morning became unforgettable. It was when this book began.

I thank God I met Homer again that summer. He was suddenly alongside me, a companion and an ally, the most truly reliable voice I had ever known. It was like discovering poetry itself, or the dead speaking. As I read and reread the *Odyssey* in translation, I suddenly felt that here was the unaffected truth, here was someone speaking about fate and the human condition in ways that other people only seem to approach obliquely; and that directness, that sense of nothing between me and the source, is what gripped me. I felt like asking, 'Why has no one told me about this before?'

The more I looked at the poems in different translations, and the more I tried to piece bits of them together in the Greek with a dictionary, the more I felt Homer was a guidebook to life. Here was a form of consciousness that understood fallibility and self-indulgence and vanity, and despite that knowledge didn't surrender hope of nobility and integrity and doing the right thing. Before I read Pope's Preface to the *Iliad*, or Matthew Arnold's famous lectures on translating Homer, I knew that this was the human spirit on fire, rapidity itself, running, going and endlessly able to throw off little sidelights like the sparks thrown off by the wheels of an engine hammering through the night. Speed, scale, violence, threat; but every spark with humanity in it.

TWO

Grasping Homer

PARIS, 11 MAY 1863, Le Repas Magny, a small restaurant up a cobbled street on the Left Bank in the Sixième. Brilliant, literary, sceptical Paris had gathered, as usual, for its fortnightly dinner. The stars were there: the critic and historian Charles Sainte-Beuve; the multi-talented and widely admired playwright and novelist Théophile Gautier; the unconscionably fat Breton philosopher, the most brilliant cultural analyst of the nineteenth century, Ernest Renan; the idealistic and rather intense Comte de Saint-Victor, a minor poet and upholder of traditional values; and observing them all the supremely waspish Jules de Goncourt, with his brother Edmond.

Magny's restaurant stood at the head of the rue Contrescarpe–Dauphine on the Left Bank in Paris.

The Magny dinners, every other Monday, were ten francs a head, the food 'mediocre' apparently, everyone shouting their heads off, smoking for France, coming and going as they felt like it, the only place in Paris, it was said, where there was freedom to speak and think. Jules de Goncourt transcribed it all.

'Beauty is always simple,' the Comte de Saint-Victor said as the waiters brought in the wine. He had a way, when saying something he thought important, of putting his face in the air like an ostrich laying an egg. 'There is nothing more beautiful than the feelings of Homer's characters. They are still fresh and youthful. Their beauty is their simplicity.'

'Oh for Christ's sake,' Edmond groaned, looking over at his brother. 'Must we? Homer, *again?*'

Saint-Victor paused a moment, went white and then very deep red like some kind of mechanical toy. 'Are you feeling well?' Goncourt said to him across the table. 'It looks as if Homer might be playing havoc with your circulation.'

'How can you say that? Homer, how can I put it. . .Homer. . . Homer is . . .so *bottomless!*' Everyone laughed.

'Most people read Homer in those stupid eighteenth-century translations,' Gautier said calmly. 'They make him sound like Marie-Antoinette nibbling biscuits in the Tuileries. But if you read him in Greek you can see he's a monster, his people are monsters. The whole thing is like a dinner party for barbarians. They eat with their fingers. They put mud in their hair when they are upset. They spend half the time painting themselves.'

'Any modern novel,' Edmond said, 'is more moving than Homer.'

'*What?*' Saint-Victor screamed at him across the table, banging his little fist against his head so that his curls shook.

'Yes, *Adolphe*, that lovely sentimental love story by Benjamin Constant, the sweet way they all behave to each other, his charming little obsession with her, the way she doesn't admit she wants to go bed with him, the lust boiling away between her thighs, all of that is more moving than Homer, actually more *interesting* than anything in Homer.'

'Dear God alive,' Saint-Victor shrieked. 'It's enough to make a man want to throw himself out of the window.' His eyes were standing out of his head like a pair of toffee-apples.

'That would be original,' Edmond said. 'I can see it now: "Poet skewers himself on street-lamp because someone said something horrid about Homer." Do go on. It would be more diverting than anything that has happened for weeks.'

Chairs were shoved back from the table, somebody knocked over a bottle of wine, the waiter was standing ghoul-faced at the door, Saint-Victor was stamping and roaring like a baby bull in his own toy bullring, as red in the face as if somebody had said his father was a butcher and his mother a tart. Everyone was bellowing.

'I wouldn't care if all the Greeks were dead!'

'If only they were!'

'But Homer is divine.'

'He has got nothing to teach us!'

'He's just a novelist who never learned how to write a novel.'

'He says the same thing over and over again.'

'But isn't it deeply moving,' Saint-Victor said imploringly, 'when Odysseus's dog wags the last sad final wag of his tail?'

'You can always tell a bully,' Edmond said quietly to his brother. 'He loves dogs more than their owners.'

'Homer, Homer,' Sainte-Beuve was murmuring through the uproar.

'Isn't it strange,' Jules said to Renan afterwards. 'You can argue about the Pope, say that God doesn't exist, question anything, attack heaven, the Church, the Holy Sacrament, anything except Homer.'

'Yes,' Renan said. 'Literary religions are where you find the real fanatics.'

Homer loomed up again at another Magny dinner the following October. They were talking about God, whether God was definable or even knowable. Renan ended up by comparing God, his particular God, in all possible piety and seriousness, to an oyster. Uniquely itself, beautifully self-sufficient, not entirely to be understood, mysteriously attractive, mysteriously unattractive, wholly wonderful: what was not Godlike about the oyster? Rolling laughter swept up and down the table.

That was when Homer emerged. To the Goncourts' horror, these modern, sceptical destroyers of faith, the most fearless critics of God that France had ever known, burst into a song of Homeric praise which made the brothers retch. The diners at le Repas Magny might have been partisans of progress, but all agreed that there was a time and a country, at the beginning of humanity, when a work was written in which everything was divine, above all discussion and even all examination. They began to swoon with admiration over individual phrases.

'*The long-tailed birds!*' [Hippolyte] Taine, [the philosopher and historian] cried out enthusiastically.

'*The unharvestable sea!*' exclaimed Sainte-Beuve, raising his little voice. 'A sea where there are no grapes! What could be more beautiful than that?'

'*Unharvestable sea?*' What on earth did that mean? Renan thought some Germans had discovered a hidden significance in it. 'And what is that?' asked Sainte-Beuve.

'I can't remember,' Renan replied, 'but it's wonderful.'

The Goncourt brothers sat back, regarding this mass expression of Homer-love with their habitual, jaundiced eye.

'Well, what do you have to say, you over there,' Taine called out, addressing them, 'you who wrote that antiquity was created to be the daily bread of schoolmasters?'

So far the brothers had said nothing, and had let the Homer-hosannas go swirling around the dining room without comment, but now Jules said: 'Oh, you know, we think [Victor] Hugo has more talent than Homer.'

It was blasphemy. Saint-Victor sat as upright as a fence-post and then went wild with rage, shouting like a madman and shrieking in his tinny voice, saying that remarks like that were impossible to stomach, they were too much, insulting the religion of all intelligent people, that everybody admired Homer and that without him Hugo would not even exist. Hugo greater than Homer! What did the Goncourts know? What idiot novels had they been producing recently? He shouted and screamed, dancing up and down the room like an electrified marionette. The Goncourts shouted back, increasingly loudly, raging at the little supercilious poet, who for some reason thought he was more in touch with the meaning of things than they ever could be, sneering at them down his peaky red nose, while they could feel nothing but contempt for the man they would think of forever after as the nasty stuck-up little self-congratulatory Homer-lover.

* * *

These conversations seem as distant as the Bronze Age. Where now is our violence on behalf of a poet? Who feels this much about Homer? The Goncourts, with their scepticism and their modernism, their contempt for antiquity, have won the day. Their prediction has come more than true: the ancient world is now the daily bread not of schoolmasters but of academics. Everyone has heard of Homer, probably of the two poems, and many have read some passages; but no one today ends up shouting at dinner about him. Mention Homer across a table and a kind of anxiety comes into the face you are looking at, a sort of shame, perhaps a fear of seeming stupid and ignorant. Almost no one loves the poems he wrote, or the phrases that recur in them.

Why should they? The place of Homer in our culture has largely withered away. I can only say that, for me, the growing experience of knowing Homer, of living with him in my life, has provided a kind of ballast. He is like a beautiful stone, monumentally present, a paternal foundation, large, slightly ill-defined, male and reliable. He is not a friend, a lover or a wife; far more of an underlayer than that, a form of reassurance that in the end there is some kind of understanding in the world. Goethe thought that if only Europe had considered Homer and not the books of the Bible as its holy scripture, the whole of history would have been different, and better.

That quality does not exist in some floating metaphysical outer sphere. It is precisely in the words he uses, and it is on that level that something like 'the unharvestable sea' is a beautiful expression. It is the twin and opposite of another of Homer's repeated, metrically convenient, perfect and formulaic phrases, 'the grain-giving earth'. And why is it beautiful? Because it encapsulates the sensation of standing on a beach and looking out at the breaking surf, and seeing in it the unforgiving brutality of the salt desert before you. Everything you are not stares back at what you are. It is a phrase which knows that, as you are looking out at that hostility, behind you, at your back, are all the riches that the earth might give, the olive and the grape, the security of home, the smell of cut hay, the barn filled with the harvested wheat and barley, the threshed grains, the sacks tight with them in the granaries, the ground flour, the bread at breakfast, the honey and oil. 'The unharvestable sea' – two words in

Greek, *pontos atrygetos* – is a form of concentrated wisdom about the condition of life on earth. It states the obvious, but also provides a kind of access to reality, both painful and revelatory. All Homer is in the phrase.

Those words occur many times in both the *Iliad* and the *Odyssey*, often poignantly. Almost at the beginning of the *Odyssey* Odysseus's son Telemachus, at the end of twenty years' waiting for his father to return, first from the war against Troy and then from his vastly extended and troubled journey home across the sea, has decided to go in search of him, to ask in the mainland of Greece, in Pylos and Sparta, if there is any news of the man most people now consider dead.

Homer, over the course of thirty-five lines, prepares the ground for the climactic words. Telemachus needs to get ready for his journey, and to do so he goes down into his father's treasure chamber in the palace in Ithaca, his *thalamos*. Upstairs, all is anarchy and chaos. The young men who are living in the palace, clamouring to marry Telemachus's mother Penelope, are eating up the goods of the household. But down here, like a treasury of the past, of how things were before Odysseus left for the wars half a lifetime ago, all is order and richness. Clothes, gold and bronze are piled in the chamber, but also sweet-smelling oils, wine, which is also old and sweet, all lined up in order against the walls. All the accumulated goodness of the land is in there. Telemachus, whose name means 'far from battle',* meets an old woman, Eurycleia, down here. She was his nurse as a child, feeding and raising him. Now that he is a man, she tends and protects these precious fruits of the earth. He asks her for the best wine to be poured out for him into small travelling jars, and for milled barley to be put into leather sacks. He must take the earth's goods out on to the sea.

But Eurycleia – and the name of this private nurse, this tender of things, means 'wide-fame' – dreads Telemachus going where his father has gone to die. A wail of grief breaks from her when he tells her his plans, and she suddenly addresses him as she had years before:

---

* It can also mean 'fighting at a distance', like an archer; so it was an appropriate name, because archery was one of Odysseus's skills and he might have wanted to pass it on to his son.

Ah dear child, how has this thought come into your mind?
Where do you intend to go over the wide earth,
you who are an only son and so deeply loved?
Odysseus is dead, has died far from home in a strange land.
No, stay here, in charge of what is yours.
You have no need to suffer pain
or go wandering on *the unharvestable sea.*

Nothing could be clearer: the unharvestable sea is not to be visited. It is the realm of death. When Odysseus does finally come home (and Eurycleia plays a key role in that return), Homer has a one-word synonym for the sea: evil. The word she uses here for 'wandering' is also dense with implication: *alaomai* is used of seamen, but also of beggars and the unhomed dead. The unharvestable sea is where life and goodness will never be found. Everything Eurycleia has devoted her life to, the nurturing and cherishing of the goodness of home, has been the harvest of an unwandering life. The man standing in front of her is one of those fruits. The unharvestable sea is a kind of hell, and in that phrase the drama of his life, her life, Odysseus's life, the life and death of those Ithacans who have not returned from Troy, of Penelope weaving and unweaving the cloth that will not be woven until Odysseus returns: all of it is bound up in *pontos atrygetos.*

For all the Goncourts' wit and scepticism, I am on the side of Renan, and Hippolyte Taine, and Sainte-Beuve, and even the ludicrous Comte de Saint-Victor. Homer, the most miraculous and ancient of survivals in our culture, comes from a time of unadorned encounter with the realities of existence. It is absurd now to call the sea 'unharvestable', but it is also beautiful and moving. For all of Saint-Victor's despised sententiousness, he was right in this. Homer's simplicity, his undeniably straight look, is a form of revelation. Its nakedness is its poetry. There is nothing here of ornamentation or prettiness, and that is its value. 'Each time I put down the *Iliad*,' the American poet Kenneth Rexroth wrote towards the end of his life,

after reading it again in some new translation, or after reading once more the somber splendor of the Greek, I am convinced, as one is convinced by the experiences of a lifetime, that somehow, in a way beyond the visions of artistry, I have been face to face with the meaning of existence. Other works of literature give this insight, but none so powerfully, so uncontaminated by evasion or subterfuge.

This book is driven by a desire to find the source of that directness and that understanding.

* * *

In the early autumn of 1816, John Keats was not yet twenty-one. He had been writing poetry for two years, living with other medical students in 'a jumbled heap of murky buildings' just off the southern end of London Bridge, working as a 'dresser' – a surgeon's assistant – in Guy's Hospital. He was miserable, good at his job but hating it, out of sorts with 'the barbarous age' in which he lived, filled with a hunger for life on a greater scale and of a deeper intensity than the ordinariness surrounding him could provide.

At school in Enfield, his headmaster's son Charles Cowden Clarke, who had ambitions himself as a poet and littérateur, had introduced him to history and poetry, immersing him in Shakespeare, Milton and Wordsworth. Clarke gave him the first volume of the great Elizabethan English epic, Edmund Spenser's *Faerie Queene*, and, as Clarke remembered later in life, Keats took to it

> as a young horse would through a spring meadow – ramping! Like a true poet, too – a poet 'born, not manufactured', a poet in grain, he especially singled out epithets, for that felicity and power in which Spenser is so eminent. He hoisted himself up, and looked burly and dominant, as he said, 'what an image that is – "sea-shouldering whales"!'

When Keats at this age saw the wind blowing across a field of barley still in the green, he jumped on a stile and shouted down at Clarke, 'The tide! The tide!' Here was a boy, born the son of a London ostler, hungry for depth, for a kind of surging reality, for largeness and otherness which only epic poetry could provide. Poetry for him, as Andrew Motion has said, was 'both a lovely escape from the world and a form of engagement with it'. It was not about prettiness, elegance or decoration but, in Motion's phrase, 'a parallel universe', whose reality was truer and deeper than anything in the world more immediately to hand. Poetry gave access to a kind of Platonic grandeur, an underlying reality which everyday material life obscured and concealed. It is as if Keats's sensibility was ready for Homer to enter it, a womb prepared for conception. All that was needed was for Homer to flood into him.

Perhaps at Clarke's suggestion, he had already looked into the great translation of Homer made by the young Alexander Pope between about 1713 and 1726, the medium through which most eighteenth- and early-nineteenth-century Englishmen encountered Homer. But it was a translation that came to be despised by the Romantics as embodying everything that was wrong in the culture of the preceding age: interested more in style than in substance, ridiculously pretty when the Homeric medium was truth, a kind of drawing-room Homer which had left the battlefield and the storm at sea too far behind.

Where, for example, Homer had said simply 'the shepherd's heart is glad', Pope had written

> The conscious swains, rejoicing in the sight
> Eye the blue vault, and bless the useful light.

From the point of view of the 1780s, Pope's Homer was about as Homeric as a Meissen shepherdess with a lamb in her lap.

This wasn't entirely fair to Pope. His preface to the *Iliad*, published in 1715, is one of the most plangent descriptions ever written in English of the power of the Homeric poems. Northern European culture had been dominated for too long by the processed and stable maturity of Virgil's *Aeneid*, the Latin epic *par excellence*, written in about 20 BC. Homer represented an earlier stage in human civilisation, a greater closeness to nature, to the potency of the sublime, a form of poetry which was not to be admired from afar but which would bind up its reader or listener in a kind of overwhelming absorption in its world. 'No man of true Poetical Spirit,' the young Pope had written, 'is Master of himself while he reads him; so forcible is the poet's Fire and Rapture.' Translation was not a calm carrying over of the meaning in Greek into the meaning in English, but a vision of the processes of the mind as a flaming crucible in which the sensibilities of translator and translated were fused into a new, radiant alloy.

Pope may have been the darling of the establishment. In his preface, he thanked a roll-call of the eighteenth-century British great – Addison, Steele, Swift, Congreve, a string of dukes, earls, lords and other politicians – but for all that, his entrancement with Homeric power is not in doubt. Homer was like nature itself. He was a kind of wildness, 'a wild paradise' in which, as the theory then was, the great stories and figures he described came into being.

> What he writes is of the most animated Nature imaginable; every thing moves, every thing lives, and is put in Action. . . The Course of his Verses resembles that of the Army he describes,
> *They pour along like a Fire that sweeps the whole Earth before it.*

This inseparability of Homer and his world is what excited Pope. It seemed to him like a voice from the condition of mankind when it was still simple, quite different from 'the luxury of succeeding ages'. Poetic fire was the essential ingredient. 'In *Homer*, and in him only, it burns every where clearly, and every where irresistibly.'

Pope grasped the essential point: unlike Virgil, Homer is no part of the classical age, has no truck with judicious distinction or the calm management of life and society. He precedes that order, is a *pre-classic*, immoderate, uncompromising, never sacrificing truth for grace.

> *Virgil* bestows with a careful Magnificence: *Homer* scatters with a generous Profusion. *Virgil* is like a River in its Banks, with a gentle and constant Stream: *Homer* like the *Nile*, pours out his Riches with a sudden Overflow.

In this preface to the *Iliad*, Pope can lay claim to being the greatest critic of Homer in English. But what of his translation? Was he able to bear out this deep understanding of Homer's 'unaffected and equal Majesty' in the translation he made? Perhaps not. Take for example a moment of passionate horror towards the end of the *Iliad*. For most of the poem Achilles has been in his tent, nursing his grievance and loathing against Agamemnon, but now that Patroclus, the man he loved, has been killed by Hector, Achilles is out to exact revenge. He is on his blood-run, gut-driven, pitiless, the force of destiny. Among his enemies on the field, he encounters a young Trojan and looks down on him with the vacancy of fate. The young warrior stares back up:

> In vain his youth, in vain his beauty pleads:
> In vain he begs thee, with a suppliant's moan
> To spare a form and age so like thy own!
> Unhappy boy! no prayer, no moving art
> E'er bent that fierce inexorable heart!
> While yet he trembled at his knees, and cried,
> The ruthless falchion [a single-edged sword] oped his tender side;
> The panting liver pours a flood of gore,
> That drowns his bosom till he pants no more.

'It is not to be doubted,' Pope had written in his own preface, 'that the *Fire* of the Poem is what a Translator should principally regard, as it is most likely to expire in his managing.' But that is what has happened here. Apart from what Leigh Hunt, the great liberal editor of the *Examiner*, called Pope's trivialising, 'cuckoo-song' regularity, he has lost something else: Homer's neck-gripping physical urgency. In the Greek everything is about the body. The boy crawls towards Achilles and holds him by the knees. It is Achilles's ears that are deaf to him, his heart and his mind that remain unapproachably fierce. The boy puts his hands on Achilles's knees to make his prayer, and then the sword goes into the liver, the liver slipping out of the slit wound, the black blood drenching the boy's lap and 'the darkness of death clouding his eyes'. Nothing mediates the physical reality. Homer's nakedness is his power, but Pope has dressed it. 'The panting liver . . . pants no more': that is so neat it is almost disgusting, as if Pope were adjusting his cuffs while observing an atrocity. Dr Johnson called the translation 'a treasure of poetical elegances'. That was the problem.

Keats had undoubtedly read Homer in Pope's translation; there are echoes of Pope's words in what Keats would write himself. But he was ready for something else. His life was constrained in the crowded and meagre streets of south London, filled with the 'money-mongering pitiable brood' of other Londoners. He had been to Margate with his brothers and had seen 'the ocean' there in the pale shallows of the North Sea, but nowhere further. In early October 1816 he went for the evening to see his old friend Charles Cowden Clarke, who was living with his brother-in-law in Clerkenwell. Cowden Clarke had been lent a beautiful big early folio edition of the translation of the *Iliad* and the *Odyssey* made by the poet and playwright George Chapman.

The two men began to look through its seventeenth-century pages. Clarke's friend Leigh Hunt, the heroic editor of the *Examiner*, in which he had just published the first of Shelley's poems to be printed, had already praised Chapman in the August issue, for bottling 'the fine rough old wine' of the original. In the next few days Keats was about to meet Hunt himself, with the possibility in the air that he too might swim out into the world of published poetry and fame. The evening was pregnant with the hope of enlargement, of a dignifying difference from the mundane conditions of his everyday life. To meet Homer through Chapman might be an encounter with the source.

It is touching to imagine the hunger with which Keats must have approached this book, searching its two-hundred-year-old pages for something undeniable, the juice of antiquity. The two of them sat side by side in Clarke's house, 'turning to some of the "famousest" passages, as we had scrappily known them in Pope's version'. Chapman had produced his translations – almost certainly not from the Greek but with the help of Latin and French versions – between 1598 and 1616. It is a repeated experience with Homer that he seems to haunt the present, and Chapman himself had met him one day in Hertfordshire, not far from Hitchin where Chapman had been born, Homer masquerading as 'a sweet gale' as Chapman walked on the hills outside the town. It was a moment of revelation and life-purpose for him, so that later he could say: 'There did shine,/A beam of Homer's freer soul in mine.' The eighteenth century had not admired it. Pope had called it 'loose and rambling', and Chapman himself 'an Enthusiast' with a 'daring fiery Spirit that animates his Translation, which is something like what one might imagine *Homer* himself would have writ before he arriv'd to Years of Discretion'. Dr Johnson had dismissed it as 'now totally neglected'. But Coleridge had rediscovered it. In 1808 he sent a copy of Chapman's Homer to Sara Hutchinson, Wordsworth's sister-in-law, the woman he loved. 'Chapman writes & feels as a Poet,' he wrote, ' – as Homer might have written had he lived in England in the reign of Queen Elizabeth . . . In the main it is an English Heroic Poem, the *tale* of which is borrowed from the Greek – . . .'

Chapman's distance, his rough-cut unaffectedness, stood beyond the refinements of the Enlightenment, as if he were the last part of the old world that Homer had also inhabited, before politeness had polluted it. Here the Romantics found Achilles as the 'fear-master', and horses after battle which liked to 'cool their hooves'. Cowden Clarke and Keats were hunched together over pages that were drenched in antiquity. Ghosts must have come seeping out of them.

Something that had seemed quaint to the eighteenth century now seemed true to the two young men. They pored over Chapman together. 'One scene I could not fail to introduce to him,' Cowden Clarke wrote later,

> the shipwreck of Ulysses, in the fifth book of the 'Odysseis' [Chapman's transliteration of the Greek word for *Odyssey*], and I had the reward of one of his delighted stares, upon reading the following lines:

> > Then forth he came, his both knees falt'ring, both
> > His strong hands hanging down, and all with froth
> > His cheeks and nostrils flowing, voice and breath
> > Spent to all use, and down he sank to death.
> > *The sea had soak'd his heart through.*

It is the most famous meeting between Homer and an English poet. Keats had read and stared in delight, shocked into a moment of recognition, of what the Greeks called *anagnōrisis*, when a clogging surface is stripped away and the essence for which you have been hungering is revealed.

At this stage Odysseus has been at sea for twenty days. For nearly two hundred lines he is churned through the pain Poseidon has wished on him.

> Just as when, in the autumn, the North Wind drives the thistle tufts over the plain and they cling close to each other, so did the gales drive the raft this way and that across the sea.

The sea is never more vengeful in these poems, never more maniacally driven by violence and rage. The raft is overturned and broken, the giant surf hammers on flesh-shredding rock. It is one of Odysseus's great tests. His name itself in Greek embeds the word *odysato*, meaning 'to be hated', and that adjective appears twice in this storm. He is the hated man on the hateful sea. This is his moment of suffering, and the sea he sails on is loathing itself.

Throughout the *Odyssey* he is the man of many parts, inventive, ingenious, with many skills and many gifts, but here is merely *polytlas*, the man who dares many things, suffers many things and endures many things. Only when a goddess-bird and then Athene herself come to his aid can he finally drag himself to the shore.

Here in a virtually literal translation is what Homer says as Odysseus emerges from the surf:

> he then bent both knees
> and his strong hands-and-arms; for sea had killed his heart.
> Swollen all his flesh, while sea oozed much
> up through mouth and nostrils, he then breathless and speechless
> lay scarcely-capable, terrible weariness came to him.

The Greek word Chapman translated in *The sea had soak'd his heart through* – the phrase which Keats loved so much – is *dedmēto*, which means overpowered or tamed. It comes from a verb, *damazo*, of immensely ancient lineage, its roots spoken in the steppelands of Eurasia at least six thousand years ago, used to describe the breaking-in of animals and later the bending of metal to your desires and needs. It is essentially the same word as 'tame' in English, or *domo* in Latin, the word for reduction, to kill in a fight, to domesticate and dominate. But in the *Iliad* it also appears as a word for seduction, or more likely the rape of girls. Young girls, enemies, heifers and wives are referred to in Homer by words that come from the same stem. So Odysseus here is tamed and unmanned by the sea. The sea has done for him. As a hero reduced to the condition of a heifer, his heroic willpower temporarily overcome, he is no better than a corpse, bloated, destroyed, owned, possessed and dominated.

Pope, encased in the language of *politesse*, fell short when faced with this challenge:

his knees no more
Perform'd their office, or his weight upheld:
His swoln heart heaved; his bloated body swell'd:
From mouth and nose the briny torrent ran;
And lost in lassitude lay all the man.

On a sofa? you might ask.

Others have tried and failed: 'For the heart within him was crushed by the sea,' wrote Professor A.T. Murray in 1919; 'Odysseus bent his knees and sturdy arms, exhausted by his struggle with the sea,' was E.V. Rieu's Penguin post-war bestseller prose version in 1945; 'his very heart was sick with salt water', wrote the great American scholar-poet Richmond Lattimore in 1967; 'The sea had beaten down his striving heart,' his successor Robert Fagles in 1996.

Keats was right. None approaches '*The sea had soak'd his heart through,*' perhaps because Chapman's English has absorbed the vengeful nature of the sea Odysseus has just experienced; has understood that his soul is as good as drowned; has not lost the governing physicality of the Homeric world, so that Odysseus's heart appears as the organ of pain; and is able to summon a visual image of a marinaded corpse, blanched and shrivelled from exposure to the water, as white as tripe. Chapman had understood *dedmēto*: Odysseus's sea-soaked heart is a heart with the heart drained out of it.

Clarke and Keats read Chapman together all night, and at six in the morning Keats returned to his Dean Street lodgings – his 'beastly place in dirt, turnings, and windings' – with Chapman looming in his mind. On the journey home across London he had begun to frame the sonnet which on arrival he wrote down. The manuscript, which he paid a boy to take over to Cowden Clarke that morning, so that it was on his breakfast table by ten o'clock, survives. The big, loopingly written words of that first morning text are not quite the same as what is usually printed.

On the first looking into Chapman's Homer

Much have I travell'd in the Realms of Gold
And many goodly States and Kingdoms seen;

Round many Western islands have I been,
Which Bards in Fealty to Apollo hold.
Oft of one wide expanse had I been told,
    Which ~~low~~ deep brow'd Homer ruled as his Demesne:
    Yet could I never judge what Men could mean,
Till I heard Chapman speak out loud, and bold.
Then felt I like some Watcher of the Skies
    When a new Planet swims into his Ken,
Or like stout Cortez, when with wond'ring eyes
    He star'd at the Pacific, and all his Men
Look'd at each other with a wild surmise –
    Silent upon a Peak in Darien –

It was the first great poem he wrote. And it is a poem about greatness, not about first reading Homer; nor even about first reading Chapman's Homer; it's about first looking into Chapman's Homer and, from one or two fragments and passages, understanding for the first time what Homer meant. It is as if that big 1616 folio were a sort of aquarium into which he and Clarke had peered in amazement, looking up at each other as they found the beauties and rarities swimming in its depths. No other version had given Keats this plunging perspective into the ancient. Politeness had dressed Homer in felicity, when his underlying qualities are more like this: martial, huge, struggling through jungle, dense, disturbing and then providing that moment of revelatory release, of a calm pacific vision emerging on to what had been fields of storm or battle. Men had assured Keats that Homer possessed such a realm, but he had been unable to see it in the translations he knew. Here at last, though, was the moment when, cresting a rise, a new and deeper, ineffably broad landscape had opened in front of him. Homer might be dressed up as a cultural convenience, a classic, but in truth he is not like that. He is otherness itself: impolite, manly, cosmic, wild, enormous.

Keats made a mistake: it was Vasco Núñez de Balboa, not Cortez, who first sighted the Pacific Ocean. He didn't correct that, but when he came to revise this poem for publication he did change a word or two, most importantly the seventh line. In the first early-October-morning version, after his night of revelation, it had been

Yet could I never judge what Men could mean,

which acts as the core of the poem, the rejection of the instruction and learning he had received, substituting it with the vast scale of the new understanding that Chapman had given him. For publication, he replaced that with

Yet did I never breathe its pure serene

which is politer and not entirely concordant with what the rest of the poem aims to mean. Further than that, he had borrowed the verb and the key adjectival noun from Pope's *Iliad*:

> The troops exulting sat in order round,
> And beaming fires illumined all the ground.
> As when the moon, refulgent lamp of night,
> O'er heaven's pure azure spreads her sacred light,
> When not a breath disturbs the deep serene. . .

Keats, on the verge of his twenty-first birthday, even as this sonnet was announcing his new discovery of Homeric depth and presence, had not shrugged off that eighteenth-century inheritance.

For all that, coursing through the sonnet is a sense of arrival in the world of riches, a sudden shift in Keats's cosmic geometry, moving beyond the drabness and tawdriness by which he felt besieged. Keats had become everybody in the sonnet's fourteen lines: the astronomer, himself, Chapman, Homer, Cortez and 'all his Men'. All coexist in the heightened and expanded moment of revelation. Pope had found fire in Homer; Keats discovered scale. And scale is what then entered his poetry, as a kind of private and tender sublime, the often agonised heroics of the heart, in which, just as in Homer, love and death engage in an inseparable dance.

Homer, or at least the idea of Homer, pools into Keats's poetry. Hostile Tory reviewers in *Blackwood's Magazine* started to call him 'the cockney Homer', but in *Endymion*, the long poem he had been contemplating when he wrote the Chapman sonnet, and which he began the following spring, his experience of that night with Cowden Clarke shapes the core phrases. People remember the poem's beginnings:

> A thing of beauty is a joy for ever:
> Its loveliness increases; it will never
> Pass into nothingness; but still will keep
> A bower quiet for us, and a sleep
> Full of sweet dreams, and health, and quiet breathing.

That is poetry as balm, even, as Andrew Motion has said, as medicine, the discipline which Keats was now abandoning for life as a poet. Keats went on to describe the ways in which beauty manifests itself in the world, the consolations it provides in 'Trees old and young', 'daffodils/

With the green world they live in', streams and shady woods, 'rich with a sprinkling of fair musk-rose blooms'. But then, at the centre of this first part of the poem, drenched in memories of Shakespeare's sweetest lyrics, comes this, the bass note of a Homeric presence, a sudden manliness, a scale of imagined beauty that encompasses the depths of the past:

> And such too is the grandeur of the dooms
> We have imagined for the mighty dead.

Homer is the foundation of truth and beauty, and Keats was happy to say that 'we' had imagined his poetry. Homer will enlarge your life. Homer is on a scale that stretches across human time and the full width of the human heart. Homer is alive in anyone who is prepared to attend. Homerity is humanity. Richmond Lattimore, making his great version of the *Iliad* in the late 1940s, when asked 'Why do another translation of Homer?' replied: 'That question has no answer for those who do not know the answer already.' Why another book about Homer? Why go for a walk? Why set sail? Why dance? Why exist?

THREE

Loving Homer

HOMER-LOVE CAN FEEL LIKE a disease. If you catch it, you're in danger of having it for life. He starts to infiltrate every nook of your consciousness. What would Homer have had for breakfast? (Oil, honey, yoghurt and delicious bread. One of the things that is wrong with the Cyclopes is that they don't eat bread.) Or a picnic? (Grapes, figs, plums, beans.) How did he feed his heroes? (Grilled meat and thoroughly cooked sausages.) What did he think of parties? (He loved them: no moment was happier for a man than sitting down to a table loaded with wine and surrounded by his friends.)

These were questions the Greeks asked. In fifth-century Athens, Socrates was impressed by Homer's decision, for example, that no hero should ever eat iced cakes: 'all professional athletes are well aware that a man who is to be in good condition should take nothing of the kind'. Protein – well salted, not boiled – was the stuff for heroes. And it had to be red meat; fish was the last resort,* and chickens had yet to arrive from the Far East: they reached the Aegean in about 500 BC, known to the Greeks as 'the Persian Bird'.

I have a way now of finding Homer wherever I look for him. No encounter, no landscape is without its Homeric dimension. In a way, Homer has become a kind of scripture for me, an ancient book, full of

---

* The Classical Greeks were baffled by Homer's dislike of fish; they thought fish the ultimate delicacy, and couldn't understand why Homer's heroes ate beef when they were so often sitting next to a prime fishing spot. This contempt for fish was perhaps a steppe-land inheritance, from the time when a large herd of meaty animals was one of the identifying marks of a king or hero.

urgent imperatives and ancient meanings, most of them half-discerned, to be puzzled over. It is a source of wisdom. There must be a name for this colonisation of the mind by an imaginative presence from the past. Possession, maybe? Mindjack? In one of his Socratic dialogues, Plato has a wonderful image for the secret and powerful hold that Homer has on his listeners. Socrates is talking to Ion, a mildly ridiculous rhapsode, a man who made his living by reciting and speaking about Homer. 'I am conscious in my own self,' Ion tells Socrates in phrases which even two and a half millennia later have a whiff of the stage, 'and the world agrees with me in thinking that I do speak better and have more to say about Homer than any other man.' If Greeks had moustaches, Ion would be twirling his.

The Socratic eyebrow rises a little, but he then tells Ion the truth, a little slyly, the Socratic wisdom masquerading as flattery. 'The gift which you possess of speaking excellently about Homer,' Socrates says,

> is not an art, but an inspiration; there is a divinity moving you, like that contained in the stone which Euripides calls a magnet. . . This stone not only attracts iron rings, but also imparts to them a similar power of attracting other rings; and sometimes you may see a number of pieces of iron and rings suspended from one another so as to form quite a long chain: and all of them derive their power of suspension from the original stone. In like manner the Muse first of all inspires men herself; and from these inspired persons a chain of other persons is suspended, who take the inspiration.

The poet, Socrates tells him, is 'a light and winged and holy thing' – Homer not as great bearded mage, but like the bird Blegen found, or a mosquito, a flitting bug – of no substance, swept here and there on the winds of poetry. 'There is no invention in him until he has been inspired and is out of his senses, and the mind is no longer in him.'

Plato affects to despise poetry, for the way it interferes with the rational mind, but it is clear that he was in love with it, moved by it as much as Ion could ever hope to be. And he identified the mechanism: there is no act of will in loving Homer. You don't acquire Homer; Homer acquires you. And so, like Ion, you hang as a curtain ring from him, who hangs from the Muse, who hangs from her father Greatness and her mother Memory.

I cannot go for a walk in the English chalklands without imagining the cold damp *Iliad*s that must have been sung there. Every burial in an English Bronze Age round barrow must have had a version of these heroic songs sung at its making. But Homer is also in the Hebrides and off the coast of Ireland. Traditions of heroic song have endured there. One eighteenth-century bard was given a lovely estate on Harris by his Macleod chief, for which he had to pay '1 panegyrick poem every year'. That is Homeric rent. Wild unadorned landscapes or places of great antiquity summon his archetypes and their stories. Pope thought that for Virgil, Homer and nature were indistinguishable, and for me Homer is also everywhere: from the North Atlantic to the plain of Troy, in the mountains of Extremadura, on the beaches of Ischia.

No shore now is without its Homeric echoes. It is one of the realms of the heroes, the great zone of liminality between land and sea, the sphere of chance-in-play. Outcomes are never certain there. It is the governing metaphor for the position of the Greeks in the *Iliad*. The Trojans are never seen on the beach, unless battling there, but that is where the Greeks are at home. It is a place of ritual and longing: in Book 3 of the *Odyssey*, the people of Pylos are making a giant sacrifice to the gods on the beach; in Book 5 Odysseus weeps on the beaches of Calypso's island for his sorrows and his distance from home. It is also the place of promise: in Book 6, his eyes rimmed red with sea-salt, he finds Nausicaa and her girls and their assurance of life, coloured by the hint of sex. It is the realm of threat, where Odysseus and his men on their descent to Hades draw up their ships in the cold and dark, in terror at the experiences they know await them. It is above all the field of ambiguity, where at the very centre of the *Odyssey*, Odysseus lands, this time still asleep, on Ithaca, fails to understand he has reached home at last, or to acknowledge that trouble awaits him, and sets off, uncertain, into the island he would like to call home.

In the *Iliad*, when Odysseus and Ajax go to Achilles in Book 9 to urge him to rejoin the fight against the Trojans, they walk there by a sea shore that is roaring with the violence and scale of Poseidon's terror:

So Ajax and Odysseus made their way at once,
where the battle lines of breakers crash and drag,
praying hard to the god who moves and shakes the earth
that they might bring the proud heart of great Achilles
round with speed and ease.

It is also the place of grief, where later in the *Iliad*, in the restlessness of his despair over the death of his beloved friend Patroclus and when sleep will not come, Achilles goes in the night to

wander in anguish, aimless along the surf, and dawn on dawn
flaming over the sea and shore, dawn would find him pacing there.

As so often in Homer, the single moment encapsulates the enormous story. Man and landscape interfuse. The dawnlit Achilles in the agony of sorrow wanders by the aimless surf: no place for Homer is more filled with tragedy than the beach. It is on the beach that Achilles builds the great funeral pyre for Patroclus, the man he loved, now dead, as Achilles will soon be.

As an extension of the beach itself, nothing is more potent in Homer than the first moments of a vessel leaving it. Leaving a beach is moving off from indecision. The set-up for departure, like the arming for battle or the preparation of dinner, is repeated time and again. These are the scenes which have the oldest form of Greek in them, and are at the deepest level of these many-layered poems. They are as old as Homer gets.

And so today a friend – Martin Thomas – stands in the shallows, his trousers rolled up, his calves in the water, hands on hips, saying not shouting the goodbye from the beach. Homeric departures are full of verbal formulae, repeated every time a boat puts to sea, describing the necessary actions. The repetitiveness is often concealed in translations, as if it were an embarrassment, and some variation were needed in the saying of these words, but their formulaic nature is important, as if the poem were an incantation, a ritual departure-charm, a way of getting ready for sea, an arming of the ship, getting the words right in the way that things on the boat must be got right.

So Martin asks, like a hero, if I am all right. Am I prepared? Have I stepped the mast properly? Is the running rigging free? Are the sheets through the fairleads? Is the rudder secured on its pintles? Is the mainsheet caught on the rudder-stock? Do I have water, something to eat, my phone?

Homeric crews almost never sail away. From the shelter of their bay or quayside, they nearly always row out into the seaway to catch the wind. So, today at home in Scotland, there has been a turn in the wind and the water in the bay is lying still, in its own calm. If I could walk on it, I would walk on it this morning. It looks more like oil than water. A blackbird half a mile away is singing in the arms of a Scots pine. A curlew I can hear but not see moans somewhere over there beside the rocks. The seawater itself is green with the reflected woods, an ink of molten leaves and boughs.

But beyond the bay, beyond its two headlands, I can see out into the sound where there is a suggestion of wind. I must row out there and follow the Homeric pattern. As I drift away from the shore, Martin walks up the beach, looks back once or twice, and the sand goes blue beneath me with the depth.

Homeric departures are often at dawn, in the calm before the wind gets up. As the day begins, the voyage begins. Everyone knows that Homeric dawn is 'rosy-fingered', but she also sometimes sits 'on her golden throne' as if she were the goddess of the glowing sky; or, beautifully, she can wear 'her veil the colour of saffron', *krokopeplos*, the crocus-cloth, the warmest colour in the world, from the stigmas of the Cretan crocus, the flush of wellbeing and luxury. And as she rises over the water in those beautiful clothes, the colour is spread across the whole of the sea beneath her, a drenching and staining of the world with the beauty of dawn. She presides over the launching, to sponsor it, but the hero of the ship must lead his men. The voyage cannot happen without human will. And so under his command but with his goddess alongside him, the hero and crew embark, loosen the stern lines that hold the ship to the shore, sit on the benches and 'strike the sea with their oars'.

That is how it is here now too. Martin is back in the house and I settle on the bench in my small boat, the main thwart, put the oars in the rowlocks and ease the blades into the green sea. I can't help but feel the ancientness of it, my own life woven into the fabric of the past. The boat slips forward in a dream of liquidity, released from ploddingness into a kind of flight. With each stroke – a pull, the bending of the shaft of the oar as it is drawn against the water, the sucking puddle as the blades exit and then their dripping on to the perfect skin of the sea – I join the continuous past. Whoever first made a boat, even a simple punt driven forward with a pole, or a dugout with a basic paddle, must have seen and felt this fluency as a kind of magic, a suspension of the earth-bound rules of existence.

But you long for wind. You imagine wind before it comes. You look for it on the water. None of this is far from praying for wind, or even sacrificing for it. Part of the Homeric ritual is to make a libation to the goddess as you leave. And the goddess whom you choose summons her own kind of wind. So Athene, never moderate, owl-eyed, all-seeing, sharp beyond all human understanding, sends a fierce wind for Telemachus as he heads out from Ithaca to find his father, a wind from the west 'that bellowed roaring over the wine-coloured sea'. His voyage is anxious, uncertain, driven by that demanding mentor.

At the same time, somewhere else in the realms of fantasy and loss, his father is being given a wind by the amorous goddess Calypso who has imprisoned him on her island of deliciousness for the last seven years. He has been sitting weeping on the shore, longing for home. Now at last she will release him, and her wind is like her, all-embracing, warm and seductive, a sleep-with-me wind sending him on his way. He spreads his sail gladly to it, a bosom of wind, wafting him away from her comforts to the world of truth and reality.

As the wind comes, they hoist 'the white sail', the sail fills, 'and the wind and the helmsman guide the ship together'. It is an act of co-operation between man and the world, a folding in of human intention with what the world can offer. The ship is a beautifully made thing, as closely fitted as a poem, as much a mark of civilisation as any woven cloth, and the wind in the *Odyssey*, when it is a kind wind, is a 'shipmate', another member of the crew. It is not the element in which you sail but a 'companion' on board. The human and divine dimensions of reality meet in it.

And now, when I am out in the sound, and the right wind comes, I think of it like that, as something else to be welcomed aboard. That coming of the wind is a moment when you can't help but smile, when the world turns in your favour. It is also a moment of extraordinary potency in Homer, never more than when in the *Iliad* the Trojans find themselves in a terrifying and difficult phase of the battle and things are against them, until they see Hector and his brother Paris coming out of the gates of the city, armed, ready to help. It is, the poem says, like that moment when the crew has been struggling for too long with the oars, and their arms are weary, and they have been praying for wind, and then, as a blessing, the wind seems to come and the weariness drops from their bodies and they can rest in its strength and power: 'So these two appeared to the Trojans, who had longed for them.'

Matching that instant of relief and triumph is another, almost at the other end of the *Iliad*, when the winds become the indispensable companions of the heroes. Achilles has made the great funeral pyre on the beach for Patroclus. Timber has been cut and carried, and the pyre is now a hundred feet in each direction. Animals have been slaughtered and the fat laid on the pyre. But it will not light, and Achilles realises he has failed to do one thing: he must pray to the two winds, the west wind and the north wind. And they come, sweeping in from their distant dwelling places, driving the clouds before them. A vast, inhuman blaze erupts in the pyre, and under the winds' fierce encouragement, one shrieking blast after another, it burns all night long, incinerating everything but the bones. Only then do the winds retire

> Back towards home again, over the Thracian sea,
> And it heaved with a long, groaning swell as they crossed it.

The wind never comes unsummoned, or in a solid block. All you feel at first is a finger or two, the faint chilling of the skin on the cheek, or stroking the nape of your neck. But then it builds a little, one finger becomes five, the canvas stirs, like a dog in a bed, begins to acquire a form, and the boat gains a sense of purpose, a coherence it had lacked as it slopped in the chop or swell. The wake slowly starts to bubble behind you, 'the gleaming wake' that runs behind Homeric ships as a sign of life and excellence, the cockpit drains gurgle with the air sucked through them, and with tiller and sheet in hand you sit up and pick your course across the sea. That is the Odyssean moment: everything liquid but directed, everything mobile but related: the sea itself, your boat in it, the air and its winds, all the possibilities. The ritual is done, the routines have been followed, and your chances are now set fair.

Of all Homeric departures, none is more poignant than when Odysseus and his men, right in the centre of the *Odyssey*, set off for Hades, to hear from the blind seer Tiresias the way home to Ithaca. Circe, 'the trim-coifed goddess', as Ezra Pound described her, has set them on their way. They have no choice. Only Tiresias can tell them the way home. They have made all their tackle secure and provided themselves with food and drink. The wind has joined the crew and is now there alongside the helmsman, guiding 'the black ship in the bright sea' as their companion. But neither Odysseus nor any of his men are making this voyage with any hint of delight. This is a journey down and under the world, into the dark places, into themselves as much as to the edge of the physical universe. As the wind holds fair for them, they sit on their benches and grieve. Big, heart-wrenching tears fall on the pale timbers of the deck. The wind is taking them towards a terrifying destination, the place of death which Odysseus has so far exercised all his wit and skill to avoid. The wind knows nothing of that and propels their ship onwards, its red-painted bows plunging and rising with each oncoming sea, the swells breaking and surging around the stempost, while above that foam of life the wind never falters or wavers:

> The wind caught the sail, bellying it out, and the blue-shadowed waves resounded under the fore-foot of the running ship as she lay over on her course and raced out to sea.

> Thus with stretched sail, we went over sea till day's end.
> Sun to his slumber, shadows over ocean.

FOUR

Seeking Homer

ALL MODERN VERSIONS OF Homer are descendants of the edition made by a French nobleman, Jean-Baptiste Gaspard d'Ansse de Villoison. In 1788, in Paris, he published the most important Greek text of the *Iliad* ever printed. Ten years earlier he had arrived in Venice, sent there by the enlightened instincts of the French crown, to trawl through the holdings of the great St Mark's library on the Piazzetta. Villoison was agog at what he found, and soon began writing ecstatic letters to his friends all over Europe. He had made the great discovery: a Byzantine

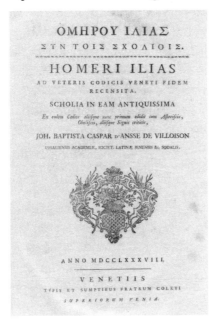

edition of the *Iliad* which seemed to derive from the scholars who had worked on it in Alexandria in the second century BC, sifting the true text from the mass of alternative readings they had gathered in the great Ptolemaic library in the city. It was, Villoison wrote, the *'germana et sincera lectio'*, the real and uncorrupted reading.

Villoison thought he had discovered the essence of a work by a single poet called Homer. But he had sown the seeds of his own demise. The idea was already in the air in the eighteenth century that Homer was not one poet but many, and that the poems were the product of a whole culture, not an individual genius. Villoison's discovery turned out to be the Copernican moment. The mass of alternative readings rejected by the Alexandrian scholars itself threw doubt on the idea of a single great original text. They had chosen to make a single Homer, but looking further back in time it seemed as if there were multiple Homers to choose from. William Cowper, the English lover and translator of Homer, read Villoison and stood aghast at the fragmentation of his hero. As he wrote to his friend the Rev. Walter Bagot in the winter of 1790:

> I will send you some pretty stories from [Villoison] which will make your hair stand on end, as mine has stood on end already, they so horribly affect, in point of authenticity, the credit of the works of the immortal Homer. . .

Homer now was not one but many, and most of them obscure. In 1795 Villoison was challenged by the young, highly analytical German scholar Friedrich August Wolf. How could Villoison tell if the decisions made by the Alexandrian editors were the right ones? Surely what Villoison had published was evidence that the *Iliad*, as they all knew it, was a set of late, corrupt and unreliable texts, brought together in one poem but with their origins in bardic songs which had been radically altered by every hand they had passed through. The originals were unrecoverable. Homer, whoever that was, could never now be known.

The scene was set for the long struggle over the so-called 'Homeric Question' raised by Wolf which has lasted ever since. 'Some say, "There never was such a person as Homer,"' the English essayist Thomas de Quincey joked in 1841. ' "No such person as Homer! On the contrary," say others, "there were scores." ' Nevertheless, the text of the *Iliad* over which the battles were fought between the lumpers and splitters, the one-Homer advocates and the scores-of-Homer advocates, the Homerophiles and Homerophobes, continued to be almost precisely the one published by Villoison in 1788.

He was not the first in the field. The first printed Greek Homer had appeared in 1488, in Florence, published by an Athenian, Demetrius Chalcondyles, who had come to Italy to teach Greek to the humanists of the Italian Renaissance. Soon other copies were being printed in Milan, Heidelberg, Leipzig, Paris and London. And behind those first printed books stands a long manuscript history. Many of the medieval manuscripts of Homer migrated late to the European libraries, because in the early Middle Ages Homer was unread in Europe. Dante had Virgil call him the 'sovereign poet', but Europeans had lost the ability to read Greek, and even though the great fourteenth-century humanist Petrarch was said to have owned a copy of the *Iliad* – he was the man who used to kiss it in reverence – he could not understand a word it said. Homer, he wrote, 'was dumb to me and I am deaf to it'.

Nevertheless, Homer continued to lurk in the European mind: pervasively there but rarely seen. Medieval *Odyssey*s are scattered through scholarly Europe, in Cambridge and London, Milan and Munich, Naples and Moscow, in Paris, Venice, Stuttgart and Vienna. There are *Iliad*s in the Bodleian in Oxford (from the twelfth century), the Bibliothèque Nationale in Paris (a copy which probably came from Mount Athos), in the Escorial and in Florence. Through these few precious manuscript books, Homer survived in medieval Christendom.

All of them derive in the end, but through routes that are now forever hidden, from the tradition of scholarship that was maintained far to the east in Greek-speaking Byzantium. The earliest complete *Odyssey* to have survived is from the late tenth century, now in Michelangelo's Laurentian Library in Florence, held as one of the greatest of treasures in those beautiful, treasure-rich halls. But slightly earlier than that, and the earliest complete manuscript of Homer anywhere, is the *Iliad* which Villoison thrillingly rediscovered in 1788 in the Biblioteca Marciana in Venice. It is an extraordinary and beautiful manuscript, 654 large goatskin vellum pages, decorated with Byzantine imaginings of the great heroes and notes enclosed within giant lyres. This manuscript, known as Venetus A, was written out in the middle of the tenth century AD in Constantinople, by a scribe who took immense pains with the work, adding in the wide margins a mass of notes and references from earlier scholars there in Byzantium, in Rome and Alexandria. It had been brought to Italy in the first years of the fifteenth century, and in 1468 deposited in the Doge's palace, until it was transferred to Sansovino's library in 1554. There are other still earlier manuscripts from the same Greek tradition surviving in the Vatican and in St Catherine's Monastery in the Sinai desert, but none of them can match the completeness of Venetus A.

From the time Villoison discovered it, that manuscript takes Homer back a thousand years to the scholarly libraries of Byzantium. A series of beautiful discoveries made in the nineteenth century by Europeans travelling in Egypt took Homer further back still. In the early years of the century, Egyptians who had dug rolls of papyrus out of ancient tombs began to offer them for sale. Pieces found their way into gentlemen's libraries across Europe. From the mid-nineteenth century onwards, Egyptologists began a more systematic search for these ancient documents, none more assiduous than the thoroughly unkempt, restlessly energetic and no-sock-wearing Englishman William Flinders Petrie. He was a man who since boyhood had understood that the careful unravelling of historic deposits layer by layer, an exfoliation of the past, was the only way to approach them. In the winter of 1887 he began to dig in the large necropolis at Hawara, in the Fayum depression to the west of the valley of the Nile.

Almost every mummy was accompanied by an image of the person, their unwavering gaze, their necklaces and earrings and carefully braided, gathered hair. With them were other artifacts, beads and vials, mirrors and, tucked in by the dead children, rag dolls with carved heads and real hair. The dolls had changes of clothes, dresses, little tables and wooden bedsteads with which the girls played. Their coffins were made of a kind of papyrus-based papier-mâché, and Flinders Petrie found within their fabric the remains of many ancient texts.

To help with those documents he had with him his old friend, an Oxford Assyriologist, the Reverend Professor Archibald Sayce. 'The floating sand of the desert,' Sayce wrote the next year, was found to be full of shreds of papyrus inscribed with Greek characters. . . They seem to have formed the contents of the office of some public scribe, which have been dispersed and scattered by the wind over the adjoining desert.

It's an image from Shelley, the world after Ozymandias: ancient texts blowing in shreds and fragments across the Egyptian desert. But then Flinders Petrie came across the greatest of all his treasures. On the morning of 21 February 1888, under the head of a woman who was not named on her coffin and was buried in an otherwise unmarked stretch of the necropolis, he found a large roll of papyrus, a papyrus pillow. This was no chance leftover. 'The roll had belonged to a lady with whom it had been buried in death,' Sayce wrote. 'The skull of the mummy showed that its possessor had been young and attractive-looking, with features at once small, intellectual, and finely chiselled, and belonging distinctively to the Greek type.'

The papyrus had been damaged in its outer leaves, but Petrie began to unfold it, as if he were looking into the innards of a wasp's nest, and peering beyond the outer covering found himself reading the Greek numbers twelve and eighty, and the names 'Agamemnon', 'Achaeans', 'Corinth'. The roll with which the young woman had been buried was the first two books of the *Iliad* and, here from Book 2, Flinders Petrie, with the sand of the Sahara blowing around him, was reading lines from the Catalogue of Ships, Homer's enumeration of the Greeks who sailed to Troy.

This Hawara Homer, written on papyrus in about AD 150, is now in the Bodleian Library in Oxford, its lines numbered by Flinders Petrie in August 1888. It is one of the most time-vertigo-inducing objects I know. In columns ranged left, the clear Greek capitals are spooled out across the reedy, vegetal surface of the papyrus sheets. There are no gaps between the words, but they are entirely legible, the relaxed and masterful calligraphy rolling on for line after line like a wave that will not break. This is a text to travel to the next world with, the strokes in each letter just curved away from straightness, so that in its combination of open 'o's and 'u's and the 'w's of its omegas, and the slight flexing in the pen strokes of its 'k's and 'n's and 't's, this is one of the greatest images of the generous and beautiful word ever made. Other contemporary manuscripts found by Flinders Petrie are far more sketchy and scratchy, less steady in their progress across the page; but this is Homer as monument, as scripture, as 'the grandeur of the dooms/We have imagined for the mighty dead'.

The most intriguing aspect of the Hawara Homer, and other papyri of the same era, is how close they are to the text of Homer as it was transmitted to the Byzantine scholars who were assembling the Venetus A manuscript eight hundred years later. By the time the unnamed woman was buried with this precious pillow in the Hawara necropolis, Homer had already become the Homer we now have.

The key phase in this creation of the Homer which Roman, Byzantine, late medieval, Renaissance and early modern Europe all thought of as the undeniable text was in the halls of the Ptolemaic library in Alexandria. Between the third and second centuries BC, a sequence of great Alexandrian editor-scholars, enormously funded by the wealth of the Ptolemies, the rulers of Egypt, created the monumental Homer that is visible in the Hawara grave, in the Byzantine codex Venetus A and in the minds of Alexander Pope and John Keats. That Alexandrian era is the narrow neck through which an earlier and rather different Homer passed.

The famous library of Alexandria was not just a gathering of texts, but far more energetic and dynamic than that, a massive multi-disciplinary research institute, an engine for establishing Alexandria as the centre of the civilised world. By royal edict from the Graeco-Egyptian dynasty of pharaohs, no ship could call at the port of Alexandria without being searched for the books it carried. Every one would be copied with unforgiving exactness and marked in the catalogue as 'from the ships'.

Occasionally the librarians held on to the original and returned the copy.

The Alexandrian library was the repository for Greek culture, the place in which the plays of the Athenian tragedians and the works of Plato and Aristotle were preserved, but it was devised and run on a Near-Eastern model. For thousands of years it had been the practice of great Near-Eastern kings to establish libraries and archives on a scale which individual Greek city-states had never come anywhere near. Alexandria fused Babylon and Nineveh with Athens and Sparta.

With thirty to fifty state-funded scholars at work in the library, the head librarian also the royal tutor, and the agents of the Ptolemies scouring the Mediterranean for copies of all books – magic, music, metaphysics, zoology, geography, cosmology, Babylonian, Jewish, Greek and Egyptian thought – the Alexandrian library was a grand central knowledge machine. It was an exercise in cultural dominance, tyranny through control of the word. By the first century BC, it was thought that the library contained 700,000 papyrus rolls, 120,000 of them poetry and prose, all stored and labelled and catalogued in their own tailored linen or leather jackets.

This industrial-scale exercise in cultural imperialism left its impress on Homer, and the key to the Alexandrian changes is in the large number of marginal notes in Venetus A. The Byzantine scholar in about 950 copied out the text the Alexandrians had bequeathed to him. In his wide margins, he wrote down many of the remarks they had made, not only about Homer but about previous commentators on him. It is Homer as a *millefeuille*: one leaf of scholarship laid on top of another for centuries. Other medieval manuscripts have their own additional notes, or *scholia*, and some of the papyrus fragments, including the Hawara *Iliad*, also have marginal notes from these editors.

It is difficult to escape the idea that the Alexandrian editors, who seem to have limited themselves to commentary rather than cuts, wanted to make Homer proper, to pasteurise him and transform him into something acceptable for a well-governed city, to make of him precisely the dignified monument which the family of the young woman in Hawara had placed beneath her head in death. There was a long tradition of treating Homer like this.

In Plato's *Republic*, written in about 370 BC, Socrates maintained that Homer would be catastrophic for most young men in the ideal city. Poetry itself was suspect, and dangerous if it disturbed the equilibrium of the citizen, but in some passages Homer stepped way beyond the mark. He quotes the beginning of Book 9 of the *Odyssey*, when Odysseus is about to sit down to dinner in the beautiful palace of the king of the Phaeacians.

Nothing, Odysseus says, is more marvellous in life than sitting down to a delicious dinner with your friends, the table noisy and the waiter filling the glasses. 'To my mind,' Odysseus says cheerfully, looking round him at his new friends who have saved him from the unharvestable sea, 'this is the best that life can offer.' Not for Socrates or his pupil Plato:

> Homer is the greatest of poets and first of tragedy writers; but we
> must remain firm in our conviction that hymns to the gods and praises
> of famous men are the only poetry which ought to be admitted into
> our State.

That frame of mind undoubtedly governed the editing process in Alexandria, and its presumptions appear at every turn. Towards the end of Book 8 of the *Iliad*, Hector is making a speech to the Trojans. It has been a long and terrible day on both sides. Among the many dead, Priam's son Gorgythion had been hit hard in the chest with an arrow.

> Just as a poppy in a garden, heavy
> with its ripening seeds, bends to one side
> with the weight of spring rain;
> so his head went slack to one side,
> weighed down by the weight of his helmet.

Night is now falling, and Hector is encouraging the Trojans to prepare themselves for the following day. He has been like a hound in the battle, pursuing the Greeks as if they were wild boar, slashing and strimming at their legs in front of him, his eyes glittering in the slaughter like the god of battle. The corpses had piled up on the field like the swathes of a hay meadow newly mown and yet to be gathered. There is scarcely room for a body of men to stand together. Now, though, Hector has summoned the Trojans 'to a place that was clear of the dead', and speaks to them of the state they are in. They should feed their horses, light fires, roast the meat of sheep and oxen, drink 'honey-hearted wine' and eat their bread. In Troy itself, the old men and the young boys should stand on the walls and the women light great fires in their houses, all to keep a watch so that the Greeks should not 'ambush' them. The word he uses is *lochos*, the same as will be used in the *Odyssey* to describe the Greeks hiding in the Trojan Horse, and which has as its root *lechomai*, meaning 'to lie down'. The implications are clear: the Trojans stand to fight; the Greeks do so cheatingly, creepingly. The ambush, the covert attack, is the kind of violence the Greeks would do. This is Hector speaking as the man of the city, defending it against the treachery of its assailants, a man who in almost every line is the voice of his community.

The Alexandrian editors accepted these noble statements without demur. In these passages Hector fitted the idea of restrained nobility which the Hellenistic Greeks required of Homer. But Hector then moves up a gear and goes on to speak of the next day and of himself. The Greeks are no better than 'dogs, carried by the fates on their black ships'. Hector will go for Diomedes in the morning, and Diomedes will lie there, 'torn open by a spear, with all his comrades dead around him'. And Hector himself will be triumphant:

> If only
> I were as sure of immortality, ageless all my days –
> And I were prized as they prize Athene and Apollo.

A peppering of special marks in the margin, hooks and dots, all carefully transcribed by the Byzantine scholars, signals the Alexandrian editors' anxiety at the vulgarity of these lines.

This apparent self-promotion and self-assertion: can that really be what Homer intended for him? In the third century BC, Zenodotus, the first librarian at Alexandria appointed by the Ptolemies, rejected the line about the fates and their black ships. Aristarchus, his great second-century successor, agreed with him. And when Hector went on to claim immortality, Aristarchus thought his words 'excessively boastful', not the done thing, and highly suspect. In Aristarchus's mind, although not entirely clearly, these lines were probably not Homeric.

It is as if these editors were trying to make Homer into Virgil, to turn Hector into Aeneas, to transform the Greek epics into tales of irreproachable moral instruction, and in doing so to reduce their emotional and psychological range. But Homer was greater than his editors, rougher, less consistent and less polite, a poet who knew that a war leader in his speech on the eve of battle will be both a man of civilisation and its raging opposite.

Compare Hector's words with the speech made by Lieutenant-Colonel Tim Collins in the Kuwaiti desert about twenty miles south of the Iraqi border on 19 March 2003, the eve of the allied invasion of Iraq. Collins had found a place where he could address the men of the 1st Battalion, the Royal Irish Regiment. In his Ray-Bans, with his cigar in his hand and a certain swagger, speaking off the cuff to about eight hundred men standing around him in the middle of a dusty courtyard, he spoke as Homer had Hector speak.

'We go to liberate, not to conquer,' Collins began, half-remembering echoes of the King James Bible, Shakespeare and Yeats, all mingling with the modern everyday in his ear.

> We are entering Iraq to free a people and the only flag which will be flown in that ancient land is their own. Iraq is steeped in history. It is the site of the Garden of Eden, of the Great Flood and the birthplace of Abraham. Tread lightly there. If there are casualties of war then remember that when they woke up and got dressed in the morning they did not plan to die this day. Allow them dignity in death. Bury them properly and mark their graves.

Alongside that restraint and magnanimity towards the enemy, and the sense that he is speaking as the representative of a great civilisation himself, is something else. 'I expect you,' he said, addressing his young soldiers, most of them from poor Catholic Northern Irish backgrounds,

> to rock their world. Wipe them out if that is what they choose . . . The enemy should be in no doubt that we are his nemesis and that we are bringing about his rightful destruction . . . As they die they will know their deeds have brought them to this place. Show them no pity . . . If someone surrenders to you then remember they have that right in international law and ensure that one day they go home to their family. The ones who wish to fight, well, we aim to please.

Hector wants his men to rock the Greeks' world. There is an element of pretension and self-aggrandisement in both of them, but the modern British officer and the Bronze Age poet both know more than the scholar-editors in their Alexandrian halls. Homer's subject is not elegance but truth, however terrible.

The Alexandrians were keen on more than a moralised Homer. Their huge and careful gathering of texts from across the ancient world and from any passing ship was a complex inheritance, a braided stream they tried to purify and make singular, to make one Homer where previously there had been many.

They did their job with scholarly decorum, sometimes deleting lines from the text they bequeathed to the future, usually in their commentaries doing no more than casting doubt on what Homer was meant to have said, marking the text with a skewer, an *obelos*, in the margin, as if to pin the error to the spot. If Homer got things wrong – killing off a warrior who then reappeared in the battle a few lines later; if he repeated a line or group of lines with no variation; if it seemed as if something had been pushed into the poem at a later date; or if Homer's ancient words simply didn't make sense to Hellenistic editors – these were all grounds for severe judgement in Alexandria. Homer had to be kept up to his own standards.

Before that Alexandrian edit, Homer was a not a single monumental presence in the ancient world, but a voluble, chattering crowd of multiple voices. Ancient authors quote lines from Homer which do not appear in the post-Alexandrian text. Occasionally a piece of papyrus will have an odd or variant equivalent for a well-known line. Different Greek cities had their own different Homers. Crete had its own, as did Cyprus, Delos, Chios and Athens. Alexandrian scholars knew versions from Argos in the Peloponnese, Sinope on the Black Sea coast of what is now Turkey, and from the great Greek colony of Massalia far to the west, beneath what is now Marseilles. There were more epics than merely the *Iliad* and the *Odyssey*, filling in the gaps of the story which the poems we know only hint at. Homer was said to have written them all. Aristotle had a different version of Homer from Plato's, and prepared another for his pupil Alexander the Great, to take with him on his world adventures into Asia. Homer ripples around the ancient Mediterranean, and even further afield, taking on local colour, not a man or a poem but flickering, octopus-like, varying, adopting the colours of the country he found himself in. None of these local versions survives as more than references in ancient scholarly notes, but they hint at a reality which would have made William Cowper's or Alexander Pope's hair stand rigid. Homer, before Alexandria, was multiplicity itself.

It's as if in that Alexandrian moment Homer's radiant, ragged beard and hair were trimmed and neatened for a proto-Roman world of propriety and correctness.

Roughness characterises the world before the great pruning. In this way Homer is unlike any historical writer. The usual idea – that copying makes a text increasingly corrupt through time – must be abandoned and the opposite assumption made. As Homer travelled on through time, passing in particular through the rigorous barbers' salon of the Alexandrian scholars, the more regular he became. In the words of Casey Dué, Professor of Classics at Houston and editor of the Harvard Homer multitext project: 'The further back in time we go, the more multiform – the more "wild" – our text of Homer becomes.' Homer is not orderly. Hope to trace him back to his essence, to the tap root, and you find yourself lost among the tangle of his branches. Homer's identity was in his multiplicity, his essence was in his lack of it, and he soon sinks back into the world from which he came.

Homer is never there. He is the great absentee, always slipping between the fingers, a blob of mercury on a bed of wax. Nothing reliable can be said about him: his birthplace, his parents, his life story, his dates, even his existence. Was he one poet or two? Or many? Were the Homers women? Samuel Butler, a great Victorian translator of the *Odyssey*, thought that its poet must have been a girl from Trapani in Sicily, 'young, head-strong and unmarried', partly because she was 'so exquisitely right' in her descriptions of 'every single one of [her] women', partly because she made such girlish mistakes. Would a man ever have thought, for example, that a ship should have a rudder at both ends? Homer does, twice, in the *Odyssey*, Book 9, lines 483 and 540.*

This Homeric unpindownability has inspired eccentrics. Craziness abounds. Medieval Italians, who could not read Greek, used to keep copies of the *Iliad* and kiss them for good luck. Lawrence of Arabia thought he was qualified as a translator of the *Odyssey* because, among other attributes, he, unlike most Greek professors, had 'killed many men'. No point in trying to read Homer unless you had blood on your hands. One scholarly work in Italian has revealed that Homer was Swedish and what he describes as the Mediterranean was in fact the Baltic. Another has recently shown that the *Iliad* is an ancient guidebook to the stars. A careful and immensely detailed study has been written by

---

* But see *The Odyssey*, Murray/Dimock (1999), which justifies Homer's apparent mistake by explaining that between the two mentions of the rudder the Greeks had turned the ship around. There was of course only one rudder, or steering oar, at the stern, but within the course of the story the vessel was facing in two different directions.

a Dutchman to show that Homer was from Cambridgeshire, the Trojan War happened on the Gog Magog hills near Cherry Hinton, 'Sparta' was in Spain and 'Lesbos' was the Isle of Wight. Henriette Mertz, a Chicago patent attorney, has shown that Calypso lived in the Azores and Scylla and Charybdis was Homer's description of tidal movements in the Bay of Fundy, Newfoundland. Nausicaa and her father lived in the Caribbean.

None of this is new. Plutarch (AD c.46–120) thought Calypso's island was five days' sail from Britain out in the North Atlantic, perhaps in the Faroes. Earlier still, many lives of Homer were written in the ancient world, some now preserved in precious early medieval manuscripts that are stored in some of the great repositories of Europe. They are rich in creative detail, but, like so much else to do with Homer, all of them were made up. In the library of the Medicis in Florence you will find a fourteenth-century manuscript which describes the way in which Homer lived and worked and sang his poems on Chios, the desiccated rusk of an island off the Aegean coast of Turkey. According to a ninth-century manuscript now in the Biblioteca Nazionale in Rome, he was born in Smyrna, on what is now the Turkish mainland. Others say in Ithaca, as the grandson of Odysseus, or so the Pythia in Delphi told the Emperor Hadrian when he enquired; or the Argolid, where Agamemnon had ruled in Mycenae; in Thessaly, in the harsh and half-civilised north of Greece, the northern zone on the edge of civility from where Achilles came; or, as a manuscript now in Rome claims, in Egypt, because his heroes had the habit of kissing each other and that was an Egyptian practice. Even, in time, the Romans themselves claimed him as one of theirs. An eleventh-century manuscript now in the royal library in the Escorial outside Madrid adds Athens to the list. Many claim he was born, or died, or at least lived for a while, on the island of Ios in the Cyclades. In other words, he came from everywhere and nowhere.

The life of Homer lurks in this way in the subconscious of the European imagination. He is present in the archives but mysteriously absent. And hanging over all the suggestions in these ancient lives, which are thought to draw on ideas of Homer that emerged in about the sixth century BC, is a deep air of doubt. Did Homer really come from any of these places? Homer, even in the tradition of the ancient lives, seems to exist as a kind of miasma, a suggestion of himself, more an idea than a man, a huge and potent non-being.

But from these muddled, uncertain texts one or two beautiful suggestions do emerge. In the ninth-century life of Homer now in the Biblioteca Nazionale in Rome, the author – himself anonymous – compiled the verdicts he could glean from the past, and quoted Aristotle from a book called *On Poets* which is otherwise now lost. 'The people of Ios, Aristotle said, record that Homer was born from a spirit, a daimon, who danced along with the Muses.' His mother, a girl from Ios, had got pregnant with the daimon. So it was as simple as that: like Jesus and Achilles, Homer was half human. And his flesh was infused not with mere godliness but with the spirit of poetry. Just as Aesop never existed but was a name around which traditional fables gathered, Homer was the name given to the poems they composed.

The word Aristotle used for this moment of fusion carries some wonderful implications. The Greek for 'dance with' is *synchoreuo*, meaning 'to join in the chorus with'. The *choreia* of which the Muses and Homer's daimon father formed a part was a singing dance – words, music and movement together. The same word meant both the tune they danced to and, by extension, any orderly circle or circling motion. Even the islands of the Cyclades, of which Ios is one, arranged as they are in a wide circle on the horizon around the sacred island of Delos, were thought to be a *choreia*. It was, in essence, any beautiful turning in motion together, especially of the stars. Buried in this half-mystical genealogy is the understanding that Homer's poems are the music of the universe.

Another life, said to have been written by Plutarch, the Greek historian of the first century AD, and perhaps genuinely drawing on Plutarch's lost books, says straightforwardly that Homer's fatherland was nowhere on earth; his ancestors came from 'great heaven' itself: 'For you were born of no mortal mother, but of Calliope.' Calliope was the Muse of epic poetry. Her name means 'beautiful voice' and she was the daughter of Zeus, the all-powerful king of the gods, and of Mnemosyne, the goddess of memory. This is not the language we now use. It is even a little off-putting, too high, too reminiscent of murky paintings on ignorable ceilings, but it says what seems to be the truth. There was no human being called Homer: his words are the descendants of memory and power, the offspring of the Muse who had a beautiful voice. The myth itself identifies something that biography and geography can only grasp at. Homer is his poetry. No man called Homer was ever known, and it doesn't help to think of Homer as a man. Easier and better is to see him abstractly, as the collective and inherited vision of great acts done long ago. The poems acknowledge that. In the first lines of both the *Iliad* and the *Odyssey*, they call on the Muse as their own divine mother, the source of authority and power, to tell the tales the teller is about to begin.

The name Homer – which is pronounced in Greek with a short 'o' and a long 'e', *Homeeros*, making it stranger than you had imagined, from a more distant world – may mean 'blind', at least in the dialect of Greek spoken on Lesbos. From the name came the tradition that Homer was blind, although that too was fiercely disputed by the ancient authors.

Or it may mean something stranger still: a 'connector', or even 'bond'. Homer, perhaps, was the man who joined together, in the way of the poet, things which might otherwise have lived apart: different elements of the inherited stories; or those stories and the audiences who listened to his telling of them.

There is another tradition, related to that one, which runs through all his ancient biographies. Homer was not his original name, perhaps only given him when he went blind or became a hostage (another possible etymology). His original name in this version was Melesigenes, perhaps because he was born by the river Meles, which runs through Smyrna, now Izmir, or more intriguingly because the name can mean 'caring for his clan'. This Homer is to be seen as the man who cared for his people, his inheritance, his race descent, the way he came into being, his origins. Homer is what looked after the source, what found, remembered and transmitted truth from the distant past. In that meaning of his name, his essence is not his smart newness, his ability to connect, but the antiquity of the tales he tells. He is the embodiment of retrospect.

All poetry is memorial. Much of it is elegy. The earliest to have been found was dug up by Victorian archaeologists in Sumer, in what is now Iraq, on a tablet marked with wedge-shaped cuneiform symbols pressed into the wet clay before it dried. The fragmentary poems in the clay were written in about 2600 BC, perhaps two thousand years before the Homeric epics were first written on papyrus. But that first written

Sumerian poetry is not about the springtime of the world. Poetry begins by looking back to the beautiful past, a song about Ashnan, the goddess of grain, and her seven sons, opening with these chantable, formulaic repetitive lines:

> *U re u re na-nam*
> *Gi re gi re na-nam*
> *Mu re mu re na-nam.*

> In those days, now it was in those days,
> In those nights, now it was in those nights,
> In those years, now it was in those years.

As far back as you can reach, poets have been looking back, their poetry living in the gap that opens between now and then. Another song, from Ur in Iraq, written down at about the same time, instructs the singer to

> attend to what is old, and not allow it to be neglected.
> Let nothing be neglected in practice,
> Let him apply himself to the art of singing
> Let the scribe stand by and catch the songs in his handwriting
> Let the singer stand by and speak to the scribe from the songs
> So that they will be made to last in the scribal college
> So that none of my praise-song should perish
> So that none of my words should be dropped from the tradition.

This song is what Melesigenes, Homer's hidden name, actually means. You might think of Homer as the skilled reteller of his people's stories. But he is more than that; the poems are the passed baton itself, ancient meaning enshrined in the remembered word.

There is one more story, often repeated in the fictional biographies of him that were written throughout antiquity, which hints at Homer's unfittedness for the ordinary world. It exists in many versions, but the most articulate has survived in a manuscript transcribed in the eleventh century AD and now in the great royal library in the Escorial outside Madrid.

Homer is at the end of his life, sitting on the beach on the Cycladean island of Ios, after a life of travelling and singing his poems in many places in the Greek world. This is not his home. As he sits there, alone and blind, he hears some fishermen coming up the beach towards him. They have been at sea, and Homer calls out to them: 'Fishermen from Arcadia [it is unexplained why it should be Arcadia in the Peloponnese when he is in the Cyclades], have we caught anything?' There is something charming, or perhaps self-ingratiating, in that 'we'. But they reply unkindly. 'All that we caught we have left behind and all that we missed we carry.' By which they mean that their fishing had been useless, but as they sat out at sea with nothing to do, they searched each other's bodies for lice. Those lice they had caught, they killed and threw into the sea; those they missed were still on them in their clothes.

It was a joke, a riddle, a tease for a blind old man, but he didn't understand it, and, crushed by the loneliness and depression that came in the wake of that failure to comprehend, he died on Ios, where he was buried under an epitaph he had written himself:

> Here the earth conceals that sacred head,
> The setter-in-beautiful-order [*kosmētora*] of heroic men,
> the godly Homer.

According to that much-repeated story, it was the triviality of the joke, a ridiculing of incapacity, even a lack of nobility in others, that finally killed him. This is Homer as the Great Outsider, blind, from beyond our ken, the figure who does not belong in the world where everyone knows everyone else, the man who has yet to enter the restaurant or the drawing room. He is outside our normality, scarcely even aware of the merry din within, with an austerity about him, a grandeur and an urgent, other reality.

Homer – allied to his neighbour and contemporary, Isaiah, another great speaker of wisdom, whose dates and identity also stretch across many generations from at least 1500 to 600 BC – is the archetype from which every great seer is descended: he is Lear on the heath, Rousseau in a reverie on his island in the Lac de Bienne, the Ancient Mariner who waylays the wedding guest at the bridegroom's door, but who will never enter that feast. Homer exists in his other world, almost unknowably separate from us in time and space, a realm whose distance allows ideas of transcendence to develop around him. His distance from us is itself an imaginative space which his own greatness expands to fill.

This is no modern effect: it was the effect Homer had on the ancient Greeks, as a voice from the distant past, even a voice from the silence, the voice of greatness untrammelled by any connection with our present mundanities. Homer doesn't describe the world of heroes: he *is* the world of heroes. As his epitaph said, he made their *kosmos*, a word which in Greek can mean order, world, beauty and honour. It is used in the *Iliad* when the commanders set their men in order for battle. It is used to describe the order in which a poet sets the elements of his tale. Those qualities are all different dimensions of one thing. Everything one might associate with the heroic – nobility, directness, vitality, scale, unflinching regard for truth, courage, adventurousness, coherence, truth – is an aspect of the cosmic and all of it is what 'Homer' means.

FIVE

Finding Homer

IT SEEMS CLEAR, FROM the kind of Greek in which the Homeric poems are written, that the main text preserved by the Alexandrians came from Athens, where Homer could be heard almost daily, in recitals by rhapsodes, professional artists who strung together choice passages from the epics, learning by heart parts of the inherited text and, in a way not entirely approved of by the traditionalists, selling their services for dinner parties or entertainments. Homer was also used as a manual in school, the poems treated as tales of great men and women, of nobility in crisis, and of the choices people must make when faced with the deepest challenges of their lives. Homer for classical Athens was an encyclopaedia of moral choice.

It was also performed with enormous elaboration at the four-yearly festival of the Panathenaia, where, at least according to Eustathius, a twelfth-century Byzantine bishop of Thessalonica, the reciters of the *Odyssey* wore sea-purple and of the *Iliad* earth-red costumes, 'the purple on account of Odysseus's wanderings at sea, the red on account of the slaughter and bloodshed at Troy'. If the *Odyssey* men were soaked in the royal purple dye of the Phoenicians and those of the *Iliad* in the blood of the heroes, nothing could be clearer about the role Homer played in classical Athens's idea of itself. At their most holy and self-conscious moment, the Athenians gathered for total immersion in the Homeric stories, drinking up the tales from which most of the great tragedies drew their plots and characters, thinking of Homer as the source of what they were.

A clan of reciters from Chios on the eastern side of the Aegean, calling themselves the Homeridae, claimed to be Homer's descendants and to have his precious poems in manuscript handed down to them by the great man their ancestor. There is no telling if there is any truth in that, but, under the Athenian surface, the main constituent of the Greek in which the epics are written is Ionic, which was spoken in Chios and other parts of western Anatolia. And there is an early piece of evidence for Chios in the so-called *Homeric Hymn to Delian Apollo*, written in Homeric hexameters, when the singer himself says:

> Remember me in after time whenever any one of the men on earth, a stranger who has seen and suffered much, comes here and asks of you: 'Who do you think, girls, is the sweetest singer that comes here, and in whom do you most delight?' Then answer, each and all of you, with one voice: 'He is a blind man, and lives in rocky Chios: his songs are forever supreme.' As for me, I will carry your fame as far as I roam over the earth to the well-placed cities of man, and they will believe also; for indeed this thing is true.

The *Iliad* also knows that country, not only the shape of the land around Troy, but the habits of the wind, the form of islands and the nature of the sea there. If Homer needs to turn for a comparison to a specific place, the choice he usually makes is there too.

Chios lies only seven miles off the Turkish coast. Its dry limestone gorges push deep into its mountains and, on the bench of flat arable land beside the sea, acre after acre is covered in olive groves, vineyards and the dark, irregular mastic bushes, the source of a clear chewable gum, much valued in antiquity.

The huge harbour at Chios town is almost empty of shipping now – a few yachts, a ferry, one or two container ships – but is still surrounded by the cafés on the port side, the banging of dominos on tables, the bales of stuff awaiting collection. Behind them are the crumbling neo-classical villas of the Chiote merchant class who in the nineteenth century made their fortunes trading around the Mediterranean. Chios is what it always has been: a commercial island, outward-looking – there are still some powerful ship-owning families here – and with its foundations resting on the products of the earth, the red wine, loved by Virgil, famous across the whole Mediterranean for its blackness, and the pungent, peppery green island oil.

Far to the south of Chios town, a rare and extraordinary ghost of the Homeric world can be recovered. A narrow road curls its way down the length of the island. Drought is all around you, a blazing sky and burningly bright rocks. In among the rocks are the cisterns, the beautiful dark and buried places of cool and conservation, an eye of water at their heart, roofed in stone, protected from the sun. In a landscape of such exposure and harshness, the cistern seems like the guarantee of continuity.

All this defines a dry world. It doesn't rain in Chios from the beginning of June until the end of October. What rain has fallen in the winter sinks into the ground and emerges from the rock reservoirs as springs. There the soil gathers and the fertility builds in a landscape which is otherwise bones. The result is a kind of sharpness, super-definition, a world polarised between the inhabited and the bare, the habitable and the desolate.

In places like this, the growing of human sustenance can only be governed by the presence of water. Where the springs emerge, *vryses* in modern Greek, is where the vegetable gardens are. 'I am going to the springs' means 'I am going to the gardens.' The roots of that word stretch far back into ancient Greek, from *bruein*, which when it describes water means 'to gush out', 'to bubble up', 'to spring'. But further than that *bruein* means 'to be full to bursting', to swell, to abound, to be luxuriant, to teem with produce. It is the verb of emergent life.

Beyond the gardens full of grapes and figs, pomegranates, plums and blackberries, those miraculous concentrations of sugar and juice in the damp corners of the island, often away from houses, the dry country stretches, the world of drought in which everything that grows infiltrates its roots between the rocks and is defended against the grazing and browsing teeth of the animals that would devour it. The leaves that survive are either bitter or armoured in thorns. Even the thorns are branched, thorns with thorns on them. Settlement here cannot choose to dispose itself carelessly as it can in a temperate or wooded country. Life must be concentrated: the city, the village, the gathered place is a necessary response to a landscape in which life is thin on the ground.

Almost at the southern tip of the island, Emporio is little more than a scatter of one or two buildings and a taverna, a stub of a quay at which the fishing boats are tied up, a looped horseshoe of a harbour, a grey beach on which the Aegean laps. Its name means 'the trading centre', the emporium, which may also have been the name of this small settlement in antiquity. Here, in June 1952, came two of the great men of Homeric studies in the second half of the twentieth century: a young English archaeologist, John Boardman, then Deputy Director of the British School at Athens, with the young architect Michael Ventris, the man who would soon decipher Linear B, the written language of Mycenaean Greece.

They walked up from the harbour – 'a well-girt man carrying nothing in his hands can today reach the acropolis from the harbour side in twenty minutes without serious loss of breath' – and high above the valley, on top of a dry, conical hill overlooking the little harbour, they found an ancient settlement, a rocky citadel, heavily walled against raiding pirates, the workmanship of the masonry, Boardman reported, 'wretched throughout'.

It was no great city, but a rather poor and abandoned village, probably built in about 800 BC, with outside the acropolis walls some small, stepped and paved, walkable streets between one- or two-roomed houses. There are stables and granaries beside them. The scale is domestic, and because nothing was built here later, everything is clear on the ground, looking much as it did when abandoned in 600 BC. The tall white spires of the asphodels glow on the stony, lizardy hillsides. Inside the acropolis walls there is a small temple to Athene (Boardman and Ventris found little votive shields in there, given by fighting men to the warlike goddess) and a *megaron*, a large columned room about sixty feet long and twenty wide, a gathering hall, with the stone bases of three wooden columns down its centre. Perhaps eighty people could have met here. It is not unlike a Saxon or Viking mead-hall, in which the sagas or *Beowulf* would have been heard or sung. It is the great house of the settlement, the only one inside the acropolis walls, and with a commanding view from its columned porch down across the hill to the harbour below. Boardman found little inside, a few pieces of pottery with a 'heavy cream slip', the handle of a wine jug, but stand in here now and you can start to feel your way towards the Homeric world of the eighth century.

The megaron at Emporio, Chios.

Beyond the lee of the island, the Aegean sparkles under the north wind. On the far shore, grey mountains step back into the Asian mainland – a promise of scale and richness outside the constraints of island life. The eighth-century sea is full of threat, and even in the sunshine, as cigarette smoke disappears in the brilliance of the light, Emporio feels carefully held back, marginal, defensive. It is cleverly designed so that the harbour can be seen from the acropolis, but the acropolis is almost invisible from the harbour. You can watch the people down there in the taverna, where the fish are smoking on the griddles, and they will not know.

Boardman thought that about five hundred people might have lived here, in about fifty houses spread over ten acres. Their lord and master would have occupied the megaron, and there the heroic songs would have been sung. There is no grandeur. It is a rough, overt power structure. The plain below the acropolis may be covered in olives and mastic bushes, and its harbour is there so that these people can reach out to lands beyond those horizons, but this miniature city is up here for protection.

Emporio is both closed and open, a place to withdraw into and one to venture out from. It is a place belonging to robber-traders, at least half-piratical, needing to rely on imported grain for its sustenance, perhaps from Egypt, perhaps from the Black Sea, and to export its wine and oil and gum for its currency, but inseparable from violence. Here it is possible to feel that Homer is the product of an essentially marginal world, away from the great civilisations, the lords of Emporio fascinated by the great but not able to count themselves among them.

If Homer was an ancient inheritance in the eighth century BC, as I believe it was, already a thousand years old, this is the sort of place in which that memory would have been treasured and nurtured, where the Keatsian sense of enlargement and the surge of greatness would have been experienced by the young men hearing the stories, no doubt inspiring their own visions of love and violence. Just as much as Athens or Alexandria, places like this would have been links in the chain.

Only the phlomis and the thorns grow on the eastern shore of Chios; the only colours are the sand-washed blue of the sea and the rust stains in the limestone of the cliffs. Here and there the cushion tufts of a low thistle show purple in its nest of thorns. On a stony path just above the sea, with a swell breaking on the shore, I found a young kid, perhaps born that spring and now laid out on a rock, dead and as dry as a parchment. It had been preserved by the drought. Its leather collar and bell was still around its neck, its yellow plastic ear-tags pinned into its ears, its hooves tucked up under its chest, where its ribs like flat, blanched pencils just protruded from the coat. The teeth were made prominent by the shrinking of the lips, but otherwise it was almost perfect, as if in the drought one day it had simply lain down and died. Touchingly, its head was turned as if it were trying to lick its own flank. The eyes were gone, and you could look through their sockets into the skull. It was the Homeric world: brutal, perfect, without euphemism, but somehow enshrining a longing for something better, softer, more forgiving.

The Homeric poems, or at least versions of them, were written down somewhere very like this, perhaps in about 725 BC, or maybe as much as a century later. Precision is almost certainly irrelevant; there can be no ruler-drawn horizon at which the written Homer begins.

If Homer is from this moment, then the poems are the product of a culture emerging from a dark age, looking to a future but also looking back to a past, filled with nostalgia for the years of integrity, simplicity, nobility and straightforwardness. The *Iliad* is soaked in retrospect. The *Odyssey* the twin and pair of it, filled with heroic adventurism and the sense of possibility, as if it were an American poem and the *Iliad* its European counterpart.

There is no doubt that the poet of the *Odyssey* knew the *Iliad*. The *Odyssey*, with extraordinary care, is shaped around the pre-existence of the *Iliad*. It fills in details that are absent from the earlier poem – the Trojan Horse, the death of Achilles – but never mentions anything that is described there. That discretion and mutuality is present on a deeper level too. So, where the *Iliad* is a poem about fate and the demands that fate puts on individual lives, the inescapability of death and of the past, of each of us being locked inside a set of destinies, the *Odyssey*, for all its need to return home, consistently toys with the offer of a new place and a new life, a chance to revise what you have been given, for the individual – or at least the great individual – to stand out against fate.

The two poems talk across that divide. The *Iliad* is rooted in the pain of Troy the singular place and the sense of entrapment that brings to everyone involved. The *Odyssey* is constantly free and constantly inventive. That difference is reflected in the two heroes. Achilles is fixed into rage, into need to fulfil his fate, fixed into having to avenge the death of his friend Patroclus. Odysseus is always slipping out, the man who has been everywhere, seen everything, done everything, but also thought of every-thing, invented everything and changed everything.

These are the two possibilities for human life. You can either do what your integrity tells you to do, or niftily find your way around the obstacles life throws in your path. That is the great question the poems pose. Which will you be? Achilles or Odysseus, the monument of obstinacy and pride or the slippery trickster in whom nothing is certain and from whom nothing can be trusted? The singular hero or the ingenious man?

The *Iliad* embraces an earlier, rawer, more heroic and more tragic past. The *Odyssey* looks forward, takes modern dealing and adventuring and casts a magic spell over it so that it becomes a strange and idealised version of the trading and colonising life. The *Iliad* is a picture of what we think we once were and maybe long to be; and the *Odyssey* a version of what we are and what we might yet be. There is no need to put a date on those perspectives: their prospect and retrospect are everlasting dimensions of the human condition. In any age, the present is no more than the saddle of level ground at the pass, an instant of revelation in front of you and abandonment behind. Like all great art, Homer is essentially transitional, emergent, hung between what is lost and what does not yet exist.

In a way that remains permanently and inevitably uncertain, the Phoenician alphabet arrived in the Greek world, probably in the ninth century BC, from the trading ports of the Near East. Powerful currents were running between the Near East and the Aegean. Craftsmen, foods, spices, herbs, precious metals, ways of working that metal, myths, meta-physical ideas, poetry, stories – all were flooding in from the east, and the alphabet came with them. Unlike the earlier complex scripts, the simple Phoenician alphabet wasn't confined to high-class scribes, and the Greeks soon adapted it to their own use, adapting Phoenician letters for vowels and for 'ph-', 'ch-' and 'ps-', which do not occur in Phoenician. Like the songs of Homer themselves, the Greek scripts they developed varied from place to place, but of all the scraps and fragments of early Greek text that have survived from the eighth century none is more suddenly illuminating than a small reconstructed object from the island of Ischia, at the far, western end of the Greek-speaking world, guarding the northern entrance to the bay of Naples.

Ischia now is a dream of wellbeing, a sharply dressed salad of an island, rising to a high volcanic peak in Mount Epomeo, rimmed in lidos and those in search of rheumatic cures, but with a lush greenness which must have seemed to any Aegean sailor like an oasis of welcome. It is a version of Calypso's island, balmy, seductive, inviting, somehow suspended from mundane realities. The sun comes up over the shoulder of Vesuvius on the mainland and lights the lemon trees and the figs. Mounds of bougainvillea and ipomoea clump and tumble down the hillsides. A milky haze hangs all morning over an almost motionless sea. Bees hum in the rosemary flowers and crickets tick over in the grass.

Ischia offered the early Iron Age Greeks more than exquisite comfort. When the first settlers came here in about 770 BC from the Aegean island of Euboea, they set up the earliest, most northern and most distant of all Greek colonies in Italy. They chose it because the northern tip of the island provides the perfect recipe for a defensible trading post: a high, sheer-walled acropolis, Monte Vico, with sheltered bays on each side, one protected from all except northerlies, the other open only to the east. Between the two a shallow saddle is rich in deep volcanic soils where a few vine and fruit trees still grow among the pine-umbrellaed villas and the swimming pools. Here, beginning in the early 1950s, the archaeologist Giorgio Buchner excavated about five hundred eighth- and seventh-century BC graves which reveal the lives of people for whom the Homeric poems were an everyday reality.

This little Greek stone town was called Pithekoussai, Ape-island, perhaps from the monkeys they found here on arrival, or more interestingly as a name suitable for people who were seen from the mainland as vulgar and adventurous traders, laden with cash, irreverent and with uncertain morals, enriching themselves on the edge of the known world (*pithekizo* meant 'to monkey about'). It was an astonishing and wonderful melting pot, four thousand people living here by 700 BC, nothing half-hearted about it, nor apparently militaristic. People from mainland Italy, speaking a kind of Italic, were living here, with Phoenicians from Tyre and Sidon, Byblos and Carthage, Aramaeans from modern Syria and Greeks. The archaeologists found no ethnic zoning in the cemetery. All were living together and dying together, buried side by side. There was little apparent in the way of ethnic gap between these people. It was a deeply mixed world. Iron with the chemical signatures of Elba and mainland Tuscany was worked here in the blacksmiths' quarter and sold on to clients in the Near East. Trade linked the island with Apulia, Calabria, Sardinia, Etruria and Latium as well as the opposite Campania shore. No other Greek site in Italy has objects from such a vast stretch of the Iron Age Mediterranean.

Buchner found no hint in any of the graves of a warrior aristocracy. The only blades were a few iron knives, awls and chisels. The leading members of the Pithekoussai world were from a commercial middle class, some with small workshops for iron and bronze, many with slaves of their own. The style of burial marks the difference between those classes: the slaves hunched foetally in small and shallow hollows, no possessions beside them; their masters, mistresses and their children laid out supine, in plain and dignified style, accompanied by simple but beautiful grave goods.

Much of their pottery came from Corinth and Rhodes, and what they didn't import, they copied. Small Egyptian scarabs were often worn as amulets by the children and went to their graves with them, along with stone seals from northern Syria and one or two Egyptian faience beads. There are some fine red pots made in the Phoenician city of Carthage on the North African coast, and silver pins and rings from Egypt. A tomb of a young woman buried in about 700 BC was found with her body surrounded by little dishes from Corinth and small ointment jars, seventeen of them, around her, a dressing-table-full. Men also had little fat-bellied oil jars with them, some no more than an inch high and an inch across, pocket offerings, maybe used in the funeral rites. A fisherman was buried with his line and net; only the bronze fish hook and the folded-over lead weights of the net have survived. These men were all buried in the way of Homeric heroes, their bodies cremated on wooden pyres, and then interred with the charred wood and their possessions beneath small tumuli.

Nothing is coarse or gross. Big-eyed sea snakes and fluent, freely-drawn fish decorate the grey-and-ochre pottery. There are flat-footed wine jugs, suitable for a shipboard table. There is one big dish decorated with a chariot wheel, perhaps another faint heroic memory. Some pots are decorated with griffins from patterns that had their distant origins in Mesopotamia, others with swastikas that probably originated just as long ago in the Proto-Indo-European cultures of the Caspian steppe.

Fusion and mixture, a kind of mental mobility, is the identifying mark of this little city. It was not a luxury civilisation, but as you spend a morning walking around the empty, cool marble halls of the Pithekoussai Museum in the Villa Arbusto, peering in at the pots, you can feel the stirring of life in this distant and adventurous place 2,700 years ago. It doesn't take much to see the wine being mixed in these bowls, poured from these jugs or drunk from these cups, nor the glittering fish hauled up in these nets or the goods loaded on distant quays and beaches and sold from here to curious buyers on the mainland of Italy.

And the museum holds its surprises. One late-eighth-century *cratēr* originally made in Attica, a bowl for mixing wine and water, depicts this world in trouble.

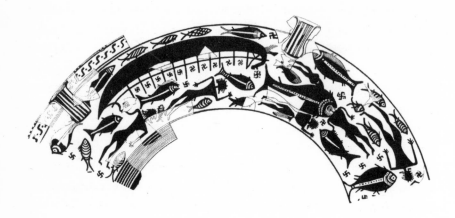

On its grey and rapidly painted body, a ship floats all wrong in the sea, turned over in a gale, its curved hull now awash, its prow and stern pointing down to the seabed. Everything has fallen out. Wide-shouldered and huge-haunched men are adrift in the ocean beneath, their hair ragged, their arms flailing for shore and safety. Striped and cross-hatched fish, some as big as the men, others looking on, swim effortlessly in the chaos. A scattering of little swastikas does little to sanctify this fear-filled waterworld. One man's head is disappearing into the mouth of the biggest fish of all. It is a disaster, fuelled by the fear the Greeks had of the creatures of the sea, alien animals which, as Achilles taunts one of his victims, 'will lick the blood from your wounds and nibble at your gleaming fat'. The scene is no new invention; it is painted with all the rapidity and ease of having been painted many times before.

There is no need to attach the name of Odysseus to this; nor of Jonah, the Hebrew prophet swallowed by a fish, his story exactly contemporary with this pot. It is merely the story of life on the Iron Age seas, the reality of shipwreck, the terror of the sea as a closing-over element filled with voracious monsters. In a later, Western picture, the large-scale catastrophe of the ship itself would have been the focus. Here it is pushed to the outer margin and made almost irrelevant; the central characters are the men, their hair and limbs out of order, the experience of human suffering uppermost. In that way, this is a picture from the Homeric mind.

Then, in a room hidden deep in the museum, you find the other transforming dimension of Pithekoussai: these people wrote. Shards from the eighth century BC are marked or painted with tiny fragments of Greek. One has the name *'Teison'*, perhaps the cup's owner. A second, on a little fragment of a cup, says *'eupoteros'* – meaning 'better to drink from'. A third, also in Greek, written like the others with the letters reading from right to left as they are in Phoenician, and with no gaps between the words, says, fragmentarily, '. . .*m' epoies[e]'*. The verb *poieo* has the same root as 'poetry', and the inscription means 'someone whose name ended in -inos made me' – Kallinos, Krokinos, Minos, Phalinos, Pratinos? This is no scratched graffito, but painted as part of the Geometric design. It is another first: the oldest artist's signature in Europe.

By 750 BC at the latest, writing had seeped into all parts of this expanding, connecting, commercial, polyglot world. Pithekoussai is not unique. Eighth-century inscriptions, many of them chatty, everyday remarks, with no claim to special or revered significance, have survived from all over the Aegean and Ionian Seas. These aren't officious palace directives, but witty remarks, sallies to be thrown into conversation.

And, as a wonderful object on Ischia reveals, Homer played his part. It was found in the tomb of a young boy, perhaps fourteen years old, who died in about 725 BC. He was Greek, and unlike most of the children was cremated, an honour paid to his adulthood and maturity. In his grave his father placed many precious things: a pair of Euboean wine-mixing bowls from the famous potters of their home island, jugs, other bowls, and lots of little oil pots for ornaments.

The greatest treasure looks insignificant at first: a broken and mended wine cup from Rhodes, about seven inches across, grey-brown with black decoration and sturdy handles. Scratched into its lower surface on one side, and not at first visible but dug away a little roughly with a burin, are three lines of Greek, the second and third of which are perfect Homeric hexameters. This is not only the oldest surviving example of written Greek poetry, contemporary with the moment Homer is first thought to have been written down, it is also the first joke about a Homeric hero.

In the *Iliad*, during a passage of brutal bloodletting and crisis for the Greeks, the beautiful Hecamede, a deeply desirable Trojan slave-woman, captured by Achilles and now belonging to Nestor, mixes a medicinal drink for the wounded warriors as they come in from battle: strong red wine, barley meal and, perhaps a little surprisingly, grated goat's cheese, with an onion and honey on the side. Hecamede did the mixing in a giant golden, dove-decorated cup belonging to Nestor, which a little pretentiously he had brought from home: 'Another man could barely move that cup from the table when it was full, but old Nestor would lift it easily.'

There are Near-Eastern stories of giant unliftable cups belonging to heroes from the far distant past. And tombs of warriors have been found on Euboea from the ninth century BC which contain, along with their arms and armour, some big bronze cheese-graters, now thought to be part of the warrior's usual field kit, perhaps for making medicines, perhaps for snacks.

So this little situation – the Nestor story, the unliftable cup, the Euboean inheritance, and the presence at a drinking party of wonderfully desirable women – has deep roots. Remarkably, they come together in the joke and invitation scratched on the Ischian cup. 'I am the cup of Nestor,' it says,

good for drinking
Whoever drinks from this cup, desire for beautifully
crowned Aphrodite will seize him instantly.

The Pithekoussaian trader was turning the Homeric scriptures upside down. This little cup was obviously *not* like Nestor's cup, the very opposite in fact: all too liftable. Its wine was *not* to cure wounds received in battle. It was to get drunk at a party. And drinking it would *not* lead on to an old man's interminable reminiscing over his heroic past. No, the cup and the delicious wine it contained would lead on to the far more congenial activity of which Aphrodite was queen: sex. This elegant little wine cup, treasured far from home amid all the burgeoning riches, gold and silver brooches, success and delight of Pithekoussai, a place supplied with beautiful slave-girls taken from the Italian mainland, was for the drinking of alcoholic aphrodisiacs. The inscription was an eighth-century invitation to happiness.

The distant past might often seem like the realm of seriousness, but the Ischian cup re-orientates that. The first written reference to Homer is so familiar with him, and so at ease with writing, that in mock Homeric hexameters it can deny all the seriousness Homer has to offer. Homer and his stories were so deeply soaked into the fabric of mid- to late-eighth-century BC Greek culture that dad-style jokes could be made about him. And that makes one thing clear: here, in 725 BC, is nowhere near the beginning of this story. The original Homer is way beyond reach, signalling casually from far out to sea.

There is only one aspect of grief associated with the sophisticated optimism and gaiety of this story, and it is inadvertent. The father offered this cup to his fourteen-year-old son in the flames of the funeral pyre, where it broke into the pieces which the archaeologists have now painstakingly gathered and restored. Death denied the boy the adult pleasures to which these toy-verses were inviting him. And that is another capsule of the Homeric condition: the Odysseyan promise of delight enclosed within the Iliadic certainty of death.

SIX

Homer the Strange

THE PITHEKOUSSAI WINE CUP marks the limits of the written Homer. It is the edge of a time-cliff: step beyond it, further back in time, and the ground falls away. In that disturbingly airy and insubstantial world out beyond the cliff face, before the eighth century BC, Homer is unwritten, existing only in the minds of those who knew him.

It is a disorientating condition for our modern culture: how can something of such importance and richness have had no material form? How can the Greeks have trusted so completely to their minds? At home in Scotland, I sometimes go up to the edge of the sea-cliff above the house, looking down to the fulmars circling in the four hundred feet of air below me. Again and again, the birds cut their effortless discs in that space, turning in perfect, repetitive circles, in and out of the sunlight, scarcely adjusting a feather to the eddies, but calm and self-possessed in all the mutability around them; and I have thought that in that fulmar-flight there may be a model of the Homeric frame of mind. You don't need to fix something to know it. You know it by doing it again and again, never quite the same, never quite differently. You may even find, in that tiller-tweaking mobility – a slight adjustment here, another there – that you know things which the rigid and the fixed could never hope to know. The flight is alive in the flying, not in any record of it. And perhaps we, not Homer, are the aberration. Of about three thousand languages spoken today, seventy-eight have a written literature. The rest exist in the mind and the mouth. Language – man – is essentially oral.

Until the twentieth century, no one had any idea that Homer might have existed in this strange and immaterial form. It was the assumption that Homer, like other poets, *wrote* his poetry. Virgil, Dante and Milton were merely following in his footsteps. The only debate was over why these written poems were in places written so badly. Why had he not written them better? Both the *Iliad* and the *Odyssey* are riddled with internal contradictions. No self-respecting poet would allow such clumsiness.

The great eighteenth-century Cambridge scholar Richard Bentley – the dullest man alive, according to Alexander Pope, 'that microscope of Wit,/ Sees hairs and pores, examines bit by bit' – thought that Homer wrote

> a sequel of songs and Rhapsodies, to be sung by himself for small earnings and good cheer, at festivals and other days of Merriment; the Ilias he made for the men and the Odysseis for the other Sex. These loose songs were not connected together in the form of an epic poem till . . . about 500 years after.

Homer was no longer a genius; he was the work of an editor-collector, perhaps not entirely unlike Professor Bentley himself. Later microscopes of wit thought there was not even one author, but a string of minor folk poets whose efforts had been brought together by the great Athenian or even Alexandrian editor-scholars. The Prince of Poets had been dethroned. The scholars had won. And so the nineteenth century was animated by the debates between Analysts and Unitarians, those who thought Homer had been many and those who continued to maintain that he was one great genius.

The argument lasted for over a century, largely because of the sense of vertigo a multiple Homer induced. If Homer was dissolved into a sequence of folk-poets, one of the greatest monuments of Western civilisation no longer existed. Nevertheless, these were the preconditions for the great discoveries about Homer made in the early twentieth century by the most brilliant man ever to have loved him.

Milman Parry is a god of Homer studies. No one else has made Homeric realities quite so disturbingly clear. Photographs show what his contemporaries described, a taut, focused head, a man 'quiet in manner, incisive in speech, intense in everything he did'. There was nothing precious or elitist about him, and his life and mind ranged widely. For

Milman Parry, 1902–35

a year he was a poultry farmer. Along with the technicians at the Sound Specialties Company of Waterbury, Connecticut, he was the first to develop recording apparatus which didn't have to be interrupted every four minutes to change the disc. He took his wife and children with him on his great recording adventures in the Balkans, and at night sang songs to them which mimicked and drew on the epic poems he had heard in the day. At Harvard, where he became an assistant professor, he took to washing his huge white dogs in the main drinking-water reservoir for the city, stalking about the campus in a large black hat with 'an aura of the Latin quarter' about him, regaling his students with the poetry of Laforgue, Apollinaire, Eliot and e.e. cummings. Supremely multilingual, at home in Serbo-Croat, writing his first articles and papers on Homer in French, this was the man who pulled Homer back from its academic desert into life.

Parry was born in June 1902, and brought up a Quaker in the sunny sterilities of Oakland, California. From that clean, germ-free youth he plunged off into ancient Greek at Berkeley, and when still there, writing the thesis for his Master's degree, jumped to the idea that Homer was neither a great poet making these poems from nothing, nor a collection of minor folk-tales somehow strung together, but the combination and fusion of those two ideas: a poet working within a great tradition which had deep roots and multiple sources. The poems were composed by a man standing at the top of a human pyramid. He could not have stood there without the pyramid beneath him, and the pyramid consisted not only of the earlier poets in the tradition, but their audiences too, the whole set of assumptions and expectations in which the poems swam. Homer, a plural noun, were the frozen and preserved words of an entire culture. At different moments in their evolution, the songs would have sounded different, but there is no need to assume that they would have been cruder or worse. At any one moment the singer is standing on the human pyramid beneath him. Hear them as they should be heard and you will have the sound and meanings of the distant past in your mind and ear.

Parry was a romantic, who loved the ancientness of the past for itself and for its stark difference from twentieth-century America. The motivations apparent in Keats are in Parry too. For the classical scholars of eighteenth- and nineteenth-century Europe, brought up in an elite and aristocratic culture, Homer may have seemed like a contemporary, his words on honour and self-sacrifice to be taken as relevant instructions for the noble life. The only task was to clean Homer up, to make Homer more like them, to classicise him, to rid him of his repetitiveness and his awkward lack of *savoir faire*, to translate him, as Pope had done, with many delightful felicities overlying the raw Greek.

For the brilliant young American from Oakland, that could never have been the starting point. Homer for Parry is almost unapproachably strange and distant. Only by recognising that distance could he be understood. Parry's guiding light was Ernest Renan, the star of the dinners at the Repas Magny. Renan had insisted on understanding the past on its own terms. 'How can we grasp the physiognomy and the originality of an early literature,' he had written, if we do not enter the personal and moral life of the people who made it, unless we place ourselves at the very point in humanity which was theirs, so that we see and feel as they saw and felt; unless we watch them live , or better, unless for a moment we live with them?

This liberal, anthropological understanding of what Homer might be – quoted and requoted by Parry in his papers – was far ahead of anything other Anglo-Saxons were thinking, and the key to that penetration of the past was in the nature of the verses themselves. Parry's central question was this: what does the nature of the poetry say about the world in which it was composed? He focused on two qualities: the way in which heroes and objects are accompanied by almost unvarying and sometimes inappropriate adjectives and epithets, the building blocks of unvarying 'formulae'; and the role of words in Homer which 'Homer' – the eighth-century BC scribe who wrote the poems down – almost certainly did not understand.

Parry was told by the Classics faculty at Berkeley in 1922 that there was no chance he would get a doctorate by following up on his Master's thesis on the formulae in Homer. It was not what an American classicist did. For a year Parry worked with his chickens, but he recognised that his future studies would find most encouragement with the anthropologists in Paris, and when he was twenty-two he went there to do his doctorate at the Sorbonne. What he set out to analyse may seem arcane, but it is in fact a route into the mind of the Bronze Age, an archaeology of the word. First, abandon any idea of the classic poet. The poems are not objects conceived by a single, gifted person, but profoundly inherited, shaped and reshaped by a preceding culture, stretching far back in time, something as much formed by tradition as the making of pots or the decoration of their surfaces. Homer is the world of tradition-shaped poetry, not of realism, as unlike reality as opera and profoundly guided by its own conventions. And the governing fact in that epic world is the music of the poetry.

The Homeric epics are essentially the music of hexameters, a Greek word that means 'six measures', because in each line there are six 'feet' for which the words must be chosen to fit the pre-existing pattern. This verse is measured language. Within each of the six feet, the language can fall in different ways. Feet made up of a long and two shorts (a phrase like 'This is the') are called dactyls, after the Greek word for a finger, *daktylos*, a word which both mimics the shape of the human finger – a long bone followed by two short ones – and is a dactyl itself. A foot of two longs ('hemlocks') is a spondee, the Greek word for a libation, an offering poured out with certainty and directness for a god, and which is a spondee itself. Most feet can be either dactyls or spondees, but the rules of epic insist that the fifth foot is usually a dactyl ('pines and the') and the final foot always a spondee. Here, with those rules in mind, is an English hexameter, by Henry Wadsworth Longfellow:

– u u | – u u | – u ^ u | – u u | – u u | – –
This is the | forest pri | meval. ^ The | murmuring | pines and the |hemlocks

Variation is always to hand: the dactylic 'murmuring' could be the spondaic 'moss-girt'. The pines have to be surrounded by hemlocks because dactylic 'rivulets' would not be allowed at the end of the line, but Longfellow could have chosen the spondaic 'wood prim-eval', to make an even weightier line,

– u u | – – | – u ^ u | – – | – u u | – –
This is the | wood prim | eval. ^ The| moss-girt | pines and the | hemlocks

But he may have felt that the breeze was not blowing through that American landscape quite as he wanted. Flexibility within the pattern is at the core of the system. This is not an iron prison but a means of making memorable music, of allowing music to carry a tale.

Each of the lines has a natural break (marked here by ^ after 'primeval') called a caesura, and the line naturally falls into two halves on either side of it. In reality there are many variations in Homeric verse, but this is the underlying structure, a combination of variety and rhythmic certainty, governing the way each line develops. It is the sound of epic, entirely unlike the way anyone would ever have spoken, but embodying for the Greeks the heroic world.

Parry established that an astonishingly high proportion of the poems composed in this rhythmically repetitive form was made up of pre-fabricated elements which had been evolved to fit the metrical pattern of the hexameter. Anyone telling the story of the *Odyssey* or the *Iliad* in verse would have had, ready to hand, words and expressions which could easily be put into this form. Just under a third of all the lines in Homer are like this, either repeated entirely or containing phrases repeated elsewhere.* Saying the same thing, or a version of the same thing, over and over again, lay at the foundations of the Homeric world.

If Alexander Pope in eighteenth-century England thought the excellence of poetry lay in 'What oft was thought/But ne'er so well express'd', Homer's ideal is precisely the opposite: saying the true things in ways that are deeply familiar: what oft was thought and almost always expressed in exactly the same way. Homer, in its genes, was set against newness, turning to the fixed music of the hexameters and the phrases inherited from the past for the validation of its truths. This is poetry which can be thought of in the same light as weaving patterned cloth or building wooden ships. The past, through endless tests, successes and failures, has come up with ways of using and joining materials that work, that are robust, reliable and true, that can cope with seas or storms at night, that have a grace and commodity about them, whose threads can glitter in the candlelight and which are, of their essence, inherited.

Nowhere is the formulaic method of the verse clearer than in the way Homer uses the name of a hero or god, attached to a descriptive adjective or phrase, to fill in the second half of a hexameter, the space between the mid-line break, the caesura, and the end of the line. You can represent the gap Homer needed to fill again and again by the phrase 'old man chewing a beanstalk'. Each of the thirty-seven most important heroes and gods of the *Iliad* and the *Odyssey* has a formula attached to his or her name which exactly fills that gap. One after another they queue up to occupy it: *polytlas dios Odysseus* – much-suffering godlike Odysseus is there thirty-eight times; followed closely by *podarkēs dios Achilleus*, swift-footed godlike Achilles; *boōpis potnia Hera*, ox-eyed goddess Hera; *thea glaukopis Athene*, goddess owl-eyed Athene; *anax andron Agamemnon*, lord of men Agamemnon – and so on through the

* There are 9,253 repetitive lines out of a total of 27,803.

whole cast. Equally formulaic phrases often fill the other part of the line – 'and so in reply he spoke', 'and so she said when smiling' – so that entire lines, and entire sequences of lines, are filled up not with words chosen for their individual strength, poignancy or relevance, but as a means of keeping the music constant, keeping the characters present and alive in the surface of the poem.

Once you grasp this core repetitive mechanism – often obscured in translations of Homer – these poems become profoundly strange, sinking back away from us in time and mentality, to a point where story and character are visible only though the mask of the formulaic, as unreal as a Noh-play, as mysterious as an unheard liturgy. The stories of the warriors at Troy and the wanderings of Odysseus become as alien as a tale told in hieroglyphs or cuneiform. This is the Renan effect, seeing the past for its strangeness, not imposing our own clarity or suppositions on something from the other end of human consciousness.

'The poetry,' Parry wrote,

> was not one in which a poet must use his own words and try [as] best he might to utilize the possibilities of the metre. It was a poetry which for centuries had accumulated all such possibilities – all the turns of language, all the words, phrases, and effects of position, which had pleased the race.

So powerful was the need to keep the music whole, that these metrically convenient phrases are often used even when they make no sense. The heavens are 'starry' in the middle of the day; linen is 'gleaming' when it is about to be washed; Odysseus is called 'much-suffering godlike Odysseus' by the shade of a man he has recently killed, now in Hades; Aegisthus, the adulterous lover of Clytemnestra and murderer of Agamemnon, is 'blameless'; ships are 'swift' when they have been turned to stone. But the hexameters roll on, sustained by these formulaic expressions, a music whose sense of its own overarching greatness matters more than any local meaning. By the time of 'Homer' – often put in quotes by Parry – the heroic epithets had become virtually meaningless. Achilles was not really 'swift-footed' when lurking in his tent for book after book of the *Iliad*, refusing to fight for the Greeks; Odysseus was not really 'suffering much' when performing as only one among many of the Greek commanders at Troy. These words, in Parry's analysis, had become useful line-fillers because that is what the music of the hexameters, the tradition itself, required. They had nothing to do with what the poem meant.

This was a radical dismantling of the inherited Homer. Ever since the Alexandrians, Europe had tried to rescue Homer from his own errors. Parry, alive with all the early twentieth century's fascination with the strange truths to be found in non-Enlightenment cultures, now plunged him back into a deeply pre-classic world, taking him apart in the process. Parry was accused of being the 'Darwin of Homeric scholarship', the man who had turned a god into an ape. But he is more like Homer's Gauguin or Stravinsky, creating a poet for a Jungian world, allowing for the validity of his pre-rational methods, finding there beauty which the classic tradition was blind to and wished to excise. Parry thought Homer beautiful in the way an African totem or a Polynesian mask might be beautiful. Europeans since the Renaissance might have looked on Homer as one of the furnishings of the gentlemanly life. Parry saw himself as no part of that tradition, and for him distance and inaccessibility stood at the root of Homer's meaning.

Parry had summoned a strange and troubling Homer from the depths, a poet entranced by his inheritance, almost blind in front of it, spooling out what the past had given him, 'a machine of memory with limited aesthetic scope', as the Californian critic James L. Porter has described him, 'his materials emerging from the deepest lava flows of epic time'. This is Homer as Hawaiian volcano, oozing the past like the juice from the earth's mantle. Parry even suggested that the poems were full of words, often in old forms of Greek, that may have fitted the music of the hexameters but which 'Homer', the Ionic poet from Chios in the eighth century BC, did not himself understand. There are 201 words in the *Iliad* and the *Odyssey* which occur only once in Homer and never again in the whole of Greek literature. That number goes up to 494 if you include proper names, their roots deep in ancient forms of Greek, many of them spoken in Thessaly in northern Greece, but which in Chios and through the Ionic fringe of Anatolia were no longer used. Many have never been translated – unintelligible to the Greeks of fifth-century Athens or third-century Alexandria, their meaning still now only to be guessed at.

But for Parry, this was all evidence of the tradition at work, of Homer being more interested in epic music than its meaning. The past must be given its due, and one aspect of that past was the unintelligibility of its language. Only then would you understand the relationship of the singer and his tradition: 'The tradition is of course only the sum of such singers. One might symbolize it by the idea of a singer who is at once all singers.' He quoted Aristotle's *Rhetoric* on the ideal for an epic poet: 'One's style should be unlike that of ordinary language, for if it has the quality of remoteness, it will cause wonder and wonder is pleasant.' Mystery is power, and the not-entirely-understood seems greater than what is clear. Parry's vision of Homer is very nearly like the unintelligible ritual of the Latin mass sung to uncomprehending peasants across medieval Europe: words which were meaningful because they could not be understood. Eliot's passing thought in his 1929 essay on Dante that 'genuine poetry can communicate before it is understood' is less radical than this. Parry sees Homer as a culture riding into the future on poetry whose deepest parts are entirely inaccessible.

His professors at the Sorbonne told him something which he hadn't quite grasped: everything he had been pursuing was a sign that Homer was not originally a written but an oral text. This formulaic composition was the mark of a sung poem, so dependent on pre-shaped elements that a singer could compose it as he performed it. Such songs were neither monstrous feats of memory nor improvisations, invented from one moment to the next, but tales told with the help of ancient formulae, devised long before, which the singer could rely on as steady metrical elements in his lines. He did not have to learn any poems, but he had to learn what the tradition could teach him, the ability to make poems on the hoof.

This may seem a presumptuous comparison, but it is clear to me that anyone who has ever stood up in front of an audience, of any kind, and made a speech, knows what is meant by composition-in-performance, particularly if you have made the speech before, or over the course of a few months have the chance of making it a few times to different audiences, in different atmospheres and for different purposes. You know, in essence, the stories you have to tell, the morals you would like to draw. You know the moments where pathos is available and those where people will laugh. You know what has worked before and what has died as it left your lips. You know, above all, but just how you know is difficult to know, how to establish a kind of gut-dialogue between you and the audience, to feel them feeling what you are saying, to understand point by point what might be the right development of the tale.

It is not improvisation, because you know at least where you might be going. You have your formulae, conscious, semi-conscious, unconscious, the tics that make you who you are, that are your inheritance. You have passages that run in familiar ways, that allow the intuition to consider the shape of what you are making, the way you might go next, the goal it must aim for. And you have your ingredients, your set terms, the passages where you need not invent, where you can say what has been said before, and those passages where invention seems to come easily to the mind, not in the sense of making up a new substance for the story, but in finding words that will work for it. All this is easier when there is some darkness in the room.

This is not to say that I speak in hexameters, or devise complex reflective schemes and ironies, that I keep in train a thousand characters over 14,000 lines. But at a very basic level I understand that between memory, the present moment and the spoken word, is a kind of three-part dance. When my children were small, we used to play this Homeric game. Last thing at night, I would tell them long rhythmic poems about our lives and our holidays, the little adventures we had in boats or trains, all designed to send them to sleep. Nothing was repeated more often than the story of taking the night train to Scotland, feeding off the atmosphere of excitement and anticipation we got from it every summer and Christmas. The poem was never quite the same from one telling to the next, but it used all the easy techniques of repetitive phrasing and a thumping rhythm which, as Milman Parry said of his own story-telling to his children when they came with him to Bosnia, are the overused recourse of the bad epic poet and almost untouched by the good.

But this is epic verse as it is made today in England, in the evening, upstairs in the bedroom, traditional, formulaic, with lumps of the culture embedded in it, full of memories, lullingly soporific. I never wrote anything down at the time, and I have written this now straight on to the keyboard as it came to mind, nothing predetermined, except the formulae and the memory of having done something like it often before:

That was the night and it was very very dark
That the children found their way to the station
and there at the station waiting in the dark
was the long long train that they knew from before.
Dark was the train and wonderfully shiny
the lights from the station shining on its flanks
and the lights in the cabins glowing inside
and there as the children stood in the station
watching the train that was dark in the night
they said to each other Can we climb aboard?
Can we find our way to our beds in the train?
And their father said No to them, No not yet.
Wait till the guard opens the doors.
So they stood in the cold and longed for the warmth
Of the long night train as it made its way north.
Together they stood and huddled in the dark
Waiting for the moment when the doors might open
and then at last they heard far away
The banging of doors and the shouting of men
as each of the guards got out his big key
and opened the doors for the night to begin.

I usually fell asleep before they did, lulled by my own pump-engine rhythm, but this is Homeric in its *parataxis*, its telling of the story with no subordinate clauses, accumulating one detail after another, its rapidity, its formulaic phrases taking up reliable positions in the pattern of the lines, its cherishing of memories and heroising of the ordinary, its love of the shared experience between speaker and listener, its cavalier way with facts.

What can you say? Only that this sort of rhythmic, inherited story-telling is part of the human organism, and that the world in which the *Iliad* and the *Odyssey* began was an outgrowth and fulfilment of this basic capacity, one in which the telling of your own great tales was not something done by a father at bedtime but in the gathering of people for whom these stories were the foundation of their lives, the thing that might last when everything else might not.

Between 1933 and 1935, prompted by his Parisian professors, Parry made his journeys through the remote mountain villages of Yugoslavia. It was quite a caravan: his assistant, a Harvard student, Albert Lord, several typists and interpreters, and Nikola Vujnović, a singer himself from Herzegovina, who would ease the way with the people they met. They met and listened to over seven hundred singers, each with their *gusle*, the single-stringed violin that accompanied the words. Almost 13,000 separate songs were written into eight hundred notebooks, and hundreds more recorded on 3,500 twelve-inch aluminium discs. When he returned to Harvard, Parry delivered to the library almost exactly a ton of archive material.

Bégan Lyútsa Nikshitch, a Turkish bard from Montenegro, 'a tall, lean and impressive person'.

The excitement was real. Here was the past made flesh and blood, stubble and cigarettes, sawing out its epics in front of them. On market day they would drop in at a coffee house and make enquiries. Were there any *guslari* nearby? Were they good? Could they come? One morning at Bijelo Polje, a small town in the hills of northern Montenegro, they found, lying on a bench in a coffee house, a Turk smoking a cigarette with an antique silver cigarette holder. He was Bégan Lyútsa Nikshitch, 'a tall, lean and impressive person' who spoke to them like a warrior from the depths of the past.

Bégan knew a certain Avdo Medjédović, a peasant farmer who lived an hour away, and he was insistent that the Americans had to hear him.

Finally Avdo came, and he sang for us. . . We listened with increasing interest to this short homely farmer, whose throat was disfigured by a large goiter. He sat cross-legged on the bench, sawing the gusle, swaying in rhythm with the music. He sang very fast, sometimes deserting the melody, and while the bow went lightly back and forth over the string, he recited the verses at top speed. A crowd gathered. A card game, played by some of the modern young men of the town, noisily kept on, but was finally broken up.

The next few days were a revelation. Avdo's songs were longer and finer than any we had heard before. He could prolong one for days, and some of them reached fifteen or sixteen thousand lines. Other singers came, but none could equal Avdo, our Yugoslav Homer.

The *guslari* always sang their long epic songs of battle and disaster with a kind of hard energy, loud, at a high pitch, the singer's whole frame gripped with the effort. This was no smooth crooning but a passionate engagement of mind and body.

It takes the full strength of the man to sing in this way. The movement of the body in playing the instrument, the laboring of the lungs needed for the breath needed for the volume of song, the strain on the muscles of the throat and mouth that go to forming the words, make the singing a toil, and a good singer after a half hour of his song is drenched in sweat.

Nothing about the sound of the *gusle* is charming, and the way in which the poems are sung has little apparent melody. The string of the instrument screeches from one line to the next, the *guslar* chants his lines without any attempt at a flourish or grace notes. This is not an exhibitionist performance. It is more serious than that, the voice of concentration, as he composes with his formulaic phrases and passages, the metre heavily emphasised in every phrase he uses. It is the words that matter, their recounting of tragedy and suffering. But the unbroken presence of the instrument is there not for its tune but for its strangeness, the signal it makes that this is another world.

Each singer sang usually for between twenty and forty minutes, sawing away at the *gusle* on his lap, singing up to twenty lines of his song every minute, more slowly at first, speeding up as he reached the crisis of the tale, and then stopping for a cup of coffee, a cigarette, a glass of burningly fierce plum raki and a visit to the loo. They didn't always get to the end of their song before the session tailed off into the night. Some singers did not even know the endings of their songs, and when they did come to the last part, they were always more various than the beginnings.

In June 1935 Halil Bajgorić, a thirty-nine-year-old stockman from a remote mountain village in Bosnia, sang them a long song about a young and resourceful hero, called 'The Wedding of Mustajbey's Son Bećirbey'. Even as he began, after a thirty-second introduction on the *gusle* alone, setting the rhythm, establishing the metre in his mind, it was clear that Bajgorić's tale was driven along by the formulaic pattern, not only at the level of individual phrases, but in the shape of scene after scene.

Bajgorić's epic is simple, but it shares many things with Homer. First, as in Homer, the adventure begins with the break of day and the waking of the hero:

> Oj! Djerdelez Alija arose early,
> Ej! Alija, the tsar's hero,
> Near Visoko above Sarajevo,
> Before dawn and the white day
> Even two full hours before dawn,
> When day breaks and the sun rises
> And the morning star shows its face.

In epic, it is not enough to say 'One morning. . .'. It needs expansion, space opening out around the story, the luxury of time expanding around the singer. And it can joke about that need for a little more time:

> When the young man got himself up,
> He kindled a fire in the hearth
> And on the fire he put his coffee pot;
> After Alija brewed the coffee,
> One, then two cups he poured himself –
> One, then two, he felt no spark,
> Three, then four, the spark then seized him,
> Seven, then eight, until he had enough.

Finally, the hero sufficiently stoked with caffeine, the formulaic sequence can begin: the preparation of 'a long-maned bay horse' for the journey, the horse made beautiful with all her trappings, 'Like a careless young shepherdess up on a mountain/Clothed in her hood and motley jacket', the fitting of the hero with his beautiful equipment, his swords and daggers, his elegant pistols, one from Venice, one from England, to the point where he can set out on his journey, swim a great river while still mounted on his precious mare – she knows what he wants without him saying so – until at last he arrives at the city where

> He quenched his thirst with dark red wine
> And he smoked two pipefuls of tobacco.

Translate the Homeric situation to the valleys of early-twentieth-century mountain Europe and the poem translates itself. That is Parry's point: this poetry was the product not of unique glowing genius, but of a world in which the spoken epic is the vehicle which carries the meanings of the past into the present, and in which the need to tell the poem again and again is itself the most powerful force in its shaping. Formulaic verse is a response to social need.

Parry was entranced by the world he had stumbled on. 'The moment he cherished most,' his student Albert Lord wrote later, occurred toward the end of one of his earliest days in the Serbian hills, during the summer of 1933. They had settled at an inland village and at length come across a *gouslar*, the first epic poet Parry had ever known, an old man who claimed to have been a warrior in youth and to have cut off six heads. All afternoon he sang to them about his battles. At sunset he put down his *gousle* and they made him repeat a number of his verses. Parry, very tired, sat munching an apple and watching the singer's grizzled head and dirty neck bob up and down over the shoulder of Nikola, the Herzegovinan scribe, in a last ray of sunlight. 'I suppose,' he would say, in recalling the incident, with crisp voice and half-closed eyes, 'that was the closest I ever got to Homer.'

It is as powerful a moment in the history of Homeric understanding as the evening when Keats and Cowden Clarke peered into Chapman's Homer, or when Carl Blegen in the summer of 1939 found the smashed fresco of the singer, destroyed in the fire three thousand years before. Parry, listening to these men and their grating instruments, their sawing voices, heard in them the transmission of epic across the generations, the thousands of years. It was the moment in which the vacuum of life before the written word had suddenly acquired a substance.

Through Nikola Vujnović, the Herzegovinian singer, Parry asked Halil Bajgorić where he had learned his songs. All came from his father, he said. But how had he actually learned to sing and play when he was a young boy? Halil described how he would sneak the *gusle* away from his father, and in another room, when his father was sleeping, he would sing a little.

Nikola: But why did you feel the need to sneak the *gusle* away from him?

Halil: Because I wanted to know how [to play], I saw there was a place for him among the people because he knew how to sing. He'd come there, when there were gatherings among us, when there were weddings, some celebrations, and I'd go with him. And he'd come there, and there would be a lot of people, and the people all made room and said, 'Singer, come on up to the front and sit by the man brewing coffee.'

Nikola: Aha.

Halil: Then, by God, I too wanted to learn to play the *gusle*.

This is how it must always have been: the father at the centre of the listening circle, the boy on the edge of it seeing his father in a different light from the usual man at home with his breakfast, the current of the heroic recognised by the boy, the stirring of ambition to have that scale of existence in his own life, the tentative beginnings in secret, his imagining of the audience, his first attempts in public, the increasing confidence with which the formulae might become his own, that miraculous sensation when he felt he could divert the stream through his own life and mind.

'The verses and the themes of the traditional song form a web in which the thought of the singer is completely enmeshed,' Parry wrote later, establishing the primacy of the tradition over the individual poet. 'The poetry stands beyond the single singer. He possesses it only at the instant of his song which is his to make or mar.' 'His to make or mar' is the idea in the mind of the young Halil, practising with his father's *gusle* in the hidden room.

They asked one singer called Ibrahim Bašić, known as Ibro, a seventy-year-old woodcutter from central Herzegovina, where he got the words for the songs. If he told a tale a second time, did he repeat it word for word? Yes, Ibro said, word for word.

Nikola: What is, let's say, a word in a song? Give me a word from a song.

Ibro: Here's one, let's say, this is a word: 'Mujo of Kladusha arose early,/At the top of the slender, well-made tower.'

Nikola: But these are lines.

Ibro: Well yes, but that's how it is with us; it's otherwise with you, but with us that's how it's said. . .But here's one, let's say this is a word: 'Mujo of Kladusha arose early' – that is a word for 'arose early'; 'Before dawn and the sun is arising' – that's also a word for 'arose early'.

Words are not individual, separated lexical objects, but poetic lines, half-lines, formulae, metrical units and story units that can slot into the song. This is building a wall not brick by brick but panel by panel. Getting up with the dawn, preparing the chariot, arming the warrior, equipping the ship, rowing for the wind, swift-footed Achilles, much-suffering Odysseus: these are the words in which Homer speaks. To repeat a song 'word for word' is to choose any one of these formulae as they come to mind. The tradition is not a fixed object like the written text of *Paradise Lost* or the *Aeneid*; it is a braided stream of possibilities pouring into the present out of the past, essentially multiple, recomposed from its given elements every time it is sung, and in that retelling conceived of as remaining the same. It is a curiously Platonic conception of a story, as if the epic's essence were in a pure, immaterial, pre-existent form, of which the actual words that are sung are an almost incidental bodying forth into our mundane reality. 'Plato thought nature but a spume that plays/Upon a ghostly paradigm of things,' Yeats said, and you could say the same of Parry's Homer: Homer thought his poem but a spume that played upon the ghostly truths that came from long ago.

Parry was convinced that he had pushed the modern understanding of Homer back beyond the eighth-century BC horizon at which writing arrived in the Greek world. He thought he knew that in the formulaic composition-in-performance of the Yugoslav *guslars* he had heard the way in which the *Iliad* and the *Odyssey* had been composed. Homer was clearly the most extraordinary practitioner – the songs from the Balkan mountains were thin and empty compared to the *Iliad* and the *Odyssey* – but this was the practice of which Homer was the master. 'The more I understand the South Slavic poetry and the nature of the unity of the oral poem,' Parry wrote late in his life,

> the clearer it seems to me that the *Iliad* and the *Odyssey* are very exactly, as we have them, each one of them the rounded and finished work of a single singer. . . I even figure to myself, just now, the moment when the author of the *Odyssey* sat and dictated his song, while another, with writing materials, wrote it down verse by verse, even in the way that our singers sit in the immobility of their thought, watching the motion of Nikola's hand across the empty page, when it will tell them it is the instant for them to speak the next verse.

Parry had crossed the boundary into the mental world occupied by Homer. He was thirty-three when he returned in triumph to Harvard with his ton of notebooks and aluminium discs. A life's work stretched ahead of him, but that December, on a visit to his mother-in-law in Los Angeles, he died in a stupid accident when a revolver mixed in with his clothes in a suitcase went off and killed him. Something resembling the book he was planning to write about Homer and the *guslari* was written much later by his assistant and student Albert Lord, after a long and fruitful career spent fulfilling the promise of the visionary man who had once led him to the Balkans.

A rainy early-autumn day in the Hebrides, the cloud down low over the islands, a sheen of wet on the grass. We have been gathering sheep for the September markets. The sea around us is bruised by the wind. Hardly a word has been spoken all morning, as the four of us have been strung out in a line across the hillside half a mile long, two or three hundred yards between each of us, our arms flailing at the gloomy and reluctant sheep. The sky is torn into shreds and patches. The only words have been the violent insults thrown at the dogs.

Now the lambs are down at last in the fank on the beach, ready to be taken off by dory and fishing boat tomorrow morning. The sheepdogs nip at them through the bars. The shepherds, Kennie, Nona and Toby, are all leaning on the hurdles of the fank and discussing the animals in front of us, their fleeces shrivelled and lank in the rain. They are not as good as anyone had hoped:

Nona: It was the wet spring that did it.
Toby: That was what kept them back.
Nona: Aye, and the dry summer.
Toby: Aye, that would have kept them back too.
Nona: And it's been cold these last few weeks.
Toby: That wouldn't have helped.
Nona: No, they are not as good as they might have been.
Toby: But there are some big ones in here.
Nona: Monsters some of them.
Toby: There's some good lambs in there.

Nona: Look at that horned ewe with her twins.
Toby: There's some very heavy lambs here.
Kennie: It'll be heavy work getting them into the dory.
Toby: [To his dog] Come into heel, will you.
Nona: You are not going to get that quality every time.
Toby: No, not every time, that's right.
Kennie: No, not every time. You can't hope for it every time.

This was a chat, a break from work, with a roll-up and a cup of tea and caps on the backs of heads, but it is the talk that has been had since the Neolithic. Its buried musicality, the repetition of its phrases, the antiphonal give and take of each repeating gesture – all of that presses up under the surface of the words. Perhaps this is the natural way we have of speaking, just hesitating on the lip of the musical, but it is a quality of language which is usually shut down and denied in a written culture.

Parry's new understanding of the Homeric poems undoubtedly pushed them into the pre-literate centuries before 800 BC. Homer comes from an oral and aural world, a world of public speech and shared listening. But how far back? And how much of that ancient world could survive in the telling and retelling? Can one really reach back through the words of Homer to that moment in about 1800 BC when the Greek-speaking people, whatever they were called, came south to the Mediterranean world of sailing ships and stone-walled cities?

There is a real difficulty: the reliability of these story-tellers. They inherited the past, they were conscious of that inheritance, but how much did they transform what they had been given? Milman Parry and his team asked the Serbian singers if their stories had any truth in them, a question, it soon became clear, which did not entirely make sense to them.

Ibrahim Bašić, the *guslar* known as Ibro, answered casually enough: everything in his songs was true, except for details he added to make them more fitting. His stories might have required heroic furniture – swords, horses – to sound right, but that didn't make them any less 'true'. It might even have made a story 'truer', more like the heroic past Ibro had in mind. These songs were epics, extensions of memory over deep reaches of time. They weren't history. They celebrated a heroic ethos and their purpose was not to preserve events. They existed in the 'now', standing as a bridge between the present moment and the distant past.

There is one extraordinary discovery from Crete, made by the American-Greek scholar James Notopoulos, a follower of Parry and Lord, that relegated the question of historical truth in ancient epics to a category that was at least moot. Notopoulos was a professor in Hartford, Connecticut. His father had been a poor Greek immigrant from the Peloponnese who became rich by building and operating theatres in small-town Pennsylvania. At Oxford, James had become entranced by Homer and by Parry's discoveries. An intense romantic, he was remembered by students gazing dreamily at the ceiling through clouds of pipe-smoke during Greek classes in Hartford. But he was also a precisionist, capable of 'making the wince into an art-form' when a pupil failed to pronounce the Greek properly or get the metre right.

In 1953, with a Guggenheim scholarship, Notopoulos travelled to the far west of Crete, one of the most heroic landscapes in Europe. In the wild and stony mountain province of Sfakia, gorges are sawn thousands of feet down into the barren, dry White Mountains. I have seen fences around sheepfolds there held up with the rusted barrels of old machine guns, and have sat eating my lunch in a café while at the table next to me a man first cleaned his automatic pistol and then fired it out of the door to see that it worked.

Notopoulos arrived only eight years after the end of a war in which the Cretans had maintained bitter and heroic resistance against the German occupiers. He found Sfakia in a 'ferment' of song. Everywhere the American ethnographer went, men were singing about the 1941 airborne invasion, the cruelty of the Germans, their burning of villages, their shooting of the innocent, the heroism of the Sfakiots themselves, the sons no less heroic than their fathers and grandfathers, and the bitter reprisals carried out by them against their own traitors and fifth columnists. The long island tradition of daring manliness, the kidnapping of brides, the maintenance of unforgivingly violent blood feuds and of loathing for the outsider – Roman, Arab, Venetian and Turk – was pouring out in this new generation of song. It is a suggestive connection:

are the years after a war the great moment for epic? With the dreadful realities of the crisis over, can the miasma of epic descend?

The mountain bards in their black tasseled kerchiefs, knee-high boots and baggy trousers sang as Parry had led Notopoulos to expect, formulaically and repetitively, composing in performance, versions of songs sung in the morning different from how they were sung at night. Notopoulos recorded them all. One of his bards was a young man, Andreas Kafkalas, only thirty-nine, particularly gifted in what Notopoulos called 'spontaneous improvisation', the ability to sing a story for the first time without rehearsal.

After one of his epics about the German invasion and occupation, Notopoulos said he was surprised Kafkalas had not mentioned anything to do with General Kreipe, the commander of the German garrison on Crete. No, Kafkalas said, but in response to the American's prompting, he thought he could sing a poem about him now. Notopoulos turned on the recording equipment and Kafkalas began. His tale was about as long as one of the shorter books of the *Odyssey*. His formulae filled whole passages of the song, all in the traditional fifteen-syllable Cretan line. How did he know, Notopoulos asked him later, to put fifteen syllables in a line? 'I didn't know the line had fifteen syllables,' he said. 'I don't count the syllables, I feel them − it's the melody that shapes the lines.' The tradition was singing through him.

The kidnapping of General Kreipe was the most famous act of bravura special operations in the whole story of occupied Crete. Two British officers, Patrick Leigh Fermor and Billy Moss, had captured him, their whole enterprise conceived in Cairo but dependent on the networks of *andartes*, the Cretan resistance fighters. One evening in late April 1944, on the road between the general's HQ at Archanes and his quarters outside Knossos in central Crete, the two Englishmen and a band of *andartes* stopped the German car, a new Opel, coshed the driver, dragged him on to the road (he was later killed) and bundled the general into the back of the Opel with a knife at his throat. The two British officers sat in the front, Moss impersonating the German driver, Leigh Fermor Kreipe himself, with the general's hat on his head.

After a terrifyingly anxious drive through Herakleion, passing slowly through twenty-two German checkpoints, inching along streets filled with the men of the garrison who had just come out of the cinema, they drove out into the wild lands at the foot of Mount Ida, abandoned the car and headed off on foot into that harsh, dry and fissured mountain. For the next twenty days, as the Germans attempted to encircle them, looking for them with spotter planes but never detecting them, the general was led west halfway across mountain Crete, the party hiding in sheepfolds and caves in the daytime, stumbling on difficult mountain paths, often in the rain, at night, until they finally came down to a small bay west of Rodakino on the south coast. There they boarded a British motor launch which had been summoned by radio and, high on excitement and triumph, with their general safely aboard, made off for Alexandria.

I have walked the whole of their route, from where they dumped the car to the little bay where they embarked near Rodakino. It took me two weeks. I slept in chapels and vineyards, I burned in the sun in the daytime, froze at night at six thousand feet on top of a snowy Ida, and was often lost in the dry, echoing gorges coming down to the valleys. Griffon vultures swung across the sky. I ate cherries in the villages and for days at a time brushed through the dry, scented smoke of the Cretan garrigue. My boots after two weeks' walking were shredded by the limestone shards of the mountains, my body crawling with lice from the places I slept, but my mind was filled with the mountain distances of that epic and beautiful island. A shepherd taught me a phrase – *Yiassou pantermi Kriti!*: Bless you, desolate Crete! – as the only words to be said when facing the long, dry emptiness of the mountains, stretching as a desert into the haze. It is a brutal world, and later that year the Germans executed ferocious, slaughtering attacks on the people of mountain Crete. In every one of the villages through which the Kreipe group passed, in between the cherry trees and the figs, the little tavernas and the shady plane trees, there is a tall marble memorial on which the names of their dead are listed.

The Leigh Fermor party never got as far west as Sfakia, but Kafkalas told his tale with only a little hesitation. He had heard it from another Cretan when in hospital in Athens. And now, he told Notopoulos, he was singing the song to him 'to fulfil the obligations of Cretan hospitality'. But the song Kafkalas sang was an intriguing oddity. Almost nothing survived in it from the original story; truth had disappeared under a slew of the heroic. A single [untrue] English general [untrue] arrives in Crete and summons a hero from Sfakia, Lefteris Tambakis, to see him. [Untrue: Tambakis was a real figure, but he had never been anywhere near this operation.] The English general draws himself up to his full height, weeps over the cruelties being done by the Germans to the people of 'desolate Crete', and reads out the order to the Sfakiot hero that Kreipe is to be captured dead or alive [all untrue – no such order existed].

For the honour of Cretan arms, Tambakis knows what to do. In disguise he goes to Herakleion and finds a beautiful girl there [he didn't]. She is the secretary to the German general [he didn't have one]. He tells her that if she helps him, her name will be immortal in Cretan memory. She will join the catalogue of heroes. She agrees and 'sacrifices her woman's honour' with the German general. Kreipe – called Kaiseri in this song – whispering across the pillow, tells her his plans. [Of course he didn't.] She passes them on to Tambakis, and Tambakis goes to meet the English general at Knossos [there was no meeting there]. The ambush is laid. The *andartes* get 'a long car' with which to block the road [they didn't], but Tambakis himself waits there on a beautiful horse [no horses were involved, but they always are in old Cretan songs]. The English general is by now pretty marginal to the story. The Cretans stop Kaiseri's car, strip him naked [they didn't], he begs for mercy for the sake of his children [he didn't, but this is a motif that usually appears at these moments in Cretan poetry], and they start on the long trek over Mount Ida. Dogs [not used] and aeroplanes, called 'birds of war', hunt for the kidnappers, but to no avail. They arrive in Sfakia [they didn't], where the people try to kill Kaiseri [they didn't] before a submarine [it was a launch] sweeps him off to Egypt. Hitler is in despair [he probably was in June 1944, if for other reasons]. 'Never before in the history of the world has such a deed been done.'

Nine years had passed between these events and this telling of them. Nothing in the *Kreipiad* is true beyond the kidnapping of a general and his leaving in a submarine. Whole characters and a different Sfakiot geography, plus the luscious fantasies of a Mata Hari seductress-spy, are laid over the top of any historical truth. If this is what could happen to a modern story in nine years, how could anyone hope that anything true might survive in the *Iliad* or the *Odyssey*?

At almost exactly the moment James Notopoulos was hearing the *Kreipiad* sung to him in Crete, and the idea was collapsing of an inheritance transmitted through song from the deepest past, precisely the opposite conclusion was being reached at the other end of Europe. In September 1953, a group of forty Celtologists gathered at a conference in Stornoway on the Outer Hebridean island of Lewis, flown in from all over Europe by the British Council. The key session in Stornoway was boringly advertised as 'Paper on Folktales with Live Illustration'. No one guessed that they were about to hear something that would turn the Parryite orthodoxy on its head.

Also asked to the meeting, as its star turn, was a seventy-year-old stonemason from a village on South Uist, two ferries and a long drive away down the Hebridean chain.

Duncan Macdonald was a small man with an air of untroubled self-possession. He was not Duncan Macdonald but *Donnchadh mac Dhòmhnaill 'ic Dhonnchaidh 'ic Iain 'ic Dhòmhnaill 'ic Tharmaid* – Duncan the son of Donald the son of Duncan the son of Iain the son of Donald the son of Norman. They were descendants of the MacRury family of hereditary bards who had sung for the chiefs of the Macdonalds at the now ruined and abandoned castle at Duntulm, on the shores of the Minch, within touching distance of the northern tip of Skye. His father and brother were story-tellers, his mother a famous singer, her brother a much-loved piper and poet. He was one of the most gifted story-tellers in twentieth-century Europe, heir to the great traditions of Celtic story-telling which stretched far back into the Gaelic past.

Anything the singers Milman Parry had found in the Balkans could be matched by this inheritance, and Duncan did not disappoint. It was not the first time he had been the focus of attention for the folklorists, and on this afternoon in Stornoway he told a tale – it was 'The Man of the Habit', lasting about an hour – which he had told to transcribers four times before, in 1936, 1944, 1947 and 1950. This afternoon the delegates were given a booklet containing a transcription and an English translation of the way he had told it in 1950.

He began, as one of his hearers said, in Gaelic that was 'polished, shapely and elegant. . .Everything he recited was given both weight and due consideration.' But, as slowly emerged, this mild-mannered stonemason's confidence in the tradition was matched by the extra-ordinary precision with which he told his tale. Scarcely a word was different from the printed version they held in their hands – a few tiny mistakes, substituting *subhachas* ('gladness') for *dubhachas* ('sadness'), one or two interjections that were different and some synonyms changed, but on the whole the seven-thousand-odd words of the story were exactly as he had told them three years earlier. On analysis, all five of his versions were as good as identical. He had learned it like this from his father, and had told it like this ever since first learning it. The family had held it in mind as a kind of remembered heirloom, a hero tale, composed at least two hundred years earlier – there is an account of it from 1817 – which remained alive not just as a plot but in precisely the same words, transmitted unaltered from generation to generation.

In a world overtaken with the Parry hypothesis of composition-in-performance, this was revelatory. Duncan Macdonald had provided another way of seeing Homer, not as the poet who had written the *Iliad* and the *Odyssey* as his own works of art; nor as the poet who adapted and transmuted what he had learned to the situation he found himself in; but a poet who worked with a curatorial exactness, resisting the changes imposed by the passing of time, preserving antiquity in detail. For this kind of poet, stories were reliquaries in which precious wisdom and cherished understandings could be kept despite all the mutability of world and time. A poem enshrined memory. Its music denied death.

In Homeric Greek this understanding of the role of poetry focuses on a particular phrase: *kleos aphthiton*, in which *a-phthitos* means without death, undying, eternal, everlasting; and *kleos*, in the most revealing of all Homeric significance-clusters, means story, fame, honour and glory. In the Homeric mind, those four things are one. The tale told is itself a form of honour; honour exists in the telling of a tale; fame is to be found in the heroes of tales; their glory in life is the substance of honour; the tale of honour is the denial of death. Only if the tale resists the erosions of time can it make any claim to be the vehicle for glory. Undying fame is both the substance and the purpose of the Homeric poems.

In the years since then, ethnographers have discovered all over the world traditions of oral poetry which do not rely on the Parry method of composition-in-performance, which are not entirely formulaic, but which trust in the power of human memory to preserve with real precision the names, stories and words of the past. Duncan Macdonald's son wrote down 150,000 words of stories he had heard from his father before he died. The great eighteenth-century illiterate poet Duncan Ban MacIntyre knew at least six thousand lines of his own poetry. According to the Scottish Homer scholar Douglas Young, there was an octogenarian crofter from the Hebridean island of Benbecula, a man called Angus McMillan, who

> had in his head more than seventy tales lasting at least one hour each, and some novels lasting seven to nine hours, one of them running to 58,000 words, which is nearly as long as Homer's *Odyssey*. . . [He] could talk for eight hours at a stretch, almost without a pause. On the nearby island of Barra, Roderick MacNed is reported to have told tales every winter night for fifteen years without ever repeating himself. On the Scottish mainland, in Lochaber, John Macdonald recorded over six hundred tales, each of them a comparatively short story complete in itself. An Irish taleteller recorded over half a million words of tales he knew.

The idea of human memory in monumental form allows one to push Homer beyond the ninth or tenth centuries BC. The epic poem, seen as the deepest of all recording mediums, releases Homer from time constraints, allowing his tales to plunge far back into the centuries before writing. It is a kind of time-release not unlike standing on a peak in Darien, seeing the Pacific widths of the past expanding before you. Parry was only partly right: it now seems clear that his model is one way, but not the only way, that Homer works. Homer unites and combines the formulaically made with the acutely remembered and the sparklingly invented. In the substance of its poetry, Homer is the inherited tradition in its multiple forms: both alive as the poem composed in performance and fixed, as monumental as the stone over a grave mound, the memorial of great things done long ago. Multiple in origin, multiple in manner and multiple in meaning, Homer in this light both knows the deep past and moves beyond it. He is both South Uist and Sfakia. And so the question emerges: what is it that Homer remembers?

SEVEN

Homer the Real

HOMER IS HAUNTED BY the threat of transience, by the way memory fails and meanings drift in the face of time. That slide into insignificance summons his tenderest and most lyrical moments. So in Book 6 of the *Iliad*, when the battle is well under way and all is in a roar, 'the terrible noise' of it stoked by the commanders on both sides, a brazen, brutal shouting, something else emerges. The Greek warrior Diomedes, second only to Achilles as a man with an appetite for killing, is pumped with rage and the need for death. He is conducting his drive, his *aristeia*, through the Trojan ranks. Death awaits anyone he meets.

Quivering with battle-lust, he comes across a young warrior from Lycia, an ally of the Trojans. This is Glaucus, whose name means 'the gleaming one', a word used by Homer to describe both the sea and the eyes of the wisdom goddess Athene. Here, surely, is Diomedes's next victim. But instead of surrender or any display of weakness, Glaucus appears to him, like other heroes, 'shining' and 'glorious'. Diomedes guesses he might be a god, and as such intensely dangerous. He isn't, he is mortal, and so Diomedes asks him about his ancestry, who his father and grandfather might have been.

It is a traditional conversation, important for a hero, as his own self-esteem is bound up with the knowledge that his victims are themselves of good lineage, but also a kind of time mark: two warriors meeting in battle are not merely themselves; they are the vehicles for their own pasts. A man is his ancestry, and just as this poem is the poem which the tradition is now singing, these men are the future which their fathers and grandfathers dreamed of.

Nevertheless, Glaucus resists the expectations. 'Why ask about my birth?' he asks Diomedes in return, and a pause, a slowness, pools out into the flow of violence and grief. The noise of war rolls on in the background, but immediately, here, in the present, with you the listener looking on, a scene unfolds that exists in its own bubble of quiet, delivering a kind of precious and individualised oasis amid all the horror. In some of the most famous lines in the *Iliad*, Glaucus reflects on the meaning of life and death:

> Like the generations of leaves, the lives of mortal men.
> Now the wind scatters the old leaves across the earth,
> now the living timber bursts with the new buds
> and spring comes round again. And so with men:
> as one generation comes to life, another dies away.

For Glaucus, all life goes back into the earth and returns again. Earth's abundance and earth's indifference are the same thing. But this resolved simplicity in the face of death, a philosophical calm and a knowledge that the armies of men gathered on the Trojan plain are 'as many as the leaves and flowers that appear in the spring', – that is not the usual Homeric attitude. Glaucus may think of himself as one leaf in the centuries of leaves, a transient phenomenon, an irrelevant individuality, but that acceptance of transience is not what most of the poem thinks, or most of the heroes in it. For them, and for Homer, impermanence is life's central sorrow and the source of its most lasting pain.

It is also what the poem itself is intended to cure. In scene after scene, Homer quietly shows its listeners that it knows more and remembers more than men usually know or are able to bring to mind. The whole of the *Iliad* is a hymn to the scale of remembering of which epic is capable. The world forgets, but the poem remembers, and that knowledge is the source of Homer's repeated sad-eyed, bloodhound irony on the nature of life. Only the gods can know as much as the poem knows.

Almost at the beginning of the *Iliad*, the first time the Trojans move out of the city and on to the plain to confront their enemies, to face either death or the possibility of renown and glory, Homer describes the landscape beyond the gates. Out on the open plain there is a tomb, a high burial mound or tumulus, of the kind which can be found across the whole of Bronze Age Eurasia, from Bahrain to Sweden and from Sussex to the deserts of Kazakhstan. It is the tomb of Myrine, a great mythological Amazon warrior queen, who conquered Anatolia and died in battle. The poet knows that, but the Trojans have entirely forgotten it. She has sunk out of their minds, and instead they think the hill is merely 'Thicket Hill', as its name *batieia* can be translated. The great mound has sunk away from memory into landscape. Only Homer and the gods know that a great woman is buried there.

> Near the city but far out in the plain, there is a steep hill with clear space around it so you can pass on either side; this men call Batieia, but the immortals call it the grave mound of Myrine.

Homer knows something else, a delicate and transient fact about Myrine. She was *polyskarthmos*, a dancer, 'much-skipping' as the word means literally, even 'very frisky', as it is a phrase used of calves and lambs playing on the springtime grass. That is what this miniature interlude means to say: epic poetry is beautiful and valuable because it redeems from the unavailably distant past such a fragile and transient thing as the gaiety and dance-steps of a long-dead warrior queen.

Human memory lasts only three generations at best, but the poem is more godlike than that. A poem is not an act of memory but of memorialisation, fixing into everlasting song what would otherwise be forgotten. Agamemnon may lust after the possessions which victory will give him, objects 'such as will remain in the minds of men who are yet to be'. But he is wrong about that. We have no idea what those looted goods were; we only know what the poem has preserved.

Epic is different from life. The present moment might be seen as a kind of blade, cutting the past from the present, severing now from then, but poetry binds the wounds that time inflicts. As Odysseus says, the Muse provides 'her own way' for poets and story-tellers, a path of song on which events from the past will continue to live in a present reality. It is inconceivable that the epics, for all the pressures of composition-in-performance, did not attend to inherited realities, beyond the moment in about 700 BC or soon after when Homer was first written down. The poems are littered with hints and suggestions of the ancient. Iron, which by the time of Emporio and Pithekoussai was the material out of which farm instruments were made, is often treated in Homer as the most precious and rare of metals, to be carried home as booty in the same class as gold and bronze, the stuff of strange dark jewellery and, as Hector says of Achilles's iron heart, capable when heated of a mysteriously powerful reddened glow. That is exactly the position of iron in the Bronze Age before 1200 BC. Homeric warriors carry 'silver-riveted swords', which are found in the graves at Mycenae from the sixteenth century BC but scarcely later. Shields either in the form of large figures-of-eight or huge towering constructions behind which a man can hide as if behind a city wall – these are both Homeric pieces of equipment which are never found by archaeologists later than the fourteenth century BC. Helmets made of boars' tusks sewn to a leather backing, each helmet requiring the tusks from at least forty boars, are found in Mycenaean graves and in Homer, but never in contexts nearer the Iron Age. This is the equipment of a profoundly ancient world.

In the *Odyssey*, Homeric bards sing to gatherings of elegant aristocrats and their followers, attentive around the formal hearth, in complex, many-roomed and multi-floored palaces, in which kings and their queens happily ordain a well-ordered life, the like of which are not found in archaeology after the cataclysms of 1200 BC, but are the baseline of the Mycenaean civilisation before it. Much of that poem addresses the agony of rootlessness, the lack of civility in an ill-governed house, the failure of Greeks to be civilised; but the rest of it portrays what looks like a Mycenaean world, a world in which the war is over and the Greeks have come to rest. These poems must at least have passed through a palatial phase for them to be so familiar with the workings and architecture of that life. And in the *Iliad* there is one element in particular of that palace environment which seems to guarantee that at least in part Homer belonged to the palatial phase of Greek Bronze Age civilisation.

In the late nineteenth century and again in the mid-twentieth century, the greatest of all Aegean archaeologists – Heinrich Schliemann, Arthur Evans and Carl Blegen – working at Mycenae, at Knossos in Crete and at Pylos in the Peloponnese (with others following on at Chania, Thebes and Tiryns), found a series of clay tablets in which some kind of writing had been scratched before they dried. Small, grey, slightly roughly made things, these tablets were clearly not public objects. They are clay notes and records for private reference, not public display.

At Pylos, they came from within a few yards of where Carl Blegen found the fragments of the wonderful fresco showing the poet with his lyre and the bird of poetry taking wing in front of him. For decades no one could interpret the scratched signs, but in the early 1950s, through a combination of American and English analysis (feeding off the cryptography techniques developed in World War II), it became clear that the language they were written in was a form of Greek that was in use between about 1400 and 1200 BC. These Linear B tablets (Linear A was a similar, earlier, Cretan script, yet to be deciphered), once they had been understood, turned out to be the checklists and store-room accounts of clerks working in the administrative offices of these early Greek palaces. They were everyday files, dealing with employees, religious functionaries, chariots and other military equipment, food stores, domestic animals, regional officials and palace servants.

Judging from impressions on the clay, they had either been kept tied together in bundles or in baskets on shelves, which had collapsed in heaps on the floor during the final conflagrations of these palaces, the heat by chance baking and preserving the clay. Nothing on any of them even faintly resembled non-bureaucratic life, let alone the energised emotional realities to be found in Homer. It was a filing system, which like the workings of most bureaucracies remained hidden from the mass of the population: an essential part of the way the world works, entirely obscure to the mass of people inhabiting that world.

In what became known as the Archive Room at Pylos, Carl Blegen, on the very first morning of his dig in 1939, began to uncover the cache of Linear B tablets. By the end of that first season, his team had found six hundred. In the southern corner of the same room, traces of burned wood and seven small and very badly corroded hinges were found. Other similar hinges had been found at Knossos by Evans in 1900. Both sets of hinges and the little nails attached to them were too small to have belonged to a box of any size. They could not have been the remains of hinged containers for the tablets, because few such tablets could have fitted inside them. No one could guess what lids or doors they were for.

Only when another discovery was made in 1982 did the significance of these tiny clues become clear. Off the coast of Lycia, at Ulu Burun, about six miles south-east of Kaş in south-western Turkey, the wreck of a Bronze Age ship was stumbled on by a local sponge diver. A piece of firewood on board, freshly cut, was dated to 1306 BC.

The objects the wreck contained provided the most time-shrinking set of insights into the world of the eastern Mediterranean in the fourteenth century BC. The ship had been sailing west towards the Aegean from the Near East, heavily laden with ten tons of large copper ingots from Cyprus and a ton of tin ingots, perhaps brought to the Mediterranean coast from the great tin mines in Afghanistan. The standard copper to tin ratio for making bronze is 10:1. The metals in the Ulu Burun cargo could make enough bronze weapons to equip an army.

Together with those bulk goods was an extraordinary collection of riches: glass ingots, logs of Egyptian blackwood – a kind of ebony – ostrich eggshells, perhaps to make cups, inlaid seashell rings, elephant tusks, more than a dozen hippopotamus teeth and the shells of tortoises which the excavators think were the soundboxes for musical instruments. Little pots contained coriander and nigella seeds, rose-scented oils, olive and almond oil. There was gold jewellery from Canaan and Egypt, and precious mugs and cups made from tin. The ship carried equipment for building, fishing and war, presumably for sale, or perhaps to be distributed as gifts to those in power, and also the personal possessions of the people on board. Most of them seem to have been either Cypriot or Canaanite, traders coming west with the luxury goods of the east, but there were three men on board who had different origins. One wore a sword of which the nearest equivalents have been found in Sicily and Albania, as well as a bronze pin, and had some spears and a stone mace, of which the nearest parallels have been found in Romania and Bulgaria, on the western shores of the Black Sea. This was a man from the shadowy north, travelling in the Mediterranean, also now making his way back west, perhaps to Greece, perhaps to his homeland.

Alongside him were two men from Mycenaean Greece, their possessions appearing in pairs, carrying with them the kind of bowls and plates they were used to at home, as well as their razors, their bronze knives, and the engraved stones, their seals, with which they signed off documents and packages by pressing the engraved surface into clay balls attached to the binding strings. From mainland Greece, many seals and sealings survive. Perhaps these two men were accompanying some of these precious goods back from the Near East to the court of their king in Greece. In Egyptian and Hittite royal documents, such ambassadorial figures, overseeing the exchange of valuable goods between brother-kings, are a constant element in Bronze Age diplomacy.

The late-fourteenth-century BC realities of the Ulu Burun wreck – all now to be seen in the beautiful, cool, darkened rooms of the museum in Bodrum – were accompanied by one other extraordinary and revelatory object: a writing tablet made out of two boxwood leaves, with ivory hinges at one side, and hollowed-out panels on the inside of each leaf into which wax could be poured to make the writing surface. The bed of each panel is roughly cross-hatched to make a good, binding key for the wax. The closed tablet could be held shut with fixings on its outer edge, and that is probably how it was when the merchant ship went down: the outer surface of the tablet is far more worn than the inside. The wax itself has entirely disappeared in the thirty-three centuries the tablet spent in the sea. Nor was any stylus found with the Ulu Burun tablet, perhaps because it was made of wood or horn, but metal ones have been discovered in Anatolia, with a writing point at one end (the Greek word *graphein*, later meaning to write, originally meant to draw with a point or to scratch), and at the other a flat spatula for revision, smearing out marks in the wax.

The mysterious hinges at Pylos and Knossos were, it now seems, the only parts of portable writing tablets that survived the fires which brought the life of those palaces to an end. But the situation those objects describe – writing as the reserve of a specialist minority in royal households; folding tablets in which written messages, unintelligible to the majority of people, could be carried abroad to foreign courts; the tablets stored for keeping in the writing offices of the palace administration – finds a vivid echo in a moment from the *Iliad*.

It is the story told to Diomedes by the Lycian warrior Glaucus when they meet in battle and Diomedes asks him who his ancestors were. Glaucus's grandfather, he says, was a beautiful young hero called Bellerophon. He was living in Corinth, at the court, when the queen of

Corinth fell in love with him. She was originally from Lycia, in western Anatolia, where her father was king. At the sight of Bellerophon she became crazed with lust, but he held her at bay. Her frustration mounted, and she came to the point where if she could not sleep with him she wanted him killed. She went to her husband and told him that Bellerophon had tried to seduce her, to sleep with her against her will. If the king had any dignity at all, he would have him murdered. The king balked at the idea of performing the killing himself, but instead

> He quickly sent him off to Lycia, gave him some fatal tokens, scratching many deadly soul-tormenting signs in a folding wooden tablet, and ordered him to show them to the queen's father, who was king of Lycia, so that he might die.

Bellerophon, without being able to read it himself, was carrying his own death warrant with him into exile. When he reached Lycia he showed the mysterious signs to the king, who was able to read them, and then subjected him to a series of murderous tests. But Bellerophon behaved so heroically, overcoming every challenge, that he emerged triumphant and came to father three children, one of whom was Glaucus's own father.

The world of this tiny, famous incident is almost Arthurian: its elevation of honour, its secret lusts in palace corridors, its conscious stepping beyond the ethics of the battlefield. It is, in fact, a deeply traditional folktale, elements of it found all across the preserved literatures of the Near East. But what of the writing, those mysterious and dangerous signs? What does this description of writing say about the Homeric moment?

The Greek king could have something written, presumably by a scribe, but Bellerophon could not read what it was. Writing was something that belonged to royal administration, not to members of the court. The text was also inaccessible to the poet telling the tale, and seems mysterious, half-magical to him. The king in Lycia could read it, or have it read to him, but still it has the quality of a spell, those many dangerous signs crammed into the folding wooden tablet Bellerophon has brought him.

This story is, in other words, an illiterate description of something written, seen more as an object than a message, its means of communication arcane and beyond ordinary understanding. It is a tiny glimpse into the Mycenaean world, profoundly different from both the Greek world after 750 BC, when ordinary wine-drinkers could scratch hexameters into wine cups, and from the Greek world between 1200 and 750, when no one could write at all and there were no palaces, or archive rooms within them. The Bellerophon tale, in other words, is the mark of the *Iliad* being at least as old as the palatial culture of Mycenaean Greece.

But that is far from the end of it. A Mycenaean palace might have been the world in which the *Iliad* – or an *Iliad* – was sung. It is not the world the *Iliad* describes, or in which it began. That world, in which a Greek warband confronts a non-Greek city; in which Greek adventurers find themselves at sea in a world of settlement and order, profoundly unlike their own mobile, predatory, unsettled lives; in which they know about gold and weaponry and fine things, but look on palaces and cities as belonging to others – that world can only have been much earlier.

Clues to these ancient ghostly layers are everywhere in Homer. As the great American archaeologist of the Bronze Age world, Emily Vermeule, Professor of Archaeology at Harvard, said of the Homer she loved, deep tradition 'floats all through the songs as dust through air'. About 20 per cent of the whole of Homer looks as if it was originally composed in a Greek that was earlier than the Greek of the Linear B tablets, i.e. before 1400 BC. That antiquity can be seen above all in the way what are called pre-verbs relate to the verbs they modify. In Linear B, as in later classical Greek, a phrase the equivalent of 'the situation described earlier' might be written as 'the aforementioned case'. In Homer (and in other early languages of the Indo-European family) it often takes the form of 'the afore case mentioned'. The pre-verb floats free of the verb. A 'predetermined outcome' can in Homer, but not in later Greek, be a 'pre outcome determined'. This small clue makes it clear that Homeric Greek is in many parts earlier than the Greek of the Linear B tablets.

It has long been a puzzle to Homeric scholars that some lines in Homer don't scan properly. But they can be made to scan if you assume that certain words had another letter in them – the *digamma* or *wau*, which was pronounced like the English 'w', which had mostly disappeared by the time of the Linear B tablets, and is absent from the text of Homer as it has been preserved. Agamemnon is *anax andron* – the lord of men – in the text that has survived; the phrase only scans if you assume that it was originally *wanax andron*. The Greek for wine is *oinos*, but its original form is more familiar: *woinos*. These words that only work in their early form include the descriptions of the giant man-encircling shield carried into battle by Ajax. That kind of shield had been replaced by a little round shield as early as the fourteenth century BC, but the Iliadic words that had originally accompanied it survived in epic. Battle equipment, word-form and verse-form all point in the same direction: Homer's foundations are in pre-palatial antiquity, a poem stretching at least as far back as the seventeenth century BC.

That is the evidence in the language, but archaeology feeds into this too, nowhere more spectacularly than in the objects discovered in the Shaft Graves at Mycenae. Go to the beautiful halls of the National Museum in Athens – make it midweek in midwinter and you will have them entirely to yourself – and what you will find there is an electrifying encounter with the past. The Shaft Grave treasures are from the seventeenth and sixteenth centuries BC. The dead and their possessions were laid on the floor of a deep shaft, which was then roofed over and a mound built above it. They are from the time before any great fortresses or palaces were built in mainland Greece. The famous gates and ramparts at Mycenae and at Tiryns are all later. The blazingly rich objects in the graves come from a Greek warrior world where all value was to be found in the glory of the individual body and its accoutrements. This is an essentially mobile world, in love with horses, chariots, ships, weaponry, hunting, adornment, beauty, gold and song. The people in the graves were undoubtedly entranced by the contemporary richness and glamour of the Minoan civilisation in Crete and the almost unimaginable wealth of Egypt. Evidence of borrowings – or thefts – from those cultures are everywhere in the grave goods. But the Shaft Grave world was not yet palatial. From all the evidence found by more than a century's intensive archaeology, it was the bodies of the great, not the city of Mycenae in the sixteenth century BC, that was rich in gold. These kings and queens must have rustled with gold, jangled with it as it hung from their ears

The battle face of the *Iliad*: brutal, excluding, potent. One of the golden masks discovered by Heinrich Schliemann in the Shaft Graves at Mycenae in 1876. (See pages 108–9)

Overleaf: Throbbing with desire for the Sirens, Odysseus, bound to his ship, resists the illusions of nostalgia. From a storage jar made in Athens in about 480 BC. (See pages 4–6)

'Battle was sweeter to them than the land of their fathers.' The sword-bearing charioteer, hunched over in his war-lust, drives against an enemy. A limestone stele from the Shaft Graves at Mycenae, c.1600 BC. (See pages 159–60)

A gold drinking cup covered in the interlaced, bind-and-release spirals which entranced Homer's world. (See pages 110–11)

A golden octopus cup from Mycenae, perhaps made by a Cretan, or taken from Crete: the liquid beauties of a southern, palatial sophistication, which Odysseus lyingly claims as his own. (See page 242)

Scales from the Shaft Graves, made of gold so thin they could only have weighed the butterfly souls impressed on them. (See pages 111–12)

A sixth-century BC *lekythos* shows the tiny mosquito of a dead man's soul half-hovering above his head. For Homer, life itself was rich, life-after-death terminally diminished. (See page 112)

The theatre of dominance: a diadem from the Shaft Graves, the gold beaten as thin as costume jewellery. (See pages 106–7)

His father's son: tiny, dead Mycenaean princelings went to their graves encased in gold, front and back, a habit of reverencing the children of the great which goes back to the steppes. (See page 169)

The miniature drama of Mycenaean daggers. The multi-metal inlays of this *niello*-work find an echo in Homer's description of the landscapes of the shield of Achilles. (See page 136)

A portable writing tablet from about 1300 BC, found in the wreck at Ulu Burun off the Turkish coast. For Homer's heroes, writing was a form of threatening magic, reserved for specialists. (See pages 101–4)

and wrists, amazed onlookers with it, standing before them in high, pointed diadems and perfect, imperishable gold foil.

This body-enriched but monumentless life is strikingly like the world of the Greek warriors in the *Iliad*. When the German businessman and romantic Heinrich Schliemann first dug into the Mycenae graves in the wet autumn of 1876, he wrote to his friend Max Müller, describing how he was reduced to *weighing* what he was finding:

> There are in all five tombs, in the smallest of which I found yesterday the bones of a man and woman covered by at least five kilograms of jewels of pure gold, with the most wonderful, impressed ornaments; even the smallest leaf is covered with them. To make only a superficial description of the treasure would require more than a week. Today I emptied the tomb and still gathered there more than 6/10 kilograms of beautifully ornamented gold leafs . . . I telegraphed today to *The Times*.

It is held up as one of Schliemann's great errors that he identified the warriors he found in those graves with the Homeric heroes. It is still thought to have been the crassest of his anachronisms, since the orthodoxy continues to think, as the classical Greeks did, that the Trojan War was fought in around 1200 BC, and that the Shaft Graves at Mycenae are at least 350 years too early to have had anything to do with that war. But that dating has nothing to secure it beyond the guesses made by the classical Greeks. Evidence of destruction at Troy itself has been found at a series of archaeological horizons from 2200 BC to 1180 BC. Any one of them might have been the war of the *Iliad*, except for this one reason: Homer in the *Iliad* describes the Greeks as a pre-palatial warrior culture, very like the world of the gold-encrusted kings buried in the Shaft Graves at Mycenae. The Greeks as seen in the *Odyssey*, which in these lights can only be the later poem, coloured by the great period of Mycenaean palaces, have clearly begun to adopt the habits and structures of the Near Eastern palace culture. Nothing of that, though, appears in the *Iliad*. There is certainly no better reason to associate Homer with the Troy of about 1200 BC than with a city many centuries earlier.

And so this book, like Schliemann, has a different suggestion to make: the Shaft Graves at Mycenae are contemporary with, or probably slightly later than, the deepest levels of the Homeric poems. The objects in the graves are their own best evidence of a pre-urban, marginal, heroic world whose inhabitants look very like the people Homer portrayed.

The faces on which Schliemann stumbled are the faces of men as they are found in the *Iliad*. The usual image of the most famous mask, with the ears laid out to the side, gives the wrong impression, reducing the severity it intends. As you can see from the creases in the gold, those ears, much of the beard and the upper rim of the mask should be folded away from the face, leaving the features naked and prominent.

It is a battle face, not a portrait of an individual but the face of the warrior king: brutal, excluding and potent, as intense as any Renaissance inquisitor, nothing more resolute than that wide, closed mouth and the jaw gripped behind it. It is the face-helmet of fixed glory. Stare into its rebarbative blankness, appeal to it and it will not respond. Its gold shines; it does not care. It can hurt but you cannot hurt it. Here is Agamemnon in his *aristeia*, his power-drive towards supremacy, his best moment, as that word means, his excellence, his moment of prowess. And in that focus of power his strange, coffee-bean eyes can be seen as either closed in self-absorption and self-regard, or slitted in concentration. There is vanity here – his moustache tips are just tweaked upwards; a little sprig of hair grows just below the lower lip – but at root this face is the pitilessness of dominance.

Hold that face in mind and read Agamemnon's demeanour in Book II of the *Iliad* as he wades through 'the slayers and the slain'. Under his violence, men fall like trees under a woodman's axe. He drives his spear through a Trojan's forehead 'and the spear was not stopped by the helmet, heavy with bronze, but passed through it and through the bone, and all the brain was splashed inside'. The next man is speared in the chest 'by the nipple', and the third killed with a sword-cut close to the ear. The next two, brothers, beg Agamemnon not to kill them. They speak to him 'weeping, with gentle words', offering him bronze and gold and iron from their father's house, but 'ungentle was the voice they heard', *ameiliktos*, meaning unsoothing, the opposite of 'darling'. He stabs one of the boys in the chest, and slices off the arms and then the head of the other with his sword, the head rolling through the surrounding crowds of warriors like a round stone. Agamemnon is a fire in the forest and a lion in the mountains. His hands are spattered with the filth of blood. The chariots of those he has killed run driverless through the battlefield, the horses 'longing for their incomparable charioteers', but those men are now lying on the earth, 'more loved by the vultures than by their wives'.

Every Trojan warrior stands away from Agamemnon, trembling like a hind that sees a lion devouring her young and can do nothing to protect them. Agamemnon is that lion, eating the inward parts of those he kills. He kills a man, Iphidamas, just married, whose wife would now have 'no joy of him', and then, in a frenzy of repetition, Iphidamas's brother, whose head Agamemnon cuts from his body with his sword. It has been a fiesta of severance, a destruction of human beings, but more than that, a destruction of human bonds. Agamemnon is edge-honed violence, his victims essentially their ligatures and sinews. It is the meeting of blade and connective tissue.

Only when wounded in the arm does Agamemnon withdraw from his unforgiving crusade. As his wound begins to dry, pain starts to afflict him.

And just as when the sharp pain strikes a woman in labour, the piercing dart sent by the bitter goddesses of childbirth, so sharp pains broke in on the strength of Agamemnon.

Those words are a measure of the grace and wisdom of this beautiful and terrifying poem. The pain suffered by the unforgiving agent of death and termination is like the pain of a woman as she gives birth to new life. What Agamemnon has done is to cut the connections between men and their fathers, men and their brothers, men and their wives, even men and their horses. But as his comparator for that slicing away of meaning, Homer summons the agony of childbirth, the root connectedness of humanity.

The Shaft-Grave Greeks, in this vision, are the people of the blade and the mask, the Trojans of the loom and the embrace. One slices and rejects, the other weaves and holds; but Homer stands beyond and embraces them both. He makes a poem of death that is itself a thing of woven beauty. That is the essential picture of the *Iliad*, a great history cloth, a tapestry of sorrow, in which the non-city is set against the city, where the marginal and contingent confronts the settled and the secure. The poem is hinged to that difference: the loved against the abused, the creative against the destructive forces of life. And the fact of the poem itself is a kind of super-weaving, a weaving of severance and weaving into one shining cloth of incomparable understanding.

You can find that love of complexity in the Mycenaean halls of the Athens museum. Take for example the interlaced spirals on one of the beautiful golden cups, almost certainly a hospitality cup for drinking on shared, ritual occasions. Its decoration dramatises those moments. The spirals are formed into upper and lower bands. Trace individual lines in the patterns and you will find that the spirals in one set of lines roll from right to left, those in the other from left to right. Each tightens into a knot, meets its opposite there, and then spirals out and on to the next encounter. At the same time lines from each band reach out and intertwine with lines from the bands above and below.

This is a culture entranced with the meeting, engaging, twisting, intertwisting and emerging of different cross-currents. Spirals are every-where, in the gravestones showing spearmen in chariots hurtling into battle, on pots and on architectural masonry, on the beautifully chiselled platforms for the thrones of Mycenaean kings, on a golden breastplate bubbling with the swirl of life. The spirals might be taken as abstractions of the waves of the sea, but they are more than that: a recognition that this pattern of bind-and-release, alternating connectedness and separate-ness, is intimate with the nature of existence, of the thinking mind, the experiencing heart, the world which weaves and severs.

In Book 14 of the *Iliad*, as deep trouble is afflicting the Greeks, Nestor, the old king of Pylos, stands outside his own shelter in the Greek camp and looks dazed at the confusion around him:

As when the open sea is deeply stirred by the ground-swell
But stays in one place and awaits the rapid onset of tearing
Gusts, not rolling its surf onward in either direction
Until Zeus drives the wind down to decide it:
So the old man pondered, his mind caught between two courses.

That is as near as poetry could get to what archaeologists have called the 'antithetical spirals' which colonise such large areas of Mycenaean decoration and thought: dynamic, self-interlacing, not fixed but entranced by the very concepts of mobility, complexity and dynamism.

But there is a delicate and fluttering sensibility here too. In Grave III, where Schliemann found the remains of three women and two children, crowned with the most astonishing sun-embossed diadems of gold foil, their dresses scattered like spring meadows with gold roundels and flowers, he also found a set of impossibly flimsy golden scales, the bar from which the two pans hung made of foil so thin that anything more than the weight of a butterfly would have bent it. And on those scales, the Mycenaean craftsmen had impressed into the metal precisely that: fat-bodied butterflies, their wings fitting the scales on which they rested.

All this makes one thing clear: there is no need to assume that this early, pre-palatial *Iliad* was some kind of brutalist crudity of bloodlust and violence, indifferent to the subtleties of moral atmosphere which are part of the deep weave of the poems. The early *Iliad* was as alert to irony, tragedy, poignancy and humanity as the *Iliad* we know. As Emily Vermeule once told a gathering of American classicists:

> Philologists often dislike, and reject, the idea that the early *Iliad* was good, and so beloved that great poetic effort and training were devoted to conserving it with all its archaisms and outmoded armor. They often prefer a late genius Homer who unified the design and gave new subtlety to the characters. This is because we still like to believe in progress, and that each generation somehow improves over the one before it; so, Homer should be as close to the civilized and lovable Us as we can make him, not some primitive singer of the remotest past. . . [But] poetically and archaeologically, early is not always the same as primitive.

Look for example at the two most pitiful and most fully realised deaths in the *Iliad*, those of Achilles's dear friend Patroclus and of Hector, the champion of Troy. The same lines are given to their moment of dying, and only to them:

He spoke, and as he spoke the end of death closed in upon him,
And the soul, fluttering free of his limbs, went down into Death's house
Mourning its destiny, leaving behind its youth and manhood.

The Greek of those lines is as ancient as any in Homer, and yet they are also among the most poignant. The little soul leaves with nothing but regret. Death is not a release into beautiful immateriality, but an expulsion from vivid life. Death is exile from light. The lovely limbs and eyes of Hector and Patroclus are now inert and glazed; the soul is nearly nothing without them.

Later images on Greek pots sometimes show a tiny, moth-like figure, more wing than body, hovering on the shoulders of the heroes who have just died. Emily Vermeule, in a connection typical of her bright genius, reported an experiment performed by a doctor in Düsseldorf who had placed the beds of his dying patients on extremely sensitive scales, so that he could measure their weight immediately before and after death. The difference, he found, was twenty-one grams, three-quarters of an ounce, the weight of the soul.

How can these objects and images not be evidence of a Homeric sensibility in sixteenth-century BC Mycenae? The love-denying mask of Agamemnon; the vision of the mayfly-soul, sadly departing the man in whose body she had found such radiant life; the antithetical interlace of a mind caught between two courses; the presence of tenderness allied in your everyday life to desperate violence.

Again and again in his similes, Homer knows that life is fragile, love suffers hurt and death comes; and that the moments on a hillside in the springtime, when the flowers are emerging in the turf, the sheep are giving milk and what looks like a mist of new leaves just breathed into the dark of a winter wood are more precious than any gathering of metal from slaughtered enemies or the rape of their wives.

There is no need to patronise the past, or to assume that we somehow have a fineness of moral vision to which the warrior culture of Homer and the Shaft Graves had no access. But can one push on beyond this moment of the early Greeks in Greece? Does Homer have his roots in anything earlier than what can be found at Mycenae? He does. But here the path bifurcates: from Greece and the Aegean, the undoubted setting of the Homeric poems, one road leads north and west into Europe and the borders of Europe and Asia; the other goes south and east towards the great palace civilisations of Crete, Egypt, Mesopotamia and the eastern shores of Mediterranean. Homer exists at the confluence of those two giant streams; in many ways his subject is what happens when those two streams meet and mingle. Homer, often seen as the template from which many later encounters of west and east are drawn, is better understood as the great meeting of north and south, what happens to northern adventurers in a southern world. That is the meeting which lies at the roots of Greek civilisation, and from which the later history of Europe stems.

EIGHT

The Metal Hero

IN THE STONE AGE, before man went in search of metal, you could have picked up nodules and nuggets of copper lying on the surface of the earth, or glimmering in the sandbanks of any stream. In some places, like the great copper body at Parys Mountain in Anglesey, copper was so thick in the ground-water that perfect branches, plant stems, leaves and nuts of the metal could be found in the dirt, where the mineral had somehow replaced the organic matter buried there.

All over Eurasia, that native copper was beaten into discs and rosettes, badges and brooches, and occasionally little needle-sharp awls and burins for working leather. In about 8000 BC in Anatolia, in Syria and northern Mesopotamia, people began to smelt it, the first smiths, magicians of heat and strangeness, drawing the metal out of the ores in which it is usually found. The heat of a pottery kiln is enough to release the metal from its oxides and sulphides, but even so the glowing emergence of a material which when cool stayed flame-bright can only have summoned a kind of awe. It may even be that the Arthurian story of the sword in the stone is a folk-memory of this emergent miracle: gleaming strength drawn from a rock.

From about 5000 BC, people all over Europe and Asia started hardening the copper, perhaps first by chance, by mixing arsenic with the metal when it was molten. But copper and these copper-arsenic alloys were rather soft, not the revolutionary material which after 3000 BC would transform Eurasia. Only then did someone, probably in Anatolia, discover that if you added tin to copper, you could produce a metal that would not only take a high shine – a brazen, visual hardness – but was physically hard, and could be sharpened to a fierce and lasting edge. This tin-copper alloy was bronze, and it would change the world. There is some tin in Anatolia, but in most places it is rare or absent, and across the bulk of the bronze-making world it had to be imported from elsewhere. Still nobody is certain where that tin for the Bronze revolution came from: perhaps from Bohemia in the Czech Republic, maybe from Cornwall, but more likely from Afghanistan. Whatever the origins of the tin, travel and connection became central to the culture of Europe. For the first time in the European Bronze Age (2500 to 800 BC), the exotic became desirable, and the distant prestigious. It became a world of interconnectedness, a culture founded on mobility, with ideas, beliefs and ways of life all travelling along the seaways and river routes of Europe and western Asia.

'The broad picture,' as the Bristol archaeologist Richard Harrison has written, 'is of a continent with an imaginative map of itself that knew, through objects from faraway places, that other worlds existed and that they shared values as well as objects.' A necklace of Baltic amber, found in a grave in Wiltshire in England, was made of beads shaped in Mycenae. The Nebra sky disc, found in central Germany, was made of Austrian copper, Cornish tin and Cornish gold. A Bronze Age wreck off the south coast of Devon carried a Sicilian sword. A piece of amber has been found at Bernstorf in Bavaria, inscribed with a word written in Linear B, the Greek spoken in Mycenae, along with gold diadems that resemble those from Mycenae itself. Afghan lapis lazuli appears in Greek graves. Folding chairs in Danish graves were made on patterns that recur in Greece and in Egypt.

Were these movements of things accompanied by people? Or was it only that objects were passed from hand to hand across Europe? Shipwrights in Bronze Age Scandinavia made craft that bear a striking resemblance to Greek prototypes. Carvings of otter-like animals on some Swedish tombs look very like the creatures engraved on Mycenaean signet rings. How did those ideas get there? Did Bronze Age Greeks actually make their way to Denmark?

The teeth of an early Bronze Age man who was buried not far from Stonehenge in southern England bear trace elements which show that he grew up somewhere in the Swiss Alps. Near him another man was buried, his relative, perhaps his son, with the same slightly faulty bone structure in his feet, whose teeth revealed that he had grown up in southern England. Cross-continental journeys were certainly possible in the Bronze Age, but was the whole of this proto-Europe alive with adventurers and travellers? Or people whose journeys were not of their own volition? Chemical analysis of the teeth enamel from twenty-four people roughly buried in a series of late Bronze Age pits at Cliffsend in Thanet in north-east Kent, from around 1000 BC, show an extraordinary set of international origins. Just over a third were from Kent (strontium and oxygen isotopes in drinking water carry unique chemical signatures), another third from southern Norway or Sweden, a fifth from the western Mediterranean, and the rest undetermined. Many of these people left their birthplaces when they were children between three and twelve years old. One old woman buried in Thanet was born in Scandinavia, moved to Scotland as a child, and at the end of a long life finished up in Kent. Almost certainly these people were slaves.

Certain clusters of human genes (the haplogroup E3bIa2) which have their heartland in the copper-mining districts of Albania, and are found in the people living there now, rarely appear elsewhere in Europe, except in two specific concentrations: one in the modern inhabitants of Galicia in north-west Spain, the other in the people of north-west Wales, both important centres of copper mining in the early Bronze Age. It seems inescapable that these genes are the living memories of Bronze Age people travelling the width of a continent to exploit the magical metal.

Bronze began to transform the Near East, and to have its effect in China, the Indus valley and the Aegean. Troy, on the far northern edge of that urban belt, became a trading city, controlling routes to the north. City-states emerged, along with writing, bureaucracies, specialist traders and central authoritarian government. Woven textiles were traded up into the Caucasus in return for copper from increasingly well-developed mines. In a belt that stretched east across the Asian continent, and of which Troy and the beautiful cities visited by Odysseus are the emblem and embodiment, urban civilisations emerged.

At the same moment, but further north, the new metal had an equally powerful effect on human history. A different, non-urban Bronze-based culture emerged. A cluster of economic, social, military and psychological changes came about in a wide swathe of country which stretched from the steppelands around the Caspian Sea through the Balkans and on into northern Europe. These changes created the civilisation of which Achilles is the symbol: not a city world but a warrior elite, ferociously male in its focus, with male gods and a cultivation of violence, with no great attention paid to dwellings or public buildings, but a fascination with weaponry, speed and violence. The heroes of this warrior world were not the bureaucrats of the cities further south, or the wall-builders, or the defenders of the gates, but men for whom their individuality was commemorated in large single burials, often under prominent mounds, on highly visible places among the grazing grounds cleared for their herds. Meat mattered in this warrior world, largely as a symbol of portable wealth when on the hoof and as the material for feasting when dead and cooked.

This semi-pastoral economic and political system was the breeding ground for a dynamic and mobile warrior culture which would eventually spread throughout Eurasia. There were many local variations and idiosyncrasies, and a complex chronology, full of time-lags, which mean that the same cultural phase occurs at different times in different places; but for all that, a single world of Bronze Age chieftainship stretched across the whole of northern Eurasia from the Atlantic to the Asian steppe. It is a world hinged to the idea of the hero, quite different from the developed, literate cultures of the eastern Mediterranean, and it is the world from which the Shaft-Grave Greeks emerged in about 1700 BC.

In his Greek heroes, Homer gives voice to that northern warrior world. Homer is the only place you can hear the Bronze Age warriors of the northern grasslands speak and dream and weep. The rest of Bronze Age Europe is silent. Echoes of what was said and sung in Ireland or in German forests can be recovered from tales and poems collected by modern ethnographers, but only in Homer is the connection direct. The relationship travels both ways. Homer can illuminate Bronze Age Europe, and Bronze Age Europe can throw its light on the Homeric world.

In places where you might least expect to find them, echoes of the world of Achilles come drifting up at you. And the weapons are at the heart of it. I have seen them now in museums in Wiltshire, in Naples and Syracuse, Bodrum, Athens and Nafplion, and in St Petersburg, Paris, Edinburgh, London and Boston, where collectors and excavators have gathered them. Anywhere you seek out Bronze Age weaponry, the same power gestures greet you from across the room: the seductive, limousine length of the blades, the oxidised green of the bronze, often now the colour of a mottled sea, the willow-leaf javelin points, the sheer length of the long swords with their golden hilts, the deep-socketed spear heads, the socket running as far back along the shaft as the spear head protrudes beyond it, the metal occasionally still wrapped in oiled cloth to preserve it.

If you look at one of these blades with Homer in mind, you see it for what it is: the tapering fineness of its double edges, coming to a point more gradually than anything in nature, those everlasting cutting edges going on and on like the leaf of a fine, imagined iris; or a slow-motion diagram of death being delivered; the strengthening midrib, narrowing along the blade but running to the very tip, so that it arrives there as delicate as a syringe; and the reinforcement at the root of the blade, a possible weak point where the shaft first narrows, vulnerable to the body of the victim twisting and kicking with the pain.

These blades are pure ergonomy, designed for a purpose, elegantly coalescing the necessary functions, the cut and the shove, two slicing edges and a penetrative rod for the best possible pushing of metal into flesh, and then the widening of the wound past the point, so that the man will bleed and die.

These are the wonder-weapons of the *Iliad*:

> They clothed their bodies in gleaming bronze and Poseidon the Shaker of the Earth, led them, carrying in his strong hand his terrible long-edge sword, like lightning, which no one can stand up to in dreadful war. Terror holds men aloof from it.

These weapons are horrifying and beautiful, repulsive and attractive in the way the *Iliad* can be, for their lack of sentiment, the unadorned facts they represent, but also for the perfection with which they are made, their seamless match of purpose and material. The swords that have been found in Mycenaean graves are always exceptionally well-balanced things, the weight in the pommel counteracting the weight in the blade so that they feel functional in the hand, body-extensions, enlarging the human possibilities of dominance and destruction. The lances would have been useful in the hunt, to be thrown or to jab at cornered prey, but these swords mark a particular horizon in human history: they are the first objects to be designed with the sole purpose of killing another person. Their reach is too short for them to be any good with a wild animal thrashing in its death terror. A sword is only any use if someone else agrees to the violence it threatens; it will get to another man who is prepared to stand and fight. Some of the most beautiful decorated swords are found scarcely used, ceremonial objects to be carried in glory. But most of the rest show the marks of battle; the edges hacked and notched where another sword clashed on to them, worn where those edges were resharpened for the next time.

An air of threat and beauty hangs about them, even in their glass cases, labelled and sanitised, consigned to a curated past. They seem sometimes like caged predators, their violence lurking a quarter of an inch beneath the surface. Anyone who has ever walked out with a gun they liked, or even a rod well set up, will know something of this, its beautiful fittedness to your needs, 'as snug as a gun', as Seamus Heaney described the pen he chose instead of it, the sense a weapon has of extending your power over the material world, its promise, or at least taunting suggestion, of what it will be like when the fish takes the hook and the rod bends, and you feel in your hand that other creature's struggle against your dominance; or when the bird you have been tracking crumples and folds with the shot, its head and wings useless, bowling towards earth, where the body lands football-like, a muffled heavy thump.

Our modern sensibility might wrinkle its nose against the pleasure the warrior world took in violence, but Homer cannot be understood unless that pleasure is also understood. Homer has a specific word for that death thump: *doupeo*, meaning 'to sound like the heavy thud of a corpse as it falls'. It is always set against its opposite *arabeo*, to rattle and clash, the sound that armour makes when a man is felled. That pairing is a formula which fills a whole line, recording again and again the death of enemies:

> *doupēsen de pesōn, arabēse de teuche' ep' autōi*
> With a thud he fell, rattling his armour around him.

The thud and the rattle mark the falling apart of a man's life, its coherence removed by death, the effect delivered by the gleaming bronze, the triumph of the new metal dominance, its penetrative masculinity and its cultivation of power. The sharpened blade transformed human relations.

Only once in my life have I had a knife held to my throat. It was thirty years ago. I was twenty-five years old and in Palmyra in the Syrian desert. In the early evening I was walking alone in the palm groves on the southern edge of the oasis, down the rutted tracks that curved through the trees beyond the ruins of the temple of Baal. The sun was coming through in rods, lighting up the bunches of fruit high in those trees, and between the shafts of light the air was soft and grey, almost milky. The warmth of the evening was feeling its way between my shirt and skin. A little boy passed me and said 'Hallo' in English, brightly and sweetly.

I was thinking how beautiful this place was after all the openness of the desert, coming as we had on a hard, rough track from Damascus, and was paying no attention to where I was wandering, kicking up the dust on the track with the toes of my boots. But the light was going, and after a while I thought I should return to where I was staying, the Hotel Zenobia, a mile or so the far side of the famous ruins, in the grid of streets of the modern town.

And so I turned back up the track, the way I had come. I could see the footprints my boots had made as I came down there. But I reached a crossing, where another track cut over, and could not immediately remember which to take. A young man, a little older than me, but shorter, with rather thick hair combed to one side, was leading his bicycle towards me. 'Hotel Zenobia?' I asked him. He looked up at me. 'Hotel Zenobia?' I asked again.

A look of understanding came into his face and he smiled, turned his bicycle around and led me along the track he had just come down. We had the usual, fruitless non-conversation between people who cannot speak each other's language. After a few minutes we came to another crossing, and he seemed a little uncertain. I looked in his face to see if I could guess where he thought we should go, but as I did so he dropped his bicycle, grabbed me by my wrists and started to push me to the ground in front of him. It was always going to be hopeless, him being the shorter, and I held him and his arms away from me. He tried to trip me, as schoolboys do, by putting his foot behind mine, but to no end. It was faintly ludicrous, the two of us there in a kind of tussling non-embrace, on some track in the middle of an oasis in the Syrian desert. But there was anxiety in his eyes, now I looked into them.

I broke free of his hold, running back the way we had come, turned right at the first crossroads and ran on, hoping but not knowing that I was on the track to get out of the palm grove and into the openness around the ruins. I ran on, the path curving here and there between the different blocks of the plantation, until I came to a fork in the road. Which way? I had no idea, and stopped, trying to recognise the route home. But as I stopped he caught up with me. I looked down at him and saw that he had a large stone in his hand; he had been thinking of throwing it at me. But the instant I saw the stone he dropped it and took out a knife, the blade no more than four or five inches long, but coming to a point, the edges honed, scratched where he had sharpened them on a file.

He raised the knife to my throat and held the point just where you would put your fingers for a pulse, where the neck begins to curve round under the jaw. I could feel the metal point on my skin, but it did not cut me. Keeping it there, he led me back down the track we had both just run along. I didn't feel any conscious fear. My breathing was slowing, my mind going cold, disconnected. He wanted to be somewhere we would not be disturbed. We turned off the track into a little patch of scrubby ground between the palm trees. There were some plastic canisters here, perhaps for oil. Neither of us spoke. He made me undress, holding the knife into the side of my neck as I did so. Surely I should have hit him then? Looking back on it now, I wonder why I didn't. Why not just hit his face with my fist, knock him down and kick him once he was on the ground? Isn't that what the warriors in Homer would have done? Break his skull, murder the man who threatened me with his knife? Wasn't that the only dignified thing to have done?

But I didn't. I behaved in the way that the 'foolish children' of the *Iliad* behave, submitting to the knife, too frightened at what that blade might do to my face and body to risk fighting him. Women and children in Homer are always called foolish because they do not risk death by confronting the enemy; they submit and suffer like sheep under a worrying dog. I knelt in the dust as he raped me, a pitiable little dog-like action from behind, the point of the knife jiggling in the side of my neck with his frantic movements, my mind observing this from afar and realising that the moment of greatest danger was not yet over: that after he had done with me, all the possibilities of loathing, resentment and shame, not to speak of the chance that I would report and identify him, might mean he would kill me.

I prepared for that moment as I felt him coming over my thighs and buttocks. It all seemed entirely prosaic, neither consciously frightening nor dramatic, not anything that would raise my pulse. This was my experience of the ordinariness of death, that everything that had made me what I was up to that moment – my father and my father's father, my love of home, of the orchards and wheatfields that the Iliadic warriors always remember, and my wife in England – all of that was now perhaps to come to an end, without strangeness or mystery, but as one of the essential facts of being and non-being, of my life being bound up with the continued existence of the pulse in my body. I felt entirely animal, as if I and my body were co-terminous, everything about me dependent on the blade of that knife not cutting into me and draining my life into the Syrian dust.

In those few minutes, I moved through the full spectrum of Homeric reactions, from the child-like stupidity of acceptance of violence to the man-like recognition that I should risk killing him in order to be myself. This was when the fight for life would happen; this was my introduction to the world with which the Homeric heroes are so familiar; their life dependent on the death of those who are out to destroy them.

We stood up, I dressed, he did up his trousers, holding the knife in his hand, and I walked back alongside him, smiling, talking about Palmyra, just out of arm's reach. We came to his bike and he picked it up, the knife still in the hand that held the handlebars. I made sure I walked with the bike between me and him. I kept talking to him, looking at him with my eyes smiling, acting ease and acceptance, waiting for the moment when he would stop again, and come for me, preparing for that, not in anything resembling rage or fear, but a stilled, intent cold-mindedness. As we walked along, I looked for the stones on the track which, when the time came, I would pick up and use to crush the skull-bones between his eyes.

It was getting dark. We passed the point where he had first caught up with me. The further we got, the safer I knew I was. We reached the edge of the palms and the blue of the open desert. He pointed me to the road I should have taken and then he turned away to the right, walking with his bike into the shadows of the trees. I went on across the desert towards the town and the hotel, where I stood for longer than I knew in the shower, recognising that I had understood something that evening: the banality of one's own death, so much less terrible than the death of someone you love; its mysterious combination of everything and nothing; its lack of beauty or poignancy; the extreme calm that threat can summon; the clarity with which, when threatened with death, you must threaten death in return.

I knew nothing of Homer then, but I know now that these are all aspects of Homeric understanding. They emerge from a world in which use and imposition are part of the everyday fabric of life. The poems are not the overheated fantasies of palace-based thrill-seekers. There's no ooh-ah here. Homer's groundedness in the plain facts of killing is one of the guarantees of its truth.

A few years later I went in deeper pursuit of this northern, non-urban, metal warrior world, led first by the hint of a footnote in a book by Adolf Schulten, the German archaeologist who devoted his life to the recovery of antiquity in southern Spain. In 1922, in the first volume of *Fontes Hispaniae Antiquae*, he made the suggestion that he knew where Hades was, the underworld, which in the middle of the *Odyssey* Odysseus and his men visit in order to learn the way home from the old, blind seer Tiresias. It was, I recognise, a quixotic thing to do, to fly there, hire a car, drive through the concrete scurf of the modern Spanish coastline, to find the place where Odysseus, a fictional character in a phantasmagorical story from the Bronze Age, was said to have encountered some of the deepest truths Homer had to offer. It is the sort of behaviour you might find in a Tom Stoppard play or a High Victorian memoir, but as things turned out, in my few days of walking around the river valleys and dry cork oak pastures on the high borders of Andalusia and Extremadura – that most-marginal-imaginable of Odyssean landscapes – I felt as if I were cutting deep trenches into the Homeric world.

When I first read the *Odyssey*, no moment was more powerful for me than Odysseus's visit to the underworld. Inner and outer landscapes were more intimately fused there than in anything I had ever read. The great man's crew of time- and sea-worn sailors have been on Circe's island, but are now cold and frightened, at the limits of the world. The coast of Hades is desolate, fringed with tall poplars and with willows whose seed falls from the trees before it is ripe. This place is everything the world of heroes is not: dark, colourless, silent and mournful.

Crowds of the dead surface to confront the crew. The ghosts, the *psyches*, shuffle towards them; their limbs are 'strengthless'. All the varieties of death emerge: the old who had suffered much, the girls with tender hearts, the brides and unwed youths, and 'great armies of battle dead, stabbed by bronze spears, men of war still wrapped in bloody armour'. They cannot speak. They do not have the life juices which would allow them to speak.

For the dead, there is no other choice than Hades. This is not punishment, but simply the place where in the end all people, however good and however holy, must go. Hell is the absence of life, the removal from the world of love and warmth which is the defining glory of life on earth. Hell is the house of loss. Only when Odysseus sprinkles in front of him all the good and fruitful things of the world – milk, honey, wine, water, white barley flour – and adds to them the hot blood of newly slaughtered lambs, and only when he allows the ghosts to sip at that life-blood, does the power of speech, the sense of human communicativeness, return to the spirits.

One by one they approach him, drink and speak: his friend Elpenor; Tiresias; and his mother. Odysseus longs to embrace them all, but as he moves to hold them, they rustle through his hands, slipping away like shadows, 'dissolving like a dream'. They are nothing in his arms. *Psyches* are merely people from whom the life-defining qualities of people, their physical presence in the world, have been stripped away. Here are people in the grey, fleshless state to which death has reduced them. It is a vision of the beautiful, the regal and the desirable sunk to nothing but rustling, flittering spirit.

As Odysseus stands there, with the tears running down his cheeks, he sees the ghost of Achilles coming towards him, the greatest of all the warriors, the fastest and fiercest among them, worshipped almost as a god by the other Greeks at Troy, and now the greatest among the dead. His face is mournful, and Odysseus tries to console him. Achilles answers coldly and passionately: 'Never try to sweeten death for me, glorious Odysseus.' The word Achilles uses for 'glorious', *phaidimos*, is used throughout Homer to describe the heroes. But here in hell, it has a particular resonance. Its roots are in the word for 'shining' or 'brilliance'. As the dead Achilles speaks, it is the world of lightlessness addressing the world of light and glimmer, the shining world from which Odysseus comes and from which Achilles is forever excluded.

This is one of the pivotal moments of the Homeric epics, the dead hero of the *Iliad* addressing the living hero of the *Odyssey*, the man of singular and unequalled heroism, who has already suffered his fate, speaking across the borders of hell with the living, slippery, 'many-wayed' man, *polytropos Odysseus*, whose life and destiny has still some glittering way to run. Death is addressing life and envying it.

Achilles makes the great central statement of the poems. 'If I had a chance of living on earth again,' the ghost says through his tears, 'I would rather do that as a slave of another, some landless man with scarcely enough to live on, than lord it here over all the dead that have ever died.' This is the Achilles whose pride had defined him in life, whose honour and sense of his own greatness had driven hundreds of men to their death, who had chosen death and a short life as the foundation of his glory. In the *Iliad*, Achilles had glowed with destructive beauty: he was a flaming star, a fire burning through a wood. His hands were 'like consuming fire, his might like glittering iron'. His eyes burned like a furnace-core. His protective goddess, the grey-eyed Athene, had lit an unwearying fire that burned over his head. At every turn in his life he was quick and unforgiving. He was elemental in his strength, like a river unsusceptible to argument or compromise. But now, for this ghost, this burned-out, ashy wraith, any taste of life, of any kind, however humble, would be preferable to the half-lit half-existence of senseless wastedness to which he is condemned. The purity of death holds no attraction for the Homeric Greeks. Their world is one in which the felt, sensed and shared reality, the reality of the human heart, is the only one worth having.

As a measure of Homer's skill as a dramatist and topographer of the emotions, he has Achilles address Odysseus again, the two of them still in tears, with the question that burns in the heart of any ghost in hell: 'But tell me the story,' Achilles says – the Greek word is *mythos*, meaning the 'word', the 'rumour', what men say, but also the plot, the pattern of the story – 'of the lordly boy.' He is referring to his son Neoptolemos, whose name means New War. Had he followed the Greeks to the wars? Had he fought as a son of Achilles might be expected to fight? Was he a boy a man might be proud of? Odysseus, drenched in love and pity for the dead hero, tells him all he knows of the beauty and courage of Neoptolemos: his calm when waiting with Odysseus in the belly of the Trojan Horse, his unwavering courage, and, perhaps more important, how the boy had ended the war unharmed and even unscarred, never stabbed by either spear or sword, but sailing home in his ship with his share of the spoils and 'a noble prize'. He does not mention that in other stories of the Trojan War, Neoptolemos was the most savage of all killers at the fall of Troy, murdering Priam at the altar of Zeus and killing Astyanax, Hector's child, by throwing him from the walls. In one version, Neoptolemos kills Priam by battering him with the dead body of his grandson.

Achilles does not hear this, but nevertheless can say nothing in response to what Odysseus does say. It is too much for any father, even the greatest of heroes. He can only walk away across this beautiful, monochrome hell, which is covered, like all stony wasteland in the Mediterranean, with stands of tall, pale asphodels. It is a moment to describe the desolation of death and the unbridgeable gap between the world of light and the world of dark. Achilles both possesses his son in his memory and knows he can never possess him again. Neoptolemos is not here, and Achilles can be nowhere else. Here, defined by death, is the central grief of experience. Odysseus tells his listeners what Achilles did next:

> So I spoke, and off he went, the ghost of the great runner,
> Loping with long strides across the field of asphodel,
> Speechless in triumph at all that I had told him of his boy.

Adolf Schulten suggested that this scene occurred at the far western end of the Bronze Age world, in south-west Spain, because that is where the goddess Circe had told Odysseus to go:

> Set up your mast, spread the white sail, and sit yourself down; and the breath of the North Wind will bear your ship onwards.

Bronze Age ships, on a broad reach, with the mainsail braced hard to port, could drive west with a north wind, the fastest of all points of sailing.

> But when in your ship you have crossed the stream of Oceanus, where is a level shore and the groves of Persephone – tall poplars and willows that shed their fruit – there beach your ship by the deep swirling Ocean, but go yourself to the dank house of Hades.

These are plain instructions. Odysseus's ship must sail beyond the gates of the Mediterranean, out through the Straits of Gibraltar, into the

Atlantic Ocean, where the tides swirl and circle in a way unknown to Mediterranean sailors, and there find a beach with strange, cold, oceanic trees whose fertility deserts them under the salt winds. These are the trees of Persephone, the queen of death who is also queen of life, a vegetation goddess taken by Hades, king of the underworld, to be his consort, and in whose kingdom she presides over the sufferings of human souls. Odysseus would know he had arrived when he found her trees whose seeds would never be ripe.

But Circe is more explicit still:

There into the ocean flow Pyriphlegethon and Kokytus, which is a branch of the river of Styx; and there is a rock, and the meeting place of the two roaring rivers.

Homer's geographic imagination understands scale and substance, and these are the giant rivers of hell: *Pyriphlegethon* means blazing or raging like a fire, used of cities when men torch them; *Kokytus* means howling or shrieking: it is the sound made by Priam and the women of Troy when they hear of the death of Hector; *Styx* means hateful and loathsome, the word used again and again for war, death and destiny. In rivers that make their way down to the great surrounding ocean, sorrow and fearsomeness slide out of the huge, dark, hidden continent called Hades.

Schulten thought he knew where this was. West of the Guadalquivir, and west of the straits of Gibraltar, two rivers flow out into the Atlantic at Huelva: the Rio Tinto, which means the red river, and the Rio Odiel. Where they meet in the estuary at Huelva, a great hoard of Bronze Age weaponry, now in Madrid, was dredged up in 1923. The confluence of those rivers is below a conspicuous rock where the monastery of Santa Maria de la Rábida has stood since the Middle Ages, and where in 1492 Christopher Columbus made his final prayers before sailing west for Cathay.

It may not be much, but there were undoubtedly Mycenaean connections in southern Spain; Mycenaean ceramics have been found at Montoro on the Guadalquivir, east of Cordoba. If there were connections to the Cornish tin supply, then the sea routes came past here. It is possible that the estuary at Huelva is Homer's gates of hell.

I was there alone one autumn, the south wind blowing warm and delicious out of Africa. There are beaches where, as it says in the *Odyssey*, 'they stowed their gear and laid the mast in the hollow hulls', waiting to see what would come to them at the ends of the earth. There is a flat shore, as Circe promised; a rock, or at least a large mound; two rivers, but neither is roaring nor made of fire. The estuary waters are brown and polluted. Slimed stumps of old quays stand up to their shins in the water. Waders teeter on the water's edge. The trees are no longer the seed-spreading willows but clumps of eucalyptus and palms in rows. Phoenician, Egyptian, Greek and Cornish objects have all been dredged from these shallow waters, but if this is the gate of Hades, the shores of a lightless eternity, you would hardly guess it.

But go inland and the landscape starts to change. Both the Rio Tinto and the Rio Odiel push on to the north of Huelva. These river valleys were one of the most important sources of metals in the Bronze Age, because the hills on either side are filled with veins and big ore-bodies of copper, tin, gold and silver. Both rivers in their upper reaches are deeply changed by the metal country they run through. The *Odyssey*, with its man-eating monsters and vicious whirlpools, is a gothic poem, full of the nightmarish and the terrifying, the imagined sufferings of its heroes, but these garishly-coloured mineral valleys share that atmosphere: the toxic, the metallic, the otherworldly, the lifeless and the threatening all fused into some kind of recipe for hell.

Stop the car, walk down to one of these riverbeds and you will find the world drenched in strangeness. It is a gaudy and bloody trench, earth transmuting into another planet. The rocks and water are both iron red. Sandbanks in the river look as if they are the hulks of abandoned iron beaches. These are not the neat pleasure-landscapes of an island kingdom, but big, harsh, continental, inherently violent. Flakes of white quartzite shine through the water between ribs of rock that veer from red to tangerine to ochre and rust to flame-coloured, flesh-coloured, sick and livid. In between those red rocks are green snakeskin copper-rich boulders, glinting grey-eyed green minerals from within the orange depths.

The rivers themselves are deeply and naturally poisoned. This is the earth polluting itself. Where it has dried it has left white chemical residues, scurfy scabmarks of receding poison tides. Only one kind of strange, green, longhaired weed can live in it. Apart from that the water is cloud-less, mineral red but entirely clear. This is a place in which almost nothing can live, in which fruit would drop before it was ripe. Those swirling fronds of green hair, seven, eight, nine feet long, are swept downstream around the flakes of rock. Underwater, the whole bed of the stream is coated in a thick dust of iron poison, iron solids precipitated from the water, a fungal metal scum. Where, in a back-eddy, the current slows, a crusted porridge of the bloody slurry gathers in the pools, and no fish rise.

An occasional dragonfly hangs its diamond-blue wings over this hell-water, but never with a mate. No songbirds. High above, some distant hawks. Perfectly white flies lie dead, caught in the mineral slicks. If Homer, in Chios, heard of this, of course he would have put Hades and Persephone here. I have never seen a place more suited to them.

At the mining town of Rio Tinto itself, there is a museum where the mysteries of this metal world are on display. If you want to rediscover the Bronze Age entrancement with minerals in the raw, this is the place. In neat, old-fashioned glass cabinets you will find some of the strangest things the natural world can offer: fractured blue-silver flakes of galena; silver-gold cubes of iron pyrites; bulbs of calcite, erupting and diseased like glaucous eyeballs. Cinnabar is a stone blood-pudding, its red shot through with purples and blacks, the background for lilac amethysts. Green malachite is here, with azurite its close cousin, a Prussian blue only to be found in Alpine gentians. Sometimes the pyrites coats the skin of a rock in what they call *calco pitita*, as if a breath of gold had been blown over the stone. But nothing is more like the jewels of a hell palace, or poetry from the depths, than the rainbow stripes of Goethite, the crust of an indigo, lilac and green-gold planet.

The extraction of mineral ores here can only have been hell. The metals were mined from the overlying rock in difficult, cramped, dangerous and unforgiving conditions. Much of the ore was loosened by setting fires in the underground chambers, the heat splitting the rock, which could then be pulled away by hand or levered off with antler picks. Otherwise, it was simply beaten with hard stone hammers that were waisted to take a rope binding, which have been found in the ancient mines, their ends battered with the work they had done before they were cast aside. Human limb bones are occasionally found beside them deep in the ancient workings.

Twenty miles from Rio Tinto, in the dry hills near the village of El Pozuelo, at a place called Chinflón, a Bronze Age copper mine remains much as it was left when the seams were abandoned about three thousand years ago. It is not easy to find, about an hour's walk from the nearest road through poor, scratchy cork oak and eucalyptus hills. This is high and silent country, nearly sterile with its metals, scarcely visited now, a universe away from the industrialised agriculture of the coast. There are deer slots in the dust of the track and the views are enormous, twenty miles in all directions over the burnt forested ridges, taking in at their limit the vast bloody gash of the modern quarries at Rio Tinto. There are pale-winged buzzards in the sky, dust seems to be everywhere and salt sweat runs into your eyes and on to your lips.

The top of the hill at Chinflón is still smothered in the grey-greenish toxic spoil from that ancient mine. Red and orange rock flakes prod up through it. Coppery grey-green lichen spreads over the stones. Because of the way the rock strata are aligned, the flakes run along the crest of the hill in a series of narrow parallel ridges, so the summit is spiked skywards, like the vertical plates on the back of a Stegosaurus. Between those flakes is where the metal-bearing veins of malachite and azurite came to the surface, and where the Bronze Age men dug away for it, mining into a series of slits, pursuing the vein as it sank away from the air and the light, scrabbling with their heavy hammers, diving after the metal like dogs down burrows.

There is a modern chainlink fence surrounding the workings, to prevent you getting at them, but you can fumble and scrape your way under it easily enough. Within the rough enclosure are the deep but narrow rock trenches cut into the earth, twenty or thirty feet long, six feet wide at their widest; others just wide enough for a ladder to lead down into their dark. They push seventy or eighty feet below the surface. Coppery, blue-leaved plants grow on the mine lip, as if the metal had entered their veins. Clots of quartzite sit there like fat in pâté. Steps are cut into the walls of these red, dark mineral hollows, the rim of each step slightly higher than its cupped floor so that the hold feels safe enough as you go down. But you descend gingerly. In one of them, nineteenth-century iron chain-ladders are set into the little cut cliff-faces, where later miners hoped to find what their predecessors had abandoned. The air feels cool as you drop into the shadow, lowering yourself into the rock-bath, the sweat cooling on your back, the mine wrapping its walls around you. At the bottom, in the half-dark the slits are wet and mossy, comforting, mysteriously juicy, liquid, the walls of Hades seeping with grief. Any noise you make is echoey. But the sides of the walls are vulnerable. There is not much a pick would be needed to dig out. Touch them and rock pebbles clatter down below you into the dark, ricocheting off the lower walls. I collected flakes of greenish, snakeskin rock, the minerals in them glimmering as they turned through the light from above.

All mines are full of spirits. In the lead mines in County Durham, the men always spoke of the rock as an animal, ready to push at you as you made your way along an adit or down a shaft. In Cornwall the tin miners called the mine spirits the Knockers, as they knocked back at any man cutting away at the metal-bearing veins. They were the mine itself speaking. In sixteenth-century Germany, according to the great Renaissance theorist Georgius Agricola, these spirits were 'called the little miners, because of their dwarfish stature, which is about two feet. They are venerable looking and clothed like miners with a leather apron about their loins.'

Most of the time the Knockers were gentle and friendly, hanging about in the shafts and tunnels, only turning vicious if the miners ridiculed or cursed them. You needed to treat them with respect. Whistling could offend them, as could intentionally spying on what they were doing. They liked to be left in the shadows or the depths of the mines, or even behind the rock, knocking from inside it. Many miners placed small offerings of food or candle grease in the mine to feed and satisfy them. If you were good to them, they would show you where to find the metal.

As Ronald Finucane, the historian of the medieval subconscious, has said, ghosts 'represent man's inner universe just as his art and poetry do'. Ghosts are what you fear or hope for. The mine, if the gods favoured you, could provide a sort of magically immediate richness not to be found in the surface world. But all was hidden until you found it. And that reward-from-nothing was reflected in the miners' attitudes to metals. In Cornwall, they thought that iron pyrites when applied to a wound would cure it. Even water that had run over iron pyrites was said to be medicinal. Cuts washed in it would heal without any other intervention. But also in Cornwall, and in the parts of the USA where Cornish tinners emigrated and took their ancient beliefs with them, Knockers were thought to be ugly and vindictive. Miners who were lamed were known to be victims of the Knockers' rage. Insult them and they could damage you for life.

It is a commanding cluster of images: lightlessness, the spirits of the underworld, the hope for treasure and happiness, wounding, cures, the half-glimpsed, the dreaded, a realm of pain and power. This is the dark basement of the Achilles world, the place that metal came from, emerging through processes that were unknown and unintelligible to most of the population, but somehow providing the power-soaked tools with which the killer-chiefs dominated the landscape.

It is at least a possibility that Homer's Hades is a nightmare fantasy fuelled by the Bronze Age experience of the mine: a place in which spirits are clearly present but not to be grasped; where life has sunk away from the sunlight to the mute and the insubstantial; to beings that are only half there, regretting the absence of the vivid sunlight above; where a mysterious sense of power lurks in the dark. 'When it comes to excavated ground, dreams have no limit,' Gaston Bachelard wrote in *The Poetics of Space*. When you are underground, 'darkness prevails both day and night, and even when we are carrying a lighted candle, we see shadows standing on the dark walls . . . The cellar is buried madness.'

There is a sense of transgression at Chinflón, a feeling that this place was once alive and that the miners hacked at its life, as if they were hunting it, digging out its goodness, a form of rough and intemperate grasping, the masculine dragging of value from a subterranean womb. No one could be in the high, lonely mine at Chinflón, with its rock walls pressing in around them, and an almost oppressive silence filling the gaps between the stones, and not sense the reality of Hades as the house of sorrows, a toxic pit where the price of glory is buried suffering.

To the north, beyond the Sierra de Aracena, a ridge of dry, flaky schists on the frontier of Andalusia and Extremadura, another dimension of the Homeric world makes itself known. Distributed across a wide province stretching over southern Portugal and south-western Spain are some of the most vivid memorials of the warrior world Homer's poems describe. They are stone stelae or slabs, cut in the Late Bronze Age, from about 1250 to 750 BC, designed to show the nature of a hero's life. Other stone stelae, many shaped to look like people, can be found all over the Bronze Age world, but these are among the most articulate. None of them remains where it was found, and Richard Harrison, the Bristol archaeologist, has written a catalogue of the hundred or so that survive, listing their modern locations: one is in a bar in the Plaza de España in the village of San Martín de Trevejo on the Portuguese border north of Badajoz; others are in Madrid, Porto, in many local museums, in a school, in a town hall, in people's gardens and houses, one used as a seat at the entrance to an estate, another as a lintel over a window. A couple were reused as gravestones in Roman antiquity, with the name of the buried men cut across the Bronze Age designs. Many are beautifully exhibited in the museum in Badajoz. No doubt there are more still lurking unseen in walls or foundations.

The beautiful, hard landscape of Extremadura is natural horse and cattle country. Long, brown distances extend in all directions. Stone corrals are topped and mended with thorns – as they are in the *Odyssey* – and little mustard-yellow damselflies dance through the grasses. The pale roads wind over the hills, tracing the contours between the olives and the cork oaks, with the *tung tung tunk tunk* of the sheep bells a constant metal music beside them. Oaks that have been stripped of their cork are now date-black, as crusty as the blood on a cut. Grasshoppers flash their amber-ochre underwings. Cattle gather in the shade. Lizards seem to be the only liquid. It is above all a stony place: whitewashed upright flakes of schist marking the boundary between estates; bushily pruned olives peering out above stone walls; stones gathered in the dry scratched fields into big cairns, little round fortresses of solid cobble.

None of this is different from the state it was in three or four thousand years ago. Stock were raised then on the wooded savannahs, as they are now. Cattle-herding was the basis for all wealth. A low understorey of grass sustained the herds under the evergreen oaks. Nothing would have been more nutritious for the autumn-fattening pigs than the fall of acorns. Wheat, barley and beans were grown then in small patches of dry farming as they are now.

In this big, open, manly environment, the stelae were often placed at significant points, where drove roads met or forked on a hillside, where they crested a pass or came down to a river crossing. Some commanded wide panoramas. They were meant to be seen. You were meant to encounter them as you crossed the country. They were created for public display. Some were attached to graves, but not a majority. These were miniature, highly individual monuments intended to mark the presence – and dominance – of great men in their place.

The stelae are, in another medium, the *Iliad* of Iberia: heroic, human, repetitive but individualised. They mark the shift away from the communal values of the Stone Age, when joint graves gathered the ancestors in a community of the dead, to a time which valued more than anything else the display of the glorious man. None is more than six or seven feet high – these aren't great communal menhirs; they are on the scale of gravestones – but they are not recumbent. There is no knightly sinking into death here. Each is a standing monument to the vigour of a person. Gods do not appear: men dominate. The man himself is often shown as a kind of stick-figure, pecked into the surface of the slab, probably with a bronze chisel, and around him are his accoutrements, the things that made him the warrior hero he knew himself to be. And the catalogue of those heroic objects is a pointer to the values of the warrior world he wanted to record. To see these images is the strangest of sensations: it is, suddenly, Homer, 1,800 miles from Ithaca, more than two thousand from Troy, drawn in pictures on Spanish stone.

First there are the astonishing shields, dominating one stele after another. In the very early examples, the shield even takes the place of the man himself, and stands there for him and his world. The shields are huge, as big as a man, round but notched at the top, made of many concentric rings, the symbol of resistance and resilience, usually shown with the handle visible in the centre. In other words, they are seen from within the world that is protected by them. These are our shields, including us. They are the shelter for the life this man dominates, and in their massive, cosmic, many-ringed roundness they symbolise the universe of wholeness which the warrior protects. They are, in other words, the simple graphical equivalent of the great shield of Achilles which Hephaestus the smith god creates for the grieving warrior chief in Book 18 of the *Iliad*.

Only because Homer survives can you understand entirely what the Iberian symbols hint at. Like the many-ringed shields of Extremadura, Achilles's shield has a threefold rim, and there are five layers to the shield, all constructed within its governing circularity: the earth and heaven, sea, sun and moon at the full, all the famous stars, marriages and feasts, dancing men, with flutes and lyres playing, an argument over the blood-price payable for the victim of a murder, with wives and little children standing on the walls of a besieged city. Fate herself appears here in a robe that is 'red with the blood of men', but this is neither a sentimental nor a tragic vision of the world: everything is here, ploughlands and cornlands, harvest and sacrifice, 'fruit in wicker baskets' and a dancing floor, like the one at Knossos in Crete, with young men and women together. In bronze, tin, silver and gold Hephaestus made a depiction of the whole world of sorrow and happiness, of justice and injustice, fertility and pain, war and peace. Many shields in Homer are described as 'the perfect circle' – a visual signal which confronts the sharp, narrow insertion of the blade. Even the Greek word for a shield, *aspis*, means the smooth thing, the thing from which roughness has been smoothed away. Achilles's shield is only the most perfect. In Homer as in Extremadura, the shield is the encompassing symbol of the warrior king.

Then come the weapons: sword, spear, dagger, bow and arrow, very occasionally a quiver, and almost invariably a chariot, with the horses attached, their bodies shown in profile, the chariot in plan, drawn like this in Portugal and Spain, but also, extraordinarily, appearing in the same way on the Bronze Age rock carvings of southern Sweden.

The weapons are the necessary instruments of the martial life, the tools for establishing central aspects of the hero complex: maleness, heroic individuality and dominance. It is what comes next that re-orientates any flat-footed view of Bronze Age warrior heroism. These killer chieftains were obsessed with male beauty. The great Greek heroes all have blond hair (unlike the Trojans, who are dark-haired), and they have lots of it, lustrous, thick hair being an essential quality of the hero. Achilles had hair long enough for Athene to grab him by it when she wanted him to stop attacking Agamemnon. Hector's hair, after his death, lay spread around him in the dust. Paris, the most beautiful of all warriors in the *Iliad* – too beautiful – so rich and thick was his hair that he looked like a horse, 'who held his head high and his mane streamed round his shoulders'. The male gods are just as thickly maned. And the beauty of the warrior chiefs is inseparable from their power as men.

All of this appears on the stelae of the Iberian chiefs. Beyond their weaponry, carefully picked out on their memorial slabs, appears all the necessary grooming and beauty equipment: mirrors, combs, razors, tweezers, brooches, earrings, finger rings and bracelets. These accessories of male beauty are not consigned to some private preparatory ritual. Making the Bronze Age warrior beautiful is central to the idea he had of himself. Here is the handsome gang-leader, made more handsome by what he wears and how his body is prepared for its appearance among men. None of this culture would be possible without the bronze blades, but those blades are not its destination; they are the means to reach what these other precious objects describe: the mirror for a powerfully present idea of the self; the comb for grooming the beautiful hair; tweezers more likely to pluck an eyebrow than to take a splinter from flesh; brooches, earrings, rings and bracelets to adorn the beautiful man. When the river gods of the Trojan plain wish to attack and destroy Achilles as he is on his rampage, clogging their streams with the slaughtered dead, one says to the other in encouragement:

His strength can do nothing for him, nor his beauty, nor his wonderful armour.

Beauty is one of the elements that make him the most terrifying of men. The mirror, the comb and the tweezers are also instruments of Bronze Age war.

There is another detail that recurs on many stones, almost the only exception to the otherwise crude depiction of the heroes' bodies. Time and again, the fingers of the warrior-hero's hands are shown outstretched, explicit and over-life-sized. His hands seem to matter more than any other part of his body, perhaps because they were the part of him with which he imposed his power on the world around him. The hand is the agent of the burning warrior self, the essential instrument of the weapon-wielding man. That is also the role played by hands in the Homeric epics. Both Hector and Achilles have 'manslaughtering hands', and it is Odysseus's hands that are steeped in blood as he exacts his final revenge on the suitors. It is as if the hands had concentrated in them all the destructive power of the warrior hero. And when, in the *Iliad*'s culminating scene of mutual accommodation, Priam the king of Troy comes to Achilles in the Greek camp, it is through the hands that the drama is played out:

> Great Priam entered in and, coming close, clasped Achilles's knees in his hands and kissed his hands, the terrible man-slaughtering hands that had slaughtered his many sons.

Homer rings those repetitions like clanging bells at moments of intensity and high purpose. And here, the word continues to boom on through the meeting. Achilles hears Priam's plea for the body of his precious son Hector to be returned to him for burial. That pleading love of the father makes him think of his own distant father in Phthia. Priam's words

> roused in Achilles a desire to weep for his father; and he took the old man by the hand, and pushed him gently away. So the two of them thought of their dead and wept.

And again, when they had finished weeping, Achilles 'took Priam by the hand' and spoke to him words of pity and shared understanding of the pain men suffer in a careless world. The outstretched fingers of the Iberian warriors also carry all that love and violence within them.

There is one further object which binds together Homer and the Extremaduran stelae. On one stone after another, alongside the killing equipment and the beauty equipment, is something at the heart of the Bronze Age warrior world: the lyre. Sometimes they are drawn many-stringed; on a few they are as large as the giant universe-shields; on many, the lyre is shown as no more than a simple frame with two or three stings across it. But all of them signify the same thing: here is the instrument with which this warrior can sing heroic songs of deathless glory. The weapon, the beauty equipment and the lyre are all integral to his world. He exists in memory; in some ways he exists *for* memory. Just as Odysseus sings the tale of his own adventures when he finds himself at dinner with the king of the Phaeacians, Achilles is a man who sings heroic songs of deathless glory. That is how the other heroes find him when in Book 9 of the *Iliad* they come to his shelter, hoping to persuade him to rejoin the battle:

> And they came to the huts and the ships of the Myrmidons [Achilles's men] and they found Achilles delighting his mind with a clear-toned lyre, fair and elaborate, and on it was a bridge of silver; this he had taken from the spoil when he destroyed the city of Eëtion. With it he was delighting his heart, and he sang of the glorious deeds of warriors; and Patroclus alone sat opposite him in silence, waiting until Aeacus's grandson should cease from singing.

It is a moment, like Glaucus's account of the leaf-generations of men, when the passage of Homeric time stops for a moment and when, in its privacy and lovingness, the world of brutality withdraws with the help of a lyre. That is what the presence of the lyres on the Spanish stelae says: Homer is not only *about* the heroic world; Homer *is* the heroic world. It is the realm of gang violence, in which pity and poetry have a central place.

If there were any doubt that song was a central part of the warrior complex, a discovery in one of the remotest parts of north-west Europe in the summer of 2012 changed all that. Archaeologists working in the High Pasture Cave on Skye found the burnt and broken remains of the bridge from a late Bronze Age lyre. Homer – or at least the forms of warrior song on which the deepest elements of Homer draw – was a universal presence across the whole of Bronze Age Europe.

The Iberian stones might be seen as a kind of heraldry, the symbol-cluster for an armed knight. But they are also the first European biographies: he drove a chariot, strung a bow and killed with it, wielded spear and sword, held the shield, was beautiful and generous, lived here, sang his song. It seems from the distribution of the stelae that each warrior territory was no more than about twenty-five miles across. Seen as a kingdom, that is exceptionally small. But seen as an assertion over the landscape by a single powerful individual controlling about 270,000 acres, it is impressive. These are not petty empires but great estates. They are gang territories, equivalent to the 'kingdoms' described in the Homeric catalogue of ships. Nowhere are there any great buildings or constructions. All focus is on the power-body of the chieftain. His men cluster around him. His individual destiny is bound up with theirs and with the fate of the kingdom. It seems unlikely that many of these 'kingdoms' outlasted the life of the man who made them. It is a place of endless, repetitive violence and competition, in which 'who your father was' is important, but not enough. Honour must be revalidated in each generation. An unused sword rusts in the scabbard, and each life follows the one before, as Glaucus said, as the leaves of each spring follow the fallen leaves of the previous autumn.

Some of the stelae show that story. One of the richest is now in the Museo Arqueológico Provincial in Cordoba. It was found in April 1968 by some farm workers at the foot of an ancient wall, a good block nearly six feet high and about thirty inches wide. They hauled it on to their tractor, carelessly smashing the sides and scratching the face of the stele, and took it to the nearby estate of Gamarrillas, thinking it might be good for building stone. But they noticed the engravings on one of its faces. By chance some archaeologists working nearby saw it for what it was and saved it.

A huge warrior figure dominates the scene, with outstretched hands and his penis hanging beneath him. He has a bracelet on one arm, and his whole torso is decorated with what might be a patterned cloth, his armour or maybe a whole-body tattoo. Even like this, scratched into limestone, he radiates significance. Of his chieftainliness there is no doubt. There is a little brooch next to his head, and his fighting equipment is gathered in the spaces around him: a spear, a shield, and a sword in his right hand, still in its scabbard. Beneath him is a comb, a shield and what may be a woven carpet. This is how he was in the glory of his life. But this stone also records his death. He is accompanied by his hunting dogs, both visibly male, and by his chariot. Around them groups of mourners hold hands, maybe dancing. There are no faces. All is in the body. This is a life that has been lived and is now over. But for all that, an atmosphere of Homeric transience is soaked deeply into these little figures. Like the epic poems, this stone is a regretful glance back to a wonderful past, which, like the man, has gone.

Most of the stelae were thrown down, taken away and dumped after they were set up. Others were deliberately effaced. But that should come as no surprise in a world of constantly shifting chiefdoms, a power-churn where no glory lasted more than a generation or two. The same circumstances that gave rise to the stelae, to the warrior-complex of which they are such vivid testimony, would also guarantee their destruction. Like the weaponry, the killing, the grooming, the insistent body-focus and the presence of the lyres, this delight in the destruction of the enemy is everywhere in Homer too, above all in the exulting over the corpse of a defeated enemy.

When one hero kills another in Homer, there is no grief or sympathy across the divide. It is a moment of triumph, when maleness achieves its undiluted self-expression. In Book 11 of the *Iliad*, as one example, Odysseus is on his destruction-drive and fixes his spear into the back of a Trojan called Sokos, thrusting it straight in between the shoulderblades, so that the point comes out of Sokos's chest. The Trojan then thumps to the ground – *doupeo* – and Odysseus stands over the dead body:

Ah Sokos, son of battle-minded Hippasos, breaker of horses, death has been too quick for you and ran you down; you couldn't avoid it, could you, poor wretch? Your father and oh-so elegant mother will not close your eyes in death now, but the birds that eat raw flesh will tear you in strips, beating their wings thick and fast about you; but to me, if I die, the brilliant Achaeans will bury me in honour.

There is no pity in this. The destruction Odysseus celebrates is wonderful to him. Nothing is more beautiful than the sight of Sokos's dead eyes staring at the sky. Odysseus is happy at the dreadfulness he has done to that man and his now-grieving family. He has destroyed the power of that dynasty and enhanced his own. There is no sense of tragedy. He has merely defaced their memory. Their stone is down and gone; his remains upright, triumphant, crowing.

Richard Harrison has emphasised the loneliness which this ideology imposed on the warrior hero. 'He is a unique and isolated figure,' Harrison has written,

> whose arm is strong and deadly; he is devoted to combat, which he actively seeks out; he is detached from ordinary social space and so is shown to be tremendously swift, able to cross time or distance between worlds; and he is a very dangerous person in society and is therefore much better detached from it and sent away on a quest where he cannot harm ordinary mortals.

That loneliness clearly attached to Hector; to Agamemnon in his pomposity, his distance from love; to Odysseus on his journeying; even to Paris, the loathed creator of the war. Heroism disconnects. And the loneliness applies to no one more than to Achilles, as profoundly isolated as any figure in world literature. In his great and terrible confrontation with Hector in Book 22 of the *Iliad*, after Hector has killed Achilles's great friend Patroclus, Achilles makes the ultimate statement of heroic loneliness, the isolation of the warrior which is also the dominant image on the Iberian stelae: a big man surrounded by his things, very occasionally by some mourners or even co-warriors, but essentially alone, trapped in the glory of his violence. 'Hector, you, the unforgivable, talk not to me of agreements,' he says, using the word *agoreue* for 'talk', the word used in the *agora*, the meeting place where citizens come to mutual accommodation. Achilles does not belong there; he belongs in the wild:

> There are no oaths sworn between lions and men, nor do wolves and lambs come to some arrangement in their hearts. They are filled with endless, repetitive hate for each other. Just so, it is impossible for you and me to be friends, nor will there be any oaths between us till one or other is dead, and has glutted Ares, the god of war, who carries his tough leather shield, with his blood.

In Celtic Ireland, on the far western edge of this hero world, where round, ridged leather shields have been dug from Bronze Age bogs, stories from the heroic age have been recorded in which the heroes gave orders that they should be buried standing upright, fully armed on a prominent hill, where they could face their enemy, awaiting the moment of resurrection when they would fight again and by this means continue to protect their people.

Those same upright warriors, continuing to haunt the living world, as enraged and violent as they were in life, also appear in the Icelandic sagas. Perhaps these are stories of the ultimate, cosmic loneliness, a measure of the inadequacy of the heroic idea, which only that weapon-less, hand-connecting moment between Priam and Achilles could hope to assuage.

NINE

Homer on the Steppes

THE ORIGINS OF THE Greeks – or at least those people who would in time become the Greeks – were not in the Mediterranean. At some point they moved south and west in search of lands they wanted to claim as theirs, but at the deepest levels they were strangers in the southern sea. Fundamentally they were northerners, their roots in the steppelands of Eurasia, the oceanic river of grass, five thousand miles long and up to a thousand wide, that runs from Hungary to Manchuria.

Homer is full of half-buried memories of that northern past, and his recollections hint at another non-Mediterranean world, far from water, far from cities, land-locked, dominated by an enormous sky, horse-rich, focused on flocks and herds and the meat they provide, violent, mobile and heroic. This steppe-world is the place from which Achilles comes. It is not the Homeric foreground, because Homer is inconceivable without sailing ships, cities and the sea – without everything which is bound up in the name of 'Troy': civilisation, the sea-borne raid, the connection to the east – but that other northern place lurks as a kind of murmured, ancestral layer, a sub-conscious.

The dates are uncertain, but the Greeks may have come to Greece at some time between about 2200 and 1700 BC. Their origins are obscure. It is possible that the last move was south from Albania. There are early graves both there and in north-west Greece which look as if they might record the movement of people who would soon be in the Peloponnese. In the way the graves are built, and from the objects they contain, they seem to be the precursors of the Shaft Graves at Mycenae. Before that, the Greeks, or the pre-Greeks, may have lived on the banks of the

144 THE MIGHTY DEAD

Danube, or elsewhere in the Balkans. And before that they almost certainly lived further to the east, perhaps in the steppe between the Black Sea and the Caspian, in what is now Ukraine and southern Russia.

Nothing is certain, and the hints are fragmentary at best. But if you withdraw a little, and look not for exactness but for the broad northern culture-world out of which the Greeks emerged into Europe, perhaps at some time around 3000 BC, things become paradoxically clearer. Clues are everywhere: in the language itself, in archaeology, in the words of the Homeric poems and in the echoes of those poems that can be found all across the Eurasian world.

Right in the middle of the *Odyssey*, when Odysseus has penetrated to the depths of Hades and is talking there, anxiously and intently, to the blind seer Tiresias, long dead, he asks him about his future, what will become of him. Tiresias knows that Odysseus is longing for nothing more than 'a sweet smooth journey home', but instead of guidance, he tells him the story of the books of the *Odyssey* still to come, the sufferings and anxieties he will undergo, the 'world of pain' he will find in Ithaca. And then the old seer says something else, strange for classical Greeks, enigmatic today.

Once Odysseus has killed the suitors in his palace, Tiresias says, he will not yet have arrived home. For his true homecoming, he must leave Ithaca again and begin a second odyssey, not a sea-journey this time but on land, another voyage in search of peace.

> You must go out one more time.
> Carry your well-planed oar until you come
> To a race of people who know nothing of the sea,
> Whose food is never seasoned with salt, strangers
> To ships with their crimson prows and long slim oars,
> The wings that make ships fly. And here is your sign –
> Unmistakable, clear, so clear you cannot miss it:
> When another traveller falls in with you and calls
> That weight across your shoulder a fan to winnow grain,
> Then plant your bladed, balanced oar in the earth
> And sacrifice fine beasts to the lord god of the sea,
> Poseidon. . .

Only then, in that sea-free place, will Odysseus's demons be stilled and the uncertainties that have haunted his life laid to rest. That northern winnowing-scene is a dream of home.

Tiresias goes on: once Odysseus has appeased the power of Poseidon, he should turn to the immortal gods, 'who hold broad heaven in their hands'. He should relinquish sea for sky. And only after that sky-world has embraced him will Odysseus be able to die 'in the ebbing time of a sleek old age', as Richmond Lattimore translated Homer's phrases, the world of the sea eased from his mind, his soul now as calm and reflective as a dark, northern, freshwater pool.

Image-ideas cluster around Tiresias's gnomic instruction. The oar becomes the winnowing fan, the sea becomes the earth, the wind which would have driven Odysseus's ship across the sea, or nearly destroyed him on his raft, becomes the breeze which sorts the grain from the chaff, as each fanful is thrown up and the lighter dust blown away. The Greek word for the winnowing fan is *athereloigos*, meaning the destroyer of bristles (*athēr*, plural *atheroi*), the husky sheaths of the grain. But *athēr* can also mean anything difficult or prickly: the spines of a fish or the barbs of a weapon. So the winnowing fan is also a smoother of barbs, a spike-remover, the tailor of life. The grains will emerge clean and pure, and the jagged world of hostility will float off on the breeze. Only here, deep in the land, will certainty be recovered. Poseidon, the god of wrongness whose origins, at least in part, are Mediterranean, as the great defender of Troy and enemy of Odysseus, the presider over storms and earthquakes, who has dominated the poems and been at the heart of their sufferings, will at last be put in his place.

Is there some historical root to this moment? Are Tiresias's words a form of archaic memory, fuelled by the idea that somewhere in the world, a long way from Greece, is a place where the troubles that afflict Odysseus and the Greeks do not obtain? Where there is no sea, nor even any hint of the sea, and which is not subject to the near constant sequence of earthquakes and tempests that besiege and break on Greece and Anatolia? Is Tiresias reaching far back to a time when the Greeks did not yet know Greece, but were living the life of semi-nomadic pastoralists, planting their grains, tending their flocks, ignorant of salt and ships? Is this, in other words, a kind of retrospective pastoral, a Greek vision of an abandoned Eden? Did life to the Greeks, at some half-acknowledged level, seem better before all the temptations and threats of the Mediterranean life disturbed their certainties? Was the movement south a transition into risk? If it was, Homer is the record of what happened when that risk was taken.

There is another remembered story of Odysseus, not in Homer, but recorded from Sophocles in some rough Latin notes of plays and myths which have otherwise disappeared. Telemachus, Odysseus's son, was one month old when Palamedes, a messenger whose name means 'the inventor', arrived from Agamemnon, instructing Odysseus to come to the war against Troy. Odysseus reacted as Achilles might have, sceptically, reluctantly, and to escape the summons pretended to be mad. He took a donkey and an ox, yoked them together on the same plough, as no man ever had or would, and when he had cut the first furrow he sowed it not with seeds but with salt. Palamedes doubted Odysseus, and to test him took the baby Telemachus and put him down on the unbroken grass in the path of the plough.

As Odysseus approached his son he turned the plough aside, bending the furrow away from his baby's flesh, and by that swerve showed he was sane. He loved his son more than he loved himself, and so had no choice but to go and suffer at Troy. He took with him a murderous loathing for Palamedes, the clever diplomat. In time Odysseus concocted accusations against him, that he was secretly colluding with the Trojans against the Greeks, and finally stoned him to death as a liar and traitor.

It is a suggestive enmity, a twin of Tiresias's promise of a final ease in the distant north. The southerner brings only years of pain. Faced with his invitation, Odysseus sows anti-seeds, not fruitful but toxic, not land-riches but sea-poison, not fecundity but sterility, not northern contentment but southern trouble. Palamedes is Mediterranean man, the inventor of counting, money, weights and measures, jokes, dice, military ranks, the letters of the alphabet and the making of wine. He represents everything the south has to offer, including submission to an overall king in Agamemnon. He is, in his slickness, the enemy. Tiresias holds out the possibility of comfort in the north; Palamedes promises only southern suffering.

No two worlds could be more different than the grasslands of the steppes north of the Black Sea and the craggy broken boundaries of the Mediterranean. In Greece every view is contained and defined by its mountains. Every place is a shard, sharp-edged, hardened and definite. Boot leather is torn into shreds there. 'Our land, compared with what it was,' Plato wrote famously of the Greece he knew, 'is like the skeleton of a body wasted by disease. The fat soft parts have gone, and all that remains are the bones.' On the steppe, the bones remain invisible, coated in a pelt of grasses on the high plateaux between the river valleys, thickening into forest and marsh where those rivers make their way to the south. The Mediterranean landscape is fiercely located, subdivided by its mountain ridges, every corner separate from every other. But look across the steppe and you see only more of what is already at your feet.

Everything is continuous there. The air you breathe is the air of the universe. Horizontality is all, and this is the continental-oceanic, a place that cares less about fixity than movement, less about detail than about the endlessness of things. And if landscapes can create mentalities as well as reflect them, it is possible to think that the steppelands lie at the root of the Achilles frame of mind: long-horizoned; looking for the profound and the eternal; attuned to the cosmic; indifferent to possessions; passionate, totalising; vertigo-inducing in its relationship to death and fate; both giving and denying significance to human desires and triumphs.

It is possible to think that in the *Iliad* Achilles speaks for that deep northern past. He comes from somewhere else. He is half divine, has no identifiable city and was brought up by a centaur in the mountains. His homeland is further north than anyone else's in Homer. His story is strangely disconnected from everything else in the *Iliad*: he will be killed before the sack of Troy, he goes off on plundering expeditions all around western Anatolia, and the whole account of recovering Helen would be complete without him.

Achilles does not fit with the world in which he finds himself. He holds himself physically and psychologically removed from the rest of the Greeks. He speaks the truth to them in a way no one else can. He is dense with both love and violence, the two bound together in his heart, his greatest love (for his friend Patroclus) summoning his greatest violence (for his enemy Hector). Those who are close to him adore him; those at a distance both fear and despise him. But his central quality is an inability to conform to what the world around him accepts as real.

In all these ways, Achilles confronts the forces of the sophisticated south and sets himself against them: he cannot tolerate the overarching kingliness of Agamemnon, he scorns the political sophistication and smooth-talking of Odysseus, he despises Hector, and like all warriors he wants to destroy the city. Homer calls him (as he does both Ares, the great northern god of war, and Odysseus) 'the city destroyer'. And when Achilles attacks the bodies of the Trojans and their horses, the image that Homer brings to mind is not individual death but 'the smoke ascending into the wide sky/from a burning city with the anger of the gods let loose upon it'. Achilles carries a pre-southern, pre-urban, pre-complicated world of purity and integrity within him.

He first appears most fully himself – before the lunacy of grief over Patroclus's death transforms him – in the speech he makes to Odysseus in Book 9 of the *Iliad*. For days the war has gone badly for the Greeks. Agamemnon has stolen Briseis from Achilles. She is the girl he loves, the 'bed-girl of his heart' as he calls her, and because of that theft, imposed by Agamemnon's assumption of greater authority over him, Achilles has withdrawn from the battle, has wished death and violence on the Greeks, and has witnessed their catastrophic failure in the war. Now Agamemnon, desperate with the successes of the Trojans, wants to make amends, to offer Achilles not only the return of Briseis but ship-loads of prizes and treasures. He sends Odysseus to make the offer, and in reply Achilles states his magnificent, troubling credo.

Just before Odysseus comes to his shelter, Achilles has been singing to Patroclus of the glorious deeds of warriors, of the heroic past. When he arrives, Achilles does what the hero should, and provides for his guests the meat from fat sheep and fat goats and the meaty backcuts of a great pig 'rich with fat'. All is ritualised and made proper, and the scene is one that would have occurred in thousands of chieftains' huts over thousands of years in the grasslands of Eurasia.

Odysseus then lists to Achilles the wonderful things that Agamemnon wants to give him: seven tripods that the fire has not touched; ten talents of gold; twenty shining cauldrons; strong horses, winners in races, that have won prizes for their swiftness; seven women skilled in noble handiwork from Lesbos, including Briseis herself, the girl Achilles loves. And there is the promise of much more, options on the future: things from Troy; more women from Troy; one of Agamemnon's own daughters as a bride; cities in Greece with lovely meadows outside them, grass as high as a horse's eye, places where men can live rich in cattle and sheepflocks.

But Odysseus is slippery, and although most of his speech to Achilles repeats exactly what Agamemnon had said to him, he does not repeat the high king's final riling words: 'Let him submit himself to me, since I am so much more kingly.' Odysseus suppresses those phrases, knowing that the steppe consciousness of Achilles will not accept an overking. Nevertheless, that subtext persists in the proposal he makes. There is something nauseating in the accumulated enticements Agamemnon offers. They miss the point. Long, long ago, in the first lines of the poem, Achilles has called Agamemnon 'the greediest, most possession-loving of men', and this list of offered possessions is a pollution of the air he breathes. He knows Odysseus is there to lie to him. He calls him 'many-wiled', the trickster. 'As I detest the doorways of Death, I detest that man who hides one thing in the depths of his heart, and speaks another.'

Instead of that clever, southern talk, he will 'speak what I want to speak'. That relentless focus on his own individuality drives the lines forward. Achilles cannot escape from the idea that Agamemnon has been sleeping with Briseis. That vision, in the present tense, haunts him. Agamemnon *has* her. He has his way with her, still, now, 'the bed partner of my heart'. The overking's cumulative greed has taken even her. He has made her an object too. He does not know the meaning of love. All Agamemnon can imagine is ownership, and all Achilles can think of is Agamemnon's repeated, horrible owning of his girl.

It is the most passionate speech in Homer, confused, proud, enraged, Achilles seeming not to know that Agamemnon has offered to give Briseis back. Instead, Agamemnon the criminal persists in his mind in an eternal present of wrongness, shameless as a deceiver, a man whose honour is rusted and corrupt. 'Hateful in my eyes are his gifts. His gifts are my enemy. I count them at a hair's worth.' Then Achilles lists the great cities of the south, the great riches of Orchomenos and Thebes, and Troy itself, 'where treasures in greatest store are laid up in men's houses'. (These phrases, in one of the ironies of Homeric archaeology, led Heinrich Schliemann to dig at Orchomenos in search of the gold Achilles despised.) But Achilles will have none of it. Gifts that numbered as many as the grains of dust and sand in the world would not persuade him to change his mind until Agamemnon 'has paid me back the pain he has done to me'. That is something which by definition Agamemnon could never do. 'All the wealth of Troy is not worth what my life is worth.'

These are great statements. They rage at the triviality of ownership. They are unforgiving in their contempt for the greedy, Christ-like in their abrasive, revelatory scouring of the facts and desires of power. Achilles speaks again of possessions, this time not the blandishments of cities but things which would have been familiar in the steppeland of the north:

Cattle and fat sheep are things to be had for the lifting,
and tripods can be won, and the tawny high heads of horses,
but a man's life cannot come back again, it cannot be lifted
Nor captured again by force, once it has crossed the teeth's barrier.

Death overwhelms every other meaning. What can matter in the face of mortality? Agamemnon is puerile and disgusting, Odysseus is a liar, Hector is pathetic: only by stepping outside the value system of the world can you find any value. It is one of the riches of Homer's characterisation of Achilles that what he says is not consistent. He toys with the idea that he might go home and marry a lovely girl, settle down and enjoy the possessions his father had won. But alongside that he recognises that we are all vagabonds on earth, nothing belongs to us, our lives have no consequence and our possessions are dross. We are wanderers, place-shifters, the cosmic homeless. This is not a modern truth, and Achilles is not some new kind of existentialist hero. It is the oldest truth of all, surviving uncomfortably into the modern world of cities and overkings, diplomacy and accommodation, the power-structures and the prolifer-ation of stuff which the Mediterranean world provides, all of it more modern than Achilles can allow himself to be. He is the voice of the northern, shiftless past, asserting the claims of a higher steppeland purity against the material greed and ignobility of the fixed and southern present.

The power of the poem lies in the understanding that these things cannot be reconciled. The *Iliad*'s subject is not war or its wickedness but a crisis in how to be. Do you, like Agamemnon, attempt to dominate your world? Do you, like Odysseus, manipulate it? Do you, like Hector, think of your family above all and weaken your resolve by doing that? Or do you, like Achilles, believe in the dignity of love and the purity of honour, as the only things that matter in the face of death? These ques-tions are urgent for Homer because the arrival of a steppe culture at the gates of a city made them urgent. There is more to the Achilles story than this: in the course of the poem he suffers, grows, loses himself in the violence of grief, and finally comes to a new and deeper understanding, but in this great speech of steppeland consciousness, Homer has bequeathed to us the first unforgiving idealist of our civilisation.

Greek is part of the Indo-European language family that stretches from Ireland to remote valleys in the deserts of western China, from Sweden to India, from Spain to Lithuania. It has been known since the late eighteenth century that the languages in this family are each other's siblings. In every one of them, common roots can be found in both vocabulary and grammar. Those connections can only mean that each of the daughter-languages has descended from a mother-language spoken somewhere in the distant past before its speakers moved off into the many corners of the continent. So a man who is my *brathair* in old Irish is my *frater* in Latin, my *brodor* in Old English, my *broterèlis* in Lithuanian, my *bratrŭ* in Old Church Slavonic, my *phrater** in Greek, my *bhrátar* in Sanskrit and my *procer* in a dead language called Tocharian B, once spoken in the desiccated valleys of Chinese Turkestan, eight thousand miles from the Irish monks and their brethren on the shores of the Atlantic. Languages that can have had no chance of having borrowed words directly from each other nevertheless demonstrate intimate family connections. They carry the marks of their own inheritance; like verbal tumuli, these words enshrine their own history.

Linguists have long realised that if they could establish the words that were shared across these vast distances – particularly by now well-separated languages – they might be able to reconstruct the world in which the original Proto-Indo-European language was spoken. This is the great paradox of language: words are the least substantial medium in which meaning can be formed, but they can preserve hints and suggestions of the ancient past when material remains scarcely can. Of course languages evolve, but words that have been transmitted only in speech can nevertheless retain something in their core which is resistant to the erosions of time.

Working over two centuries, linguists have been able to create an astonishingly detailed shared word-picture of the Proto-Indo-European world of about five thousand years ago, the world from which Achilles came. It sounds, first, like a dream environment, teeming with life: wolves, lynxes, elk and red deer, hares, hedgehogs, geese and cranes, eagles and bees, beavers and otters (their name the same word at root as both 'water' and 'hydro') have cognates in all of the Indo-European languages. There are no shared words for laurel, cypress or olive: this cannot have been a Mediterranean place. But cattle and sheep are both there. This is a milky, yoghurty existence, with words for butter, cheese, meat, marrow and

---

* This word, from the same root as the others, in fact means something like 'clansman' in Greek. The usual Greek word for brother is *adelphos*, meaning 'from the same womb'.

manure, for steer, calf, ox, cow and bull. These people were lactose-tolerant, feeding off the all-important transfer of nutrients (via hay and cheese) from summer grass to winter food. A verb for the driving of cattle, and a word for a large cow-sacrifice, are spread across the whole Indo-European language-world. The original word for a dog is closely bound up with the word for sheep: the first Indo-European dogs look as if they were sheepdogs, and the word for sheep, with the root *pec-* (as in pecorino, the Italian sheep cheese), is related to the word for wealth (as in pecuniary). It seems as if the riches of these people might have been in the animals they kept.

The language does not describe a completely mobile world. They had pigs, which are no good for nomadic pastoralists (both 'swine' and 'pork' are Proto-Indo-European words), because pigs refuse to be driven in the way sheep and cattle happily will be, and so the Proto-Indo-European people must have been at least partly settled, with places in which the words for grain, sowing, quern, plough, sickle, yoke and oxen all had a part to play. So their world oscillates between the mobile and the fixed, the rooted and the rootless, the raid or the drive away from home, and the companion sense of home and hearth.

The language family to the north of Proto-Indo-European, Proto-Uralic, spoken by the hunter-gatherers in the forests of northern Eurasia, has no words for any buildings beyond their tents. But Proto-Indo-European is not quite like that. They had words for house, hearth, post, door, doorpost, hurdle, wattle, wall and clay. Their buildings were clearly substantial, wooden, closable. They also had a word for 'refuge' or 'fort', but no word for city. Nor is there any hint in the language of anything resembling public architecture: no temple, no palace, no public square.

Their villages were clusters of houses, and the word for a village was the same as the word for a clan. The language makes the point clearly enough: what mattered about these places was not the buildings but the people within them. This is not a monumental world, but one centred on the lives of clannish groups of families. They had metals. They spun thread, wove cloth and sewed. And they had wheeled vehicles, and boats for crossing rivers and lakes, with oars but no sails.

This re-imagining of a distant world is one of the triumphs of linguistics. None of these claims about the Proto-Indo-European way of life is a guess; all are founded on a careful analysis of the inherited languages. And the reconstruction has penetrated beyond the physical. It is clear that the culture was male-dominated, that individuals considered themselves heirs of their fathers and that girls left their native homes to live in the houses of their husbands and their husbands' families. The word for 'to marry' – when applied to men – is intimately connected with the word for 'to lead'. Men 'led' women to the marriage bed.

It seems likely that young men in the Proto-Indo-European world were organised into warrior bands, perhaps raiding parties, and they used bows, arrows, clubs, cudgels and swords. Society may have been organised into three ranks: farmers, priests and a warrior elite, out of which the chieftains and even kings emerged. The word for king embodies the principle of order, a meaning still implicit in the English word 'rule', with a connection between 'rex' and 'right', between ordaining the world and possessing it, but there is also evidence in the inherited languages of a powerful sense of hospitality and its duties. 'Guest' and 'host' are different descendants of the same root,* a measure of the mutuality buried within them. The mutual giving of gifts, the swearing of oaths and the expectations of loyalty from that behaviour are all evident in the descendant languages. Trust was part of the Proto-Indo-European moral consciousness.

It is possible to push further in, beyond their external lives. Linguists can reconstruct a Proto-Indo-European word for belief, *kred-dhehl*, whose descendants have reached us in the form of 'creed' and 'credo'. That original compound word seems to have meant 'heart-put/place', so that belief is the place where you put what matters most to you. There is, in other words, clear linguistic evidence of a commitment to otherness, a mental life beyond the self. But not much of a pantheon can be re-established. Nearly all the gods of Olympus in Homer are Mediterranean borrowings; the only undoubted exception is Zeus, the male sky god, whose name means 'the sky', with a further derivation buried within that, as the word for sky comes from a root which means 'the shining'. God is the shining father, life is lived in his light, and when the great heroes are described in Homer either as 'brilliant' or as 'godlike', the

* In French they're exactly the same word – *hôte*.

connection is the same: they are glowing in a light derived from the power of that shining sky. The sky is the great permanence. In its divine brilliance, there is no change.

Beneath that steppe-sense of the governing sky there is a parallel and contradictory aspect of the Indo-European mind. In every daughter-language from Iranian to Hindi, to Hittite, Greek and Roman, all the Romance, Slavic and Germanic languages, Irish and the other Celtic languages, finite verbs are forced into a precise tense. Nothing in Indo-European can escape being located in the time at which it occurred. In other languages, such as the Chinese language family, there are no tenses, and it is possible to blur those distinctions, for actions to be described without it being clear when they happened. Not in the Indo-European languages: this particular form of consciousness is trapped in an awareness of time passing. Homer's and Achilles's agonies over the transience of glory; the very fact of epic poetry as a way of denying the effects of time; even the creation of the tens of thousands of Bronze Age tumuli marking the landscapes of Eurasia from Bahrain to County Clare: all are products of that time-dominated frame of mind, the awareness of the passing of things which lies at the deepest levels of the way we think. It is the governing polarity: the sky persists in a way that is outside time; nothing that is done on earth shares that eternity. Homer is framed around that recognition, and it is one in which, for example, the idea of a Messiah could never have originated. There is no closing the gap between the eternal and the transitory. Gods and goddesses might sleep with men and women, and have children with them, but those heroic children can only ever be mortal.

Grief and triumph; a sense of irony and even tragedy; an overwhelming and dominant masculinity, thick with competitive violence; a small but hierarchical society, strung between a semi-nomadic way of life and one that was settled in small wooden houses; a vivid background in the natural world; a valuing of cattle and meat; in love with horses; no understanding of the city or of any relationship to the sea: all of that is implicit in the shape of this reconstructed language, and all of it looks very like the background to the world of the Greeks in their camp on the Trojan shore.

But where and when can this world be located? That question is still far from being answered. There is plenty of evidence, but none of it adds up. Language cannot be attached to pre-literate archaeological remains, and modern genetic evidence is still too confused for any clear outline to be derived from it.

Nevertheless, it seems clear from the memories embedded in the daughter-languages that the Proto-Indo-Europeans came from a place where they could grow crops (or at least harvest wild ones) and maintain herds of grazing animals on extensive pastures. They could not have been desert, mountain or forest people. They did not live in the arid south or the frozen north. There is a word in the original language which might mean beech tree, birch tree or oak tree. And another which might mean salmon, or maybe sea trout, or maybe trout. This looks like a temperate, river-valley existence. But the grazing animals would have required expansive grasslands too. They have a word for bee, but there are no bees east of the Urals, so they can only have been on the western, European side of those mountains. The presence of many farming words means that they must have been farming before about 2500 BC, which is thought to be the last possible moment before the original group broke up and scattered across Europe and north Asia.

These clues scarcely pinpoint a region, and people's idea of the ancient homeland of the Proto-Indo-Europeans, their *Urheimat*, has wandered all over Eurasia. Originally it was thought to be in Afghanistan, but it has migrated from Bactria to the Baltic, to the Pripiat marshes in Poland, to Hungary and the Carpathians in general. The Nazis, identifying their race-vision with this linguistic category, and preferring the term 'Aryan' (the name of an Indo-European people in Iran) to 'Indo-European', located the homeland in Germany. Some still favour Armenia in north-west Anatolia, but a modern consensus has for the time being settled on the steppes between the Black and Caspian Seas.

For the purposes of understanding the roots of the Homeric vision, it doesn't much matter where this notional homeland was. The elements of a river-valley-plus-grazing landscape extends across the whole of the western steppe, from the Danube to the Caucasus and beyond. And fascinatingly, there, in the remains of settlements, and in the burial mounds, or kurgans as they are called in Russia, which decorate the landscape, archaeologists have discovered many objects and signs of life which look distinctly as if Achilles had passed that way.

Of all the steppe-Homer linkages, the most powerful is the horse. It was probably domesticated on the steppe in about 4200 BC, first as food and then to be ridden. A man on foot in the modern Eurasian steppe can shepherd no more than two hundred sheep; one on a horse can manage a flock of five hundred. It was a revolutionary difference. This early riding was not yet the militarised pastoral nomadism associated with the Scythians or the Mongols. Nothing of that kind would emerge until after 800 BC, but the speed of the horse, the invention of the bit and the bridle, the control they gave to a rider, the ability to accumulate great reservoirs of meat, to raid and withdraw from pedestrian settlements, all of it changed people's lives and would change history.

The great grasslands of the steppe were now available to a mobile, horse-mounted people in a way no one could have attempted before. Giant flocks were grazed on the giant grasslands. The men who could control them became leaders and chieftains. Mobility and glamour had arrived, and the horse was a version of power which the great men tamed and dominated (both descended from the same Proto-Indo-European root, *demha*). The careful husbandry of the Neolithic farmers was now overlaid with the rush and glamour of horse-based life. The human steppe cultures began to revere the power of the horse, fusing their visions of human power with equine beauty. The word at the root of 'equine' means quick in Indo-European languages, and the horse and its speed, the ripple and sheen of horse muscle, became central to these people's idea of greatness.

The disconnected limbs of the horses that appear all over later prehistoric Europe, on coins or in hill-figures, are the horse seen in this magic, de-materialised way. They are more spirit than body, often with huge, disproportionately alert eyes, their whole being prancing, all curve in their haunches, all muscle in their neck and back, the tension in them not unlike the tension in a ship under sail at sea. Tautness, urgency and stretch are their governing qualities. Here the horse is something like the wind, not dominated by man but co-existing with him, an extension of the possibilities of life.

Some clues to this world of the horse can be found at a timber town, not that large, about 150 yards across, at a place called Sintashta, on the banks of the wide, gravelly Sintashta river, sweeping down through the grasslands east of the Urals and on the borders of Kazakhstan. A timber-reinforced wall with gates and towers surrounded the buildings, with a V-shaped ditch outside it. Inside there were about fifty houses (some have been eroded away by the river since), and in all of them people had been making bronze and copper swords, knives and axes.

It was clearly a violent, warrior society, with the need for weaponry and a defensive enclosure. In the nearby cemetery, more than half of all the people were buried with weapons, including nearly all the men, but some were also buried alongside something else, quite new: war chariots with light, spoked wheels. They are the oldest chariots to have been discovered, dating from about 2100–1800 BC, precisely the same moment as this book has been arguing for the genesis of the *Iliad*. The Sintashta people cannot be the ancestors of the Greeks – who must already have been far to the south-west – but to archaeologists it looks as if they might have been the ancestors of those Indo-European-speaking people who were making their way east of the Urals and on to northern India.

Sintashta – and some twenty equivalent settlements have now been found – is a cousin to the Homeric world. Here, as in Patroclus's tomb in the *Iliad*, whole horses were sacrificed at the burials. Drivers were buried with bone, disc-shaped cheek-pieces, critical elements in the kind of bridle needed for tight control of chariot horses. There are some flint blades in the graves, which are thought to have been made for javelins – those light spears which can be thrown by a warrior on the ground or from a chariot. The chariots themselves are clearly fast, light war machines, quite different from the heavy transport wagons which had been around on the steppe for a thousand years. These have spoked not solid wheels about three feet in diameter, and are designed to be driven at a gallop. The chariot itself would have been skeletal, consisting of little more than a few struts. In the *Iliad* it is possible for one man to pick up a chariot to move it out of the way.

This is a combination of things that is deeply Homeric: chariot races fill the last but one book of the *Iliad*, at the funeral games Achilles stages for Patroclus, where skill in driving, in turning corners, could only have been achieved with the new cheek-piece bridles. At the same time, it is clear from the funerals of both Hector and Patroclus that these were giant communal events, great crowds of people attending the funerary rites of the heroes. Here too at Sintashta, one burial has the bones of six horses, four cows and two rams killed for the death of the great man. Archaeologists have calculated that those animals would have provided two pounds of meat for each of three thousand participants. It so happens that the giant kurgan near this animal feast would have taken, it is thought, three thousand man-days to build, just as in Homer the people of Troy and the men of the Greek camp build for many days the funeral pyres for their fallen heroes. Horses, chariots, bronze weaponry, multiple animal sacrifices, massive meat feasts, chiefdoms, wall-defended camps, huge funeral rituals, spectacular communal display: the *Iliad* and Sintashta belong to one culture world, and that world is the Indo-European steppe.

One last intriguing element appeared at Sintashta: some great men were clearly celebrated in death, and their fame consolidated by a great communal outpouring of love and grief. Glory gathers around these funerals. But in life there is no such distinction visible in the wooden houses at Sintashta, no palaces, no apparent grandeur, no hierarchy in the buildings. Here then, in Sintashta, were warrior chiefs who loved speed, who loved horses, who loved fame, but were not focused on the riches or comfort of the places in which they lived. They were, in other words, not Agamemnon but Achilles, the choosers of glory in battle, not men who were greedy for possessions. Here in Sintashta were not only the cousins of the Greeks but the world from which Achilles came.

Horses mattered to the Homeric Greeks: both Poseidon and Athene were horse gods, drawing on the power of unpredictability, the horse's muscled body, the possibility they always seem to harbour of violence and suddenness, the fire in the eye. This deep Indo-European horse-experience explains its prominence in Homer. It is an inheritance from the steppelands which can otherwise seem a little mysterious. No fighting happens on horseback in Homer. It is ships, not horses, that have brought the Greeks to Troy. Chariots are used in battle as little more than taxis. The Trojans are city people on the shores of a strategic waterway from the Aegean to the Black Sea; horse mobility is not at the practical heart of their lives. And yet horses rule in Homer.

Achilles, Nestor and even Odysseus are deeply connected with them. Achilles even has a herd with him at Troy. His horses speak and weep. He is at times, in the speed of his running, compared to 'a prize-winning horse' himself. And it is one of his own horses, Xanthos, who tells him of his death to come. But it is the Trojans and their allies whose lives are drenched in the image and potency of the horse. The Trojans were Indo-Europeans too, having arrived in Anatolia earlier than the Greeks, and despite their city existence they continued to practise some of the habits of the steppe world from which they had come. They are, as fellow descendants of the steppe, the great horse people of Homer. The finest horses of all belong to the Trojan allies from Thrace, a region which for Homer stretches north from the Aegean with no boundary. Those horses are in effect the spirit of the north, whiter than snow, as fast as the wind, terrible, shining like the sun.

'Breaker of horses' is one of the Trojan epithets. Hector, in one of the most beautiful of all warrior similes in the *Iliad*, is

like a horse that has fed his fill at the manger, who breaks his halter and runs over the plain, wanting to bathe in the fair-flowing river, and feels exultation in his limbs, holding his head high while his mane floats streaming around his shoulders and he glories in his own splendour as he runs to the pastures and the dwelling places of the mares.

The horse is what the hero might dream of being. Aeneas has horses that come from a line bred by Zeus, the great sky god of the north. The Trojans sacrifice live horses in the river Scamander that flows past their walls. And the horse dominates the names of Trojan warriors. Quick

Horse, Raid Horse, War Horse, Black Horse and Good Horse all go out to battle for Troy, sounding like a band of Comanches.

This is the shared horse-matrix out of the north which allowed the Greeks to imagine the best thing they could give the Trojans, the one irresistible gift which that city could not refuse. The Trojans would surely see it as a gift from Poseidon Hippios, their great horse-god protector, the wall-maker: a wooden horse that looked like a fortress itself. It took one to know one: the great unifying and shared belief of these two cultures was the giant creature they both feared and revered. It does not appear in the *Iliad*: Homer's great war poem stops short of that moment. Only in the *Odyssey*, in retrospect, is the tale told, twice, each time slightly different, each immersed in tenderness and sorrow.

First Menelaus, the husband of Helen, the aggrieved man from whom Paris stole his wife and thus began the war, tells Telemachus, Odysseus's son, what happened. It was a trick, a hollow ambush, a mark of Odysseus's cleverness, the product of his 'dear, steadfast heart'. But as Menelaus tells the tale, he remembers only his wife's enigmatic and mysteriously intimate behaviour. The Trojans have hauled the horse into the city, and at night Helen walks around it. It is a thickly sexualised moment: she is close up to the body of the horse, touching it with the tips of her fingers, murmuring gently through the timbers to what she guesses must be the Greeks inside, speaking to each of them in the voice of the wives they have left behind, like a sorceress becoming one by one their loved and longed-for women away in Greece. What treachery is this? They are there to cheat the Trojans, but only for Menelaus is the voice truly of his wife. And she is the wife who betrayed him. Is this intimacy now an attempt to betray them all again?

Nor is Helen alone. She is accompanied by a Trojan, Deïphobus. He is the brother of Hector and Paris, and is now Helen's latest husband, with whom she sleeps reluctantly and whom she is now also longing to betray. Violence and desire, treachery and strangeness, the threatening closeness of the horse, one of the gods of trouble, fills this scene like an acid, corrosive fog.

The second time we hear the story, Odysseus is with the Phaeacians, who are the epitome of civilisation and wholeness, at a dinner lit with braziers, where a bard is ready to tell any tale the stranger wants to hear.

Odysseus asks him to tell the story of the building of the Trojan Horse. The bard obliges, but goes on to describe the horror of the sacking of Troy, when Odysseus, accompanied by Menelaus, goes looking for Deïphobus. When they find him they cut him horribly, as Virgil described it in the *Aeneid*: 'his whole body mutilated, his face brutally torn, his face and hands, the ears ripped from his ruined head, his nostrils sheared by a hideous wound'.

Odysseus cannot bear the tale he now hears. As he listens, 'he melted', Homer says, in a word used for snow in heat, sugar in water, a cloud giving up its rain, flesh falling from a long-dead body, or of a creature that pines away for a companion it has lost. Homer does not stint in describing the depth of Odysseus's grief:

> As a woman weeps, lying on the body
> Of her dear husband, who died fighting for his city and his people,
> As he tried to beat off the day of pitilessness,
> And as she sees him lying and gasping for breath
> And winding her body around him
> She cried high and piercing while the men behind her
> hit her with the butts of their spears
> and led her away to captivity to work and sorrow
> and her cheeks were hollow with her grief.
> Such were the tears that Odysseus let fall from his eyes.

Nowhere in Homer is the harrowing of war seen more entirely. The horse has summoned the deepest of encounters with the nature of reality. Odysseus is the sacker of cities, the mutilating criminal himself, over whose crimes he now weeps like the victims whose life he has destroyed. Reflexivity, mutuality, empathy: none of those words approach the levels of human understanding here. It is the transcription of an unbearable reality. Every person here – the bard, the king, the warrior, the weeping widow, the traveller – is understood. The poem's embrace is universal.

Homer then has the bard – a blind man whose name is Demodocus, which means 'People-Pleaser' – say something that drives far into the centre of what Homer means and why Homer matters:

The gods did this and spun the destruction of people
For the sake of the singing of men hereafter.

The song, this poem, this story, is the divine purpose of the war. The war happened so that the poem could happen.

It is the most extraordinary Homeric wink. The Phaeacians are enjoying this, it says, and you are enjoying it too, aren't you? Despite yourself, you love this account of grief, and that pleasure in tragedy is the purpose of the Homeric poems. The poems recognise the dreadfulness of the events they describe; they also understand the pleasure to be derived from hearing of those events. Nothing is theorised, nor is that contradiction resolved, but from these words we understand that the beauty of the poems depends on the horror of what they say.

This is the flagstaff statement in the very first paragraph of Simone Weil's great 1939 essay on the *Iliad*, 'The Poem of Force':

> Those who had dreamed that force, thanks to progress, belonged only to the past, have been able to see in the *Iliad* a historical document; those who know how to see force, today as yesterday, at the centre of all human history, can find there the most beautiful, the purest of mirrors.

'*Le plus beau, le plus pur des miroirs*': that is what the Phaeacian bard was saying. There is no hiding in the *Iliad*, no deceit, no flinching from the view of horror, no reluctance to record the bitter jokes in the face of blood, no sweetening of dismemberment, no pretence that, when the stomach wall is cut, innards do not lurch out on to knees and laps, no forgetting that brains spatter from a spear-mangled head, nor the way wounded, dying men scratch and jerk their life out as they scrabble uselessly at their killers' feet – the word Homer uses means to clutch at, to gather like men picking up the harvested grains – no screen to shield you from the fire, no metaphor to pretend this isn't the way that men behave, no glaze to cloud 'the purest and most beautiful of mirrors'. It is clarity, summoned here by the great horse, that makes the words of the *Iliad* the most disturbing ever written.

* * *

Achilles has inherited his life from the steppe. Inflation, scale, ambition had come with the horse and its breaking. It was the archaic companionship on which the steppe cultures were built. Equipped with horses and with their carts and heavy wagons, the steppe people could move. They were perhaps driven west by an increasing aridity on the steppe, which reached a peak of dryness in about 2000 BC, perhaps drawn by the richness of European soils. Wherever they went, they made their burial mounds, which are now to be found all over the steppe and beyond, at Marathon and Troy, on Salisbury Plain and in Denmark, all over Germany, and in Greece, and were probably once above the Shaft Graves at Mycenae which were flattened only late in antiquity.

Those burial mounds, or kurgans, are houses for the greater dead, articulate if silent earth equivalents of epic poetry, the memory capsules of giant lives lived in giant landscapes. They first started to appear on the southern steppelands of Eurasia in about 3800 BC, and contain the tutelary objects ancestral to the equipment of the Greek heroes: copper spirals, often in pairs, to hold the braided hair of a single man, the glamour trappings of the decorated body, imported copper beads, almost certainly sewn to clothes which have now disappeared, along with thin sheets of metal like foil armour, and equally thin, insubstantial tubes of copper rolled into cylinders. They had axes with them, and copper pendants made in the shape of beautiful freshwater mussel shells. Other shells were carved out of alabaster, and some of the steppeland heroes wore belts of freshwater mussels themselves, each shell carefully perforated where a thread joined it to the others.

In northern Ukraine, at a place called Karagod a few miles short of the border with Belarus, just in the fringe-zone where the southern steppe merges into the coniferous forest of the *taiga*, there is a small Bronze Age tumulus. The afternoon I was there, a blanket of silence hung in the sunshine. The sandy soil was rutted and dug up by wild boar into raw scrapes. But they were only minor interruptions. The continuous grasslands stretched away in front of me, just as Tolstoy said, the same on the horizon as they were at our feet, full of small, undemonstrative flowers: creamy white scabious, lady's bedstraw, mauve-blue campanulas, the dots of brighter paint in the endless, blond, receding grass.

As I walked through them, green grasshoppers danced up like the bubbles off a newly poured glass of champagne. In the binoculars there was nothing but glow and haze, a slow motility in the distant air, as if the world itself were simmering. I have never been anywhere filled with such languorous, labile beauty. Bugs skittered over the puddles, but everything else slowed in the heat. Cattle grazed in the distance, their legs dipped and narrowing into the pool of haze, while the swallows and sand-martins wove in and out of them as if pursuing some hidden, threaded path. A kind of vanilla sweetness wafted from the lime trees, and wild raspberries grew and fruited beneath them. There were patches of lily-of-the-valley in the shade of young oaks. A wide, slow river came sliding out of the north, as unconcerned as a cow at its cud, and by the reedy riverbanks the damselflies performed and danced, pairs of dark wings on electric bodies. The breeze blew up the underside of the willow leaves, silvering them, and in the wind the edges of the water-lilies curled up too, lifting one lip away from the water.

Is there anywhere as seductive, as reflective, as this glow-thick grassland? It seems on these continental afternoons as if this might be the remembered nature of the Homeric world, the place to which Tiresias's deep memory was returning. On the evening I was at the kurgan near Karagod, a small posse of horses, roans and greys, ten or eleven of them, their manes and tails swinging in the breeze, came down through the willows and alders in front of me. They were not large animals, but independent, swaggering, ganglike, uncowed by work, brushing through the reedbed at the fringe of the river and on through the grass which like their manes and tails was being stirred by the wind from the east.

They stood half-turned in front of me, a hundred yards away. I don't know if these were wild horses, but the gap between us was electric, its charge full of suggestion and threat. It reminded me of the moment in Edwin Muir's famous 1950s post-nuclear-war vision when late in the summer strange horses came into his collapsed world. These animal companions had returned to join the human beings.

> We did not dare go near them. Yet they waited,
> Stubborn and shy, as if they had been sent

By an old command to find our whereabouts
And that long-lost archaic companionship.

That remembered paradise appears again and again in Homer, not as part
of the present scene of war and trouble, but as the ground against which
that grief-ridden existence is compared. War occupies the raging foreground at Troy, the violence of the sea fills the *Odyssey*, but peace lies in
the back of the mind and constantly breaks through into the surface of
the poetry. Sleep sits in a pine tree in the likeness of a singing bird. Hector
looks down at his baby son and thinks he is as beautiful as a star. Nature
is often violent in these comparisons too, filled with wolves, lions, eagles,
hawks and vultures, troubled by ferocious rivers and gales over the sea,
but throughout Homer the world of peace consistently resurfaces as a
place of reproach and yearning, both memory and possibility.

In one comparison after another, windows are cut through the war
into that calm-drenched past. The chariot horses of Achilles trample the
dead like cattle stepping on the threshing floor, crushing the barley.
Menelaus and Agamemnon work their way through the Trojan ranks
side by side like a pair of oxen struggling hard as they plough a fallow
field. Homer is so in love with this idea of nature as a giant reservoir of
stability that at one point in the *Iliad*, mid-battle and mid-crisis, he
describes Hector, just at the point he is charging, armed and shouting,
at the Greek enemy, as 'a snowy mountain'. Some critics have thought
Homer might have meant an avalanche by this, but there is nothing in
the Greek to justify that. It can only be that the horror of war summoned,
as a kind of longing, an image of nature, vast, still and beautiful, in which
violence had no part to play.

It was an Edenic afternoon as I sat on the kurgan and listened to the
corncrakes and the quails. The kurgan itself is on a little rise overlooking
its shallow valley, a small act of local domination. It is filled no doubt
with a warrior and his few possessions. No one has ever excavated this
mound, but if it follows the usual pattern, his relatives and descendants
are pushed in at the side, over the generations, not disturbing him, but
clustering around him, borrowing his significance, some perhaps placed
here as human sacrifice around the great man, just as the twelve Trojan
boys are sacrificed by Achilles at the grave of Patroclus.

Foxes and badgers have made their home in that kurgan now, and beside a small thorn tree its anciently stored earth pours out of the lip of their dusty entrances. Here, or at Troy, or in Epirus in north-west Greece, or on the downs in England, in Denmark, or on the chalk hills above Dover, every tumulus hints at the same story. These tombs are tattoos, or, more, scarifications, permanent marks, intended to make the skin of the planet meaningful. As epic poetry in turf, their aim is to deny time, making something lasting and resonant in a world which otherwise promises only transience. Every tumulus carries within it the memory of the songs sung when it was made. They are mourning mounds. Every one is invested with that moment of grief. Richness is buried there, because richness is what has died with the great person they contain. And if the earth can say nothing, poetry will remember what was said in these places.

The words for tomb, womb and cave all stem from the same Proto-Indo-European root, and so the tumulus can be seen as a kind of earth home, a womb for a birth into an otherworld, one of the dark places where the barriers are down between this world and the next. To put the body in the earth is to lead it towards that other world, closing it off from the present and the living with stone slabs or baulks of timber. It both connects and separates the living and the dead.

Inside the tumulus it is both homely and strange. The body is laid out on its back, sometimes with its knees raised, sometimes in a crouched or foetal position. Powdered ochre covers the bones. Outlines of men's feet and other signs are painted in ochre on the tomb floors. Under the body was laid a blanket made of reeds, or woven fabrics, skins or felted wool. This is a bed; death was a little sleep.

The tumulus cemetery and settlement at Usatovo, near Odessa on the north-west coast of the Black Sea, from the years around 3000 BC, looks as if it might have been made by the deep ancestors of the Greeks. These people were still herders and horseback pastoralists of the coastal steppes, but in touch with other worlds in Europe to the west and the Caucasus to the east, perhaps paddling along the Black Sea coast in sailless dugouts, or trading and warring with the neighbours on long horseback journeys across the grasslands. Beads and buttons of Baltic amber accompanied them in death, alongside Anatolian silver and Near Eastern antimony.

The great men were buried with axes, adzes and chisels. Others had their copper thrusting-daggers with them, many of the blades with a stiffening central rib to strengthen the weapon as it entered the flesh, that ancestral gesture which lies at the heart of the *Iliad*. And these are not utilitarian objects; some of the daggers are silver-plated. Already there was glory in violence.

These tumuli entombing the proto-heroes spread west along the coast of the Black Sea as far as the Danube delta, many of them heaped up over small stone houses for the dead. Those around the river Ingul, in southern Ukraine, north-east of Odessa, some of which are as late as 1900 BC, look increasingly like predecessors of the Greeks.

In those Ingul tumuli, the dead, like the Greeks at Mycenae, were laid in their tombs wearing masks. Some are full reconstructions of the face, some no more than coverlets for the eyes, all made not of gold as those of their Mycenaean descendants would be, but of unfired clay, coloured with ochre, or with ash or finely powdered bone to whiten the fabric, to make flesh of the clay. From the smooth form of their underside, it is clear that the clay of these masks was put on the flesh of the dead face, before it had rotted. Through this coloured earth, in the few days after death, the person was made permanent. That must have been the hope or the assumption. Mouths and eyes are modelled in the clay. Some of the heads have been given skull caps of tar moulded on to the hair.

If there can be any doubt that this culture was already focused on the individual and his destiny, or that the Homeric agonies over human transience were already present in these ancient steppeland lives, here is undeniable evidence of it. But, just as in Mycenae, this attitude to death, the person and his preservation was not addressed merely to the warrior himself. There are women and children in these tombs, also masked like their men, treated with respect, considered significant. And so the vision of heroism here is not exclusively male, but more broadly genetic. It is the transmission of meaning across the generations that guaranteed value in their world. Women and children were core components of an understanding of life which depended on breeding and inheritance. Perhaps that was only to be expected in people whose wealth was measured in the size and wellbeing of their herds, but this is the matrix from which the one important part of the Homeric worldview emerged: it is a world not of palaces and institutions but of warriors and their families. It is at least possible that in these graves the Russian archaeologists have also found the spiritual and mental predecessors of Achilles.

Poetry itself supports that idea. Across the whole of the Indo-European world, echoes and repetitions of shared attitudes and phrases continually resurface. Scholars have pursued Homeric phrases through an entire continent of poetry and have come up with a set of attributes which seem to stem from those early beginnings.

Homer's idea that poetry brings 'undying fame' to the hero is not his at all. It appears in exactly that formula in Iranian and northern Indian epics. Heroes with *kleos* or *klutos*, the words for fame or glory, built into their names are known in Greek (Hera*kles* means 'the fame of Hera', the goddess of marriage and women) but also in Indo-Iranian, Slavic, Norse, Frankish and Celtic (including *Cluto*rix – whose name, like a wrestler's, means the 'King of Fame' – a fifth-century AD chieftain known only from his tombstone now built into the wall of the church in the little village of Llandissilio in the middle of Pembrokeshire).

Poetry and war are joined in this: both are fame businesses. The same epithets are attached to these fame-seeking heroes across the whole enormous continent: he was 'man-slaying' in Ireland and Iran, and 'of the famous spear' in Greece and India. He stood as firm and immovable in battle as a mighty tree in Homer, Russian and Welsh. Like the Greeks, Irish heroes raged like a fire. In Anglo-Saxon, Greek, Vedic and Irish, that rage could emerge as a flame flaring from the hero's head. Proto-Indo-Europeans saw the great man as a torch. Across the whole of Eurasia his weapons longed for blood, even while this bloodseeking vengeance-wreaker was to his own family and clan, wherever they might be, the 'herdsman of his people' and their protective enclosure. There were no city walls in this world; the hero himself was their protection and their strength.

From one end of Eurasia to another, men stand like trees but enemies are also felled like trees, in the way a carpenter or woodsman would fell them. When death arrives, a darkness comes on the hero. Life itself for the Proto-Indo-European consciousness is inseparable from light, especially the light of the sun, and that is the energy the heroes share with the universe. For all of them, courage is not something that appears casually in everyday life. Only when battle summons them, and when the noise of battle reaches up to heaven, as it does in all these daughter-traditions, does courage appear and the hero find himself 'clothed in valour'.

These phrases, which are shared between Homer and the poets who sang to their manlords across the widths of Eurasia from the Atlantic to the Himalayas, are the creases in the mind of the Proto-Indo-European people from whom we are all descended. They are the oldest of the ancestral thoughts to which we can have access. We are their heirs, just as Homer was their heir, a descendant of the steppelands.

Memories of this pre-Greek world lingered on for the Greeks, first in the knowledge that they were not one people, but an agglomeration of families and their leaders, speaking something like the same language but never unified. Homer thinks of the Greeks as a gang of bees, alive, investigative, aggressive, buzzing with their needs and desires but never one unitary mass. This is not the army of a single nation. They are, as Nestor tells Agamemnon, different tribes and gangs, who must be organised clan by clan, people by people, listening to their leaders, scarcely integrated, resistant to overall kingship. These are in origin the groups of steppeland warriors who have come south to the more tightly organised world of the centrally ordained city.

More intriguing still is the geographical residue in Homer's language. The sea has no place in the most ancient layers of Greek. There is no Proto-Indo-European word for the sea, beyond a root that means something like pond or lake. *Thalassa*, the Greek word for sea, has no reliable etymology. It may have come from the language spoken in Greece before the Greeks arrived there. The sea was an alien environment, and when Homer speaks of it the only way he can treat it is as a steppeland. The phrase that recurs repeatedly in both Homeric poems, neatly filling the second half of a hexameter, is *ep' eurea nota thalasses*, meaning 'on the broad backs of the sea', or 'on the sea's broad ridges'. Warriors set out across the sea's broad ridges for battle or for home. The ships drive like horses across them. Poseidon, the sea god who is also the horse god, finds his own horses stabled in his extraordinary palace deep in the sea, glittering with gold, 'imperishable for ever', unlike the world over which he presides. He drives them across his own wet steppeland:

He harnessed to the chariot his bronze-shod horses
Flying footed, with long gold manes streaming behind them,
and he put on clothing of gold about his own body
and took up the golden lash, carefully constructed,
and climbed into his chariot and drove it across the waves
And about him the sea beasts came up from their deep places
and played in his path
And acknowledged their master as the sea stood apart before him
rejoicing. The horses flew on with all care
and the bronze axle beneath was not wetted
until they carried him fast to the ships of the Achaians.

That glorious drive of the sea-horse god, a baroque ceiling waiting to be painted, is a gilded stampede across the sea as if across the endless grasslands of the north. *Nota* could mean the backs of men or animals, of a boar, of horses and eagles, but also the great wide surface of the land. It is the word for that steppe continuousness, the only model on which the early Greeks could base their understanding of the sea.

The sea-as-land penetrates far into the poems. When Aeneas is remembering the time before there was even a city at Troy, he thinks of it as a place where great fortunes were made in the raising of horses. So beautiful were they that the north wind – that essence of mobility from the distant north, gusty, with the cold of the north at the back of it – fell in love with them, disguised himself as a black stallion, coupled with them, and the Trojan mares gave birth to twelve magical young horses. They could not only run along the top of the ears of the ripened corn, miraculously not breaking the grains from their stems, but then beautifully

They would play across the sea's wide ridges
Running the edge of the wave where it breaks on the grey salt sea.

Land and sea are continuous in this imagery. Blowing ears of corn and the curling break of a swell coming ashore are the same thing. When Nestor gives advice to his son on the driving of chariots, the relationships to the horse and to the ship effortlessly coalesce:

It is by cunning and craft that the helmsman holds his swift ship
On its track, though buffeted by winds, over the wine-dark sea.
By cunning and craft the charioteer beats charioteer. . .
And holds his horses steady in his hand, watching the lead horse.

What the wind does for the ship at sea, the horses do for the chariot on the plain. It is Penelope who says with regret that it is 'fast-running ships which serve as horses for men on the salt sea'. And when Odysseus is finally on his way back to Ithaca, the ship taking him there is not only as fast as a chariot at full speed; it mimics one:

Just as in a field four stallions drawing a chariot all break together at the stroke of the whip, and lifting high their feet lightly beat out their path, so the stern of the ship would lift and the creaming wave behind her boiled in the thunderous crash of the sea.

There is an overbrimming technological energy in those lines. It is the sensation you get whenever a boat accelerates at sea – imagine Homer's delight at a RIB with a pair of 200-horsepower Yamahas on the back – its sudden, gut-felt harnessing of liquid power. The speed of the chariot and the ship were transforming men's experience of the world. And there are signs in Homer of a real excitement at the idea of machinery. In the *Odyssey*, the ideal king Alcinous has beautiful metal dogs made by Hephaestus, the smith god, to guard the entrance to his palace, which will live and bark for ever. When Hephaestus is making Achilles's wonderful new armour, he has magical-mechanical robotic golden girls to help him, automata which can carry and talk and think, as well as automatic tripod tables which under their own power wheel in and out of the dining room of the gods.

The myths of Daedalus and Icarus, dazzling inventors of hubristic, dangerous machines, labyrinth-traps and wings that melt in the heat of the sun, are probably associated with this arrival of the new technology in the Aegean world. This is the first moment of European entrancement with the life-expanding potential of technology, but anxiety over the new machinery surfaces in the *Iliad* too. In Book 5, in the first great battle of the poem, the Greek warrior Meriones pursues a Trojan called Phereclus. He strikes him in the right buttock

the point
pounding under the pelvis, jabbed and pierced the bladder –
he dropped to his knees, screaming, death swirling about him.

This one grievous ending, like all the others at Troy, was due to what Phereclus had learned. Without him, Paris would never have been able to go to Greece to steal Helen, nor the Greeks come to claim her from Troy, as Phereclus was the great shipwright

> Who had the skill to craft all kinds of complex work
> Since Pallas Athena loved him most, her protégé
> who had built Paris his steady, balanced ships,
> trim launchers of death, freighted with death
> for all of Troy and now for the shipwright too.

* * *

The synchronicity is extraordinary: the technology of the new chariots, probably from the north, and the technology of the sailing ship, certainly from the south, seem to have arrived in the Greek world at about the same time, perhaps at around 1800 BC. That is also the most likely moment for the Greek arrival in the Mediterranean. High-speed chariots, high-speed sailing ships and a warrior culture from the north all come together in the Aegean at the same moment, which is also the moment that the Homeric poems are born. This newly energised world is the meeting of cultures that Homer records.

There are some intriguing linguistic linkages. The word which in a whole range of Indo-European languages means the pole at the front of a wagon or chariot to which the horses were attached (it is a 'thill' in English) became the word in Greek for the rudder post of a ship. The word for the tiller or the helm of a boat is also at root the same word as the rings on a yoke. The word for the loops attached to the yoke through which the beasts' heads were put is also the word for the cross-bar connecting the double steering-oars at the stern of a ship.

The Greek word for rudder can also be applied to reins. At this most fundamental level, the sailing ship was the sea-chariot for the Greeks, and the sea was the liquid steppe. And all of them became intimate with heroism.

There had been sea craft long before in the eastern Mediterranean, of extraordinary antiquity. There were people on Crete, which has been separate from the mainland for at least five million years, making hand axes and stone scrapers 130,000 years ago. They can only have arrived by boat or raft, probably from Anatolia. The whole civilisation of the Cyclades was created and connected by straight-hulled, low-freeboard, paddled canoes, of which the earliest representation that survives was made in about 2800 BC. No sail appeared in the Mediterranean until about 2500 BC (it had probably been invented in the Indian Ocean), when sailing ships are found travelling along the coast between Egypt and the Levant, bringing raw materials into what the archaeologist Cyprian Broodbank has called 'the colossal vortex of consumption' of the Egyptian state.

Judging by depictions on Minoan seals from Crete, and also by the increasing spread of luxury Egyptian and Near Eastern objects into Crete and Cyprus, these sailing ships were pushing up towards the Aegean by about 1950 BC. They were quite different from the old paddled canoes, with a deep, curving plank-built hull, a tall mast, held in place with rigging, as well as a sail and a steering oar. They were the most complicated and sophisticated constructions the Aegean world would ever have seen. And above all, they brought speed and power to the sea world. A hand-paddled canoe had been able to cover perhaps ten to twenty miles in a good day. A sailing ship might go a hundred. On a beam reach, the fastest point of sailing for a ship of this kind, the leading edge of its sail hauled far forward, it might achieve seven or eight knots. They could carry tons of cargo, where a canoe could have taken little more than the men needed to paddle it. A high-hulled sailing ship could live in the kind of waves which would swamp a canoe. For the first time people could experience storms at sea and survive to tell the tale.

Nowhere in Homer is this amazement with the ship more overwhelming than when Odysseus finds himself washed up in Book 6 of the *Odyssey* on the shore of Scheria, the island of the Phaeacians. Scheria is the Homeric equivalent of Southern California, or at least the urbanised, enriched, technological world of the Near East, filled with people who are living the enviable life: a city with beautiful harbours, wonderful gardens, orchards surrounding their palaces, no suffering or grief in their lives, playfulness, elegance, riches, the presence of power buried under a coat of luxuries and ease.

The north meets the south here: Odysseus is never more ragged, never treated more as a wanderer from God-knows-where, and his hosts are never more beautifully organised, more integrated as a single contented orderly world. These are the polarities of the Homeric experience. The Phaeacians are what the Greek wanderers dream of being. Homer introduces a stream of them to Odysseus (whom they consider a pirate and a drifter), and just as the Trojans are alive in their horse names, the Phaeacians can scarcely be distinguished from their ships and the sea. Odysseus stands there encountering (in Robert Fagles's translations) a stream of muscled young men: Topsail, Riptide, Rowhard, Seaman and Sternman, Surf-at-the-Beach, Stroke-Oar, Breaker and Bowsprit, Racing-the-Wind, Swing-Aboard, Shipwrightson, Seagirt the son of Greatfleet and Broadsea the son of Launcher. The king's own sons are called Ship-Famous, People-Dominator and simply Sea.

Could Homer have made it any clearer? Here, in the sea-based city, the delight and riches of an urban life are derived from the magic of the sailing ship. And the heart of the Phaeacian ships' excellence, to an open-mouthed Greek, hopelessly provincial in these upholstered surroundings, is their ability to sail *on thought alone*. Alcinous, the king, explains how it works in this floating, gravity-free world:

> Our ships can sail you home.
> They have no rudders as those of other nations do,
> but can understand our thoughts and our desires; they know all the
>   cities and countries of the world,
> and can cross the sea through mist and cloud,
> never any danger of wreck or harm with them.

The ships are as miraculous as Achilles's weeping-talking horses. They are 'as quick as a bird, as quick as a darting thought'. But perhaps embedded here is a memory of the ignorant northerners' first encounter with the miracle of the sailing ship. No need to paddle it to make it travel across the sea. Just arrange its parts as they need to be arranged, make a libation to the right goddesses, and on thought alone the ship will sail to the ends of the earth and back.

These rocket ships, as Cyprian Broodbank has said, 'drastically shrunk maritime space'. They were adventure machines. Egypt could be reached from Greece in four days. Sudden arrival and sudden violence was now a possibility. They could sail to windward, or at least within fifty degrees of the wind, in a way paddlers would find difficult and exhausting. Life had speeded up. The whole geography of the sea and its surrounding lands had changed. It was as revolutionary as the invention of the steam engine. And that excitement and amazement at the wonder of the sailing ship and its transforming effects on the dynamics of life has soaked deep into the fabric of the Homeric poems. In Homer's hands, sailing ships became the vehicles of heroes.

It is never quite said explicitly in Homer, but it is assumed that this sense of boat-perfection has become for the Greeks one of the joys of life. Ships are always fast, or well-balanced, or well-made. The word usually translated as well-balanced, *eisos*, has a moral and psychological dimension to it, and means equal, or properly shared like a feast, or well-balanced in mind. The wisdom of Odysseus is described as *eisos*, his wholeness and beauty as self-sufficiently itself as a well-made ship. Those adjectives contribute formulae that slip the sea-craft into the verse form, but they are also a kind of repetitive admiration for the wonder of ships. Menelaus remembers how fast they were when at last, at the end of the war, the Greeks left Troy for home. It was fast ships that repeatedly brought wine from Greece to the warriors in their foreign camp. Homer recounts the variety and strength of the different bands of men that went to Troy by remembering the numbers of ships in which they travelled. It is the ships, as Ajax reminds them, which are their only guarantee of getting home dryshod. It is the ships they must defend, and around the ships is where the fiercest fighting rages. The sea might be salt and bitter, so wide in places that even seabirds cannot cross it, but the well-benched ships, the hollow ships, the ships whose hulls are black with waterproofing tar, the ships equipped with all the gear that strong-benched ships carry, these are the foundations of their lives in the southern sea.

So, each time now the wind fills in, and you roll the headsails out and get the main up, and you feel the boat starting to gather way, to pick up its skirts, unable to resist the pull of the wind, you will know something essential of the Homeric world. Here under the bow you can listen, like the Phaeacians carrying Odysseus home, to the water surge and fall, that repeated hoosssh-hoosssh of a hull at speed. And here, as you make your way between the blue islands, the boat heeled far over and the curves of the headsails bellied out to leeward, you can begin to know and sense the power of possibility in the well-balanced, well-benched ship, equipped with all it needs, acquiring the world, stretching the idea of what it means to be alive, leading men to adventure, home or war.

TEN

The Gang and the City

THE GREEKS ARE CAMPED on the edge of the beach, a gang of men divided between themselves, with no secure leadership, the atmosphere angry and uncertain, no constancy in their arguments or their dealings with each other, no faith in their purpose, no substance in their loyalties and no women with any significance beyond their sex. They are living in rough sheds built against their ships. The rigging has rotted. They are surrounded by loot but sleep on the skins of wild animals. Dogs eat the dead. Dogs are everywhere on the battlefield. They chew at the genitals of the corpses and birds clap their wings over the remains. If you walk across that realm of death at night, you must pick your way through 'the abandoned weapons and the black blood'. The Greeks confront the realities of life and death with unadorned directness. No family, no safety, no home, no sense that virtue is rewarded or frailty sheltered. No prospect of dignity in old age or security when weak. No meaning beyond the presence of force.

They have been here too long, and the language vibrates with its own violence. The burningly angry killer-chief Achilles says that Agamemnon, his nominal leader, is dog-eyed, dog-faced, shameless, greedy, a wine-drinker, with his heart as flaky as a deer's. Agamemnon calls Achilles 'the most savage man alive, violence itself, beyond all feeling'. Anger and disgust ripple through their 'shaggy breasts', in the roughness of their hearts. In private they are tender about themselves and their girls, but here they overbrim with hate, each longing for the other's 'black blood to come pumping out on to my blade'. They stand nostril to nostril in mutual loathing. This is a gang world, marginal, desperate and tragic, a place of outsiders. Civilisation it is not. Like all gangs, they have their meetings and their discussions, their insistence on hierarchy and obedience. And this fight between the leaders feels ugly and unwelcome, deplored by the old men. Nevertheless, it is an organic part of who the Greeks are, one aspect of the anarchy and violence that crouch just beneath the surface of every interaction between them. The Greeks are the barbarians in this story.

Across the plain, Troy is different. Here are the people of a city, full of conviction, with well-ordered relations, allies who remain true to each other, a king to whom all give respect, brothers, sisters, wives, parents and children all living in a mutually dependent, interlocked system, with institutions that seem permanent. Noble women lead graceful lives. There are arguments within the family, there are hints of luxury and softness, but this is a place where not merely the bodies of slaughtered animals but woven and embroidered cloth, the flexible and intricately constructed thing, is the offering they make to the gods.

The Trojans are at home and the web of their connections is wound closely around them. When Hector, their young war leader, mid-battle, returns to the gates of the city,

> the wives and daughters of Troy came crowding up around him,
> asking for their sons, brothers, friends and husbands.

This is the network the Trojans are embedded in. Hector goes into the city, to the palace of Priam, his father, and enters

> that magnificent structure
> Built wide with porches and colonnades of polished stone.
> And deep within its walls were fifty sleeping chambers
> masoned in smooth, lustrous ashlar, linked in a line
> where the sons of Priam slept beside their wedded wives;
> and facing these, opening out across the inner courtyard,
> lay the twelve sleeping chambers of Priam's daughters,
> where the sons-in-law of Priam slept beside their wives.

It is the geometry of coherence – of repetition and continuity – of people understanding and responding to the virtues of mutual accommodation, the opposite of the shiftless place of the Greeks outside. So this is the confrontation: gang against city, individual violence against domestic order.

The wind blows unbroken across the plain, and among the Greeks unbridled maleness meets in erect competition or tensed stand-off. The sexuality is inescapable. It takes the old Greek war-leader Nestor to say it. When persuading doubters not to return to Greece before Troy falls, he gives them the plain invitation:

> Let no man hurry to sail for home, not yet. . .
> Not until he has slept with the wife of some Trojan.

Only sex with the enslaved wife of a dead enemy could justify the grief and trouble they have endured over Helen. The symbols at the heart of the city of Troy are those elegant, well-swept corridors of polished stone and the beautiful woven cloth its people give their gods; for the Greek camp it is edge-sharpened bronze and the unsheathed phallus.

The *Iliad* is not shut into the Trojan plain; it loves mobility; its gods and goddesses fly across the islanded world of the Aegean with effortless fluency and a wide surveying sense of its geography. The poem often travels away to Olympus, the home of the gods, to Africa and to other mountains where the gods take up temporary residence. Minor deities are sometimes caught between flights, rushed off their feet, in transit from Anatolia to Egypt, or to a dinner party in the house of the west wind. But the poem *never* goes to Greece. No scene is set in a Greek house. Greek places are referred to with formulaic adjectives – 'rocky', 'with-many-ridges', 'sheepy' – but with none of the overwhelming sense of reality that clusters around Troy and its rivers, its woods, springs, washing places and even individual trees and burial mounds. In that poetic sense, at one of the deepest levels of the poem, the *Iliad* portrays the Greeks as a long way from home.

It is true that they occasionally refer to the places they come from, but the psychological weight in those references is not to buildings or cities. The Greeks look back with longing and a sense of loss to their families, their distant fathers, and their fathers' fathers, their wives and children, the brotherhood of their clans, the hearths which are defined by the people who gather round them, not to any palaces. They love their land, which gives them food and sustenance, its wheat-bearing fields and lovely orchards, but not the kind of deeply instituted fixity and built wealth they have come to get their hands on at Troy. What they miss, in a phrase that is repeated again and again, is 'the loved earth of their fathers'. But in Greek there is no distinction between 'fatherhood' and 'fatherland'. The word for them both is *patra*, and it can apply in Homer to a shared descent, a cousinage, a sense of family or clan. Fatherhood is fatherland and blood and heart is home.

Even the loved earth of the fathers is trumped by something else in the Greek mind. When the great owl-eyed goddess Athene, terrifying in her power, carrying her magic *aegis* or breastplate, moves through the Greek army, putting a deep hunger for violence in their hearts, allowing them to fight without rest, home itself drops into insignificance:

> And now sweeter to them than any return
> In their hollow ships to the loved earth of their fathers
> Was battle.

The word Homer uses for the deliciousness of that violence in battle is *glukos*, sugary, even sickly, used of nectar and sweet wine, of the people you love. Battle, in many ways, is the Greek home. As the agents of severance, they are themselves severed from home. The most delicious thing they can imagine is a world of unrelenting violence.

'Beware the toils of war,' Sarpedon the Lycian hero says to Hector, 'the mesh of the huge dragnet sweeping up the world.' Buried inside that terrifying image of war trawling for the lives of men, its net stretched from one horizon to the other, ushering the mortals into the cod end, is the Greek word for flax, the thread which the Fates use at the beginning of each of our lives to spin our destinies. And so the metaphor makes an assumption: war is part of destiny. It is not an aberration or a strangeness. It is, for Homer, a theatre in which the structure of reality is revealed.

Simone Weil and many others have read the *Iliad* as an anti-war poem. But to see it as a polemic in that sense is to reduce it. Homer knows about the reality of suffering but never thinks of a world without conflict. On the shield of Achilles, the smith god Hephaestus creates dazzlingly opposed images of the good world and the bad, set against each other. But even in the good world of justice there is still murder and violence. We might long for peace, but we live in war, and the *Iliad* is a poem about the inescapability of it.

All of that lies behind the *Iliad*'s massive oversupply of suffering. The poet's conception that the Greeks have been on this beach for nine long, dreadful years – a historical absurdity – stands in for eternity. This is how things are. This is how things have always been. This is how things are going to continue to be. War is the air a warrior society must breathe. And alongside that everlastingness of grief, its repetitive return, is a deeply absorbed knowledge that suffering can only be told in detail. No counting of casualties will do; no strategic overview will understand the reality; only the intimate engagement with the intimacy of pain and sorrow can ever be good enough for the enlightenment which is Homer's purpose.

Scholars have worked out that 264 people die in the course of the *Iliad*. It doesn't seem enough. One atrocity in some villages on the northern borders of Syria, one night-time drowning of African refugees in the Mediterranean, one week of car bombs in Baghdad – any of them can outdo it. Only the epic engagement with Atē, the blind goddess of ruin, whose name means both wrongness and wickedness, can tell what those figures conceal. People are pitiably weak in the face of ruin, pathetically hoping that their prayers for happiness might prevail. That is why the goddesses of prayer in the Homeric universe are broken, tragic figures:

> they limp and halt,
> they're all wrinkled, drawn, they squint to the side,
> can't look you in the eye, and always bent on duty,
> trudging after Ruin, maddening, blinding Ruin.
> But Ruin is strong and swift – She outstrips them all,
> loping a march, skipping across the whole wide earth
> to bring mankind to grief.
> And the Prayers trail after, trying to heal the wounds.

Christians might think of prayer as something that can summon divine power; Homer knows different. 'Of all that breathe and crawl across the earth,' Zeus himself says, 'There is nothing alive more agonized than man.' The term the great god uses is *oïzuroteros*, more miserable, from the word for a wailing lament, the unbroken, everlasting, ululating cry that echoes from one end of the *Iliad* to the other.

When the poet is reaching for a comparison that will sharpen the pity of life and the futility of killing, it is fish that repeatedly drift into his consciousness. Perhaps because they are so disgusting, nibbling at the bodies of the dead; perhaps because a fish is so unable to look after itself when caught on a hook, in a net or on a spear, both fish and fishermen are for Homer absurd.

Fish gasping for the sea are not simply poignant in their hopelessness. In the *Iliad*, fishing is the source of some of Homer's bitterest and jokiest comparisons. When Patroclus, the friend and childhood companion of Achilles, his great intimate in a world where no one else seems to love him, borrows Achilles's armour at a moment of great crisis for the Greeks in the war at Troy, and strides out into the mass of the Trojans, he pins them against the ships drawn up on the sand. This is his *aristeia*, his moment of greatness, his time of horror. Patroclus rampages through the Trojan bodies, repetitively and brutally.

> Patroclus kept on sweeping, hacking them down,
> making them pay the price for Argives slaughtered.

One poor Trojan, Cebriones, a bastard son of Priam the king of Troy, is killed by Patroclus with a stone smashed into the front of his skull. Both Cebriones's eyes fall out into the dust at his feet and the body, jerked into death, somehow dives out of the chariot to join them. The beautiful, elegant, much-loved Patroclus mocks the corpse:

> Hah! look at you! Agile! How athletic is that, as if you were diving
> into the sea. You could satisfy an army if you were diving for oysters,
> . plunging overboard even into rough seas as nimbly as that.

Corpse as oyster-diver: ridiculous victim, vaunting killer. At one point, in describing Patroclus's safari, Homer sinks to nothing but a list of the names of those he destroys:

> Erymas and Amphoterus and Epaltes and Tlepolemus son of Damastor
> and Echius and Pyris and Ipheus and Euippus and Polymelus, son of
> Argeas: corpse on corpse he piled on the all-nourishing earth.

Patroclus moves on, as Robert Fagles translated Homer's phrase for the unstoppability of this, 'in a blur of kills'. But then the rapidity, the appetite for more, stops and stills for a moment, and dwells on the detail of one particular death, one moment of heroic prowess:

> Next he went for Thestor the son of Enops
> cowering, crouched in his beautiful polished chariot,
> crazed with fear, and the reins jumped from his grip –
> Patroclus rising beside him stabbed his right jawbone,
> ramming the spearhead square between his teeth so hard
> he hooked him by that spearhead over the chariot rail,
> hoisted, dragged the Trojan out as an angler perched
> on a jutting rock ledge drags some fish from the sea,
> some precious catch, with line and glittering bronze hook.
> So with the spear Patroclus gaffed him off his car,
> his mouth gaping round the glittering point
> And flipped him down facefirst,
> dead as he fell, his life breath blown away.

Man as fish, body as rag doll, killing as a form of acrobatics, the absurdity of the slaughtered corpse: this is vertigo-inducing, a plunge into the black hole of reality, fuelled by the mismatch of sea-angling with war. Christopher Logue, the most brilliant of all modern interpreters of Homer, drove these lines further into domestic savagery:

> Ahead, Patroclus braked a shade, and then and gracefully
> As patient men cast fake insects over trout,

He speared the boy, and with his hip as pivot
Prised Thestor out of the chariot's basket
As easily as lesser men
Detach a sardine from an opened tin.

The first fighting does not begin until 2,380 lines into the *Iliad*, but thereafter the blood flows, increasingly, with an increasing intensity and savagery, until the climax comes in the crazed berserker frenzy of Achilles's grief-fuelled rampage through the Trojans. The culmination is in the death of Hector, when steppe-man finally meets and kills the man of the city. The Greeks might think battle sweet, their warriors might see battle not as a burden but a cause for rejoicing, but Homer does not.

Now the sun of a new day struck on the ploughlands, rising
Out of the quiet water and the deep stream of the ocean
To climb the sky. The Trojans assembled together. They found
It hard to recognize each individual dead man;
But with water they washed away the blood that was on them
And as they wept warm tears they lifted them on to the wagons.
Great Priam would not let them cry out; and in silence
They piled the bodies on the pyre, and when they had burned them
Went back to sacred Ilion.

The Greek words translated here by Richmond Lattimore as 'hard to recognize' carry multiple meanings. *Chalepos* – hard – means both emotionally painful and difficult to do; it is a word that can be applied either to grieving or to rough ground over which you cannot help but stumble as you walk. *Diagnonai* – to recognise, like diagnosis – means to distinguish or discern, to sort out a single important thing from a confused mass, to find individuality amidst the blood and muck of the heaped-up bodies. So the phrase can mean either that it was physically difficult in the mounded carnage to make out who it was that was dead; or that finding your own dead amid the mass of others was the most harrowing of experiences. Or both. Those hot, silent Trojan tears, *dákrua thermà*, allied in these lines with the deep calm of the ocean and the water which washes the blood away, are among Homer's greatest legacies

Opposite: The Mycenaean citadel of Tiryns: heroic architecture designed to mimic the walls of the first Hittite-influenced cities besieged by the Greeks. (For giant walls as part of Troy's metaphorical geography, see pages 202–4)

The eighth-century BC wine cup from Rhodes, found on Ischia, with the first surviving Greek hexameters – and the first Homeric joke – scratched into its surface. (See pages 65–7)

Odysseus, half-dead from days at sea, emerges naked and a little rough to find Nausicaa on the shore. A fifth-century BC Athenian party cup shows the scene which, in Chapman's translation, first convinced John Keats of Homer's greatness. (See pages 20–2)

The *Iliad* in Extremadura: a Late Bronze Age stele now in Badajoz shows a warrior, his sword and the giant shield marked with the concentric rings of the cosmos. (See pages 133–41)

A shield-like piece of Bronze Age horse harness found in the Wiltshire Avon, ritually stabbed and perhaps symbolically killed. Repetitive, insertive killing is at the heart of Homer's tragic vision. (See pages 199–202)

Metal heroes: Extremaduran figures with shield, swords, bow, spear and two objects central to the hero-complex: a bubble-handled mirror, for beauty, and a musical instrument, for epic song. Both men have large, 'man-slaughtering hands'. (See pages 133–41)

The Rio Odiel, north of Huelva in southern Spain: waters poisoned with the metals that make this a candidate for Homer's Hades. (See pages 128–30)

Southern story-telling: the multiple scenes on silver gilt bowls produced in the Near East (this one from Cyprus c.725–675 BC but showing Egyptian, Assyrian and Phoenician stories of battle and triumph) provide a possible model for Homer's description of the shield of Achilles. (See page 136)

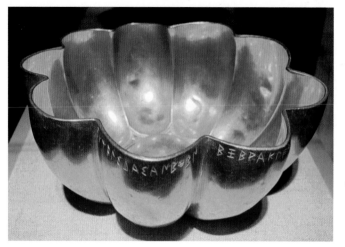

A golden libation bowl from Olympia, now in Boston. Only when Odysseus on the shores of Hades pours all the good juices of the earth on to the ground can the dead reacquire the ability to speak. (See page 125)

The shape of the south: fluency and fragility in a Kamares eggshell-ware cup from the temple-palace at Phaistos on Crete, c.1900 BC, just as the Greeks were entering the Mediterranean world.

The luxurious world of Sinuhe: an Egyptian ivory cosmetics container in the shape of a duck with fish on her back. (See pages 208–10)

Caravaggio's first painting of David as he ties a cord around the hair of Goliath's severed head, painted in 1599 and now in the Prado, Madrid. The triumph of godliness over Homeric self-importance. (See pages 223–7)

Odysseus's instrument of revenge: a Mycenaean dagger now in the British Museum, found on Ithaca. Its hilt resembles Near Eastern examples of a kind Odysseus would have been given by the Phaeacians (See pages 244–7)

'The sweetest place any man could imagine': wild pear tree in blossom on spring meadows at the southern end of Ithaca, March 2007. (See page 241)

A Cretan bath from the mid-fourteenth century BC, one of the elements of Mediterranean civilisation most greedily adopted by Homeric Greeks. (See pages 214–16)

The transforming grace and power of the sailing ship:
Dionysus on a reach, on a fifth-century Attic *kylix* now
in Munich (See pages 175–8)

to us, the persistent belief, amidst all this damage, that there is value and beauty in human ties.

Homer's portrait of the Greeks at Troy fits the historical situation in the centuries after 2000 BC, when newly empowered northern warriors, equipped with sailing ships and chariots, could batten on the walls of a rich trading city in north-west Anatolia, clamouring to get at its women and its goods. But it is also a portrait of something more enduring: a well-set-up, well-defended establishment is under attack from outsiders who long for, envy and wish to destroy it. The siege at Troy, often seen as a kind of war, as if these were two states battling with each other, is in fact more like a gang from the ghetto confronting the urban rich. Outsiders and insiders, nomadic and settled, the needy and the leisured, the enraged and the offended: the hero-complex of the Greek warriors is simply gang mentality writ large.

Iliadic behaviour echoes through modern urban America. As the criminologists Bruce Jacobs and Richard Wright have documented from the streets of St Louis, Missouri, American gang members talk about themselves, their lives, their ambitions, their idea of fate, the role of violence and revenge, in ways that are strangely like the Greeks in the *Iliad*.

Revenge is at the heart of their moral world, a repeated, angry and violent answer to injustice, to being treated in a way that does not respect them as people. There appears to be no overriding authority or legitimacy on the streets of St Louis. Authority resides in the men themselves and their ability to dominate others. 'This desire for payback,' Jacobs and Wright say, 'is as human and as inevitable as hunger or thirst.' Crime itself on these streets becomes moral, and revenge a form of justice.

Like the Greeks, these gangsters are 'urban nomads', not set up in their elaborate houses, but living nowhere in particular, 'staying' or 'resting their head' in different places according to mood or what is going on. They are rootless, dependent on themselves, displaying their glory on their bodies, in their handsomeness, their jewellery and in the sexiness of the women on their arms and in their beds.

They can only rely on themselves: 'maintaining a reputation for toughness dominates day-to-day interaction'. And because any act of revenge has to deter the enemy from taking revenge in his turn, there is an accelerator built into the process. Any insult, any slight, any suggestion that you are not a man worthy of respect summons severe, intense and punitive retaliatory violence. Achilles longs to kill Agamemnon after he has humiliated him in public over a slave girl he loves. The St Louis gangsters take revenge without a thought.

One evening, a man called Red knocked into a stranger at a bar by mistake and spilled his glass of cognac on him. In response, the stranger 'bitch-slapped' him, not with a closed fist but with an open hand, usually reserved for women. 'Everyone was watching,' Red said, 'so it made me look bad.' Red left the bar and waited in the dark in the parking lot. When the man came out he shot him, not once but several times. This is the only way in a warrior society that you can be yourself, or protect the fragile boundaries of the self, forever under attack from those around you who are all feeling the same.

Homer usually talks with a mysterious decorum about acts of extreme and horrifying violence, perhaps as a product of the poem evolving over generations, so that a kind of linguistic dignity is laid over the top of the violence itself; but have no doubt, the words of the gangsters reflect a Homeric reality, nowhere more than in Book 10 of the *Iliad*. The behaviour that book describes is peculiarly horrible, a stripping away of any skin of dignity and nobility. Like 'two lions into the black night/ Through the carnage and through the corpses, the war gear and the dark blood', Odysseus and Diomedes slink off towards the Trojan line.

They come across a young Trojan, Dolon, out in the night, and set off to chase him, 'like two rip-fanged hounds that have sighted a wild beast, a young deer or a hare'. They catch him and he stands in front of them in terror, gibbering and in tears. The two Greeks interrogate him, smiling, getting out of him any information they can, but he knows what is to come. He begs for his life, reaching up to the chin of Diomedes, asking for mercy, but Diomedes

struck the middle of his neck
With a sweep of the sword, and slashed clean through both tendons,
And Dolon's head – still speaking – dropped in the dust.

This is the most shocking moment in Homer, part of a hideous murder-run in the dark, with many dead, and booty taken, including wonderful horses and chariots, at the end of which Odysseus laughs aloud, has a swim in the sea and then a beautiful bath. Its amusement and delight at violence leaves a hollow in the reader's heart, which is scarcely filled by the way the Greeks 'vaunt' over the bodies of the people they have killed, calling them fools, telling the world of their own excellence, their right to stand over the dead and damaged body of the rival. This is also how gangsters 'trash talk'. 'I got your punk ass,' Bobcat tells one of his victims,

> and now look at you . . . Now if you'd paid this cheese [money], you'd have been all right, but now you fucked up, you bleeding and shit . . . you talking about your ribs broke. Now what the fuck?

Words are a way of making it hurt. This is the hero delivering justice, telling his victim, and his audience around him, just how powerful he is in the world. 'Catching and punishing those who have wronged them makes offenders feel mighty,' Jacobs and Wright say, 'while at the same time it masks their objective impotence.' 'I had an adrenaline rush,' one of their informants told them about a particularly horrible piece of violence, 'like I was the shit, like I was in control.' 'I felt like I was in some pussy,' another said after using a baseball bat to break the legs of a man who had vandalised his car. 'You know [like I] busted [a] nut' – or ejaculated.

This elision of self-enlargement, sexual gratification and extreme violence to other men's bodies lurks in the sub-text of Homer. A theatre of sex and violence is at the heart of both the *Iliad* and the *Odyssey*: the stolen woman Helen; the twice stolen woman Briseis (once from her family, all of whom Achilles has murdered, once from Achilles who came to love her); the recurrent boast that the Greeks will kill the Trojan men and take their women, as they have taken other women from other cities; the sexual battening on Penelope by the suitors; the savage retribution exacted by Odysseus on those who have wanted to have sex with Penelope, and then on the women of his own household who have had sex with those suitors. This is a core reality in Homer, which finds its explicit echoes in gangland.

Colton Simpson, from South Central LA, was fourteen in 1980. His mentor Smiley, his 'road dog', his running mate, glows to him like a hero, just as Achilles and every Indo-European hero has always glowed:

> When he smiles it's as if the light, the sun behind him, fills me, fills each and every one of us standing there before him.

When the law is no good, the only justice that makes sense is retaliatory, and that is the governing ethic of the Greeks in the *Iliad*. It is the dark heart of the gang on the beach, where *personal affronts attack identity*, where *counter strikes tend to be excessive*, where *minor slights are interpreted as major blows to character*, where warriors *rely on the honor that accrues to those who demonstrate prowess in disputes*, where *honor is accumulated much like real capital and bringing someone down for what he did to you, raises your worth in the eyes of your peers*, where *intolerance earns respect* and *strength is protective*. Every one of those phrases in italics is used by Jacobs and Wright to describe life in the murderous slums of St Louis, Missouri; every one also describes the world of the *Iliad*.

The city itself floats in the half distance, a dream world of order, where the warrior is not constantly under test, where he can rely on those who are around him and who love him. The marginalised gang members, shut out beyond its walls, can only look on with envy and loathing.

Violence in the warrior gang is a means to survive and prosper. Without violence they would shrivel and fade, beaten by the city, by the pointy heads and the Brahmins. Violence is only doing what justice requires them to do. Violence is their destiny. And it should come as no surprise that these gangs must also have their epics. 'No one forgets who was killed where and for what purpose,' the Berkeley sociologist Martín Sánchez-Jankowski has written.

> Some Chicano gang members can tell you who was killed twenty years ago, before they were born, because this history has been passed down to them, these members have attained a degree of immortality, which mutes the fear of death and much of its inhibiting power.

The gangs treasure *kleos aphthiton*, deathless glory, because in their vulnerability and their transience, the way in which there is nothing beyond their bodies and the memory of their actions, they need it more than anyone who is lucky enough to live in the law-shaped, law-embraced, wall-girdled city.

There is a code of conduct within the gang, as there is among the Greeks. Neither rape nor fighting with weapons was allowable within any of the thirty-eight gangs studied by Sánchez-Jankowski. The same kind of sanction exists within the Greek camp, although the natural fissiveness of all gang life is reflected there too. Achilles and his men come within a whisker of leaving Agamemnon's coalition. Nevertheless there is a rawness in modern gang life and their talk – the gang term for a gaping wound is 'a pussy' – from which Homer holds back. The LA gang world takes delight in the explicit elision of sex and violence, dominance and abuse, in a way that Homer buries and dignifies. The latent sexuality that is threaded through the poems never quite breaks surface. Homer can be horrifyingly direct and concrete, but is never ugly, as if the language has been washed and cleansed in the centuries over which the poems evolved. The trash talk of the Greeks on the beach is conveyed in terms that could be heard in the halls at Pylos. The words of the desperate men in South Central LA and East St Louis perform some archaeology on that Homeric language, stripping away its civility, exposing the body and the suffering beneath; but that should not be seen as some kind of return to truth. Homeric truth, the meaning of Homer, is about the integration and fusion of qualities, the acquired wisdom of Homer knowing warrior rage intimately but seeing and hearing it through the words of the city.

For the Greeks, the great urban civilisations of the Mediterranean lay temptingly and glitteringly to the south, and you might wonder why, of all the places they might have chosen for their encounter with the city, Troy became Homer's focus. Is there any evidence that in the years of the Greek arrival, in the centuries around 2000 BC, Troy was the site worth sacking?

It was certainly not the richest, biggest or most powerful city of the Near East. Seen from the churning dynamos of money and power in

Egypt and Mesopotamia, or from the great port cities of the Levant, Troy, on the far north-western corner of Anatolia, can have seemed like little more than a regional outpost of the urban world, a place that did indeed have a citadel and a lower city, but which was nevertheless on the very margins of the urban universe. But seen from the other direction, 'in the eyes of its northern neighbours', as the Oxford and Sheffield archaeologists Andrew and Susan Sherratt memorably put it, 'Troy must have been the brightest light on the horizon'. It sat at one of the great crossroads of antiquity, performing the role later filled by Byzantium-Constantinople-Istanbul, controlling the routes between both the Aegean and the Black Sea and Anatolia and south-east Europe. The persistent north winds that blow across windy Troy, and a steady north–south current through the Dardanelles, meant that no sail-driven ship could make its way north there. Every cargo had to be landed. Every precious object coming west from Anatolia of necessity passed through this four-point pivot. Every movement from the north into the Mediterranean, and every Mediterranean desire to reach the Danube, the gold of Transylvania, the great rivers of the Pontic steppe and the copper mines that lay beyond them, or the metals coming from the Caucasus – all had to come through Troy.

The great Trojan treasures found by Heinrich Schliemann are now in Russia, where they were taken by the Soviets at the end of World War II. The silver and gold vessels, the bronze, the jewellery and the astonishing carved stone axes were buried in Troy perhaps as early as 2400 BC or as late as 1800 BC. Schliemann named what he found 'Priam's Treasure', and from the very beginning was ridiculed for imagining that the levels of the city in whose ashes they emerged, Early Bronze Age Troy II, a thousand years or more before the conventional date of the Trojan War, could have had anything to do with Homer's Trojan king.

But just as at Mycenae, Schliemann's suggestion is worth considering. He had found a burnt layer along with a gate and a tower, and considered them 'the ruins and red ashes of Troy'. In just the same way, his assistant Wilhelm Dörpfeld later settled on Troy VI, destroyed in about 1300 BC, and the Cincinnati archaeologist Carl Blegen came down in favour of Troy VIIa, which came to an end soon after 1200 BC. That remained the modern consensus under the huge German excavations from 1988 to 2003 led by Manfred Korfmann. But, as the British archaeologist Donald Easton has written, these were 'three different sets of material evidence all supposed to prove the same identification and authenticate the same event'. There is nothing to associate Homer with any archaeological remains at Troy. The only pointer towards a date around 1200 BC is the guess made by Herodotus in his history. But his guesses, and those of other classical Greeks, were stabs in the dark at a time when no one knew how to date the distant past. There is certainly no better reason to associate Homer with the Troy of about 1200 BC than with a city a millennium earlier. And if finds are anything to judge by, the later Troys seem to have been poorer than the city Schliemann identified as Priam's. Just as it is possible to imagine that the warriors in the Shaft Graves at Mycenae are themselves not the ancestors of the Homeric heroes but their sons and grandsons, there is nothing inherently unlikely in Schliemann's suggestion that the Trojans of about 2000 BC were living in the city to which the Greeks laid siege.

Nothing found in later levels of Troy can in any way match what Schliemann found here. It was a mass of gold and silver: six gold bracelets, two gold headdresses, one gold diadem, four golden basket-earrings, fifty-six golden shell-earrings, and 8,750 gold beads, sequins and studs.

Sophia Schliemann, aged 22, wearing 'The Jewels of Helen', Athens 1874

The jewellery was probably made in Troy. A great deal of evidence for smelting and casting has been found in the city. But these treasures are also signs of Troy's connections north and south. The tin they used for their bronzes probably came from Afghanistan. The beautiful golden basket-shaped earrings which Schliemann found are identical to others that have been found in Ur in Mesopotamia. There is amber here from Scandinavia, even a bossed bone plaque of a kind found at Castelluccio in Bronze Age Sicily.

Troy was the great entrepôt at the interface of the northern and southern Bronze Age worlds. The only way that Afghan tin and the Mesopotamian ways of working gold could have made their way to Bronze Age Transylvania and Hungary was through the Trojan gateway. No equivalent of Troy existed further north or west. Only the palace centre at Knossos in Crete could rival the extent of Troy in the centuries after 2000 BC. Just as the Vikings and the Crusaders would later lust after the riches of Byzantium and Constantinople, the Greeks longed for Troy.

Another treasure, now in the Boston Museum of Fine Arts, and with an obscure history, provides yet more spectacular hints at what any Greeks, or proto-Greeks, might have found at Troy if they had arrived there in the centuries around 2000 BC. The Boston treasure seems to have come from 'northwest coastal Turkey', the province of Troy itself. It was made in about 2300 BC, and consists of the gold ornaments to be buried with a noble woman: heavy lion-headed gold bangles, sun and moon discs to decorate a dress or headdress, golden pins, hair rings and diadems, finger-rings and gold ribbons.

These objects add to the reality of early Trojan glamour, but the most intriguing aspect of them is that they are probably Egyptian, or made by an Egyptian craftsman who had come to Troy, perhaps bringing Egyptian gold, to decorate a queen of Troy in a way she knew she deserved. He brought with him the motifs of the crouching lions and the lotus flower which were familiar at home in the Egyptian Old Kingdom, and which came north trailing clouds of imperial glory.

Of all the objects that might be thought contemporary with the arrival of the Greeks in the world of cities, none can match the dazzling, hieratic power of the four Trojan hammer-axes which are now in

Moscow. They are wonderful, high-polish, metal-mimicking, power-concentrating objects, three in a kind of jade, one in beautiful, gold-flecked Afghan lazurite. They were stolen by Schliemann in 1890, the last year of his life, from the part of the site at Hissarlik that belonged to his rival and enemy, the English diplomat and antiquarian Frank Calvert.

But the squalor of that recent history is somehow appropriate. Schliemann named his son Agamemnon, and in that choice declared himself the heir of 'the greediest, most possession-loving of men'. You only have to look at these hammer-axes to feel some kind of desire to own them. Their smooth, cool solidity, the creamiest of surfaces in the hardest of materials, was surely designed for display and allure, even for envy. The beauty of violence is embedded in the ritual of their presence. Look at them with any kind of object-lust and you will find yourself looking through the eyes of Agamemnon.

Here in these objects, smuggled out of Turkey by Schliemann, legitimately wanted by the Turks, held on to by the Germans, hidden by the Nazis, taken by the Russians, then hidden again for almost fifty years, now also claimed by the distant heirs of Frank Calvert, you can see, far more than in the dusty, abused walls of Hissarlik, exactly what the marauding Greeks were after. Everything here concentrates a power which it then emanates. This is beauty and exoticism as instruments of control, embodying the core function of a great city, drawing in the rich and strange, then displaying it as a sign of dominance.

If the plain on which the Greeks are camped is the zone of severance and 'the pitiless bronze', the city is the realm of jointness and connection, a place for weaving. In Troy, woven cloth becomes the medium for Homer's story. And in that detail there is an astonishing linkage between the archaeology of Troy and the city portrayed in the *Iliad*. From Schliemann onwards, archaeologists have found powerful evidence of an almost unparalleled scale of cloth-making in the city, at all levels of Trojan society. In the ashes of Troy II, which Schliemann identifed as Priam's city, he found a small round clay box, and in it the remains of a linen fabric decorated with tiny blue-green faience beads and a spindle full of thread. Carl Blegen in the 1930s found hundreds of tiny gold beads around the remains of a loom which had been set up with a half-finished cloth on it. And in Troy as a whole, these early levels of the city have produced over ten thousand clay spindle whorls, small weights attached to a spindle, whose momentum helped the process of spinning. It is a historical truth that Troy spun and wove.

When Helen first appears, the woman at the heart of the story, the Greek who was stolen by Paris the Trojan prince, whose infidelity began the war, who has come to love the Trojans but still longs for her homeland, who feels guilt and passionate desire for Paris but regret for the home and family in Greece she has lost, who is in other words an amalgam of severance and connection, she is in the hall of her house weaving.

On her loom is 'a great cloth' that is called *marmareēn* in some versions, in others *porphyreēn*. These are powerful, laden words, both intimately connected with her history and with the sea. *Marmareos* can mean gleaming or twinkling like sunlit, wind-stirred water; *porphyreos* heaving, or surging like a sea swell, or gushing like blood, or pouring in like death in battle, lurid like a rainbow, which for the Greeks was a portent of bad things to come, or purple like the ink of the cuttlefish. It is as if Homer has concentrated in those phrases the whole sea-tragic story of the war, and Helen's own catastrophe within it. Into the weft of her cloth, of a double fold, she is working many woven images 'of the endless bloody struggles/the horse-taming Trojans and the bronze-armed Greeks/had suffered for her sake at the god of battle's hands'.

Helen, even as she remembers the source of her grief, becomes like Homer the weaver of the tale. As he tells it, she is weaving it. Dressed in shimmering linen, with two of her attendant girls beside her, she goes to the ramparts of the city, where the old men, singing like cicadas in the treetops, look at her and see in her face 'how terribly like the immortal goddesses she is to look on', that pun on the destruction that beauty can bring embedded in the Greek. Then, amidst the horror of war, looking down from the closed ramparts at the armies drawn up below them on the open geometries of the battlefield, Priam the king of Troy does the beautiful thing, drawing Helen near to him, binding her in, weaving the reassurances of civility around her.

Come over here, where I am dear child, and sit down beside me,
To look at your husband of time past, your friends and your people.
I am not blaming you: to me the gods are blameworthy
Who drove upon me this sorrowful war against the Achaians.

This is love as a kind of weaving, a bringing together of the things that war has separated. The shuttle of the weaver travels to and fro, but the blade merely plunges in. The making and maintaining of a city is a multiple act, reflexive and responsive, in the way that the killing of an enemy, the one-way journey of a soul out through the teeth and down to Hades, could never be. That is why the offering that the Trojans make to the great goddess Athene is made of cloth:

> The queen herself went down to the vaulted treasure chamber where her robes were, richly embroidered, the handwork of women from Sidon, on the far eastern shores of the sea, who Paris himself had brought from Sidon, as he sailed over the wide sea on that journey on which he brought back high-born Helen. The best and the thickest with the finest embroideries, which shone like a star, gleaming and brilliant, they took as an offering to Athene.

These are the treasures of the innermost place in Troy, the *thalamos*. These are its essential materials. It is a place of women and children, rich with fineness brought from the east, from the great urban civilisations of which Troy was the furthest outpost, far to the north-west, of their heartland in West Asia and Egypt. Here too, Homer is describing the meeting of worlds. This is what lies at the heart of the distant towers seen from the Greek camp on the shore, and it is here that the poem demonstrates its love and admiration for the marvellousness of women and womanliness.

In the Greek camp, women are traded as commodities. A woman and a tripod are put up in one lot as a prize for a chariot race, where a tripod is thought to be worth twelve oxen and a good serviceable maid-of-all-work four. That is not the atmosphere in Troy, or in the most erotic scene in the *Iliad*, where Hera, the queen of the gods, prepares herself for love. Troy is much closer than the Greeks to the gods. There is a shared atmosphere between the city and Olympus, and the beauty of cloth, the essentially Trojan material, slides easily over into heaven. Alongside the delicious ointments with which Hera burnishes her body, she dresses slowly, seductively. It all happens inside her private chamber on Olympus, the doors closed with a secret bar, a female inwardness. She smooths her body with exotic oils, the perfume drifting down from heaven in a mist of scented rain over the surface of the earth, while around her shoulders she wraps the 'ambrosial robes' that Athene has made for her. They are smooth and satiny, with many figures embroidered on them, and she pins them across her breast with a golden brooch, circling her waist with a sash, before borrowing from Aphrodite, the goddess of love, the magic breastband which has woven into it all the hidden powers of longing and desire, 'the whispered words that can steal the heart from any man'. Weaving knows secrets which the heartless bronze could never hope to grasp.

There is a wariness in Homer about these delicious feminised delights of the city. They are not from the world of the warrior on the plain. When Nastes of the Karians, one of the Trojan allies from elsewhere in Anatolia, turns up for battle like a girl for a party, in golden clothes, 'poor fool', he is soon dead:

> He went down under the hands of the swift-running Ajax
> and fiery Achilles stripped him of his gold in the river.

It is a wet, messy killing as Achilles, the agent of nature, takes his revenge. Alongside pathetic Nastes is Paris, whose lust was the cause of the war, and who is now an empty urban fop, a pretty boy, beautiful, woman-crazed, a Hollywoodised warrior, happier in scented rooms, in bed with his beauty, than out fighting where his city might need him to be. His helmet is embellished with a richly embroidered chin strap, with which he is very nearly choked to death by a Greek, before a god rescues him and whisks him away to his boudoir. Homeric distrust of the potential for unmanliness in the city, whose beauties and order are nevertheless deeply desirable, is never far beneath the surface.

These polarities sharpen as the war deepens. The Greeks become increasingly animalistic. The Trojans are increasingly identified with the great walls that will save them from the savages at their gates. Group battle scenes give way to a sequence of individual tragedies. The shedding of blood is now close-focus. Dark underlayers bloom, and a persistent suggestion heaves up, just beneath the surface, that these men are cannibals.

Something of this has been there from the start. Agamemnon has said that the Greeks should not hesitate to kill Trojan babies. Zeus accused Hera of wanting to walk in through the gates of Troy and eat Priam and his children and the other people there, to take them raw, to glut her anger. But by the middle of the poem, the levels of body-abuse have steepened and animality has entered the battle.

> Idomeneus stabbed Erymas straight through the mouth with the
>   pitiless
> bronze, so that the metal spearhead smashed its way clean up
>   through
> the brain, and the white bones splintered,
> And the teeth were shaken out as he hit him and both eyes filled up
> With blood, and as he gaped he spurted blood through his nostrils
> And his mouth, and death's dark cloud closed in about him.

The Myrmidons, the men Achilles has brought here from Phthia, are

> like wolves, who tear at raw flesh,
> in whose hearts battle-rage knows no end,
> who have brought down a great antlered stag in the mountains,
> and then feed on him, till their lips and cheeks are running with
>   blood,
> and who then move off in a pack, the crowd of them,
> to drink from a spring of dark water,
> lapping with their narrow tongues along the black edge of the water,
> belching up the clotted blood, their bellies full and their hearts
>   unshaken.

The Greeks begin to lose the fight. Achilles refuses to stir from his tent. His beloved Patroclus takes his armour and wears it so that the Trojans might think Achilles himself has returned to the battle. The trick works, the Trojans take fright and Patroclus starts to push them back from the ships. But he goes too far; Hector kills him and he lies dead in the dust. Standing over his body, in the midst of battle, Hector makes the great statement of the city against the plain.

> Patroclus, you thought perhaps of devastating our city,
> Of stripping from the Trojan women their day of freedom
> and dragging them off in ships to the beloved land of your fathers.
> Fool! Now vultures will eat your body raw.
> Idiot! Not even Achilles could save you now.

The armies fight over the body of Patroclus with a new and horrible intensity, a struggle that lasts for hundreds of lines. In the fight, the beautiful Trojan Euphorbus is killed by Menelaus, and his lovely hair, braided with gold and silver, like the body of a beautiful wasp, is soaked and clotted with blood, civilisation drenched in war. Menelaus now, with the battle frenzy in him, is like a mountain lion that has caught a delicious cow, the best cow, and is 'mauling the kill, gulping down the guts that are inward'. Hector strips the armour from Patroclus, the glorious armour which Achilles had lent him, and drags at the body, meaning to cut the head from the shoulders 'and give the rest to the dogs of Troy'. He promises huge rewards to those who can drag back to the city the now naked body of Patroclus, who has become his own flesh, stripped of meaning, nothing but meat for the dogs and birds.

The Trojan warrior Hippothoos, meaning Quickhorse, tries to get the straps of his shield around the tendons in Patroclus's ankle so that he can pull him back to the dog-feast in the city, but Ajax shafts him in the head, and Quickhorse's brain 'oozed out from the wound along the socket of the spear, all mingled with blood'. In this horror flensing-yard scene, a Greek dies with a spear under the collarbone, a Trojan with a sword in the guts 'so that he clawed at the dust with his fingers', and another Greek with a spear in the liver under the midriff.

The desperate struggle is for the flesh of Patroclus, simply to possess his physical remains, the grisliest possible tug-of-war, stretching the body in the way people pull and stretch at an ox-hide to make usable leather of it,

with so many pulling, until the bull's hide is stretched out smooth,
so the men of both sides in a cramped space tugged at the body
in both directions; and the hearts of the Trojans were hopeful
to drag him away to Ilion, those of the Achaeans
to get him back to the hollow ships.

On different warriors, the blood runs from their hands and feet, 'as on
some lion who has eaten a bullock'. Menelaus is like a mosquito

who though it is slapped away from a man's skin, even
so, for the taste of human blood, persists in biting him.

Hector, hanging on to the body of Patroclus like 'a tawny lion who
cannot be frightened away from a carcass he has in his claws', is
desperate to pull the body back to Troy so that he can 'cut the head
from the soft neck and set it on sharp stakes'. This is not your elegant,
noble, neoclassical Homer. This is rawness itself. Bloodthirsty Ares, the
god of war, the metaphor not yet dead, has become the governing force
in a battlefield which wants more than anything else to drink human
blood.

This is the environment into which Achilles now drives, grief-mad
from the death of Patroclus. He will not eat, as civilised men sit down
and eat, but wants to feast on the body of Hector. Like a man with a
rifle at a fairground booth, he pops out death to twenty-three Trojans
in a row: a spear in the middle of the head, a spear through the side of
the helmet, another in the head, one in the back, one in the back and
out through the navel, one in the neck, one in the knees with a spear
and then finishing him off with a sword, one with a spear, another with
a sword, one with a sword in the liver, a pike in one ear and out the
other ear, a sword in the head, a sword in the arm then a spear in the
arm, beheading with a sword 'and the marrow gushed from the neckbone',
a spear in the belly and a spear in the back, and then seven men whose
deaths are remembered only in their names.

As he wearies momentarily of killing, he takes twelve young men alive,
to sacrifice on the pyre of Patroclus:

He dragged them up on the banks, dazed like fawns,
lashed their hands behind them with well-cut straps –
their own belts that cinched their billowing war-shirts,
gave them to friends to lead away to the beaked ships.
And back he whirled, insane to hack more flesh.

He is beyond humanity now, and has become 'an unlooked for evil'. His sweetness and capacity for love have left him. To the pitiable Lycaon he talks with all the reason of a madman.

Now there is not one who can escape death, if the gods send
Him against my hand in front of Ilion, not one
Of all the Trojans and above all the children of Priam.
So, friend, you die too. Why moan about it?
Patroclus is dead, who was better by far than you are.
Do you not see what a man I am, how huge, how splendid
And born of a great father, and the mother who bore me immortal?

Everyone must die, so why don't you die? 'Die on, all of you,' he tells the Trojans, 'till we come to the sacred city of Ilion, you in flight, and me killing you from behind.'

Even as the universe of the battlefield becomes a careless and pitiless place, the allure and goodness of the besieged city become ever more precious. This is where the grand spatial geometry of the poem comes to its sharpest point. Achilles is the untrammelled world of the plain. 'I will not leave off my killing of the proud Trojans,' he says, 'until I have penned them in their city.' He is polarising the world he controls until they are indeed all running and shuffling towards the high, wide walls Poseidon built for them – all except Hector, their champion, who must remain out on the plain with his killer.

Homer binds the Trojans to the physical facts of their city. Priam, Hector's father, the human embodiment of Troy's virtues, becomes co-terminous with the city's walls and gates:

The aged Priam had taken his place on the god-built bastion,
And looked out and saw gigantic Achilles, where before him

The Trojans fled in the speed of their confusion, no war strength
In them. He groaned and descended to the ground from the bastion
And beside the wall set in motion the glorious guards of the gateway:
'Hold the gates wide open in your hands, so that our people
In their flight can get into the city, for here is Achilles
Close by stampeding them.'

This is the Iliadic confrontation at its sharpest. The city gates must close
the Trojans in while Achilles is out in the plain, 'fierce with the spear,
strong madness in his heart and violent after glory'. Everything in the
Iliad comes into pincer-intimacy in these lines. The warriors join their
'beloved parents, wives and children' inside the gates,

For they dared wait no longer outside the walls and the city

because on the plain Achilles is running free and dangerous across the
open ground. Only Hector, the isolated Trojan, remains outside the walls,
'shackled by destiny', awaiting the climactic meeting with the inhuman
violence of the gang-man Achilles.

Metaphorical geography has the poem in its grip here. This is not the
meeting of Achilles and Hector; it is the deathly confrontation of two
ways of understanding the world. The key words clang through the
poetry: 'city', 'battlements', 'walls', 'Ilion', 'gates', 'crowded', 'city', 'wall' and
'city' again, all within twenty lines of the beginning of Book 22, and all
set against that other world, the flatlands, the open plain, the *pedion*,
over which Achilles runs like a prize-winning chariot horse, half-human,
gleaming, looking like the Dog Star, a beacon of hate, sheathed in metal,
the bronze in which he seems to be made shining brighter than any
other star, a being radiant with horror, bringing evil and pain to men.

Homer never seems more real or more terrible than when Priam
stands on his walls and talks pleadingly down to his son Hector standing
outside the gates below him. Hector is terrifyingly alone, when the
understanding of Trojans is that community is safety. 'Come into the
walls, my child,' Priam says to him, 'so that you might save Trojan men
and Trojan women.' And then the old king makes a speech of
Shakespearean poignancy and power:

> I have looked upon evils
> And seen my sons destroyed and my daughters dragged away
> 　　captive
> And the chambers of marriage wrecked and the innocent children
> 　　taken
> And dashed to the ground in the hatefulness of war, and the wives
> Of my sons dragged off by the accursed hands of the Achaians
> And myself last of all, my dogs in front of my doorway
> Will rip me raw, after some man with stroke of the sharp bronze
> Spear, or with spearcast, has torn the life out of my body;
> Those dogs I raised in my halls to be at my table, to guard my
> Gates, who will lap my blood in their savagery and anger
> And then will lie down in my courts. For a young man all is
> 　　decorous
> When he is cut down in battle and torn with the sharp bronze, and
> 　　lies
> Dead, and though dead all that shows about him is beautiful; but
> 　　when an old man is dead and down, and the dogs mutilate
> The grey head and the grey beard and the parts that are secret
> This for all sad mortality is the sight most pitiful.

The dogs eating his genitals, like blood on the gold-laced hair, is Priam's vision of the triumph of Achilles, the triumph of the gang over the city, the anarchy of violence over the generations of people and the bonds which tie them. Hector's mother, Hecabe, from the parapet above, holds out her breasts to him, bared and open. 'Sweet branch,' she calls to him, 'child of my bearing', 'look upon these and obey. From inside the wall beat off this grim man.'

Hector's sense of honour, his debt to his city, will not allow him to go inside 'the lovely citadel', and the fatal race begins. He and Achilles run round and round the walls, Hector in flight, Achilles in pursuit. It is like a dream, Homer says, when your running brings you no closer to your prey, nor takes you further from your terror-pursuer; and it is a dream hell out on the plain, where there can only ever be one destiny. Sometimes Hector shelters under the walls, but Achilles gets between him and the wall 'and forces him to turn back into the plain'.

With unrelenting consistency, Homer applies his geography: city is goodness and connection, plain is horror and terror; city is Hector's weakness, plain Achilles's strength; city is the realm of the Trojan families, their women and children, while the plain belongs to Achilles alone – during this climax of grief the other Greeks have disappeared from view.

When finally Hector pauses, tricked by Athene, Achilles catches up with him and they talk. Achilles plunges for cannibalism. I want, he says,

> to hack your meat away and eat it raw for the things that
> you have done to me.

There can be no surprise. Achilles spears Hector in the soft part of the neck, just where the armour opens a little white mouth of skin, 'and clean out through the tender neck went the point'. And once he has killed him, the abuse to which he subjects Hector's body is to drag him *fast* behind his chariot. Hector's hair and head are tumbled and wrecked in the dust, and this physical action is the emblem of the gang-man's triumph, the imposition on the man of the city of the dirt of the plain.

With Hector's death the city's fabric is irreparably torn. Hector's mother casts aside her 'shining veil'. His wife, Andromache, does not at first hear the news. She is weaving a cloth in the inner room of her high house, a red folding robe with figures embroidered on it, not unlike the cloth Helen had been working so many thousands of lines ago. Andromache calls out to her handmaidens to prepare a bath for Hector, for when he comes back from the fighting. Then she hears the mourning and wailing of the other women, and the shuttle with which she had been weaving drops from her hand. Running to the ramparts, she sees Hector's body dragged around the city walls, his head in the dirt, Achilles triumphant. She collapses, 'gasping the life breath out of her', while all the woven things fall from her, the circlets around her head and breast, the cap she is wearing, even as the threads of Troy tighten around her and 'her husband's sisters and the wives of his brothers held her up among them'. In their house, she then remembers, there are all kinds of clothing, 'fine-textured and pleasant, wrought by the hands of women', ready for Hector. 'All of these I will burn up in the fire's blazing,' Andromache says. 'They are no use to you.' The woven and the severed: the heart of Homer's meaning.

The *Iliad* might have ended there, with the victory of the plain over the city, but it doesn't. Troy is about love, children and home. Its lifeblood is in the virtues of human community, of not claiming the ultimate against your enemy but finding it in you to say that whatever he has done, humanity is shared. Troy is a desire for wholeness, a desire that wholeness might survive the necessary violence, that there is no 'tragedy of necessity'.

The poem ends before Troy falls, but Homer orchestrates something subtler and richer than the hideousness of any military triumph. After Achilles kills Hector, the whole of the city goes into horrified despair and mourning. The women wail, the men cover themselves with dung scraped up from the streets. This moment of hopelessness is the pit of the poem. Achilles is still threatening to eat Hector's body raw. It looks as if everything the city enshrines means nothing in the teeth of the Greeks' triumph. Priam resolves to go to their camp across the plain to find Achilles and beg him for the body of his son.

The old king slowly prepares and gathers carts full of the best that Troy can offer, including beautiful cloths: robes, mantles, blankets, cloaks and tunics, as if wanting to drown Achilles in the woven. But that is the point. Priam is going to take the city out into the plain. That has been the place where in book after book, death after death, the wrong thing has been done. Priam's journey is a kind of healing laid across that theatre of horror. He travels slowly, at night, with his mule carts: no heroic northern chariots here. He comes at last into the shelter of Achilles's camp, and without announcement the old king kneels down next to Achilles, clasps his knees and 'kisses his hands, the terrible man-slaughtering hands, the hands that had shed so much blood, the blood of his sons'. That old man's kiss is the moment of arrival. Achilles thinks of his own father in Phthia, and comes to understand something beyond the world he has so far inhabited. Both men give way to grief.

> Priam wept freely
> For man-killing Hector, throbbing, crouching
> Before Achilles's feet as Achilles wept himself
> Now for his father, now for Patroclus
> And their sobbing rose and fell in the house.

Food is cooked for them, mutton souvlaki:

> They reached out for the good things that lay at hand
> And when they had put aside desire for food and drink
> Priam the son of Dardanus gazed at Achilles marveling
> now at the man's beauty, his magnificent build –
> face-to-face he seemed a deathless god . . .
> and Achilles gazed and marveled at Dardan Priam,
> beholding his noble looks, listening to his words.

They gaze at each other in silence, and that exchange of admiring looks is the *Iliad*'s triumph. Priam has brought the virtues of the city into Achilles's heart. Hector will now be returned to his father and will be buried with dignity outside the city. In that way, Troy has won the war. Achilles, the man from the plains, has absorbed the beauty of Priam's wisdom, of his superhuman ability to admire the man who has killed his sons, and from the mutuality and courage of that wisdom, its blending of city and plain, a vision of the future might flower. Achilles will soon be dead, Troy will soon be broken, the Trojan men will soon be slaughtered, Priam among them, horribly murdered by Achilles's own son, their women abused and enslaved, but here, in poetry, in passing, a better world is momentarily – or in fact everlastingly – seen.

ELEVEN

Homer's Mirror

IT IS POSSIBLE – just – to look at Homer the other way round, and to hear the story of the Greeks arriving in the Mediterranean not as the Greeks told it in Homer but as the inhabitants of the literate, bureaucratic, authoritarian civilisations of the Mediterranean littoral told it themselves.

Nothing survives which describes Achilles or Odysseus directly, but there is a handful of Egyptian, Hittite and Hebrew texts which deal with people and habits occupying precisely the culture space of Homer's Greeks: northern Indo-European warriors arriving in a world where they do not belong, where they seem like barbarians, people who don't quite know how to behave. These unsympathetic versions of the Homeric story are strangely unsettling. Suddenly here is Achilles as his enemies might have seen him; Odysseus described by the smart, rich, complacent city-folk; Greek heroism as gang hooliganism; the Greek habit of woman-theft as nothing but rape; the beautiful volubility of the Homeric warrior looking pompous and absurd. Here, in this new light, are the Homeric tales with 'Homer' – the dignity, understanding and tragic beauty of the poems – stripped out of them.

The Tale of Sinuhe is a short poetic biography of an Egyptian civil servant. It is a miraculous survival, the oldest version preserved on a re-used roll of papyrus, buried in the tomb of a government official in the Egyptian city of Thebes on the west bank of the Nile in about 1800 BC. Probably looted from the tomb, it found its way to a London auction room in AD 1843, and versions of it are now preserved on fragments of papyrus in the British Museum and in Berlin. It had been popular in

Egypt up to about 1000 BC, but until the Victorian Egyptologists deciphered it, no one had read Sinuhe's story for three thousand years.

It is from almost exactly the moment the Greeks were arriving in the Mediterranean, piratical, violent men, hungry for the gold that soon enough would appear on the bodies and in the graves at Mycenae, but comes from a frame of mind perfectly opposed to theirs. This elegant, melancholic verse novel from the richest culture in the ancient world may be the contemporary of the first versions of the *Iliad* and the *Odyssey*, but it loves nothing about them.

Sinuhe's Egypt is a huge state structure. He is part of the great service industry attending to the god-pharaoh's well-being, a court official – 'a writing-man' is the Egyptian term – and a bureaucrat. It was the best possible job he could have. 'Be a scribe,' a contemporary papyrus instructed its young readers. 'Your limbs will be sleek, your hands will grow soft. You will go forth in white clothes, honoured, with courtiers saluting you.'

The Homeric assumption that suffering and conflict lie at the heart of existence, that life is essentially uncomfortable, is simply absent from Sinuhe's world. His life is framed around repetitiveness, stability, normality, precision and security. Everything is measured and known. His tale begins on 'the 7th Day of the 3rd Month of the Nile Flood Season, in the 20th year of the Pharaoh's reign'. The rough estimates of Homeric time, the wide, veering guesses at the date of the Homeric stories, the generations that pass unrecorded – all that belongs to a different conceptual universe. For Sinuhe – whatever the historical truth – the pharaohs had ruled as far back in time as it was possible to imagine. Peace had prevailed, one pharaoh had succeeded another, cosmically great, unaddressably powerful, each handing the throne to his successor in a single direct linear sequence. The heart of happiness for these Egyptians was submission to that authority. The pharaoh 'makes those born with him plentiful', Sinuhe says. 'He is unique, god-given. How joyful this land, since he has ruled. He extends his borders. He is the lord of kindness, great of sweetness. Through love he has conquered. His city loves him more than its own members.' Set that alongside the description of Agamemnon and his gift-giving in the *Iliad* and you suddenly see him as a would-be pharaoh, a provincial satrap with ambitions beyond his reach, vulgarly attempting pharaonic status in the face of Achillean integrity.

The life of the Egyptian poor was miserable. They could expect to die when they were thirty-five, thousands lived in workhouses, obliged to sweat out their days in forced labour camps for the pharaonic regime and its monumental ambitions. But above them a bureaucratic middle class, Sinuhe's class – perhaps 1 per cent of the population was literate – managed the culture of continuity. In their linen-dressed elegance, the sense of overwhelming crisis and disruption which colours the deepest levels of the Homeric world was not even considered. Life was continuity. There was no need to be heroic, nor did the Greek hunger for honour play any part. For the ancient Egyptians, goodness consisted of service to pharaonic authority. As there was no distinction between that authority and the government of the universe, this life could be considered a kind of ante-room to heaven. The more silent and stable it could be made, the better.

Sinuhe loves the white linen he wears every day, and all the order in the Residence where he works. He is no self-sufficient hero. No existential crisis, or anxiety about his individual identity or destiny, ever pursues him. Sinuhe is a 'Follower' and 'True Acquaintance' of the pharaoh. His life is defined by the authority he serves. One of his tasks is to look after the pharaoh's children, but at the moment his story begins, this steady, beautifully organised life is destroyed by a flash of panic. He hears something, a report of the old pharaoh's murder in the palace. He thinks he should not have heard it, and worried in this totalitarian state that he might somehow be caught up in the repercussions, or even held responsible, he runs for his life, away from Egypt, north to the borders of Syria, and on across them, travelling at night, hiding at the edges of fields until at last he comes to a part of the world called Upper Retjenu.

It is the Egyptian name for Lebanon, and maybe for the places beyond it. But Retjenu as a word is not a Semitic form; it does not belong in the Near East. It is Indo-European, probably from the language spoken by the Lycians, warrior inhabitants of south-west Anatolia, known to Homer as allies of the Trojans. Sinuhe, in other words, has found himself far out in the wilds surrounded by the warrior culture of the north. He has arrived in the land described by Homer. It was not the sort of world he was used to. It was a good country, he says, with figs and grapes, more wine than water, honey and oil, with all kinds of fruit on its trees. Barley was there, and emmer-wheat, and 'numberless were its cattle of all kinds'. It was called Iaa, the 'rushy place', damp, fertile, rich in pastures, a million miles from the Egypt into which he had been born.

The experience was horrifying at first. 'This is the taste of death,' Sinuhe says, panicking at the disorder around him. All the calm of Egypt had gone. But then Sinuhe fell in with a chieftain, a warrior prince, a Diomedes or Sarpedon, and the chieftain did what heroes do in these circumstances: gave him plenty of cooked meat and wine, and delicious roast birds. They went hunting together, and from the great herds of cattle without which the Indo-European chieftains felt naked he gave Sinuhe 'milk in every cooked dish'. The mark of Homeric civilisation: beef in white sauce.

And so Sinuhe went native. He abandoned his white linen for armour. He turned warrior. 'My children became heroes/Each man subjugating his tribe.' Battle, which was absent from the life of an Egyptian bureaucrat, something that happened out here in the rawness of life on the frontiers, away from the deep calm of the central Egyptian state, now became the norm. He plundered cattle and carried off men and women as slaves. He killed again and again as the Indo-European hero must do, and in the heart of his lord and chieftain he 'attained high regard. He loved me, knowing my valour.'

Then the crisis: the naturally fissive atmosphere of the Indo-European warrior band broke into the open, and a situation not unlike the opening scenes of the *Iliad* suddenly erupted.

A hero of Retjenu came to provoke me in my tent;
he was an unmatched champion who had conquered all the land.
He said he would fight me, he planned to rob me, and had a mind
    to plunder my cattle, on the advice of his tribe.

Honour, rivalry, dignity, the brutally assertive self, the demands of violence, contempt for communality: suddenly you are in the world of the Greeks outside Troy, but portrayed in an Egyptian tale. It doesn't take much to imagine the shudder of anxiety in listeners at a party in Thebes one balmy evening in 1850 BC, just as the sun was setting over the western desert and the shadows were lengthening over the Nile. Did people out there really behave like this?

Sinuhe accepted the challenge, triumphed over the nameless hero, shooting him in the neck with an arrow and then killing him with his own axe, shouting his own vaunting war-cry over the fallen hero's back. But he was still an Egyptian, asking, in one of the most resonant questions for this moment in human history: 'What can establish the papyrus on the mountain?' That is also the great Homeric question. What place can civilisation have in a world dominated by the brute geological facts of violence and dominance? How fragile are the fibres of papyrus when set against the great rock-thrusts of the heroic world? Could these two ways of being ever be compatible?

Sinuhe was so successful as an Indo-European warrior that he ended up with more cows than he knew what to do with. Even so, an everlasting longing for Egypt lingered in his heart. 'What matters more than my being buried in the land where I was born?' he asked. Somehow, the pharaoh heard of Sinuhe's longing, and soon enough an invitation arrived from him for Sinuhe to return to Egypt, where he would be honoured and forgiven. Sinuhe gave his property to his eldest son in Retjenu, and returned to Egypt where he 'touched the ground between the sphinxes' and came face to face with the god-king he revered.

'Act against yourself no more,' the pharaoh tells him, and as he hears the words, Sinuhe feels himself re-absorbed into the fabric of Egyptian society. The king says 'he shall not fear', and Sinuhe is recreated as a courtier. He abandons himself to the happiness of the king's grace, prostrating himself before the pharaoh. Here in 'the enduring security of the state' is the beauty of order to which he is at last allowed to return. He is rewarded with the things he has been dreaming of all the years he was away in the Homeric world:

> I was appointed to the house of a prince
> And costly things in it, with a bathroom in it,
> And mirrors,
> Clothes of royal linen
> Myrrh and kingly fine oil
> With officials whom the king loved in every room

And every serving man at his duty.
The years were made to pass from my limbs
I became clean shaven and my hair was combed
I was clad in fine linen
I was anointed with fine oil
I slept in a bed.
It is his majesty who has caused this to be done.
There is no other lowly man for whom the like was done.
I was in the favours of the king's giving
Until the day of landing came.

The 'day of landing' was the Egyptian phrase for the moment of death, the time when a human being at last achieves the goal of a perfect life, and Sinuhe's return to Egypt is like a return to heaven. For all his adventuring, Egypt had originally made him what he was. Only there could he be himself again, and only by submitting to the Egyptian powers could his day of landing be good.

Our Odyssean frame of mind looks on that moment of Sinuhe's re-absorption into his native world not as a scene of triumph but of diminution, a surrender of the vital if agonised self to the emasculated certainties of a beautifully bathed, shaved, linen-coated 'Follower'. Was it really worth exchanging his florid Indo-European hair and beard, that fullness of self-assertion, for the bland comfort-soup of a happy 'landing'? Or are we, as Homer's heirs, merely crisis-addicted? Why not accept with Sinuhe, and the profoundly impressive longevity of Egyptian civilisation, that the world of white linen and pharaonic tyranny is a better place than the discomforts of Retjenu and the threatening behaviour of 'heroes'? Are those heroes not in the end exactly as the Egyptians saw them, little more than human hyenas, repetitively needing to establish their sexual, genetic dominance of the pack? Surely human life has more to it than the Homeric tragedy of necessity? Or to put it in a typically Sinuhesque way: is that necessity really necessary? Why not accept the virtues of modesty and the realities of power?

No Homeric character could ever have behaved like Sinuhe, or have thought that his destiny was so bound up with the blessing the pharaoh and his court could bestow on him. Sinuhe ends up with a single answer:

it is better to be at home, to submit, to recognise that power is god. Across the whole of the *Iliad* and the *Odyssey*, there is nothing singular like this. The Homeric view of the world is essentially traumatic and multiple. All is in contention; power is something to be fought for, not accepted; the gods themselves are at each other's throats; nature may stand there as a beautiful background, but it too is drenched in conflict and pain. The claims of individual triumph can never be reconciled with the claims of communal love and society. We live in the great and eternal war between those principles, *Timē* and *Aretē*, honour and virtue, self and other. Achilles sees that war as the source of human tragedy, Odysseus as the opportunity for self-advancement. And beyond them both stands Homer, the great voice of understanding, regarding us all, refusing to decide.

The Tale of Sinuhe is a mirror image of Homer, exploring the polarities of city and warrior-world from the opposite direction. But there are also parallels between them. Sinuhe could be seen as the Egyptian Odysseus, the hero thrust out into the wilds, gaining wisdom there, doing well but longing for home, finally returning, full of apprehension, to the place he longs to call home. And in one marvellous detail, they are clearly part of the same thought-world. Both, on reaching home, become themselves again by having a bath.

The bath for Homer is always a gesture of welcome, the physical metaphor for the domestic embrace. Perhaps the most famous bath in Greek antiquity is the one in which Clytemnestra murdered Agamemnon on his return to Mycenae after the war. But that is not a Homeric story: it is the bleak invention of Aeschylus in the *Oresteia*. For Homer, whether it is the bathing of Odysseus after battle, or Telemachus on his visit to Nestor at Pylos, the bath is always beautiful and integrative, a moment of absorption.

Intriguingly, there is nothing uniquely Greek about this. The Homeric word for a bath, *asaminthos*, like hyacinth and labyrinth, comes from an unknown, non-Indo-European language spoken in the Mediterranean before the Greeks arrived there. It may have been the language of Minoan Crete. The unwashed Greeks coming down from the north borrowed the word as they borrowed the thing and the habit. The story of the hero returning home to the deliciousness of a bath is distributed all across the eastern Mediterranean and Mesopotamia. It is a shared symbol of homeliness and wellbeing. Gilgamesh, the ancient king of Uruk in south Iraq, who had also been journeying in the wilderness, in search of wisdom, cleansed its filth from his body as he came home to the city,

> washing his long hair clean as snow in water. . . throwing off his furs and letting the sea carry them away, so that his fair body could be seen. Let the band around his head be replaced with a new one. Let him be clad with a garment, as clothing for his nakedness. When he gets to his city, when he finishes his journey, may his clothes show no sign of age, but still be quite new.

When Jacob returns in Genesis to Canaan, he tells his household first to 'wash yourselves and change your clothes', because in this shared Near-Eastern culture, the thought-world to which the Homeric Greeks were so anxious to belong, no homecoming could be complete without the cleanness and sense of renewal which a bath can give you. Sinuhe, Gilgamesh, Jacob and Odysseus all soaked themselves in the same delicious soapiness.

You can still find beautiful baths in the palaces on Crete and at Pylos, Mycenae and Tiryns on the mainland. Some are adorned with fish and the wavy lines of comforting water. Among the austere stoniness of those excavated sites, the baths become emblems of the longing to which the Homeric mind was prey. Nothing could be more inviting, more soaked in the desire for peace and civilisation in a troubled world. They are the opposite term to Odysseus's sufferings on the open sea. Here the water will merely lap at his limbs, the giant sea-bream on the walls of the bath are his cohabitants in their shared springwater pool, the painted sea-waves no more than the memory of grief.

So it is when Odysseus has at last made the frightening witch Circe submit to his will, he can allow her maid servants, the 'daughters of the springs and the woods and the sacred rivers which run down to the sea', to prepare him a bath. One of these girls

> brought in the water and lit a roaring fire under the big cauldron so that the water grew hot. When the bright copper was boiling, she

eased me into the bath and washed me with water from the great cauldron, hot and cold mixed as I desired, allowing it to run over my head and shoulders, washing the pain and weariness from my heart and limbs. When she had washed me and rubbed me with oil, she dressed me in a warm fleece and a shirt around my shoulders and led me to the hall, where she had me sit on a silver-studded chair with a stool to rest my feet.

But there is this difference: lying in their baths, Sinuhe, Gilgamesh and Jacob could all know they were returning to a home they could trust. Singularity and obviousness clusters around their bathrooms. But Homer is subtler than the Egyptian, Mesopotamian or Hebrew story-tellers, because complexity and multiplicity, the fusion and stirring of meanings, is central to his purpose. Odysseus, when slipping into the delicious, erotic balm of Circe's bath, is still years and miles from home, his 'mind wandering, far away, lost in grim forebodings'. Circe is only the illusion of home and love, the wish-fulfilment version to which the traveller will always succumb. Her bath is a taunt and a punishment. Odysseus – and his listeners – must wait for the real thing.

A sidelight equivalent to Sinuhe's is thrown on the Homeric Greeks in the astonishing archive of 30,000 cuneiform clay tablets that has been recovered from the capital of the Hittites at Hattusa, near Bogaskale in central Anatolia. Contrasts and parallels abound here too. The Hittites were another Indo-European people who came south into Anatolia during the centuries after 2000 BC, infiltrating and then taking over the territory of the non-Indo-European Hatti, finally pushing on their southern frontier against the fringes of the great Mesopotamian powers and even the Egyptian empire.

Such close contacts with the ancient civilisations to the south meant that the Hittites adopted the literate, urbanising habits of the Near East far earlier than the Greeks. By the time of the Shaft Graves at Mycenae, the Hittites were already running an enormous, bureaucratically organised empire, with a network of military roads strung across it, stretching from Lebanon to the shores of the Aegean.

They kept their records in both Hittite and Akkadian, the Babylonian language that had become the *lingua franca* of diplomacy and government across the whole region from central Anatolia to the Tigris and the mouths of the Nile. The clay cuneiform tablets found at Hattusa are the file copies retained by the Hittite foreign office after the original treaties, usually on bronze or occasionally silver or iron tablets, had been sent to the other parties.

They give glimpses of an embracing power-world which carries echoes of life in the palaces at Troy, the fifty sons and sons-in-law gathered around Priam, the overwhelming nature of inheritance and the sense of greatness rippling down from its kingly source. The quasi-medieval atmosphere at these gatherings could not be further from the high-risk anarchy barely an inch below the surface at any meeting of the Greek chieftains. One Hittite treaty, as its tablet records, was concluded in a great and ceremonial meeting

> in the city of Urikina in the presence of Crown Prince Nerikkaili; Prince Tashmi-Sharumma; Prince Hannutti; Prince Huzziya; Ini-Teshshup, king of the land of Carchemish; Ari-Sharrumma, king of the land of Isuwa; Amar-Mushen, uriyanni; Halpa-ziti, commander of the troops of the right; Prince Heshni; Prince Tattamaru; Prince Uppara-muwa, overseer of the golden grooms; Prince Uhha-ziti; Sahurunuwa, chief of the wooden-tablet scribes; Hattusa-Kurunta, general; Prince Tarhunta-piya; Lugal dLamaa, commander of the troops of the left; Ali-ziti, chief of the palace servants; Tuttu, chief of the storehouse; Palla, lord of the city of Hurma; Walwa-ziti, chief of the scribes; Alalimi, chief of the cupbearers; Kammaliya, chief of the cooks; and Mahhuzzi, chief of the offering officials.

Whether it is Victorian India, Tenochtitlan, medieval Bohemia, shogun Japan, the world of *The Leopard* or Bronze Age Anatolia, this is the air breathed in any court, dense with rank, title, glamour, precedence and surely a hint, here and there, of what is called, even now in palaces, Red Carpet Fever: excitement at being connected with the royal.

That self-importance surfaces in Homer in the overbrimming superciliousness of the Phaeacians, condescendingly welcoming the shipwrecked seafarer Odysseus to Alcinous's regal halls. The Phaeacians 'never suffer strangers gladly'. They don't like him much, nor he them. Even here, as he is accepting their hospitality, Homer gives him the traditional epithet he shares with Achilles and Ares the god of war: *ptoliporthos Odysseus* – city-ravaging Odysseus.

They guess he might be captain of a ship full of men who are *prēktēres* – an interesting word, with its origins in the verb for 'to do', meaning that Odysseus comes over to the Phaeacians not as a nobleman who can play athletic games but as the leader of a band of practical, pragmatic practisers of things, merchants in other words, dealers, or as Robert Fagles translated it 'profiteers', freebooters who blurred the boundary between trader and pirate.

Nothing irks Odysseus more powerfully than the suggestion that he is merely a sea-robber or tradesman. Is he not a hero? Has he not fought at Troy? Has he not suffered at sea? But the suspicion won't go away. When he and his crew find themselves facing Polyphemus the Cyclops, the same idea recurs. 'Strangers, who are you?' the Cyclops asks them. 'Where do you come from, sailing over the sea-ways? Are you trading? Or are you roaming wherever luck takes you over the sea? Like pirates?'

Perhaps this is a reflection in Homer of a reality which the poems do their best to conceal. Odysseus and the other Greek chieftains might think of themselves as noble kings, the fit subjects for epic. Homer does its best to portray them as that. The civilised states of the Mediterranean saw them as anything but. What were they but the 'much-wandering pirates' Odysseus sometimes talks about, taking what they could from the wealth of the world around them, hugely status-rich in their own eyes, virtually status-less in the eyes of those they were coming to rob? It is exactly how Odysseus himself describes his behaviour as he leaves Troy. 'From Ilium the wind carried me,' he tells the Phaeacians, 'and brought me to the Cicones.' This was a tribe, allied to the Trojans, who lived at Ismarus on the shore of the Aegean, somewhere north of Samothrace. 'There I destroyed the city,' he goes on quite straightfor-wardly, using a term to mean that nothing was left, 'and killed the men. And from the city we took their wives and many possessions, and divided it among us, so that as far as I could manage, no man would be cheated of an equal share.' It is one of the moments in which Homer coolly reveals the limitations of Odysseus's mind. Our hero thinks he is telling his hosts how excellently he behaved, ensuring that unlike Agamemnon he did not mistreat his men. But he is blind to the significance of the actions preceding this exemplary fairness, the piratical destruction of an entire city and the enslaving of its women.

The same uncertain status of the pirate-king lies behind one of Odysseus's most famous sleights of hand. He and his men are suffering at the hands of the Cyclops. The Cyclops wants to know who Odysseus is. In his answers, he says that his name is 'Nobody'. The Greek for that is either *outis*, which sounds a little like *Odysseus* if spoken by a drunk or slack-jawed giant; or *mētis*, which also sounds like the Greek word for cleverness, craftiness, skill or a plot. When Polyphemus calls for help, the other Cyclopes ask who has hurt and blinded him. 'Nobody!' he answers, or 'Cleverness!' and so his friends – and the audience – can only laugh.

It is a nifty trick, but the story means more. Odysseus is indeed a nobody, essentially homeless, for all the illusions of an Ithaca floating somewhere beyond the unreachable horizon. His own naming of himself as a Nobody is an oblique and dreamlike reflection of exactly what the Phaeacians think of him. He may be king of Ithaca, the son of Laertes, a man whose fame has reached the sky, but that is not how the world of the *Odyssey* treats him. Everywhere he arrives anonymous, not somebody but nobody. Even when he comes home, he is more beggar than king, unrecognised by wife, son, subject or retainer. That double status is at the heart of the *Odyssey*: it may describe a historical situation – the marginality of people who were heroes to themselves – but it also addresses a permanent human condition. My own world may cultivate me, ennoble me, even heroise me, but what possible significance beyond the confines of home can those labels have? What possible standing could Odysseus have 'in the city of Urikina, in the presence of Crown Prince Nerikkaili'?

In about 1350 BC, a treaty was drawn up between the Hittite Great King and a man known as Huqqana. He was from Hayasa, a region on the frontiers of the Hittite empire, in north-eastern Anatolia, in what would later become Armenia. Hayasa, in a way similar to the condition of Greece in the centuries after 2000 BC, was an agglomeration of tribal chiefs, with no overarching or supreme leader. Because of this, and because of its incipient and eruptive anarchy, it was not, as far as the Hittites were concerned, part of the civilised world. The Hittite Great King, who referred to himself as 'My Majesty', had married off his sister to Huqqana in a form of political alliance, but there was anxiety in the air. How could he be sure that Huqqana, this man from beyond the borders of acceptability, would behave?

The expectations were not good. The Hittite king called his new brother-in-law 'a low-born dog'. Huqqana mustn't gossip, which he would be tempted to do.

> Given that they now bring you up to my palace and that you hear about the customs of the palace it is important! You shall not divulge outside the palace what you know or what you hear.

More problematic was the question of sex.

> Furthermore this sister, whom I, My Majesty, have given to you as your wife, has many sisters from her own family as well as from her extended family. For us the Hittites, it is an important custom that a brother does not take his sister or female cousin sexually. It is not permitted. Whoever does such a thing is put to death. Because your land is barbaric, it is in conflict [without law]. There a man quite regularly takes his sister or female cousin. But among the Hittites, it is not permitted.

Huqqana has to learn that he should treat women courteously and with dignity, an instruction that brings with it echoes of the distinction in the *Iliad* between Greek and Trojan treatment of women.

Then, strikingly in the middle of all this treaty language, the Great King of the Hittites tells Huqqana a story, or at least reminds him of one, which can't fail to drive the point home. Huqqana, when he came to the palace, was to be careful around the women he met there. 'When you see a palace woman, jump out of the way and leave her a broad path.' Did he remember the story of Mariya, clearly someone who had once been close to him, perhaps another chieftain from Hayasa?

And for what reason did he die? Did not a lady's maid walk by and he look at her? But the father of My Majesty himself looked out of the window and caught him in his offence, saying 'You – why did you look at her?' So he died for that reason. The man perished just for looking from afar. So you beware.

Just as the *Tale of Sinuhe* re-orientates the Homeric vision of the hero, and allocates him effectively the role of thug, the story of Mariya, the Hayasa warrior chief who dared look at one of the lady's maids of the Hittite court, puts the skids under the bland assumption, underlying much of that Iliadic world, that women were for the taking.

Other intriguing historical realities appear in these Hittite documents. They are late on in this story. By the fourteenth century BC, the Mycenaean Greeks had established their palaces on the mainland, had become at least administratively literate themselves, and were now dominant in Crete and across the Aegean. They had entered a form of existence which had absorbed much of the organised state apparatus and mentality of the Mediterranean world. By now they were as Trojan as the Trojans.

All that, in the lightest of touches, is confirmed in the Hittite documents. In a treaty drawn up in about 1250 BC between the Great King of the Hittites and the king of Amurru, in northern Lebanon, the Great King, as ever, tells his treaty partner how to behave.

If the King of Egypt is My Majesty's friend, he shall be your friend. But if he is My Majesty's enemy, he shall be your enemy. And the Kings who are my equals in rank are the King of Egypt, the King of Babylonia, the King of Assyria and the King of Ahhiyawa.

That last name should leap out at you. After many decades of acrimonious scholarly debate, it is now generally accepted that Ahhiyawa is the Hittite transcription of Achaea, the Homeric name for Greece, and that the king of Ahhiyawa's inclusion in this most distinguished list of the great powers of the late Bronze Age is a mark of the Mycenaean triumph. That great quasi-imperial status does not reflect the atmosphere of the *Iliad*, nor of Odysseus the homeless, the wandering albatross of the southern sea. By the time these treaties were being drawn up, the Greeks were no longer the outsiders; they had become members of the Mediterranean power network.

Not that that peace prevailed. The margins of these states were ragged and contested, and the great kings were always planning and making moves against each other in the crush zones between their empires. On the western margins of Anatolia, where the king of Ahhiwaya could wield most power, he consistently troubled the allies of the Great King of the Hittites. At some time before 1400 BC, a Hittite ally in the far west of the Hittite zone of influence, Madduwatta, was attacked by a king of 'Ahhiya' and driven out of his lands, at least until the Hittites came to his aid. When the old Hittite king died, his son wanted to remind Madduwatta of the service that had been done to him:

> The father of my Majesty saved you, together with your wives, your sons, your household servants and together with your infantry and your chariotry. Otherwise dogs would have devoured you from hunger. Even if you had escaped you would have died of hunger.

The most fascinating word in this extraordinary document is the name of the ruler of Ahhiya: he is called Attarissiya. That is not a Hittite name, nor is it exactly Greek, but it may well be what 'Atreus' sounded like to a Hittite – the name in Homer of the father of Agamemnon and Menelaus, itself perhaps a derivative of *atrestos*, 'the untrembling, the fearless'.

From these few threads some kind of fabric can be woven, describing a tense, mutually suspicious and occasionally violent relationship between the Greeks and the Hittite empire. Attarissiya had invaded Hittite territory with foot soldiers and a hundred chariots, and had also fought alongside Madduwatta in an attack on Cyprus. Another warrior, the Greek king's brother, the Hittites called Tawagalawas or Tawakalawas, which is the way they might have heard the name of a Greek called Eteocles (which happens to be the name of Oedipus's son). A letter also survived in the foreign office archives in Hattusa, from a Greek they knew as 'Kagamunas' or perhaps 'Katamunas', a name which has been interpreted as Kadmos, the greatest of the Thebans.

It is a like a picture of the post-Homeric world, one that the rulers of the great Mycenaean palaces might perhaps have recognised, but surviving only in the most fragmentary and enigmatic of splinters. Part of this jagged Greek–Hittite boundary of the thirteenth century BC was a pair of places called in the documents 'Taruisa' and 'Wilusa'. Hittite scholars are now certain that these are the names of places referred to by Homer as Troy and Ilios. They may be two places conflated in the *Iliad*, or a region and its capital. In a treaty with the Great King of the Hittites, the king of Wilusa is addressed as 'Alaksandu'. That is a Hittite version of a Greek name, Alexandros, the alternative name which the *Iliad* gives to Paris, Priam's son. By the time of these late documents, Troy had become a Greek-governed city, absorbed into the Greek world, at archaeological levels where shards of Mycenaean pottery have also been found. If there had ever been a Trojan war, it had already happened, and the Greeks had won.

The relationship remained tense between the Hittite king and the Greek prince at Troy, and the treaty includes some significant instructions sent out to this marginal kinglet from the imperial capital far to the east. The Hittite administration was keen to impose the written word as the medium of communication between them and the modern test of authenticity. 'People are treacherous,' the Great King told Alaksandu.

> If rumours circulate, and someone comes and whispers to you 'His Majesty is undertaking something to do you down, and will take the land away from you, or will mistreat you in some way,' write about it to My Majesty. And if the matter is true, when I, My Majesty, write back to you, you shall not act rashly.

That sounds like an instruction from the urban to the oral world, from the literate Near East to a culture which had yet to think of writing as a central aspect of government. It is one of the great transitions of history – the Homeric horizon, caught at the very moment the Greeks were crossing it.

A third, suddenly re-orientating view of these relationships appears in, of all places, the Old Testament. Just at the moment the Greek king

Attarissiya was raiding Anatolia and Cyprus, in the thirteenth and twelfth centuries BC, and establishing settlements which archaeologists have been uncovering in the last few decades, the cities around Gaza in southern Canaan were taken and occupied by people whom the Jews called the 'Philistines'. They had been drawn to the markets and the grassy downland of southern Palestine, where beautiful pear and almond orchards surround the mudbrick villages and where cattle and horses can graze on the clover and young barley of the open plains. Their lands – Philistia – are now the gentle, hilly farmland of south-western Israel. 'Philistine' in Hebrew means 'the invader' or 'the roller-in', and from the style of their rock-cut chamber tombs, the pottery they made once they had arrived in Canaan and from the form of their own names, it looks as if these Philistines, arriving from out of the west, were Mycenaean Greeks, cruising the Mediterranean seas, searching out new lands, ready to fight whoever they found there.

The war in Canaan between Greek and Hebrew was long and grievous, but at its symbolic climax, as depicted in the First Book of the Prophet Samuel, the readers are treated to one of the most hostile depictions of Homeric warrior culture ever written. The Philistines had taken up position on a hillside at Socoh in the rolling agricultural country of the Judean foothills, a few miles west of Bethlehem. A champion came out of the Philistine camp, a man called Goliath, to challenge the Israelites drawn up on the opposite hillside.

Goliath is a huge, clumsy, half-ludicrous, threatening and contemptible figure. He is, even in the earliest and least exaggerated manuscripts, six feet nine inches tall, wearing the full equipment of the Homeric hero: a bronze helmet on his head, bronze armour on his chest, bronze greaves on his legs and carrying a sword and dagger of bronze. Everything about him is vast. His armour weighs nearly ten stone, the head of his spear fifteen pounds.

Massively over-equipped, a cross between Ajax and Desperate Dan, Goliath stands there shouting across the valley at his enemies:

Why do you come out to do battle, you slaves of Saul? I am the Philistine champion; choose your man to meet me. If he can kill me in fair fight, we will become your slaves; but if I prove too strong for

him and kill him, you shall be our slaves and serve us. Here and now
I defy the ranks of Israel. Give me a man,' said the Philistine 'and we
will fight it out.'

The front-row stolidity of the Greek, his philistinism, his need to spell
everything out, to put his own self-aggrandisement into endlessly self-
elevating words – all of that comes out of Goliath like the self-proclaiming
spout of a whale. But this is exactly what in the *Iliad* one Greek warrior
after another liked and needed to do. Shouted aggression, the Homeric
haka, was the first act of any Greek battle.

'When Saul and the Israelites heard what the Philistine said, they
were shaken and dismayed.' It was not in them to make the symmetrical
response – you shout at me, I'll shout at you – which is one of the
foundations of the Homeric system. And so a painful and faintly ludicrous, asymmetrical situation developed.

Morning and evening for forty days the Philistine drew near and
presented himself,

standing there, twice a day for a month and a half, shouting across the
valley like a giant bronze cuckoo-clock.

The shepherd boy David, the youngest of his family, whose brothers
are in the Israelite host facing the Philistines, is told by his father Jesse
to take some loaves and cream cheeses to their commander. He arrives
there, and to his amazement sees and hears Goliath shouting away. 'Who
is he,' David asks, 'an uncircumcised Philistine, to defy the army of the
living god?' That is not a Greek question. A Greek would have understood
what Goliath was saying, and would have responded by strapping on his
armour. Defiance and the locking of horns was no more than a recognition of Homeric reality. When Saul, the king of the Jews, finally accepts
that David might respond to the challenge of the Greek giant, he tries
to dress him in his own armour. David accepts it meekly, but then hesi-
tates and proclaims his difference.

'I cannot go with these because I have not tried them.' So he took
them off. And he picked up his stick, and chose five smooth stones

out of the brook, and put them in a shepherd's bag which he had with him as a pouch. He walked out to meet the Philistine with his sling in his hand.

It is a version of the Homeric arming of the hero and the single-combat meeting of warriors, the *monomachia* between Paris and Menelaus, Hector and Ajax, Achilles and Hector, which anchors the whole of the Homeric experience. But this is more like a parody of it than a borrowing. The unprotected boy, with his shepherd's bag and stick, crouches down in the brook running between the two embattled hillsides, and with his fingers in the water, picks out the plain smoothness of five good stones. No love affair with bronze, no sharpness, no self-enlargement. In everything David does, and in every lack he suffers, there is one implied and overwhelming fact: the god of the Israelites. In his presence the difference between armour and armourlessness, bronze and flesh, is like smoke in wind.

> And the Philistine came on and drew near unto David and the man that bare the shield went before him. And when the Philistine looked about, and saw David, he disdained him; for he was but a youth, and ruddy, and of a fair countenance. 'Am I a dog that you come out against me with sticks?' And he swore at him in the name of his gods. 'Come on,' he said, 'and I will give your flesh to the birds of the air and the beasts of the field.'

David told him that he would kill him and cut off his head,

> and all the world shall know there is a god in Israel. All those who are gathered here shall see that the LORD saves neither by sword nor spear; the battle is the LORD's and he will put you all into our power.
>
> And David put his hand in his bag, and took thence a stone, and slang it, and smote the Philistine in his forehead, that the stone sunk into his forehead; and he fell upon his face to the earth.

Is there any wonder that this story has lasted as long as Homer? Those forty days of shouting, all the grandeur of bronze, the whole rhetoric of assertive Homeric heroism, is now clogged with the mud filling Goliath's mouth and nostrils. A painting by the young Caravaggio, now in the Prado, of David after the death of Goliath is, in this way, one of the most beautiful commentaries on Homer that has ever been made. It is Caravaggio's least violent and most understanding version of that subject. Michelangelo had shown David on the Sistine Chapel ceiling with his sword in mid-swipe over Goliath's neck. Titian had painted a butcher's view of the cut neck itself. Caravaggio himself would later paint ferocious and tragic images of David holding the severed head (a head which bears the painter's own grieving features), but this first David of his is soaked in calm. The boy looks as if he is about twelve years old. His body is wrapped in a loose white cloth. His lower legs are bare and his feet inelegant, the toes slightly misaligned, with dirt under the nails and a soreness around them. Nothing is idealised. Goliath's vast dead hand remains clenched on the ground, and blood has dried on his big severed head, around the wound left by David's slung stone, the puncture through which the heroic balloon has collapsed.

What survives in the painting is the beauty of the boy, his intentness on the knot as he ties a cord around Goliath's hair, his simplicity, his seriousness, his lack of bombast. He kneels on the giant Greek chest, from which the head has been cut, as if on a workbench, blood just staining his hand, his own face in shadow, a face of humility, the heroism entirely inward. This is the view of Greek heroism given us by the Hebrew scriptures: weak and bombastic compared to the clarity and strength of the pious mind.

TWELVE

Homer's Odyssey

NOTHING CAN BE RELIED on in Odysseus's world. His stories of impossible monsters – Scylla, Charybdis, the Cyclops, the Sirens – are all told as if true. Others with real places and people – Egypt, Sicily, the Cretans – are clearly Odysseus's own lying tales. Odysseus is an unblinking fraud who in the passing of a smile will slip from deceit to the defence of honour and back again. At his most soothingly and persuasively elegant, his words 'fall like winter snowflakes'. But he is no weakling. His grandfathers were raw and primitive men: Autolycus, whose name means 'the wolf himself', and Arceisius, 'Bear Man'. He comes from nature but is a multiple of multiples: *polymētis*, many-skilled; *polymechanos*, very ingenious; *polytlas*, much-enduring; and best of all *poikilomētis*, dapple-skilled, with so much woven into him that he shimmers and flickers like an embroidered cloth.

So uncatchable is Odysseus that when the poem describes his state of mind, you can never be certain where to find him. When he is lying in bed, anxious and unable to sleep, Homer says he is 'tossing backwards and forwards, like a sausage that a man is turning backwards and forwards above the burning coals, doing it on one side, then the other, wanting it to cook quickly. So Odysseus was turning backwards and forwards, thinking what he should do.' *Entha kai entha*, backwards and forwards, hither and thither, literally 'there and there': Homer repeats the phrase three times in five lines. It must be branded on his hero's heart. But is Odysseus the cook or the sausage? Is he turning or being turned? Is he the passive victim of his life or its principal actor? Or both?

It is fitting that at the beginning of the *Odyssey*, this slippery figure is nowhere to be found. He is away, an absence, the longed-for man-not-there. Twenty years have passed since he left for the war in Troy. The other heroes have returned home. Only Odysseus remains missing. No one has seen him these last ten years. Meanwhile his queen, Penelope, is surviving surrounded by a herd of young men from Ithaca, and the rival kings of nearby islands, all of them clamouring for her hand, her body and her husband's kingdom. She keeps them at bay, flirtatiously but reservedly, while her son Telemachus is humiliated and reduced by these wine-swilling, pork-consuming parasites. The word for them in Greek is *mnester*, which means a man with something in mind, a man with intentions.

With the help of Athene, Telemachus escapes their clutches for a while, and goes to ask for news of his father in the great palaces of the Peloponnese, at Pylos and at Sparta, where the old heroes tell him what has happened: his father is a prisoner on the distant island of Ogygia, where the love-nymph Calypso holds him in her sway. Only after four books and 2,222 lines does Odysseus, the hidden man, first appear.

Calypso's isle of voluptuousness is the earth's navel. She promises her captive, as all lovers do, immortality and agelessness, and she presides over him as the goddess of longing. Her hair hangs about her eyes as seductively as it does around the face of the dawn. Her island is hilly and forested, and her delicious cavern, where the scents of sweet-smelling cedar fill the air, where the owls and cormorants sit chattering in the luxuriant growth at its mouth, and the vines hold out bunches of grapes that ripen as you watch – what is this but the entrancingly shaggy cavern of desire? She is Courbet's *Origine du Monde*. Fresh streams run down through her meadows starred with violets, thick with beds of what was either 'parsley' or 'celery', a refuge 'at which any immortal god who came there would gaze in wonder, their heart entranced with pleasure'.

One spring morning, on the south-east coast of Sicily just north of Syracuse, I went somewhere which, for that day anyway, seemed to be filled with Calypso's overbrimmingly desirable spirit. It is known now as Penisola Magnisi, but was called Thapsos by the ancient Greeks. A low, flat island, about a mile long, just off the coast, is joined to the mainland by a narrow sandy neck. To north and south of that neck there is shelter and good holding, whatever the wind, the classic early Greek recipe of twin harbours. The rim of the mainland beside it is now a mess of modern oil refineries and tanker-loading bays, but Thapsos has remained uninhabited. Walk along the sand of the tombolo towards it, keep your eyes looking out to sea, and you can find yourself in a virtually untouched Odyssean world.

This little island holds the earliest of all signs of the Greeks in the west. They were here in the sixteenth century BC, as the Shaft Graves were still being dug at Mycenae, moving out into the Mediterranean as they had already come south to the Aegean. Archaeologists have found Mycenaean, Cypriot and Maltese pottery here, mixed in with local Sicilian jars and plates. It was somewhere, I thought, where I could start to come close to Odysseus on one of his distant shores.

But coming to Thapsos that beautiful morning, with the Mediterranean glittering beside me, it was impossible to think I could be here for the Bronze Age, for Odysseus, or for anything that was not part of the astonishing present, because the island that morning was awash with flowers. The true wild sweet pea, the great-grandfather of all sweet peas grown in the world, was here, its heady scent mixed with the amazing, sugary wafts of the sweet alyssum that was growing in clumps among the limestone, smelling from yards away like plates of honey sandwiches.

It was said by the Roman historian Diodorus Siculus that Sicily smelled so powerfully of wildflowers that hounds there used to lose the scent of their prey and wander about 'at a loss, sniffing the air with half-closed eyes, while the quarry grazed happily several miles off'. But Thapsos looked wonderful too: wine-dark stonecrop on the edges of the limestone flakes, clouds of borage everywhere, a purple-pink haze spangled with blue stars. Spires of viper's bugloss stood among them like the banners of festival knights, and all of this surrounded by a floor of brilliant pink little Mediterranean campions, *Silene colorata*, with banks of yellow marigolds and wild tangerine chrysanthemums beyond them.

Odysseus came to hate Calypso's island. He had been there too long, and by the time the poem finds him there he is weeping on the beach, pining for home, far from floweriness and Calypso's beguilements. Out on the other side of Thapsos, facing Greece and the sparkle of the sea, is this island's own version of the landscape of regret and loss. Here on the rocky, sea-stripped and flowerless coast is where the first Greeks in Sicily buried their dead. They made small, low, rock-cut tombs, deftly slipped into the limestone, each entrance coming in from the direction of the sea, the hollow of the tomb itself cut out of the depth of the rock. There are about three hundred of them, like the burrows of small rock-dwelling creatures, and two things strike you: they imitate in form the great tholos tombs of Mycenae and Pylos, the Tombs of Agamemnon and Clytemnestra, as Schliemann called them, with their giant ceremonial entrance courts or *dromoi*, the towering portals and the huge corbelled vaults of the tombs themselves. That heroic vision of the dead has been transported here to the distant west, but no grandeur has come with it. These Thapsos tombs are poverty itself, desperate scrapings on a rocky shore, filled with dreams and illusions of home but little else. The walls of the *dromoi* here are often no more than eighteen inches high, the doorway accessible only if you squirm inside, the vaulted space no taller than a crouching man.

Into this island of desperate and beautiful changelessness Homer suddenly injects the opposite, the great mobilising presence of the poem, the god who, alongside Athene, presides over Odysseus's whole being: the quicksilver dazzle of Hermes himself. He arrives as the messenger of Zeus, bringing a shock of life, 'swooping down from Pieria [the home of the Muses], down from the high clear air, plunging to the sea and skimming the swells, like a shearwater who hunts along the deep and deadly ways of the barren salt sea'.

Hermes does everything Odysseus might think of doing: he is the god of the thief, the shepherd, the craftsman, the herald, the musician, the athlete and the merchant. He is at home with all kinds of cunning and trickery, charms and spells. He is the god who invented music and discovered fire. Dangerous magic and a kind of phallic potency glimmer around him like static. He is at home outside the limits of normality and stability, and so he is the god of boundaries and thresholds, of roads and doors, of transitional and alien places, of mines and miners, of the ability to make and transform the fixities and pre-arrangements of the world. This is the god who watches over comings and goings. It was Hermes, in disguise, who led Priam across the Trojan plain to the Greek camp and his world-altering encounter with Achilles. He is the god of politics and diplomacy, the great persuader, the maestro of difference, and all of that makes him the god of Odysseus.

Hermes delivers transformations, and so the *Odyssey* flicks to its other mode: the sea and its islands are not to be a prison, but a place where movement and change are more possible than anywhere. Hermes tells Calypso that Odysseus must leave her island and begin his journey home. And to leave, he must build himself a raft from the great trees that surround her. The very forest which had made this place into a desire-trap, all that fringing luxuriance, is now seen as timber. Odysseus seeks out the deadest, driest, most juiceless trees he can find, because those are the ones that will 'float lightly' – but also surely because those are the most unCalypso-like – and they fall quickly to his axe.

Nothing in the *Odyssey* is described with more love or care than Odysseus making his raft. It comes together in parts, orderly, concrete, precise: axe, adze and augers, pegs and mortises, ribs, decks and gunwales, mast, yard and steering oar, braces, halyards and sheets. Odysseus assembles it just as Homer assembles his song, so that the ship becomes a poem of the sea. If her parts are right, and their relationship right, then she will sail. Calypso provisions the raft with delicious drink and food for his journey, and summons her warm and generous wind, a following wind, the only one that could take him home. He embarks – you can smell the new-cut wood – his spirits high, gripping the tiller, seated astern, his eye on the sail which fills above him.

Now Odysseus enters his crowning moment. He is the master mariner, the great soul, godlike, commanding his own craft *technēentos*, a word that blurs the boundaries of 'skilfully', 'cunningly' and 'magisterially'. He steers by the stars, as Calypso had told him, keeping the Plough and the Great Bear, of which it is a part, on the left hand, to the north. For seventeen nights he sails with the west wind behind him like this. 'Sleep never fell on his eyelids as he watched the stars above him', seeing the Plough wheeling around the North Star and 'never bathing in the waters of the ocean', while the Plough in turn is watching Orion on the other side, the two of them circling each other in eternity, 'the axis always fixed'.

You only have to sail by the stars once or twice for that connection to remain with you for the rest of your life. I can never now look up at Cassiopeia, the five bright stars of her 'W', and not think of those hours in a driving and stormy night that I kept them in the shrouds of the *Auk*, as we headed north in a storm off the south of Ireland. Nor Orion without seeing him as he was when we made our way out with the tide one summer night into the Minch, and that most hero-like of constellations stood as a warrior high to the right of us, his belt and sword glittering and jewelled, his bow up and arced to the south-west, the arrow aimed high at the heart of the Pleiades.

This exposure of Odysseus to the stars is the closest I ever feel to him, knowing that the experience of being out there, alone at sea at night, for all the changes in technology that three or four thousand years might have brought, with the sky arrayed above you and the sea and its threats dark and half-hidden, is materially the same for me as it was for him. It is the most cosmic experience of the world I know, when the universe seems not like a background but a reality, and when the scale of earthliness shrinks to nothing much. There is no history here. I am in the Bronze Age, and as Odysseus stays awake, keeping sleep at bay, watching the movements of craft and sea, I do the same, and he and I are momentarily and marvellously intimate.

But constancy is not the note of the *Odyssey*, and again Homer flicks the switch. Odysseus is within touching distance of Scheria, the island of the Phaeacians who will take him home, its mountains 'reaching towards him now, over the misty breakers, rising like a shield', when Poseidon spots the raft and decides to kill him. It is one of Homer's majestic aerial views, the little raft far below him in the expanse of sea, Poseidon's eye in the heaven far above, the midge-like fragility of our greatest man surrounded by the vast rolling dark expanse of ocean.

The storm which then erupts and blows through the next 160 lines is no dignified passage of heroic verse. It is vicious, almost formless, repetitively destructive. Every prop of every storm in every European imagination, from Virgil to Ovid and on through Shakespeare and the great composers, is brought into play here. Poseidon summons every contradictory wind. He stirs and grinds at the surface of the sea, brings clouds to hide the land, so that even the sea itself becomes invisible. Giant waves come bearing down on Odysseus, and sweep though his whole being. His knees weaken, his heart melts, his giant and commanding spirit quakes before Poseidon's chthonic power.

Poseidon is 'dark-maned', horse-like, the enemy of the civility and coherence embodied in Odysseus's beautiful raft. The verse, which had been making such steady progress on Odysseus's starlit voyage, now churns with anxiety. Odysseus wishes he had died at Troy. At least then his death would have been heroic, not the pitiable ending now facing him.

The raft loses direction. Odysseus's hand slips from the steering oar as Poseidon's waves tower and break above him, spinning his raft in a circle. The hero is thrown into the sea, where the clothes that Calypso had given him grow heavy with the water and drag him under. Wave after wave drives him down. Only his mind, the great organ of Odyssean existence, stays whole in this frenzy of natural violence, and as he surfaces at last, spewing seawater from his mouth and with the sea streaming from his head like the torrents running from the boss of a fountain, he lunges after the raft, knowing it as his place of safety, the only way he can escape 'death's decision'. But Poseidon does not release him. Here and there, to and fro, *entha kai entha*, the sea-king drives him, urging on the south wind and the north wind, the east wind and the west wind, as each in their turn try to shake from Odysseus his last rags of coherence.

He is hanging on to life; the tightly-bound raft and the woven cloth, the made things of a civilised existence, are part of the longed-for or remembered worlds. They are too fragile to last out here. He is beset with troubles, and death seems near at hand until at last, mysteriously, a seabird, *aithuia* in Greek, perhaps a shearwater, or another fishing bird, maybe a tern or a small delicate-limbed gull like a kittiwake – no one has ever been sure – alights on the wave-swept platform of the raft and speaks to him.

It is one of the Homeric moments at which the distance between then and now shrinks away. You can imagine the listeners around the poet, fixed in their attention to this overturning crisis, with nothing in their minds but the predicament of Odysseus at sea, taken up with their anxiety for this man so helplessly exposed to Poseidon's rage, now, quite suddenly feeling their hearts contract with love and sympathy at the arrival of the speaking bird. Here, maybe, is a moment of hope.

It is an experience all deep-sea sailors will have had. You are out in a storm, the boat rolls and pitches, thirty degrees one way then the other, the seas coming at you in a pattern you wish would end, the battering and shrieking of the wind unstoppable in your ear. Every surface is broken. The winds cannot leave the sea alone. What has already been ploughed and folded is ploughed and folded again. No structure in the sea remains whole. Not even a breaking wave is allowed to break, but the wind strips the spume from the wavetop and blows it in a half-element, half-air, half-sea, wildly down and across the wind, as if the air were now clouded with cataracts or a sudden blast of winter. Inconstancy and capriciousness rule. There is no permanence. Nothing in a storm can be inherited from one moment to the next. But if there is one fact that a storm seems to impose − it is not physically or meteorologically true, but this is the experience − it is the sea's mysterious dominance from below. A storm-driven sea appears to acquire a vitality and viciousness, a desire to do damage, which has nothing to do with the wind but comes from inside its own enraged, destroying body. If you ever have that sensation, it is when you are meeting Poseidon.

Out of that turmoil and trouble, enacting the repeated Homeric principle of enlightenment through the arrival of the opposite, comes the delicacy and tailored perfection of the seabird. It is a sign of grace and goodness, never more than when one alights on the deck or boom beside you. I have had swallows do that, far from land, and once, briefly, a tiny dark storm petrel, a speck of life in the middle of death.

I cannot believe Homeric sailors did not also stand at the taffrails of their beloved ships watching the birds in their wake. Seabirds are too beautifully present in the poems for them not to have seen them like that, god-like in their lightness above the rolling weight of the sea. I have watched them for days, equipped as they are with their own more perfect version of hull and sail, reaching and tacking beside you in the wind, dropping and climbing among the peaks and valleys below them, their primaries sometimes just nicking and flicking the surface of the sea, until without warning they make a decision, and turn one wing up into the wind, exposing their belly to it, thrown upwards like a cyclist on the steepest part of a banked track, and are pulled away, high and fast, in a rapid downwind run, which they end by curving slowly round to windward again, pure authority, taking up station, living with the fluency and command their liquid world requires.

Odysseus's visiting tern is Leucothea, the white goddess. She was once a mortal girl from Thebes, with, as Homer says, 'the most beautiful ankles', but has been adopted now by the gods as one of theirs. She gives Odysseus a holy veil, full of the magic of the woven cloth. He is to tie it around his chest, abandon the raft and swim for shore. With those instructions she leaves him, plunging into the sea 'like a diving tern, and the dark wave hid her'. But Odysseus, who has already refused the offer of immortality from Calypso, and whose mind is still searchingly alive, does not obey. He trusts his own raft too much to abandon it so far from shore, and with that Poseidon and the storm submit him to the next phase of horror. The earth-shaker summons a killer wave, its crest overarching, vaulted, Homer using a word he uses elsewhere to describe caves and dark bowers roofed with trees, so that the wave becomes like a vast dark hall of destruction, which he then lands on Odysseus as a sledgehammer of vengeance.

The raft is smashed and Odysseus sunk, but he emerges and climbs on to one of the scattered planks which he then rides in the sea 'like a horse'. Because finality dominates the *Iliad*, that poem introduces men in order to kill them, brought on one after another like the shambling line of an Aztec sacrifice: the many will always end in the same one place. But Odysseus meets death time and time again, and each time springs up whole and new, as if resilience were running in his veins: his central understanding, the great evolution from the *Iliad* to the *Odyssey*, is that the one needs to be many.

The storm continues for another two days. The life-spirit in Odysseus is squeezed to near-empty. His ability to survive has faced its greatest test. But then at last the wind drops and calm spreads across the sea. Still, though, the groundswell is running, and Odysseus is lifted by one of those long, rolling waves high enough to see the land of Scheria and salvation within touching distance.

Just like the kind of joy that children feel when their father has been lying ill in bed, dying, taut with pain, wasting away under the grip of some angry, powerful affliction, and at last those pains begin to ebb away and they can feel a warmth and ease come back into the air of the sick room around him, so to Odysseus did that land and its trees seem welcome, swimming towards them now, hungry to plant his feet on the earth itself.

For Odysseus, the missing father, the man whose son knows he is dead and gone, land itself has become fatherly, the embrace of what feels like home reaching out to him. But here, at a moment of arrival and the promise of simplicity, Homer gives the gimballed world of the *Odyssey* yet another spin. The poem might long for land, but will always remain at sea, and as Odysseus gets as near the shore as a man's voice will carry, he hears the vast, destructive surf breaking on what he realises is an iron coast, no harbours, no anchorages, all high headlands, reefs and cliffs. The hexameters, sounding as strange as a Hawaiian war chant, as heavy and hissing as the sea itself, play out what he hears:

kai dē doupon akouse	*poti spiladessi thalassēs*
and then the boom he heard	on the slippery reefs of the sea
rochthei gar mega kuma	*poti xeron ēpeiroio*
for roared the great wave	on the dry land of the mainland
deinon ereugomenon	*eiluto de panth' halos achnē*
terrible the deep belching	as folded up all things in sea surf

With the brightness of Athene in his mind he casts off again and finally, thankfully, finds a place where the all-male cliff gives way and a fair-flowing river, the emergent inwardness of the land, allows him entrance and he can rest at last, 'Spent to all use, and down he sank to death./ The sea had soak'd his heart through.'

Of course he does not die, and from that masterfully orchestrated sequence of island, raft, storm, bird and shore – the realms of impotence, potency, threat, grace and survival – the great central section of the *Odyssey* floods out: Odysseus's meeting with the princess Nausicaa, his coming to the deeply Asiatic palace of Alcinous her father, where he tells his tales to the assembled company. Together they constitute an enormous, cumulative exploration of human consciousness, island by island, point by point, each story exploring another dimension of what it is to be alive. In this world of flux, every island shapes the life that is in it. Arrive at any of them, push your dinghy ashore on the beach, and a different atmosphere obtains: welcome, comfort, strangeness, violence. The vocabulary of beach, rock and wood may be the same, but every island uses it in a different way, to seduce or dismember you, turn you into a pig or promise you immortality, devour your friends or make you forget that anywhere else ever existed.

The *Odyssey* is a drama of oscillation, between inner and outer, urbanity and wildness, enclosure and exposure, the memory of home and the rewards of distance, a life that is 'heartsick on the open sea' and the mixed, erotic terror-allure of the women Odysseus finds wherever he goes, their welcome, their way with drugs and potions, the caves and grottoes of their inner selves.

When he arrives at the seductions of Circe's island – her name means 'the encircler' – he finds there the poisoner-witch and the best cook in Homer. She has ever more deliciousness to offer, and with her charms seduces his men and turns them all into pigs. Odysseus knows that this is a dangerous nowhere, out in the middle of the full circle of the sea where they cannot know where the sun sets, nor where it rises, until Hermes, his great ally, the spirit of cleverness and ingenuity, gives him both an antidote to all her potions and the best possible advice: hold your sword to her throat and get her to promise that she will not make a pig of you, as she has your men.

Odysseus arms himself with all the sharpness of Hermes, then penetrates deep inside Circe's world, in through the doors of her palace, into her beautiful rooms and her jewelled chair, only then suddenly to draw his sword 'from his thigh', to dominate her as she kneels terrified before him. She must promise no spells, no enchantment, the freeing of his men, stripping their piggishness away, and with those promises, with his dominance secure, he mounts her in 'her surpassingly beautiful bed of love'.

The erotic vibrates as the underlayer of each encounter, the male fear of enclosure in endless dialogue with the male longing to be enclosed. In Hades, whose name means 'the unlit' or 'the unseen', this dance of attachment and detachment takes on its own sad colours. Everything that matters on earth, all love, life, growth and hope, is extinguished here and reduced to a grey, wraith-like half-existence, life without life. Achilles says he is surrounded there not by the dead but by the *kata-phthimenoisin*, the deader than dead, the dead's own dead. It is the darkest of all the *Odyssey*'s inward places. There Odysseus watches the lightless ghosts walk by. There is no glory in them. They are too thin for that, evaporating as his arms try to close around them.

He sees his mother first, a longed-for shadow of the woman he knew and held, then a sequence of queens, all mortal and all dead, all of them beautiful and all once lovers of gods, each of them walking past him in sombre parade. They are attendants on Persephone, the great queen of Hades itself, her own presence in the gloom of this dark cavern an emblem of all the heartache and the thousand natural shocks that flesh is heir to: she is a vegetation goddess and she belongs in the bright lit world above, but Hades had abducted her, and in that single act had brought winter to the earth.

These queens are all mothers of heroes, and one by one they remember their moments of intimacy with the gods: Tyro, thinking of when Poseidon in the shape of a giant wave took possession of her at a river's mouth; Antiopē remembering Zeus coming to her on the vast plain where their sons would later build the city of Thebes; the mother of Heracles thinking of his conception, then his wife remembering their own moments of love together; the mother of Oedipus appears, grieving at having slept with her own son; and Iphimedeia, who 'lay in the sea-Lord's loving waves' . . . and on, too many for Odysseus to remember or tell, even though

His story held them spellbound down the shadowed halls.

Behind them all, not present here but looming over the whole performance, stands the one great figure of the noble and absent queen: Penelope, Odysseus's own wife, away, not dead, but waiting for him in Ithaca. Every one of these queenly wraiths is an image of the woman he longs for. She is the queen of all queens, filled with intelligence, fortitude and wit, the match for Odysseus in her greatness. Every one of these ghosts is a translation of Penelope into another form. They all speak of the moment when longing was over and intimacy was real, and every one of them now looks across the gulf of death to the time a god made love to them. Desire, longing, separation and greatness all appear in them arrayed before Odysseus like a frieze, every one the ghost of his own lost wife.

After the monstrous-beautiful Sirens, Odysseus comes to the limb-consuming Scylla and her friend the body-gulping Charybdis. Scylla is a six-headed, rock-bound, man-eating monster, with guts made of dogs' heads, who plucks you from above; Charybdis a vast-mouthed, in-sucking, whirl-water hell-fiend who will pull you down below. Veer too far from Scylla, and Charybdis will have you. Too far from Charybdis, and Scylla will pick off your sailors. Too far in or too far out, which fate will you choose? Together they are the nightmare of female threat, either picking your life away or drowning you in who they are. Everything Odysseus loved about women in Hades is here thrown into reverse. But Odysseus makes the wise man's choice: risk Scylla, because where Charybdis will swallow you whole, Scylla may eat a man or two, but the ship will survive. This is Odysseus's virtue: in the face of life's impossible choices, he is able to navigate between the whirlpool and the rock.

His inner self reflects that outer wisdom. More than any other Homeric hero, Odysseus is not at one with himself. His mental world is storm-wrecked, and these outer landscapes are a projection of that broken core. But every arrival carries its lesson. 'Many were the people whose places he saw and whose minds he learned,' Homer says at the very beginning of the *Odyssey*. Odysseus may long 'for his return and his woman', but the heart of the poem is this contingency, the absence of any overriding permanence. It is the first depiction we have of 'the fascinating imaginative realm', as Milan Kundera called the novel, the great descendant of the *Odyssey*, 'where no one owns the truth and everyone has the right to be understood'. Abstract certainties do not apply here. Anything you might have thought true may well be false. Anything that might have seemed good can seem bad in another light. And of nowhere is that truer than the island that is Odysseus's destination, the dream of Ithaca, the place Odysseus would like to call home, 'the sweetest place any man can imagine', but which on arrival, exactly halfway through the *Odyssey*'s twenty-four books, turns out to be its very opposite.

* * *

Ithaca is not what the phrase 'Greek island' brings to mind. There is nothing of the drought-stripped bareness of the eastern Aegean, nor of the dry Asiatic pelt of the Trojan plain. Ithaca is green and wooded, more Tuscan than Greek. There are some wonderful harbours, but little good grass or arable land. It largely consists of mountains dropping to the sea. Wild pear trees blossom beside the spring meadows, but it is 'rocky Ithaca', the kind of island that has always thrived on trading or raiding but would be poor if reliant on its own resources. There are springs in the woodlands, where daisies grow in the stony turf. Magenta anemones spangle the meadows in May, and a little later in the year you can find the churchyards filled with white and purple irises. I have been there at the end of winter, which is when Odysseus arrives, and I have known nights as cold as the one in which he has to borrow a cloak to keep warm. Like him, I have sat late over an olive-wood fire, using the prunings from the vines as kindling, drinking glasses of deep black red Mavrodafni, huddled over the logs in a cold room, so that my face burned and my back froze. There was snow on the mountain paths that year, the wind was turning up the pale underside of the olive leaves and the air was more silver than golden, clarified, a distillate.

It's part of the geometry of the poems that Ithaca is like this. It is a northern country, on the northern and western edge of the Greek world, a long way from the cultivated, semi-Asiatic eastern Aegean heartland that Homer knew best. That exaggerated marginality fits Odysseus, the pirate-king of a country which is out on the edge of things. But it is a country he loves. The Phaeacians bring him here across the sea. He is asleep when he arrives, and they carry him ashore still sleeping. He wakes the next day and doesn't know where he is. He can't recognise Ithaca. Only at the prompting of Athene does he realise that this is home, and then, on seeing it, he 'bends to kiss the life-giving soil'.

The *Odyssey* throughout has taunted its listeners with images of palatial comfort and luxury. The Phaeacians are in effect the model of a rich, successful Near-Eastern kingdom. Their palaces, gardens and orchards all read like scenes from an Assyrian relief. Egypt has floated just off-stage as the reservoir of gold, the Greek dream of material well-being. The kings and queens of Pylos and Sparta live embedded in authority and sumptuousness. Even Circe seems to live in a beautifully equipped palace.

Odysseus does not arrive home to find a place like that. His kingdom is in chaos, not the lovely, sweet, green, untroubled oasis he longs for it to be. It is riven with difficulty, and that tension – between the desire and the reality, between 'Ithaca' the beautiful and Ithaca the real – leads on to the fierce conclusion of this great poem. It is no easy or sentimental re-meeting of the loved one and the loved place. Homer says 'there is nothing sweeter to a man than his own country'. That is what we want to think is true. But in Ithaca the poem enacts the opposite: nothing is more troubled than a man's own country, even if that is where the desire for sweetness is strongest.

Odysseus has repeatedly appeared as the impoverished northern wanderer not entirely at home in the Mediterranean world. Now he comes home as the broken king, the outsider with few allies. The only weapons he has are tricks of deceit and concealment, and Athene makes sure she strips him of any sign of nobility:

> She withered the handsome flesh that was on his supple limbs
> And thinned the fair hair on his head.
> She put the skin of an old, old man over his whole body
> And dimmed the two eyes that had been so beautiful.

Now he is at home, he has never been more at sea. But he is not at a loss. He tells lying stories about who he is and where he has come from, gradually working his way towards the confrontation that will bring him victory, slipping into his own palace much as the Trojan Horse that he devised was slipped into the citadel at Troy. Homer shapes Odysseus to be the universal man, dressed in rags, stronger for appearing weaker, but even in that disguise he consistently pretends to come not from the margins of the Homeric world – he is no northern vagabond – but from one of its centres of riches and power: Crete, the focus of the great palatial culture which Sir Arthur Evans, the English excavator of the palace complex at Knossos in the early years of the twentieth century, called the Minoan. Odysseus describes his island in the middle of the wine-dark sea as a fair, rich land, surrounded by water, with so many men in it they could not be counted and ninety cities, including 'Knossos, where Minos reigned'.

Odysseus has become the man who knows the world, who has been a great warrior at Troy, a great traveller to dimensions of existence few other men will ever encounter, an absorber of the Cretan civilisation, now preparing to perform his great and terrifying act of revenge. He has lost nothing in all his journeying. He has become the agent of a new fused culture, the man who will establish civility in his city by bringing war into it. He looks at Ithaca with eyes that are rimmed red with sea-salt, the hardened eyes of the returning king. He is the agent of reduction, there to remove the fat, and the irony of Odysseus's return is that the nearer he gets to his own house, the more uncompromisingly like Achilles he becomes, wanting to strip away the muddle and complexities and return Ithaca to an essential, Iliadic condition.

Set against this powerful and threatening presence is Penelope, his incomparable queen, the greatest woman in Homer. She does not yet know that her husband has at last returned. Her halls are filled with the suitors. Everything about them reeks of luxury and abuse, but she is withdrawn and self-protective. The epithet Homer uses of her most often is *periphron*, meaning wise, or more exactly that she has a mind which encompasses all sides of a question, not exactly wary or circumspect, but 'understanding the whole', filled with an enveloping intelligence. Penelope's mind is one of the most precious places in Homer, the inner citadel of virtue and value. She is deeply identified with the well-being of her house. When she appears in front of the suitors, she always stands by the columns of the beautiful hall, as if she were one of them herself, 'shining among women' just as the upper chambers to which she retires shine within the palace. This is the great woman who, as she descends her stairs, looks like Artemis and Aphrodite, the greatest of the goddesses, the queens of the wildland and of love.

Her heart is of iron, and like her husband she has 'a well-balanced mind'. Like him, she can deceive and manipulate her enemies, but also like him, she is passionate in her love for her lost spouse, and weeps bitterly over him. Like him, she lies awake at night and her troubles crowd around her throbbing heart. In one of Homer's most beautiful similes, she says that just as

the nightingale of the greenwood sings so sweetly when the spring is newly come, sitting perched in the thick and leafy trees, pouring out her rich voice in quavering and bubbling notes, even so my heart is stirred to and fro in doubt.

Odysseus's great phrase, *entha kai entha*, to and fro, there and there, is hers too; but have midnight thoughts and the fluttering anxieties of a troubled mind in the dark ever been so beautifully described?

Like all the great women in Homer, she weaves, no cloth more famous than the one she is making as a shroud for her father-in-law Laertes, weaving it every day, unweaving it every night, not only to keep the suitors at arm's length but as an emblem of her command in her world. She is a queen regnant, her fame reaching heaven for the way she rules over men, upholds justice, sees that the fertile earth brings forth wheat and barley, that her orchards are heavy with fruit and her flocks with young. All this, Homer says, comes from her 'good command' – one word: *euēgesia* – while her people 'grow in goodness under her'.

This is Homer's architecture of crisis: a great woman, her husband in disguise, a gang of young men who do not realise that the beggar is their king, witnessing their abuse and their vulgarity, eating his food, drinking his drink and sleeping with his serving-women. The tension builds over four long books of the poem, an unavoidable sexual metaphor at work: the king wolf has been away, the she-wolf is under siege, the promise of blood is in the air.

Odysseus is troubled. He knows that he must bring war into his own house, but when he longs to do violence to those servant-women who have betrayed him, anxiety reverberates within him.

> Just as a bitch stands over her young puppies,
> growling at a man she does not know,
> thinking she would attack him,
> so Odysseus's heart growled inside him.

He has to punch his own chest to keep it in order. But is Odysseus the growling heart? Or the man who keeps his heart down? Is he one of the puppies that needs protection? Or the bitch doing the protecting? Or even the man who is threatening the puppies. There is no primitive simplicity here: as Homer portrays it, complexity ripples through every contour of the human heart.

When the terrifying reprise of the *Iliad* erupts into the poem, it brings with it an almost orgasmic release of destructive energy, a balloon of mesmeric violence in which Odysseus slaughters all 108 of the young men. It is a frenzy of killing, an orgy of revenge that leaves the floors of the palace swimming in blood. The most horrible moment of the *Iliad*, when Odysseus and Diomedes kill Dolon even as he is begging for his life, and his head is still speaking as it lands in the dust: those same actions and words are repeated here with one of the more pathetic of the victims. Odysseus ends slobbered with their guts, his thighs shiny with their blood, filthy with it, 'like a lion that comes from feeding on an ox at the farmstead, and all his chest and cheeks on either side are stained with blood and he is terrible to look at; even so was Odysseus dirty with their blood and filth, his feet red, his hands and arms red with it'.

Any idea that this is a tale of diverting fantasy is buried under the horror. Odysseus emerges from the tumult and goes through his house, looking for any sign of life from the suitors, any stirring of a limb, so that none might escape.

> He found them one and all, mired in blood and dust, all of them like
> fishes that the fishermen have drawn in their meshed nets from the
> grey sea on to the curved beach. And all the fishes, longing for the
> waves of the sea, lie upon the sand. And the sun shines forth and takes
> from them their life.

Their glazed stupidity is nothing more than the measure of Odysseus's triumph. It is a moment of ecstatic slaughter, a huge gratification, filled with delight that he has done it and destroyed his enemies. He has won and has his woman back, his house and land and life. There is no euphemism here. Melanthius had been Odysseus's goatherd, but had betrayed him with the suitors:

> They led him out though the doorway and the court
> And cut off his nose and his ears with the pitiless bronze
> And tore out his genitals for the dogs to eat raw
> And cut off his hands and his feet in the anger of their hearts.

I have read these lines on Ithaca, listening one summer night to the nightingales in a thicket nearby, rocked back by this arrival of war in the house: no political solution sought, no compensatory agreement arrived at, feeling horrified that for all Odysseus's subtlety and fineness, he has ended up as a cannibal-minded kill-dog. Nothing in Homer is more troubling. You might have thought you knew this poem and its hero, but these scenes push far out into strange territory. Is this, in the end, for all our ships and palaces, our poetry, our beautiful cloths and veils, how we are, predatory carnivores snarling our dominance over mounds of filth-spattered corpses?

Odysseus has the place cleaned. He gets the serving-women of the house to purify it, fumigating it, using a hoe to scrape up the horror, behaving as the sanitising angel, instructing the women to carry out the dead bodies of the men they have been sleeping with. After the work is done, he identifies the twelve women he considers guilty of that sexual crime, finds 'the cable of a dark-prowed ship', a piece of marine equipment, and ties it high up outside the house, around a pillar and some rafters, just high enough so that if someone was attached to it, their feet would not quite reach the ground.

> Just as when in the evening long-winged thrushes or doves, trying
>   to reach their roosting place for the night,
> fall into a snare set in a thicket,
> finding the bed that greets them filled with hate,
> even so the women held their heads out in a row,
> and nooses were placed around their necks,
> so that they could die most pitiably.
> They writhed a little with their feet but not for very long.

It is, in Odysseus and Telemachus, a moment of pure pitilessness and, in Homer, of pure pity. Homer loves birds. Athene has been there, just a moment before, as a swallow up in the rafters of the palace. The word Homer uses for the pitiability of the girls' death, *oiktista*, is always used to describe the mournful notes of the song of the nightingale, Penelope's own heart-bird. There can be no doubt where Homer's sympathies lie. The suffering of those poor hanged girls, strung up with their feet quivering and kicking under the noose, their toes an inch or so from the ground beneath them, summons all the ghosts of Beslan, Srebrenica and

Aleppo. An air of trouble thickens around this crime, and any identity you might have felt with Odysseus is threatened by it. An unbridgeable distance seems to open between us. It is a step too far, an ancientness too far. But Homer is on our side of the divide, and it is clear that if Odysseus thinks he can solve life's problems by the ferocious imposition of moral authority, Homer, the poem, knows you cannot.

All that remains is for Odysseus to be at one again with Penelope. She tests him, famously, with the suggestion that they should move their bed from 'the well-built bridal chamber' where it had been ever since he left for Troy. She knows, and he knows, but she does not yet know that the man in front of her knows, that the bed can never be moved, because Odysseus had built it around a living, long-leafed olive tree that had been growing in the courtyard for more years than anyone could remember. Their marriage bed was no temporary construction, but built for continuity and fixity, not afloat on the world but rooted in it. Odysseus, the great story-teller, had made it from living, inherited materials, had cut it and trimmed it and had beautified it with gold, silver and ivory inlays. The bed, in other words, like the raft he made, is another version of the great epic poem, made and remade, the reshaping of an inheritance to a new and ever more beautiful purpose.

When Penelope sees that Odysseus knows what she knows, that theirs is a marriage of true minds, and that their companionship is in the knowledge of the world they share, 'her knees were loosened where she sat, and her heart melted, and in tears she threw her arms around his neck and kissed his face'.

This is what, in the most literal translation that makes sense in English, Homer says:

As when the land appears welcome to those who are swimming, after Poseidon has smashed their strong-built ship on the open water, pounding it with the weight of wind and the heavy seas, and only a few escape the grey water by swimming to the land, with a thick scurf of salt coated on them, and happily they set foot on the shore, escaping the evil; so welcome was her husband to her as she looked at him, and she could not let him go from the embrace of her white arms.

These verses dance around the edges of tenderness. Odysseus has returned from the sea, his eyes red-rimmed with salt, but Penelope recognises him as her homeland, the shore on which she can at last set foot after having been too long adrift on the chaos of her life. Understanding comes in seeing things from the other side. The language is clotted with formulae, the stock phrases used in every part of the poem: the strong-built ship, the grey water, the description of the sea merely as evil, her white arms. These are the words of antiquity, a frame of inherited sobriety and seriousness for the emotion that can scarcely be contained within them. What is painfully and marvellously real lies within the embrace of what is profoundly shared and ancient.

Conclusion

The Bright Wake

HOMER DOES NOT PROVIDE any kind of guidance to life if the lessons derived are the usefulness of violence, the lack of regret at killing, the subjection and selling of women, the extinction of all men in a surrendering city or the sense that justice resides in personal revenge. That recipe for gang hell has always been troubling to the civilised. Pope was shocked at the 'spirit of cruelty which appears too manifestly in the *Iliad*'. William Blake blamed Homer for desolating Europe with wars. Joel Barlow, the American friend of Thomas Paine and advocate of Enlightenment virtues, lectured the governing classes of a misguided Europe on how Homer was satisfactory as a poet,

> but he has given to military life a charm which few men can resist, a splendor which envelops the scenes of carnage in a cloud of glory, which dazzles the eyes of every beholder. Alexander is not the only human monster that has been formed after the model of Achilles; nor Persia and Egypt the only countries depopulated for no other reason than the desire of rivalling predecessors in military fame.

What is valuable and essential in these poems is the opposite of that: the ability to regard all aspects of life with clarity, equanimity and sympathy, with a loving heart and an unclouded eye. Homer knows more than the people in the poems can ever know. He knows more than the Greek warriors on the Trojan beach, and more than the citizens of Troy.

He even knows more than Odysseus, and can look down on Odysseus, despite his failings, with paternal love. Homer matters because Homer, in a godlike way, understands what mortals do not. He even understands more than the gods, who emerge from the poems as sometimes terrifying but unreliable, intemperate and eventually ridiculous beings. That is his value, a reservoir of understanding beyond the grief and turbulence of a universe in which there is no final authority.

I am aware of how twenty-first-century this sounds – Homer with no trust in the metaphysical; a multiculturalist, able to empathise with both gang and city; a fusionist, seeing in Odysseus a man who might bring together the virtues of both worlds; even a liberal and feminist, who has a deep understanding of the dignity and beauty of women, their central role in human destiny. Nevertheless it is a picture of Homer that seems true, and it is not a sentimental vision. The depiction of wrongness is fundamental to it. In a review of the harsh, extremist essays of Simone Weil, Susan Sontag speculated on why these dark Homeric qualities are so necessary.

> There are certain ages which do not need truth as much as they need a deepening of the sense of reality, a widening of the imagination. I, for one, do not doubt that the sane view of the world is the true one. But is that what is always wanted, truth? The need for truth is not constant; no more than is the need for repose. The truth is balance, but the opposite of truth, which is unbalance, may not be a lie.

Homer's embrace of wrongness, his depiction of a world that stands at a certain angle to virtue, is the heart of why we love him. He does not give us a set of exemplars. These poems are not sermons. We do not want Achilles or even Odysseus to be our model as men. Nor Penelope or Helen as women. Nor do we want to worship at the shrine of Bronze Age thuggery. What we want is Homeric wisdom, his fearless encounter with the dreadful, his love of love and hatred of death, the sheer scale of his embrace, his energy and brightness, his resistance to nostalgia or to what the American philosopher Richard Rorty described as 'belatedness'. Most literature and philosophers, Rorty wrote, put value only in the past.

Nietzsche, at his worst, gestured towards some narcissistic and inarticulate hunks of Bronze Age beefcake. Carlyle gestured towards some contented peasants working the lands of a kindly medieval abbot. Lots of us occasionally gesture in the direction of the lost world in which our parents or our grandparents told us they grew up.

Homer doesn't do that. There is no sense that he has come late to life. The poems may enshrine the past, but they exist in a radiant present, and in that way are hymns to present being. The English poet Alice Oswald has described recently how Homer is infused with this glowing sense of reality. Ancient critics 'praised Homer's *enargeia*', she wrote in the Foreword to *Memorial*, her beautiful and stripped-down translation of the *Iliad*, 'which means something like "bright unbearable reality". It's the word used when gods come to earth not in disguise but as themselves.' *Enargeia*, a noun derived from the Greek word *argos*, meaning bright or shining, is 'the quality of having brightness in it', of being vividly there. For Greek rhetoricians *enargeia* was a necessary aspect of description or *ekphrasis*, a word that literally means 'a telling out'. And that pair of terms encapsulates the Homeric ideal: Homer's greatness is in its telling out of the embedded vivid, the core of life made explicit. Homer is not Greek; he is the light shining in the world.

He provides no answers. Do we surrender to authority? Do we abase ourselves? Do we indulge the self? Do we nurture civility? Do we nourish violence? Do we love? Homer says nothing in reply to those questions; he merely dramatises their reality. The air he breathes is the complexity of life, the bubbling vitality of a boat at sea, the resurgent energy, as he repeatedly says, of the bright wake starting to gleam behind you.

Acknowledgements

THIS IS TO THANK everyone who, over many years, knowingly or not, has helped me along Homer's tangled paths.

George Fairhurst; Vassilis Papadimitriou; Gavin Francis; Robert Macfarlane; Ali Serle; Juliet Nicolson; Rebecca Nicolson; Aurea Carpenter; Andrew Palmer; Paul Johnston; Alexandra Chaldecott; Ivan Samarine; Jim Richardson; Oliver Payne; Claire Whalley; Koenraad Kuiper; Liz Broomfield; Mary Keen; Laura Beatty; Martin Thomas; Matthew Reynolds; Matthew Rice; Nicholas Purcell; Philip Marsden; Robert Sackville-West; Richard Klein; Sarah Longley; Sigrid Rausing; Stephen Romer; Thomas Pennybacker; Casey Dué; David Sansone; Garry Fabian Miller; Charlie Burrell; Issy Burrell.

Sofka Zinovieff is the best friend, guide and companion anyone could wish for. Tim Dee took me to all sorts of Homeric places in a way that transformed my understanding of Homer. Caroline Alexander came and talked about my Homeric ideas for many vigorous and illuminating hours. David Anthony provided supremely helpful signposts to the world of the steppe.

I would particularly like to thank Kylie Richardson of Trinity Hall, Cambridge and Matt Hosty of Jesus College, Oxford for the care and trouble they took in saving me from the worst of mistakes. Needless to say, they bear no responsibility for those that remain.

At William Collins, Susan Watt, Helen Ellis, Robert Lacey and Joseph Zigmond have provided unstinting support and expertise. Arabella Pike has been the sort of editor any writer longs for: careful, considerate, encouraging, responsive, generous and above all able to summon the better book that always seems to lurk just beneath the surface. Many thanks also to Hilary Bird who compiled the index

George Capel has been my stalwart friend and ally throughout, and there is nothing I could say to thank her enough.

Above all I would like to thank Sarah and the children for putting up with Homer, who is not the easiest of house-guests, for quite so long. This book is dedicated to them.

Sarah Raven
Molly Nicolson
Rosie Nicolson
Benedict Nicolson
William Nicolson
Thomas Nicolson

Text Permissions

Gary Beckman (ed.), excerpts from *Hittite Diplomatic Texts, Second Edition*. Reprinted with the permission of the Society of Biblical Literature.

Jeremy Black, excerpt from Sumerian poem from 'Some Structural Features of Sumerian Narrative Poetry' in *Mesopotamian Epic Literature: Oral or Aural?*, edited by M.E. Vogelzang and H.L.J. Vanstiphout. Reprinted with the permission of The Edwin Mellen Press.

Edmond and Jules de Goncourt, excerpt from *The Goncourt Journals*, edited and translated by Robert Baldick. Copyright © 1962 by the Estate of Robert Baldick. Used by permission of New York Review Books.

Excerpt from A. Heidel, trans., *The Gilgamesh Epic and Old Testament Parallels*. Copyright 1946, 1949 by The University of Chicago. Reprinted by permission of The University of Chicago Press.

Homer, excerpt from *The Iliad*, with parallel translation by A.T. Murray, revised by W.F. Wyatt. Copyright © 1999 by the President and Fellows of Harvard College. Reprinted by permission of Harvard University Press.

Excerpts from *The Iliad of Homer*, translated by Richard Lattimore. Copyright 1951, © 2011 by The University of Chicago. Reprinted with the permission of The University of Chicago Press.

Excerpts from *The Iliad*, translated by Robert Fagles. Copyright © 1990 by Robert Fagles. Used by permission of Viking Penguin, a division of Penguin Group (USA) Inc.

Excerpts from *The Odyssey*, with parallel translation by A.T. Murray, revised by G.E. Dimock. Copyright © 1999 by the President and Fellows of Harvard College. Reprinted with the permission of Harvard University Press.

Excerpts from *The Odyssey*, translated by Richard Lattimore. Copyright © 1965, 1967 by Richard Lattimore. Reprinted by permission of HarperCollins Publishers Inc.

Excerpts from *The Odyssey*, translated by Robert Fagles. Copyright © 1996 by Robert Fagles. Used by permission of Viking Penguin, a division of Penguin Group (USA) Inc.

Christopher Logue, excerpt from 'The Iliad: Book XVI. An English Version' from *War Music*. Copyright © 1997 by Christopher Logue. Reprinted by permission of Farrar, Straus & Giroux, LLC and Faber and Faber, Ltd.

Edwin Muir, excerpt from 'The Horses' from *Collected Poems*. Copyright © 1960 by Willa Muir. Reprinted with the permission of Oxford University Press, Ltd. and Faber & Faber, Ltd.

R.B. Parkinson (ed. and trans.), excerpt from 'The Tale of Sinuhe' from *The Tale of Sinuhe and Other Egyptian Poems 1940–1640 BC*. Copyright © 1997 by R.B. Parkinson. Reprinted by permission of Oxford University Press, Ltd.

Milman Parry, excerpts from *The Making of Homeric Verse: The Collected Papers of Milman Parry*, edited by Adam Parry. Copyright © 1971 by Oxford University Press, Inc. Reprinted by permission of Oxford University Press, Ltd.

Notes

Preface

xviii 'poet of a boom': For most of the early twentieth century, in the wake of
the discoveries at Troy and Mycenae made by the romantic German busi-
nessman/archaeologist Heinrich Schliemann, Homer was thought to
describe the palatial Mycenaean world of c.1450 to c.1200 BC. Sir Moses
Finley, in *The World of Odysseus*, London, 1954, demolished that idea and
considered Homer a product of the ninth or tenth centuries BC. For a clear
and comprehensive discussion of the current orthodoxy which considers
Homer an eighth-century poet and his use as 'an archaeological artifact',
see Ian Morris, 'The Use and Abuse of Homer', *Classical Antiquity*, Vol. 5,
No. 1 (Apr. 1986), pp.81–138. Gregory Nagy in *Homeric Questions*, 1996,
argued that the poems did not reach their definitive form until the sixth
century BC, but the archaeologist Susan Sherratt's 'Archaeological Contexts'
in John Miles Foley, ed., *A Companion to Ancient Epic*, Blackwell, 2005,
pp.119–42, insists on the syncretism of early Mediterranean cultures. Their
core characteristic was the fusion of stories and ideologies. The Homer
poems, she says, are the clearest example of 'the ideological bricolage' of
different cultures spread across the whole of the eastern Mediterranean
and over a time period that stretches from at least 1800 to 800 BC (p.139).
In the Mediterranean everything was borrowed and shared, and that meeting
of cultures is both Homer's subject and his method. Sherratt's point is that
no picture of Homer can be pinned to a particular moment in that long
millennium, nor could it be complete without looking for a deep prehistory
to the epics, back to the beginning of the second millennium BC, or further.

In the 'social fluidity and instability' of that deep past were stories and questions which would have appealed to the audiences of the equally troubled ninth and eighth centuries BC more than the steady bureaucratic calm of the intervening palatial period of the late Bronze Age (p.138).

xix 'Epic's purpose': See the many essays in John Miles Foley, ed., *A Companion to Ancient Epic*, Blackwell, 2005

xix 'a revelatory fresco': This is the watercolour reconstruction made for Blegen by the Anglo-Dutch artist and architect Piet de Jong, first published in Carl W. Blegen, 'The Palace of Nestor Excavations of 1955', *American Journal of Archaeology*, Vol. 60, No. 2 (Apr. 1956), pp.95–101, plate 41 (b&w). Mabel L. Lang, in *The Palace of Nestor at Pylos in Western Messenia, Volume 2: The Frescoes*, Princeton, 1969, after a decade of heroic work with burnt and intransigent materials, reconstructed the fragments differently, and separated the bard from the bird. But there is no certainty here. Emily Vermeule, in her review of that book in *The Art Bulletin*, Vol. 52, No. 4 (Dec. 1970), pp.428–30, was sceptical about Mabel Lang's reconstruction.

xx 'leaving Homer's own': See Casey Dué, '*Epea Pteroenta*: How We Came to Have Our *Iliad*', in Casey Dué, ed., *Recapturing a Homeric Legacy: Images and Insights From the Venetus A Manuscript of the* Iliad, Center for Hellenic Studies, Washington, 2009, pp.19–30

xxi 'the neon edges': Christopher Logue, *War Music*, 2001, p.54

xxi 'Warm'd in the brain': Alexander Pope, *Iliad* 20.551

xxi 'like furnace doors': Christopher Logue, *War Music*, 2001, p.193

xxii 'sometimes travels beside': George Seferis, 'Memory 2', lines 5–9, from Logbook 3, in *Complete Poems*, trans. and ed. E. Keeley and P. Sherrard, 1995 (2009), p.188. Seferis may have been thinking of the cosmic power of Apollo himself, the god of truth and poetry, becoming a magical dolphin in the *Homeric Hymn to Delian Apollo*: 'In the open sea Apollo sprang upon their swift ship, like a dolphin in shape, and lay there, a great and awesome monster, and none of the crew gave heed so as to understand; but they sought to cast the dolphin overboard. But he kept shaking the black ship every way and made the timbers quiver. So they sat silent in their craft for fear, and did not ease the sheets throughout the black, hollow ship, nor lowered the sail of their dark-prowed vessel, but as they had set it first of all with oxhide ropes, so they kept sailing on; for a rushing south wind hurried on the swift ship from behind.' Eventually the god-driven ship grounded on the beach at Crisa, not far from Delphi, and 'like a star at noonday, the lord, far-working Apollo, leaped from the ship: flashes of fire flew from him thick and their brightness reached to heaven'. As translated by H.G. Evelyn-White in *Hesiod, Homeric Hymns, Epic Cycle, Homerica*, Loeb Classical Library, Vol. 57, Harvard University Press, 1914, pp.395ff.

xxii 'As the wings': George Seferis, 'Memory 2', line 10, from Logbook 3, *Complete Poems*, p.188

Chapter 1: Meeting Homer

1 'Robert Fagles': Homer, *The Odyssey*, trans. Robert Fagles, introduction and notes by Bernard Knox, New York, 1996

2 'Who would want': *Odyssey* 5.100–1

2 'What he thinks': *Odyssey* 10.472–4

3 'sea-blue': *Odyssey* 8.84

3 'the man of twists': *Odyssey* 1.1

4 'starred with flowers': *Odyssey* 12.159, Fagles 12.173. The Greek adjective *anthemoenta* means strictly no more than 'flowery', and it is Fagles who has beautifully poeticised this phrase. But if Homer is, in the end, neither a pair of poems nor the single author of them, but a living tradition, then that kind of enrichment of the inherited text seems the right thing to do.

5 'We know all': *Odyssey* 12.189–91, Fagles 12.205–7

6 'That is what': Carol Dougherty, in *The Raft of Odysseus: The Ethnographic Imagination of Homer's* Odyssey, Oxford, 2001, pp.71–3, has a wonderful discussion of Odysseus's 'metapoetic ship' as a vehicle for the heroic life.

Chapter 2: Grasping Homer

9 'Beauty is always': The following scenes are based on, but expanded and adapted from, *The Goncourt Journals by Edmond and Jules de Goncourt*, ed. and trans. Robert Baldick, *New York Review of Books*, 1962 (2007) pp.83–5, 118–19

11 'I can't remember': The point that Renan failed to remember may have been that the word usually translated as 'unharvestable' was said by the second-century AD Graeco-Roman grammarian Herodian, in a marginal comment on Homer's text, to mean 'never worn out', or 'unresting', and so in several

nineteenth-century translations the phrase became 'the restless sea'. Most modern translations prefer 'barren' or 'unharvestable', perhaps on the grounds that Homer doesn't do cliché.

13 'Almost at the beginning': *Odyssey* 2.337–70

14 'Ah dear child': *Odyssey* 2.363–70 (Murray/Dimock, adapted)

14 'Each time I': Kenneth Rexroth, *Classics Revisited*, 1968, p.7

15 'a jumbled heap': John Keats, sonnet, 'O Solitude', lines 2–3

15 'the barbarous age': Quoted in Andrew Motion, *Keats*, 1997, p.10

15 'Edmund Spenser's *Faerie Queene*': Spenser, *Faerie Queene*, Book 2, Canto xii, line 204; Motion, *Keats*, p.52

15 'The tide!': Motion, *Keats*, p.93

15 'both a lovely': Ibid., p.63

15 'a parallel universe': Ibid., p.41

16 'The conscious swains': Pope's translation of the *Iliad*, 8.559

16 'No man of true': *The Iliad of Homer, Translated by Alexander Pope, Esq*, W. Baynes & Son, 1824, p.4. For an illuminating modern discussion of translation as a kind of alchemical process, see Matthew Reynolds, *The Poetry of Translation: From Chaucer and Petrarch to Homer and Logue*, 2011

17 'What he writes': *The Iliad of Homer, Translated by Alexander Pope, Esq*, p.4

17 'In *Homer*': Ibid.

17 '*Virgil* bestows': Ibid., p.12

17 'unaffected and equal': Ibid., p.18

18 'In vain his youth': *Iliad* 20.537–46

18 'It is not to be': *The Iliad of Homer, Translated by Alexander Pope, Esq*, p.17

18 'a treasure of': Samuel Johnson, 'Life of Pope' (1779), in *The Works of the English Poets, from Chaucer to Cowper*, J. Johnson, 1810, Vol. 12, p.112

18 'money-mongering'; sonnet to Haydon, quoted in Motion, *Keats*, p.119

18 'the ocean': Keats, 'Sonnet I. To My Brother George', August 1816, from Margate

19 'the fine rough': Motion, *Keats*, p 109

19 'turning to some': Charles Cowden Clarke, 'Recollections of Keats' (1861), in *Recollections of Writers*, 1878, pp.120–57

19 'There did shine': Quoted in Andrew Laing, *The English Poets: Selections with Critical Introductions*, ed. Thomas Humphry Ward, 1880, Vol. 1, p.510

19 'loose and rambling': *The Iliad of Homer, Translated by Alexander Pope, Esq*, p.17

19 'now totally neglected': Johnson, 'Life of Pope', p.112

19 'Chapman writes & feels': S.T. Coleridge, 'Notes on Chapman's Homer', in *Notes and Lectures Upon Shakespeare and Some of the Old Poets and Dramatists: With Other Literary Remains of S.T. Coleridge*, Vol. 2, p.231

20 'cool their hooves': A phrase later borrowed by Christopher Logue for the moment when the two armies sit down to watch the duel between Paris and Menelaus:

> Now dark, now bright, now watch –
> As aircrews watch tsunamis send
> Ripples across the Iwo Jima Deep,
> Or, as a schoolgirl makes her velveteen
> Go dark, go bright –
> The armies as they strip, and lay their bronze
> And let their horses cool their hooves
> Along the opposing slopes.

20 'Just as when': *Odyssey* 5.328–30 (Murray/Dimock, adapted)

20 'he then bent both knees': *Odyssey* 5.453–7

21 'As a hero': See J.P. Mallory and D.Q. Adams, *The Oxford Introduction to Proto-Indo-European and the Proto-Indo-European World* (Oxford Linguistics), 2006, p.136

22 'his knees no more': Pope, *Odyssey* 5.606–10

22 'For the heart': Murray/Dimock, parallel text, Loeb Classical Library, Harvard University Press, 1919 (1995, 2002), *Odyssey* 5.454

22 'Odysseus bent his': Homer, *The Odyssey*, trans. E.V. Rieu, revised by D.C.H. Rieu, 1946, 1991, p.83

22 'his very heart': Richmond Lattimore, *The Iliad of Homer*, University of Chicago Press, 1951, 5.454

22 'The sea had': Homer, *The Odyssey*, trans. Robert Fagles, introduction and notes by Bernard Knox, New York, 1996, 5.502

22 'beastly place': Quoted in Motion, *Keats*, p.74

22 'On the first': This early draft, differing from the published version, is in the Houghton Library, Harvard University, MS Keats 2.4 A.MS.

25 'The troops exulting': Pope's *Iliad* 8.553–65

25 'the cockney Homer': J.G. Lockhart, 'On the Cockney School of Poetry, No. V', *Blackwood's Edinburgh Magazine* (Apr. 1819), p.97

25 'A thing of beauty': Keats, 'Endymion', Book I, 1–5

26 'And such too': Ibid., 20–1

Chapter 3: Loving Homer

27 'they don't eat bread': *Odyssey* 9.191

27 'Grilled meat': *Odyssey* 20.25–8

27 'no moment was': Odyssey 9.5–11

27 'all professional': Plato, *The Republic*, Book 3

28 'Mindjack': 'Mindjacking' is a term invented by the cyberpunk novelist William Gibson

28 'I am conscious': Plato, *Ion*, 380 BC, trans. Benjamin Jowett; see also Penelope Murray and T. Dorsch, *Classical Literary Criticism: Plato: Ion; Republic 2–3, 1; Aristotle: Poetics; Horace: The Art of Poetry; Longinus: On the Sublime*, 2000, p.1

28 'The gift which': Plato, *Ion*, 380 BC, translated by Benjamin Jowett; see also Murray and Dorsch, *Classical Literary Criticism*, p.5

28 'There is no invention': Plato, *Ion*, 380 BC, trans. Benjamin Jowett; see also Murray and Dorsch, *Classical Literary Criticism*, p.5

29 'I panegyrick poem': See Macaulay's *History*, Vol. 2, p.32, describing the Homeric world of the late-seventeenth-century Highlands and islands: 'Within the four seas and less than six hundred miles of London were many miniature courts, in each of which a petty prince, attended by guards, by armour bearers, by musicians, by an hereditary orator, by an hereditary poet laureate, kept a rude state, dispensed a rude justice, waged wars, and concluded treaties.' Also David Stevenson, *Highland Warrior: Alasdair Maccolla and the Civil Wars*, Edinburgh, 1980, for the re-emergence of a warrior society in the power vacuum created by the failure of the Scottish crown. The warrior world emerges not at a moment in history, but at a certain phase of human social and political arrangements.

29 'the people of Pylos': *Odyssey* 3.5–6

29 'Odysseus weeps': *Odyssey* 5.151

29 'he finds Nausicaa': *Odyssey* 6.1ff

29 'draw up their ships': *Odyssey* 11.20

29 'Odysseus lands': *Odyssey* 13.195ff

30 'So Ajax and': *Iliad* 9.182–4, Fagles 9.217–21

30 'wander in': *Iliad* 24.12–13, Fagles 24.15–16

31 'on her golden throne': *Odyssey* 10.541

31 'her veil the colour': *Iliad* 23.227

32 'that bellowed': *Odyssey* 2.421

32 'He spreads his sail': *Odyssey* 5.268

32 'and the wind' *Odyssey* 11.10

33 'So these two': *Iliad* 8.1–8

33 'Back towards home': *Iliad* 23.229–30 (Lattimore, adapted)

34 'the black ship': *Odyssey* 11.1–14

34 'red-painted bows': *Iliad* 2.637

34 'The wind caught': T.E. Shaw, *The Odyssey*, 1932, quoted in Rodelle Weintraub
    and Stanley Weintraub, 'Chapman's Homer', *The Classical World*, Vol. 67, No.
    1 (Sep.–Oct. 1973), pp.16–24

34 'Thus with stretched': Ezra Pound, 'Canto 1', 9–10

Chapter 4: Seeking Homer

36 *'germana et sincera'*: Joh. Baptista Caspar d'Ansse de Villoison, Homeri Ilias
    ad Veteris Codicis Veneti Fidem Recensita, 1788, p.xxxiv

36 'I will send': Robert Southey, ed., *The Works of William Cowper*, 1836, Vol. 6,
    p.266

36 'No such person': Thomas de Quincey, 'Homer and the Homeridae', *Blackwood's
    Edinburgh Magazine*, No. 312 (Oct. 1841), pp.411–27

37 'sovereign poet': Dante, *Inferno* 4. 88

37 'Medieval *Odyssey*s': For the most illuminating account of the early texts of
    Homer see M.L. West, ed. and trans., 'Lives of Homer', in *Homeric Hymns
    etc.*, Harvard University Press, 2003, pp.296ff

38 'Flinders Petrie found': William M. Flinders Petrie, *Hawara, Biahmu, and
    Arsinoe*, London, 1889. Plate xix shows many of these objects.

38 'The floating sand': Ibid., Chapter 5, on the papyri, written by Sayce, p.39

39 'The roll had belonged': Ibid., p.35

39 'This Hawara Homer' (photograph): P. Hawara 24–28 (Bodleian Libr., Gr. Class.
    A.1 (P)). *Iliad* 1.506–10, 2.1–877, with many lacunae. Found in the cemetery at
    Hawara in the Fayum on 21 February 1888 by W.M. Flinders Petrie. http://
    ipap.csad.ox.ac.uk/Hawara-bw/72dpi/Hawara_Homer%28viii%29.jpg

42 'Phaeacians': *Odyssey* 9.8–10

42 'Homer is the greatest': Plato, *The Republic*, 607 a 2–5

42 'Just as a poppy': *Iliad* 8.306–8

43 'to a place': *Iliad* 8.491

43 'In Troy itself': The Venetus A scholia on this passage are analysed by Graeme Bird in 'Critical Signs – Drawing Attention to "Special" Lines of Homer's *Iliad* in the Manuscript Venetus A', in Casey Dué, ed., *Recapturing a Homeric Legacy: Images and Insights From the Venetus A Manuscript of the Iliad*, Center for Hellenic Studies, Harvard, 2009, pp.112–14

43 'dogs, carried by': *Iliad* 8.526–40, Fagles 8.617–28

45 'We go to liberate': BBC News, 20 March 2003: 'UK Troops Told: Be Just and Strong', originally from a pooled report by Sarah Oliver, *Mail on Sunday*

46 'Alexandrian scholars': See Richard P. Martin, 'Cretan Homers: Tradition, Politics, Fieldwork', *Classics@* 3, © 2012, The Center for Hellenic Studies, Washington, DC

47 'The further back': Casey Dué, 'Epea Pteroenta: How We Came to Have Our *Iliad*', in *Recapturing a Homeric Legacy: Images and Insights From the Venetus A Manuscript of the Iliad*, Harvard, 2009, p.25

47 'young, headstrong': S. Butler, *The Authoress of the Odyssey*, 2nd edn 1922, p.142

47 'Would a man': Ibid., p.9, referring to *Odyssey* 9. 483, 540. But see the footnote on pp.350–1 of *The Odyssey*, Murray/Dimock (1999), which justifies Homer's apparent mistake.

47 'killed many men': David Garnett, ed., *The Letters of T.E. Lawrence*, London, 1938, letter no. 431, 31 January 1931, pp.709–10

47 'in fact the Baltic': Felice Vinci, *Omero nel Baltico*, with introductions by R. Calzecchi Onesti and F. Cuomo, Rome, 1998

47 'guidebook to the stars': Florence and Kenneth Wood, *Homer's Secret Iliad: The Epic of the Night Skies Decoded*, 1999

48 'Homer was from Cambridgeshire': Iman Wilkens, *Where Troy Once Stood*, 2nd edn 2009; a theory first developed by Théophile Cailleux, a Belgian lawyer, in *Pays atlantiques décrits par Homère. Ibérie, Gaule, Bretagne, Archipels, Amérique*, Paris, 1878 and *Théorie nouvelle sur les origines humaines. Homère en Occident. Troie en Angleterre*, Bruxelles, 1883

48 'Henriette Mertz': Henriette Mertz, *The Wine Dark Sea: Homer's Heroic Epic of the North Atlantic*, 1964

48 'everywhere and nowhere': M.L. West, ed. and trans., 'Lives of Homer', p.433

49 'The people of Ios': Ibid., p.435

50 'In the first lines': See ibid., p.413. Pseudo-Plutarch is quoting the epigram-matist Antipater of Thessalonica, fl. c.20 BC

50 'He is the embodiment': See for example ibid., p.429

51 '*U re u re na-nam*': Quoted M.L. West, *The East Face of Helicon*, 1999, p.61

51 'attend to what': J. Black, 'Some Structural Features of Sumerian Narrative Poetry', in M.E. Vogelzang and H.L.J. Vanstiphout, eds, *Mesopotamian Epic Literature: Oral or Aural?*, Lampeter, 1992, pp.71–101

51 'one more story': See M.L. West, 'Lives of Homer', pp.399, 411, 421–3, 437–9, 441–3, 447–9, for versions of this story

52 'Here the earth': See ibid., p.448

Chapter 5: Finding Homer

54 'the purple on account': Eustathius 6.8, quoted in M.L. West, *The Making of the* Iliad*: Disquisition and Analytical Commentary*, Oxford, 2011, p.75; impos-sibly expensive editions of Eustathius's commentaries are M. van der Valk, ed., *Eustathii Archiepiscopi Thessalonicensis Commentarii ad Homeri Iliadem Pertinentes ad Fidem Codicis Laurentiani Editi*, 4 vols, 1971–87

55 'Remember me': H.G. Evelyn-White, trans., *Hesiod, Homeric Hymns, Epic Cycle, Homerica*, Loeb Classical Library, Vol. 57, Harvard University Press, 1914, pp.165–6

57 'a well-girt man': John Boardman, *Excavations in Chios 1952–1955: Greek Emporio*, The British School at Athens. Supplementary Volumes, No. 6, 1967, pp.iii–xiv, 5

57 'wretched throughout': Ibid., pp.iii–xiv, 4

62 'Giorgio Buchner': Giorgio Buchner, 'Recent Work at Pithekoussai (Ischia), 1965–71', *Archaeological Reports*, No. 17 (1970–71), pp.63–7; D. Ridgway, *The First Western Greeks*, Cambridge, 1992; G. Buchner and D. Ridgway, *Pithekoussai, La necropoli: Tombe 1–723. Scavate dal 1952 al 1961*, Rome: Accademia Nazionale dei Lincei, 1993

62 'to monkey about': Catherine Connors, 'Monkey Business: Imitation, Authenticity, and Identity from Pithekoussai to Plautus', *Classical Antiquity*, Vol. 23, No. 2 (Oct. 2004), pp.179–207

63 'Much of their pottery': For images and information on the exhibits in the Museo Archeologico di Pithecusae in the Villa Arbusto on Ischia see http://www.pithecusae.it/colonia1.htm

64 'will lick the blood': *Iliad* 21.122–7

64 'voracious monsters': In 1934, part of the scapula of a young fin whale (average adult length sixty feet) was found in a well in the area that would later become the Agora in Athens. The pottery alongside it was slightly earlier than the Attic *cratēr* found in Ischia. Terrifyingly vast fish undoubtedly swam in the Odyssean world. This shoulderblade was probably used as a cutting surface, perhaps by a butcher or fishmonger. John K. Papadopoulos and Deborah Ruscillo, 'A Ketos in Early Athens: An Archaeology of Whales and Sea Monsters in the Greek World', *American Journal of Archaeology*, Vol. 106, No. 2 (Apr. 2002), pp.187–227.

65 'someone whose name': From Kate Monk, *Onomastikon*, 1997. http://tekeli. li/onomastikon/Ancient-World/Greece/Male.html

65 'Eighth-century inscriptions': Rufus Bellamy, 'Bellerophon's Tablet', *Classical Journal*, Vol. 84, No. 4 (Apr.–May 1989), pp.293, 299

65 'the first joke': Another scratched inscription on a mid-eighth-century wine jug unearthed in Athens may be slightly older. It was probably given as a prize in a dancing competition, and carries the beautiful verse '*hos nun orchēston panton atalotata paizēi*': 'Whoever of all these dancers now plays most delicately' – would, the implication is, receive this jug as a prize. This Greek Renaissance writing begins with dance and delight and competition. B. Powell, 'The Dipylon Oinochoe Inscription and the Spread of Literacy in 8th Century Athens', *Kadmos*, Vol. 27 (1988), pp.65–86.

66 'during a passage': *Iliad* 11.632–7

66 'dove-decorated cup': D. Ridgway, 'Nestor's Cup and the Etruscans', *Oxford Journal of Archaeology*, Vol. 16 (1997), pp.325–44

66 'giant unliftable cups': M.L. West, 'Grated Cheese Fit for Heroes', *Journal of Hellenic Studies*, Vol. 118 (1998), pp.190–1

66 'the joke and invitation': Not everyone agrees it was a joke. See Christopher A. Faraone, 'Taking the "Nestor's Cup Inscription" Seriously: Erotic Magic and Conditional Curses in the Earliest Inscribed Hexameters', *Classical Antiquity*, Vol. 15, No. 1 (Apr. 1996), pp.77–112

Chapter 6: Homer the Strange

68 'essentially oral': M.S. Edmondson, *Lore: An Introduction to the Science of Folklore and Literature*, New York, 1971, p.323

69 'a sequel of songs': R. Bentley, *Remarks Upon a Late Discourse of Free Thinking*, London, 1713

69 'quiet in manner': William C. Greene, 'Milman Parry (1902–1935)', *Proceedings of the American Academy of Arts and Sciences*, Vol. 71, No. 10 (Mar. 1937), pp.535–6

70 'the first to develop': Albert Lord, *The Singer of Tales*, Vol. 1, 2000, p.x

70 'an aura of': Harry Levin, 'Portrait of a Homeric Scholar', *The Classical Journal*, Vol. 32, No. 5 (Feb. 1937), pp.259–66

71 'How can we': Renan's long essay on *L'Avenir de Science*, Paris 1892, p.292, quoted by Milman Parry in Adam Parry, ed., *The Making of Homeric Verse: The Collected Papers of Milman Parry*, Oxford University Press, 1987, pp.2, 409

73 'This is the forest': Henry Wadsworth Longfellow, *Evangeline: A Tale of Acadie*, 1847, line 1

74 'and so on through': Parry, *The Making of Homeric Verse*, p.39

75 'The poetry was': Ibid., p.425

76 'Darwin of Homeric scholarship': Ibid., p.xxvi

76 'a machine of memory': James I. Porter, 'Homer: The Very Idea', *Arion*, Third Series, Vol. 10, No. 2 (Fall 2002), pp.57–86

76 'up to 494': Steve Reece, 'Some Homeric Etymologies in the Light of Oral-Formulaic Theory', *The Classical World*, Vol. 93, No. 2, Homer (Nov.–Dec. 1999), pp.185–99; M.M. Kumpf, *Four Indices of the Homeric Hapax Legomena*, Hildesheim: 1984, p.206; M.W. Edwards, *The Iliad: A Commentary*, Cambridge, 1991, Vol. 5, p.55

77 'But for Parry': Parry, *The Making of Homeric Verse*, p.21

77 'The tradition is': Ibid., p.450

77 'One's style should': Aristotle, *Rhetoric*, 1404 b 10

77 'genuine poetry': T.S. Eliot, *Selected Essays*, 3rd edn 1999, p.238

77 'not originally a written': Parry, *The Making of Homeric Verse*, pp.xxiii–xxiv

78 'You have your formulae': Ibid., p.448

80 'almost exactly a ton': http://chs119.chs.harvard.edu/mpc/index.html

81 'a tall, lean': From the draft of a text intended for a popular audience written in 1937 by Parry's youthful assistant Albert Lord. http://chs119.chs.harvard.edu/mpc/about/intro.html

81 'Finally Avdo came': Ibid.

81 'It takes the full': Parry, *The Making of Homeric Verse*, p.457

82 'Each singer sang': Ibid., pp.458, 460

82 'In June 1935': Halil Bajgorić, 'The Wedding of Mustajbey's Son Bećirbey', Parry no. 6699: www.oraltradition.org/static/zbm/zbm.pdf

83 'The moment he': Harry Levin, 'Portrait of a Homeric Scholar', *The Classical Journal*, Vol. 32, No. 5 (Feb. 1937), pp.259–66

84 'But why did you': From Parry, Conversation 6698, in *An eEdition of 'The Wedding of Mustajbey's Son Bećirbey'*, as performed by Halil Bajgorić, ed. and trans. John Miles Foley, on www.oraltradition.org

85 'The verses and': Parry, *The Making of Homeric Verse*, p.449

85 'They asked one': John Miles Foley, *Traditional Oral Epic: The Odyssey, Beowulf, and the Serbo-Croatian Return Song*, University of California Press, 1993, pp.44

86 'Plato thought nature': W.B. Yeats, 'Among School Children', 6 1–2, *The Tower*, 1928

86 'The more I understand': Parry, *The Making of Homeric Verse*, p.451 (written in January 1934), quoted in Richard Janko, 'The Homeric Poems as Oral Dictated Texts', *The Classical Quarterly*, New Series, Vol. 48, No. 1 (1998), pp.1–13

87 'written much later': Lord, *The Singer of Tales*

87 'It was the wet spring': A conversation I have described before, in *Sea Room*, 2001, p.292

88 'everything in his songs': Foley, *Traditional Oral Epic*, p.44; Parry, Conversation 6598

89 'making the wince': See http://www.recordingpioneers.com/RP_NOTOPOULOS1.html

89 'bitter and heroic resistance' See turcopolier.typepad.com/sic_semper_tyrannis/files/arion_odysseus.doc

89 'He found Sfakia': James A. Notopoulos, 'The Genesis of an Oral Heroic Poem', *Greek, Roman and Byzantine Studies*, Vol. 3 (1960), pp.135–44

93 'the opposite conclusion': Maartje Draak, 'Duncan MacDonald of South Uist', *Fabula*, Vol. 1 (1957), pp.47–58; William Lamb, 'The Storyteller, the Scribe, and a Missing Man: Hidden Influences from Printed Sources in the Gaelic Tales of Duncan and Neil MacDonald', *Oral Tradition*, Vol. 27, No. 1 (2012), pp.109–60

93 'heir to the great traditions': See The Calum Maclean Project, Department of Celtic and Scottish Studies, University of Edinburgh, http://www.calum-maclean-project.celtscot.ed.ac.uk/home/; Lamb, 'The Storyteller, the Scribe, and a Missing Man'

94 'polished, shapely': http://calumimaclean.blogspot.co.uk/2013_02_01_archive. html

94 'On analysis': Maartje Draak, 'Duncan MacDonald of South Uist'

95 'ethnographers have discovered': Douglas Young, 'Never Blotted a Line? Formula and Premeditation in Homer and Hesiod', *Arion*, Vol. 6, No. 3 (Autumn 1967), pp.279–324

95 'had in his head': Ibid.

Chapter 7: Homer the Real

97 'the terrible noise': *Iliad* 6.105

98 'Like the generations': *Iliad* 6.146–50, Fagles 6.171–5

98 'as many as the leaves': *Iliad* 2.468

99 'Near the city': *Iliad* 2.811–14 (Murray/Wyatt, slightly adapted)

99 'epic poetry is': Jonas Grethlein, 'Memory and Material Objects in the *Iliad* and the *Odyssey*', *Journal of Hellenic Studies*, Vol. 128 (2008), pp.27–51

99 'such as will remain': *Iliad* 3.287

99 'the Muse provides': *Odyssey* 8.479–81

100 'in the same class': *Iliad* 9.364

100 'Achilles's iron heart': *Iliad* 20.372. This is a translation of the phrase *aithōni sidērō*, which might also mean more prosaically 'shining iron'.

100 'a profoundly ancient world': See for example Susan Sherratt, 'Archaeological Contexts', in John Miles Foley, ed., *A Companion to Ancient Epic*, Blackwell, 2005, pp.119–42

101 'had found six hundred': C.W. Blegen and M. Rawson, *The Palace of Nestor at Pylos in Western Messenia, Vol. I: The Buildings and Their Contents*, Princeton, 1966, I, 6, pp.95–100; C.W. Blegen and K. Kourouniotis, 'Excavations of Pylos, 1939', *American Journal of Archaeology*, Vol. 43 (1939), p.569

101 'No one could guess': Ione Mylonas Shear, 'Bellerophon Tablets from the Mycenaean World? A Tale of Seven Bronze Hinges', *Journal of Hellenic Studies*, Vol. 118 (1998), pp.187–9

102 'A piece of firewood': Christoph Bachhuber, 'Aegean Interest on the Uluburun Ship', *American Journal of Archaeology*, Vol. 110, No. 3 (Jul. 2006), pp.345–63

103 'a moment from the *Iliad*': *Iliad* 6.119–236

104 'He quickly sent': *Iliad* 6.168–70

104 'What does this description': T.R. Bryce, 'The Nature of Mycenaean

Involvement in Western Anatolia', *Historia*, Vol. 38 (1989), pp.13–14; Rufus Bellamy, 'Bellerophon's Tablet', *Classical Journal*, Vol. 84 (1989), pp.289–307; Shear, 'Bellerophon Tablets from the Mycenaean World?'; Byron Harries, '"Strange Meeting": Diomedes and Glaucus in *Iliad* 6', *Greece & Rome*, Vol. 40 (1993), pp.133–47; T.R. Bryce, 'Anatolian Scribes in Mycenaean Greece', *Historia*, Vol. 48 (1999), pp.257–64

105 'a tiny glimpse into': Not everyone agrees with this view of Homer's Greeks – or in this distinction between Greek and Trojan. From the *Odyssey* comes all kinds of evidence that the Greeks were at home in palaces: Nestor and Menelaus live in elaborate and comfortable set-ups at Pylos and Sparta, full of warmth and ritualised hospitality. Even Odysseus's home on Ithaca, while clearly not a major citadel, has *megara skioenta*, 'shadowed halls', like the rich Near Eastern palace of Alcinous in Scheria. These hints and suggestions can be taken as a sign that the *Odyssey* was deeply coloured by its transmission through the palace centuries of the Mycenaean period, when the cultural expectations of a great man's equipment had come to include a palace establishment.

The *Iliad*, perhaps because the circumstances of war did not encourage it, remained more resistant to these later influences. It is true that even in the *Iliad* Mycenae is described as *euktimenon ptoliethron*, a well-founded citadel (2.569–70), *polychrysos*, 'rich in gold' (11.46), and elsewhere, like Troy, *euruaguia*, 'with broad streets' (4.52). But these are no more than marginal suggestions. The poetic weight of warriorhood in the poem remains firmly on the Greek side, and the poetic weight of civility and urbanness firmly on the Trojan. Hector is undoubtedly a ferocious warrior, but he is nearly alone as such among the Trojans, who do not entirely admire him for it. Paris and Priam on the other hand represent two contrasting dimensions of urban civility – wise government and a tendency to foppishness – and appear as they do, not because of the circumstances in which they find themselves, but because of their essential natures. The same is true of Achilles: he will be the unaccommodated man in whatever circumstances he finds himself. For all the surrounding realism and nuance, these are the polarities the *Iliad* dramatises.

105 'floats all through': Emily Townsend Vermeule, 'Jefferson and Homer', *Proceedings of the American Philosophical Society*, Vol. 137, No. 4, 250th Anniversary Issue (Dec. 1993), pp.689–703

105 'in many parts earlier': M.L. West, 'The Rise of the Greek Epic', *Journal of Hellenic Studies*, Vol. 108 (1988), pp.151–72

106 'but the Iliadic words': Ibid.

107 'There are in all': E. Meyer, 'Schliemann's Letters to Max Müller in Oxford', *Journal of Hellenic Studies*, Vol. 82 (1962), p.92. Letter dated 24 November 1876

107 'he identified the warriors': He claimed in a telegram to a Greek newspaper that on exposing one of the gold-encrusted kings he felt that 'This corpse very much resembles the image which my imagination formed long ago of wide-ruling Agamemnon' (Cathy Gere, *The Tomb of Agamemnon: Mycenae and the Search for a Hero*, London, 2006, p.76). He never said, as is usually reported, that he had 'gazed on the face of Agamemnon', nor was he referring to the wonderful gold face-mask now universally referred to as the Mask of Agamemnon. That handsome, moustachioed, boulevardier king, the most famous face of the Bronze Age, belonged to another grave. Immediately before sending his telegram, Schliemann had looked at a dead body 'whose round face, with all its flesh had been wonderfully preserved', eyes and teeth all there. That face had also been covered in a gold mask, but it is a strange thing, clean-shaven, as round as a football, fat-cheeked and pig-eyed, an image of regality that has never been explained. (see Gere, p.79, for an illustration of the gold mask from Shaft Grave 4 of Grave Circle A, Mycenae, 1550–1500 BC.)

107 'Nothing of that': Homer does not describe burials of the kind that are found in the Shaft Graves at Mycenae. The Homeric hero is always cremated on a pyre, and his remains put in a container that is then buried within a large tumulus. That is a form of interment that is found all over the Indo-European world, but not in Greece, at least until the eighth century BC (see Miss H.L. Lorimer, 'Pulvis et Umbra', *Journal of Hellenic Studies*, Vol. 53 (1933), pp.161–80). Different Indo-European peoples at different times both cremated and buried their dead. So this is a conundrum: are the burial practices in Homer evidence of their being very late poems, no earlier than the eighth century BC? Or is this evidence of some deep memory of early Indo-European traditions which also gave rise to cremation for heroes in Scandinavia, and to people in India and Iran? See Mallory and Adams, *Encyclopedia of Indo-European Culture*, p.151.

108 'the slayers and the slain': *Iliad* 11.83–162

108 'ungentle was': *Iliad* 11.137: *ameiliktos d'op akousan*

109 'And just as when': *Iliad* 11.269–72 (Murray/Wyatt, adapted)

110 'As when the open sea': *Iliad* 14.16–20 (Lattimore, adapted)

111 'Philologists often dislike': Emily Townsend Vermeule, 'Jefferson and Homer'

112 'He spoke, and': *Iliad* 16.856–7, 22.362–3 (Lattimore, adapted)

112 'The difference': Emily Vermeule, *Aspects of Death in Early Greek Art and Pottery*, University of California Press, 1979, p.9: 'Now a doctor in Düsseldorf has succeeded in quantifying the soul by placing the beds of his terminal patients on extremely sensitive scales. "As they died and the souls left their bodies, the needles dropped twenty-one grams."' She was quoting Dr Nils-Olof Jacobson, 'Life After Death', *Boston Globe*, 19 December 1972. The claim that the weight of the soul is twenty-one grams was first made in 1901 by a group of American doctors, including Duncan MacDougall of Massachusetts, who carried out experiments reported in the *New York Times* in March 1907.

Chapter 8: The Metal Hero

114 'Parys Mountain': For a full account of Parys Mountain, see Bryan D. Hope, *A Curious Place: The Industrial History of Amlwch (1550–1950)*, Wrexham, 1994

114 'In about 8000 BC': B.W. Roberts, C.P. Thornton and V.C. Piggott, 'Development of Metallurgy in Eurasia', *Antiquity*, Vol. 83 (2009), pp.1012–22

114 'Only then did someone': Evgenii N. Chernykh, *Ancient Metallurgy in the USSR: The Early Metal Age*, trans. Sarah Wright, Cambridge University Press, 1992

115 'It became a world': Kristian Kristiansen and Thomas B. Larsson, *The Rise of Bronze Age Society: Travels, Transmissions and Transformations*, Cambridge University Press, 2005, pp.108–9, 114, 123–4

115 'The broad picture': Richard J. Harrison, *Symbols and Warriors: Images of the European Bronze Age*, Bristol: Western Academic and Specialist Press, 2004

115 'patterns that recur': See Kristiansen and Larsson, *The Rise of Bronze Age Society, passim*

115 'Were these movements': See ibid., pp.142–250

115 'The teeth of': A.P. Fitzpatrick, *The Amesbury Archer and the Boscombe Bowmen*, Salisbury: Trust for Wessex Archaeology Ltd, 2011

116 'Chemical analysis': Pippa Bradley, 'Death Pits at Cliff End', *British Archaeology*, Vol. 131 (Jul.–Aug. 2013)

116 'It seems inescapable': Stephen Oppenheimer, 'A Reanalysis of Multiple Prehistoric Immigrations to Britain and Ireland Aimed at Identifying Celtic Contributions', in B. Cunliffe and J.T. Koch, *Celtic from the West*, Oxford: Oxbow, 2010, p.142

116 'A different, non-urban': Philip L. Kohl, *The Making of Bronze Age Eurasia*, Cambridge University Press, 2007, pp.126ff

119 'They clothed their': *Iliad* 14.384 ff

119 'as snug as': Seamus Heaney, 'Digging', from *Death of a Naturalist*, Faber, 1966

120 '*Doupēsen de pesōn*': e.g. *Iliad* 4.504, 17.50

123 'their life dependent': See Vermeule, *Aspects of Death in Early Greek Art and Poetry*, pp.99–101, 112–15

124 'Adolf Schulten': A. Schulten, *Fontes Hispaniae Antiquae*, Vol. 1, 1922, p.90

124 'Inner and outer landscapes': Circe's description at *Odyssey* 10.510. Odysseus comes to the shores of Hades at *Odyssey* 11.22

125 'dissolving like': *Odyssey* 11.208, Fagles 11.237

125 'Never try to': *Odyssey* 11.408ff

126 'through his tears': It's not certain that he's weeping – *olophuromai* usually means 'lament, be sad' – but this is likely to be the sense.

126 'like consuming fire': *Iliad* 20.372

126 'But tell me': *Odyssey* 11.491

127 'murdering Priam': This was the scene, transmitted through the *Aeneid*, when Neoptolemos was slaughtering his way through Troy, 'And all his father sparkled in his eyes', that caught Hamlet's imagination: the young Greek was

    total gules; horridly trick'd
    With blood of fathers, mothers, daughters, sons,
    Bak'd and impasted with the parching streets,
    That lend a tyrannous and damned light
    To their lord's murder. (*Hamlet* 2.ii.457–61)

127 'So I spoke': *Odyssey* 11.538–40, Fagles 11.613–16

127 'Set up your mast': *Odyssey*, 10.506–7 (Murray/Dimock, slightly adapted)

127 'But when in': *Odyssey* 10.508–12 (Murray/Dimock)

128 'There into the ocean': *Odyssey* 10.513–15 (Murray/Dimock)

130 'The extraction': http://www.parquemineroderiotinto.com/

131 'at a place called Chinflón': The mine at Chinflón is at 37°40'N, 6°40'W; see
    B. Rothenberg and A. Blanco-Freijeiro, 'Ancient Copper Mining and
    Smelting at Chinflón (Huelva, SW Spain)', *British Museum Occasional Paper*,
    20 (1980), pp.41–62; for bronze mining see Ben Roberts, 'Metallurgical
    Networks and Technological Choice: Understanding Early Metal in Western
    Europe', *World Archaeology*, Vol. 40, Issue 3 (2008), pp.354–72; Anthony F.
    Harding, *European Societies in the Bronze Age*, Cambridge University Press,
    2000, pp.197–241

132 'In Cornwall': M.A. Courtney, 'Cornish Folk-Lore', Part 3, *The Folk-Lore
    Journal*, Vol. 5, No. 3 (1887), pp.177–220; James C. Baker, 'Echoes of Tommy
    Knockers in Bohemia, Oregon, Mines', *Western Folklore*, Vol. 30, No. 2 (Apr.
    1971), pp.119–22

132 'called the little': Georgius Agricola, *De Animantibus Subterraneis*, 1548

132 'represent man's inner': Ronald Finucane, *Ghosts*, Prometheus, 1996, p.1

133 'their ancient beliefs': Agricola, *De Animantibus Subterraneis*; Courtney,
    'Cornish Folk-Lore', Part 3; Finucane, *Appearances of the Dead*; Baker, 'Echoes
    of Tommy Knockers in Bohemia, Oregon, Mines'

133 'When it comes to': Gaston Bachelard, *The Poetics of Space*, Beacon Press,
    1958 (1994), pp.18–20

134 'a catalogue': Harrison, *Symbols and Warriors*. The stelae in the Archaeological
    Museum in Badajoz represent perhaps the richest of all collections. Others
    are in Cordoba, Huelva, Seville and Madrid, and in Portugal.

134 'topped and mended': *Odyssey* 14.10

134 'None of this is different': Harrison, *Symbols and Warriors*, pp.12, 24

136 'red with the blood': *Iliad* 18.538

136 'fruit in wicker': *Iliad* 18.568

136 'the perfect circle': Menelaus's, for example, in *Iliad* 17.6

136 'obsessed with male beauty': M. Eleanor Irwin, 'Odysseus's "Hyacinthine
    Hair" in *Odyssey* 6.231', *Phoenix*, Vol. 44, No. 3 (Autumn 1990), pp.205–18

137 'who held his head': *Iliad* 6.509–10

137 'His strength can do': *Iliad* 21.316–18

138 'Great Priam entered in': *Iliad* 24.477–9 (Murray, adapted)

138 'roused in Achilles': *Iliad* 24.507–8

139 'And they came': *Iliad* 9.185–91 (Murray/Wyatt)

139 'Archaeologists working': http://www.aocarchaeology.com/news/the-lyre-bridge-from-high-pasture-cave

139 'It seems from': Harrison, *Symbols and Warriors*, p.104

140 'A huge warrior figure': Ibid., pp.298–9; Catalogue number C80, found at Ategua, Cordoba. Now in the Museo Arqueológico Provincial de Cordoba

141 'Ah Sokos': *Iliad* 11.450–5 (Lattimore, adapted)

142 'He is a unique': Harrison, *Symbols and Warriors*, p.116

142 'Hector . . . talk not': *Iliad* 22.261–7

143 'the heroes gave orders': Harrison, *Symbols and Warriors*, p.116

Chapter 9: Homer on the Steppes

144 'The origins of': J.P. Mallory, *In Search of the Indo-Europeans: Language, Archaeology and Myth*, London, 1989

145 'And before that': N.G.L. Hammond, 'Tumulus-Burial in Albania, the Grave Circles of Mycenae, and the Indo-Europeans', *Annual of the British School at Athens*, Vol. 62 (1967), pp.77–105

145 'Right in the middle': *Odyssey* 11.119–37

145 'You must go out': *Odyssey* 11.121–30, Fagles 11.138–49

147 'recorded from Sophocles': R. Scott Smith and Stephen M. Trzaskoma, trans., *Apollodorus' Library and Hyginus' Fabulae: Two Handbooks of Greek Mythology*. Indianapolis: Hackett, 2007, *Fabula*, p.95

148 'Our land': Plato, *Critias*

149 'It is possible': M.L. West, *The Making of the* Iliad*: Disquisition and Analytical Commentary*, Oxford University Press, 2011, p.42

149 'the smoke ascending': *Iliad* 21.522–3 (Lattimore)

149 'the speech he makes': *Iliad* 9.308–409

150 'rich with fat.': *Iliad* 9.205–8

150 'Odysseus then lists': *Iliad* 9.264–98

150 'Let him submit': *Iliad* 9.160

150 'the greediest': *Iliad* 1.122

150 'As I detest': *Iliad* 9.312–14 (Lattimore, adapted)

151 'Hateful in my eyes': *Iliad* 9.378ff

151 'All the wealth': *Iliad* 9.401–2

151 'Cattle and fat sheep': *Iliad* 9.405–9 (Lattimore)

152 'But alongside that': *Iliad* 9.400

152 'These questions': See: Adam Parry, 'The Language of Achilles', *Transactions and Proceedings of the American Philological Association*, Vol. 87 (1956), pp.1–7; M.D. Reeve, 'The Language of Achilles', *The Classical Quarterly*, New Series, Vol. 23, No. 2 (Nov. 1973), pp.193–5; Steve Nimis, 'The Language of Achilles: Construction vs. Representation', *The Classical World*, Vol. 79, No. 4 (Mar.–Apr. 1986), pp.217–25; W. Donlan, 'Duelling with Gifts in the *Iliad*: As the Audience Saw It', *Colby Quarterly*, Vol. 24 (1993) p.171; Dean Hammer, 'Achilles as Vagabond: The Culture of Autonomy in the "Iliad"', *The Classical World*, Vol. 90, No. 5 (May–Jun. 1997), pp.341–66

153 'Those connections': For these and many of the examples in the following pages of reconstructed and inherited words in the Indo-European family, see the outstanding J.P. Mallory and D.Q. Adams, *The Oxford Introduction to Proto Indo-European*, Oxford, 2006

153 'words that have been': For an overview of the Indo-European world see Benjamin W. Fortson 4, *Indo-European Language and Culture: An Introduction*, 2nd edn, Chichester, 2010

153 'the same word at root': See Mallory and Adams, *The Oxford Introduction to Proto Indo-European*, p.138. The reconstructed root for 'otter' in PIE is *udrós*, with descendants in Latin, English, Lithuanian, Russian, Greek, Iranian and Sanskrit. That reconstructed word is itself formed from the word for 'water', *wódr*.

154 'A verb for the driving': J.P. Mallory, *In Search of the Indo-Europeans*, London, 1989, pp.117–18: 'the frozen expression "to drive cattle" is found in Celtic, Italic and Indo-Iranian'. Sanskrit and Greek share a word for the special sacrifice of 'one hundred cows': the Greek word is a hecatomb, but I don't know the Sanskrit word!

154 'It seems as if': Ibid., p.118: 'It has long been regarded as reasonable that there was an irreversible semantic development that led from a word "to comb" and a noun "sheep" (the woolly animal) to livestock in general and finally to wealth, hence German *Vieh* "cattle" and English *fee*. More recently, however, this was challenged by Emile Benveniste who argued that the semantic development should indeed be reversed and begin with the concept of "movable possessions" which, under the influence of later cultural development, was gradually specified to sheep.' The PIE root is reconstructed as *péku*. See Emile Benveniste, *Indo-European Language and Society*, Florida, 1973.

155 'The word . . . applied': Mallory, *In Search of the Indo-Europeans*, p.123: 'Many Indo-European languages do employ the same Proto-Indo-European verb *wedh* – "To lead (home)" when expressing the act of becoming married from a groom's point of view.'

155 'That original compound': Mallory and Adams, *The Oxford Introduction to Proto Indo-European*, p.323

156 'In other languages': Bernard Comrie, *Tense*, Cambridge, 1985

158 'It was probably domesticated': For the transforming role of the horse in steppeland life see David W. Anthony, *The Horse, the Wheel, and Language: How Bronze-Age Riders from the Eurasian Steppes Shaped the Modern World*, Princeton University Press, 2007

158 'both descended from': Mallory and Adams, *The Oxford Introduction to Proto Indo-European*, p.134

158 'or in hill-figures': The White Horse at Uffington (illustrated), not merely scratched into the turf but deliberately constructed with chalk rammed into deep trenches, nearly in the form it still maintains, has been dated to the Bronze Age, perhaps as early as 1400 BC, and has been regularly maintained ever since. David Miles and Simon Palmer, 'White Horse Hill', *Current Archaeology*, Vol. 142 (1995), pp.372–8. Images of horses on Celtic Iron Age coinage (the illustration is of a gold *stater* coined by the Gaulish Parisii c.70–60 BC) draw as much on that tradition as on Mediterranean examples.

159 'a place called Sintashta': Anthony, *The Horse, the Wheel and Language*, pp.371–411

159 'they might have been': Ibid., pp.371–411, 452–57

160 'it is possible for': *Iliad* 10.505

160 'at the funeral games': The chariot race at Patroclus's funeral games are at *Iliad* 23.286–534

160 'build for many days': They took nine days bringing in the timber for Hector's funeral pyre. *Iliad* 24.783–4

160 'both Poseidon and Athene': M. Detienne and A.B. Werth, 'Athena and the Mastery of the Horse', *History of Religions*, Vol. 11, No. 2 (Nov. 1971), pp.161–84

161 'a prize-winning horse': *Iliad* 22.22

161 'whiter than snow': *Iliad* 10.436, 547

161 'like a horse that': *Iliad* 15.263ff

161 'The Trojans sacrifice': *Iliad* 21.132

161 'dominates the names': Grace H. Macurdy, 'The Horse-Taming Trojans', *Classical Quarterly*, Vol. 17, No. 1 (Jan. 1923), pp.50–2

162 'tells Telemachus': *Odyssey* 4.271ff

162 'The second time': *Odyssey* 8.499ff

163 'his whole body': *Aeneid* 6.497–9

163 'As a woman weeps': *Odyssey* 8.523–32 (Lattimore, adapted)

164 'The gods did this': *Odyssey* 8.579–80 (Lattimore, fundamentally)

164 'Those who had dreamed': Simone Weil, '*L'Iliade ou le poème de la force*', in *Les Cahiers du Sud* (1940). See also Simone Weil and Rachel Bespaloff, *War and the* Iliad, trans. Mary McCarthy, *New York Review of Books* (2005), p.3

164 'the word Homer uses': *Iliad* 13.393

166 'We did not dare': Edwin Muir, 'The Horses', from *One Foot in Eden*, 1956

167 'Sleep sits': *Iliad* 14.290

167 'beautiful as a star': *Iliad* 6.399–403

167 'like cattle stepping': *Iliad* 20.495

167 'a snowy mountain': *Iliad* 13.754

168 'Usatovo, near Odessa': D.Ya. Telegin and David W. Anthony, 'On the Yamna Culture', *Current Anthropology*, Vol. 28, No. 3 (Jun. 1987), pp.357–8

170 'a world not of palaces': Katarzyna Slusarska, 'Funeral Rites of the Catacomb Community: 2800–1900 BC: Ritual, Thanatology and Geographical Origins', *Baltic-Pontic Studies*, Vol. 13 (2006), Poznań

170 'Scholars have pursued': For many of these references see M.L. West, 'The Rise of the Greek Epic', *Journal of Hellenic Studies*, Vol. 108 (1988), pp.151–72

171 'as Nestor tells': *Iliad* 2.362

171 '*ep' eurea nota thalasses*': *Iliad* 20.228, etc.

172 'He harnessed to': *Iliad* 13.23–31 (Lattimore)

172 'When Aeneas is remembering': *Iliad* 20.217

172 'They would play': *Iliad* 20.228–9 (Lattimore, slightly adapted)

173 'It is by cunning': *Iliad* 23.316–18, 325

173 'fast-running ships': *Odyssey* 4.708–9 (Lattimore)

173 'Just as in a field': *Odyssey* 13.81–5 (Lattimore)

173 'beautiful metal dogs': *Odyssey* 7.91–4

173 'robotic golden girls': *Iliad* 18.372ff

174 'the point pounding': *Iliad* 5.66–8, Fagles 5.73–5

174 'Who had the skill': *Iliad* 5.60–14, Fagles 5.66–70

174 'At this most fundamental': For these transitions see Mallory and Adams, *The Oxford Introduction to Proto-Indo-European and the Proto-Indo-European World*; and Anthony, *The Horse, the Wheel and Language*, pp.371–411, 452–7

175 'They can only have': Thomas F. Strasser et al., 'Stone Age Seafaring in the Mediterranean, Plakias Region for Lower Palaeolithic and Mesolithic Habitation of Crete', *Hesperia*, Vol. 79 (2010), pp.145–90

175 'the colossal vortex': For the transforming arrival of the sailing ship, see the concluding chapter of Cyprian Broodbank, *An Island Archaeology of the Early Cyclades*, Cambridge University Press 2000, p.345

175 'And above all': Ibid., p.345

176 'Topsail, Riptide': *Odyssey* 8.130–9, Fagles

176 'Our ships can': *Odyssey* 8.556–63

177 'drastically shrunk': Broodbank, *An Island Archaeology of the Early Cyclades*

177 'Menelaus remembers': *Odyssey* 3.158

177 'It was fast ships': *Iliad* 7.467–75

177 'It is the ships': *Iliad* 15.502ff

Chapter 10: The Gang and the City

179 'the abandoned weapons': *Iliad* 10.469

179 'the most savage': *Iliad* 1.146

179 'shaggy breasts': *Iliad* 1.189

179 'black blood': *Iliad* 1.303

180 'the wives and daughters': *Iliad* 6.237–8 (adapted from Murray/Wyatt)

180 'that magnificent': *Iliad* 6.242–9, Fagles 6.289–97

181 'Let no man': *Iliad* 2.354–5 (Murray/Wyatt, slightly adapted)

181 'formulaic adjectives': *Iliad* 2.540, etc.

182 'They love their': *Iliad* 14.120

182 'And now sweeter': *Iliad* 2.450–4

182 'Beware the toils': *Iliad* 5.487–8, Fagles 5.559–60

183 '264 people': C.B. Armstrong, 'The Casualty Lists in the Trojan War', *Greece and Rome*, Vol. 16, pp.30–1, gives 238 named casualties and twenty-six unnamed, sixty-one of whom are Greek and 203 Trojan.

183 'they limp and': *Iliad* 9.502–6, Fagles 9.610–17

184 'Of all that breathe': *Iliad* 17.441–7, Fagles 17.509–15

184 'Patroclus rampages through': Patroclus begins his tragic and destructive drive at *Iliad* 16.284

185 'Next he went': *Iliad* 16.401–10, Fagles 16.477–89

185 'Ahead, Patroclus': Christopher Logue, in '*The Iliad*: Book 16. An English Version', *Arion*, Vol. 1, No. 2 (Summer 1962), pp.3–26; a revised version in Logue's *War Music*, Faber, 2001, p.154, is subtly different from this.

186 'The first fighting': At *Iliad* 4.446

186 'a cause for rejoicing': *Iliad* 7.189

186 'Now the sun': *Iliad* 7.421–9 (Lattimore)

187 'Bruce Jacobs and Richard Wright': Bruce A. Jacobs and Richard Wright, *Street Justice: Retaliation in the Criminal Underworld*, Cambridge University Press, Cambridge Studies in Criminology, 2006

187 'This desire for': Ibid., p.25

187 'urban nomads': Ibid., p.12

187 'maintaining a reputation': Ibid., p.32

188 'Everyone was watching': Ibid., p.76

188 'Book 10 of the *Iliad*': This book, the *Doloneia*, is widely thought to be an addition to the *Iliad* which does not belong naturally with the rest. It doesn't fit easily into the story, and is written in an often bizarre Greek. One possible conclusion is that 'it was added to the epic not long after its monumental composition by a different poet, who knew the *Iliad* as a fixed text and took care to fit his tale to the *Iliad* situation, but had his own distinctive way of using the poetic materials' (M.M. Willcock, 'The Poet of the Doloneia: Studien zur Dolonie by Georg Danek', *Classical Review*, New Series, Vol. 39, No. 2 (1989), pp.178–80). The 'Homer' of the *Iliad* and the 'Homer' of the *Doloneia* were different poets, but both can only have been drawing on the same braided tradition.

188 'two lions': *Iliad* 10.297–8 (Lattimore)

188 'like two rip-fanged': *Iliad* 10.360–1 (Lattimore)

188 'The two Greeks': *Iliad* 10.400

188 'struck the middle': *Iliad* 10.455–7 (Lattimore)

189 'calling them fools': *Iliad* 16.833, 11.450–5, 2.870

189 'I got your': Jacobs and Wright, *Street Justice*, p.35

189 'I felt like I was': Ibid., p.36

190 'When he smiles': Colton Simpson with Ann Pearlman, *Inside the Crips*, St Martin's Press, 2005, p.14

190 'No one forgets': Martín Sánchez-Jankowski, *Islands in the Street: Gangs and American Urban Society*, University of California Press, 1991, pp.140–1

191 'Neither rape nor': Ibid., p.79

192 'Troy must have': D.F. Easton, J.D. Hawkins, A.G. Sherratt and E.S. Sherratt, 'Troy in Recent Perspective', *Anatolian Studies*, Vol. 52 (2002), pp.75–109

192 'The great Trojan treasures': D.F. Easton, 'Priam's Gold: The Full Story', *Anatolian Studies*, Vol. 44 (1994), pp.221–43

192 'The silver and gold': Christoph Bachhuber, 'The Treasure Deposits of Troy: Rethinking Crisis and Agency on the Early Bronze Age Citadel', *Anatolian Studies*, Vol. 59 (2009), pp.1–18; Mikhail Treister, 'The Trojan Treasures: Description, Chronology, Historical Context', in Vladimir Tolstikov and Mikhail Treister, eds, *The Gold of Troy*, 1996, pp.225–9

192 'from the very beginning': Susan Heuck Allen, 'A Personal Sacrifice in the Interest of Science: Calvert, Schliemann, and the Troy Treasures', *The Classical World*, Vol. 91, No. 5, The World of Troy (May–Jun. 1998), pp.345–54

192 'the ruins and red': Meyer, 'Schliemann's Letters to Max Müller in Oxford'

193 'three different sets': D.F. Easton, 'Heinrich Schliemann: Hero or Fraud?', *The Classical World*, Vol. 91, No. 5, The World of Troy (May–Jun. 1998), pp.335–43

193 'Schliemann's suggestion': J.B. Carter and S.P. Morris, eds, *The Ages of Homer: A Tribute to E. Townsend Vermeule*, p.5. Burkert: 'The Greeks knew no date for the Trojan war. This makes modern attempts to match ancient Greek dates with archaeological remains an exercise in illusion.'

194 'The Boston treasure': MFI Boston, Inv 68116–68139, Centennial Gift of Landon T. Clay. The museum bought it in 1968 from George Zacos, a Greek dealer in antiquities, based in Basel, who could not say where he had got it. It may have been looted from an otherwise unknown tomb in Turkey.

194 'four Trojan hammer-axes': James C. Wright, 'The Place of Troy Among the Civilizations of the Bronze Age', *The Classical World*, Vol. 91, No. 5, The World of Troy (May–Jun. 1998), pp.356–68

195 'stolen by Schliemann': Susan Heuck Allen, 'A Personal Sacrifice in the Interest of Science'

195 'his son Agamemnon': He became a member of the Greek Chamber of Deputies, and briefly the Greek Minister in Washington, DC

195 'a linen fabric': Elizabeth Wayland Butler, *Women's Work: The First 20,000 Years: Women, Cloth and Society in Early Times*, Norton, 1994, p.212

195 'tiny gold beads': Ibid., p.213

196 'a great cloth': *Iliad* 3.125ff . The word for cloth can mean 'web', 'loom-beam', or even 'mast'.

196 'shimmering linen': *Iliad* 3.140

197 'Come over here': *Iliad* 3.161–5 (Lattimore)

197 'The queen herself': *Iliad* 6.287–95 (Murray/Wyatt, slightly adapted)

197 'women and womanliness': See *Iliad* 16.100, where the Greek warriors refer to the battlements of Troy as its 'veil'

197 'A woman and a tripod': *Iliad* 23.262–4

197 'twelve oxen and': *Iliad* 23.702–5

197 'prepares herself for': *Iliad* 14.165ff

198 'the whispered words': *Iliad* 14.217

198 'He went down': *Iliad* 2.870

199 'kill Trojan babies': *Iliad* 6.57–60

199 'Zeus accused Hera': *Iliad* 4.35

199 'Idomeneus stabbed': *Iliad* 16.345–50 (Lattimore, adapted)

199 'like wolves': *Iliad* 16.156–62 (Lattimore, adapted)

200 'Patroclus, you thought': *Iliad* 16.830–7 (Lattimore, adapted)

200 'soaked and clotted': *Iliad* 17.51

200 'mauling the kill': *Iliad* 17.64

200 'and give the rest': *Iliad* 17.125–7, 241

200 'He promises': *Iliad* 17.241

200 'the straps of his shield': *Iliad* 17.290

200 'oozed out from': *Iliad* 17.297–8

200 'under the collarbone': *Iliad* 17.309

200 'so that he clawed': *Iliad* 17.315

200 'in the liver': *Iliad* 17.349

201 'with so many': *Iliad* 17.393–7 (Lattimore, adapted)

201 'as on some lion': *Iliad* 17.540–2

201 'who though it is': *Iliad* 17.571–2 (Lattimore, adapted)

201 'a tawny lion': *Iliad* 18.162

201 'cut the head': *Iliad* 18.177 (Lattimore)

201 'he pops out death': *Iliad* 20.386ff

202 'He dragged them': *Iliad* 21.29–32, Fagles 21.33–8

202 'an unlooked for evil': *Iliad* 21.39

202 'Now there is not': *Iliad* 21.103–9 (Lattimore, slightly adapted)

202 'Die on': *Iliad* 21.128–9 (Lattimore, slightly adapted)

202 'I will not leave off': *Iliad* 21.225

202 'The aged Priam': *Iliad* 21.525ff

203 'fierce with the': *Iliad* 21.540

203 'shackled by destiny': *Iliad* 22.5

203 'Come into the': *Iliad* 22.56–7 (Lattimore, slightly adapted)

204 'I have looked upon': *Iliad* 22.61–76 (Lattimore)

204 'Sweet branch': *Iliad* 22.87, 82

204 'like a dream': *Iliad* 22.199

204 'and forces him': *Iliad* 22.198

205 'to hack your meat': *Iliad* 22.347–8 (Lattimore)

205 'and clean out': *Iliad* 22.327

205 'gasping the life': *Iliad* 22.440

206 'All of these': *Iliad* 22.510

206 'robes, mantles, blankets': *Iliad* 24.228, 580

206 'kisses his hands': *Iliad* 24.478ff

207 'Priam wept freely': *Iliad* 24.509–12, Fagles 24.594–9

207 'They reached out': *Iliad* 24.628–32, Fagles 24.738–44

Chapter 11: Homer's Mirror

208 'the Egyptian city of Thebes': A place, incidentally, known to Achilles for its riches: *Iliad* 9.381–4

209 'Sinuhe's story': R.B. Parkinson, ed. and trans., *The Tale of Sinuhe and Other Egyptian Poems 1940–1640 BC*, Oxford University Press, 1997 (2009), p.1

209 'Be a scribe': Quoted Barry Kemp, *Ancient Egypt: Anatomy of a Civilisation*, Routledge, 2007, p.163

209 'Peace had prevailed': Ibid., p.62

210 'It is Indo-European': Carleton T. Hodge, 'Indo-Europeans in the Near East', *Anthropological Linguistics*, Vol. 35, No. 1/4, *A Retrospective of the Journal Anthropological Linguistics: Selected Papers, 1959–1985* (1993), pp.90–108

212 'the enduring security': Kemp, *Ancient Egypt*, p.24

212 'I was appointed': Parkinson, *Sinuhe*, p.42

213 'It is his majesty': Ibid., p.43

214 '*Timē* and *Aretē*': See Margalit Finkelberg, '*Timē* and *Aretē* in Homer', *Classical Quarterly*, New Series, Vol. 48, No. 1 (1998), pp.14–28 for a long and elegant discussion of this core Homeric tension.

214 'The bath . . . is always': J.M. Cook, 'Bath-Tubs in Ancient Greece', *Greece and Rome*, Second Series, Vol. 6, No. 1 (Mar. 1959), pp.31–41; Steve Reece, 'The Homeric *asaminthos*: Stirring the Waters of the Mycenaean Bath', *Mnemosyne*, Fourth Series, Vol. 55, Fasc. 6 (2002), pp.703–8

215 'washing his long hair': Gilgamesh Epic 11: 239–55, trans. A. Heidel, *The Gilgamesh Epic and Old Testament Parallels*, Chicago, 1949, p.90

215 'When Jacob returns': Gary A. Rendsburg, 'Notes on Genesis XXXV', *Vetus Testamentum*, Vol. 34, Fasc. 3 (Jul. 1984), pp.361-6

215 'wash yourselves': Genesis 35.2

215 'brought in the water': *Odyssey* 10.357–67

216 'mind wandering': *Odyssey* 10.374

216 'The Hittites were': See Mallory and Adams, *The Oxford Introduction to Proto-Indo-European and the Proto-Indo-European World*

217 'in the city of Urikina': Gary Beckman, ed., *Hittite Diplomatic Texts*, 2nd edn, SBL Writings from the Ancient World series, Society of Biblical Literature, 1999, p.113

217-18 'never suffer strangers': *Odyssey* 7.32

218 '*ptoliporthos Odysseus*': *Odyssey* 8.3

218 '*prēktēres*': *Odyssey* 8.162

218 'Where do you': *Odyssey* 9.252–4

218 'much-wandering pirates': *Odyssey* 17.425

218 'There I destroyed': *Odyssey* 9.39–42

219 'In about 1350 BC': Beckman, *Hittite Diplomatic Texts*, p.26

220 'Given that they': Ibid., p.31

220 'Furthermore this sister': Ibid., p.32

221 'And for what reason': Ibid.

221 'If the King': Ibid., p.106

221 'it is now generally accepted': Hans G. Güterbock, 'Hittites and Akhaeans: A New Look', *Proceedings of the American Philosophical Society*, Vol. 128, No. 2 (Jun. 1984), pp.114–22

222 'The father of': Beckman, *Hittite Diplomatic Texts*, p.154

222 'the untrembling': M.L. West, 'Atreus and Attarissiyas', *Glotta*, 77. Bd., 3./4. H. (2001), pp.262–6

222 'A letter also survived': Adrian Kelly, 'Homer and History: "Iliad" 9.381–4', *Mnemosyne*, Fourth Series, Vol. 59, Fasc. 3 (2006), pp.321–33

223 'Hittite scholars': Güterbock, 'Hittites and Akhaeans'

223 'If rumours circulate': Beckman, *Hittite Diplomatic Texts*, p.90

224 'it is clear': T. Dothan, *The Philistines and Their Material Culture*, 1982; T. Dothan and M. Dothan, *People of the Sea: The Search for the Philistines*, 1992; L.E. Stager, 'The Impact of the Sea Peoples in Canaan (1185–1050 BCE)', in T.E. Levy, ed., *The Archaeology of Society in the Holy Land*, 1995, pp.332–48; Seymour Gitin, Amihai Mazar and Ephraim Stern, eds, *Mediterranean Peoples in Transition, Thirteenth to Early Tenth Centuries B.C.E.*, Jerusalem: Israel Exploration Society, 1998

224 'at its symbolic climax': The David and Goliath story is in 1 Samuel, Chapter 17. For a brilliant discussion of it see Azzan Yadin, 'Goliath's Armor and Israelite Collective Memory', *Vetus Testamentum*, Vol. 54, Fasc. 3 (Jul. 2004), pp.373–95

224 'six feet nine inches tall': See J. Daniel Hays, 'Reconsidering the Height of Goliath', *Journal of the Evangelical Theological Society*, Vol. 48, No. 4 (Dec. 2005), pp.701–14. In the Septuagint manuscripts and in the Dead Sea Scrolls, Goliath's height is given as 'four cubits and a span', which is six feet nine inches. Later versions make it six cubits and a span, which is nine feet nine inches. The average height of Semites in the ancient Near East was about five feet. One warrior in the Shaft Graves at Mycenae has been measured at five feet five inches. See A.J.N.W. Prag, Lena Papazoglou-Manioudaki, R.A.H. Neave, Denise Smith, J.H. Musgrave and A. Nafplioti, 'Mycenae Revisited: Part 1. The Human Remains from a Grave Circle', *Annual of the British School at Athens*, Vol. 104 (2009), pp.233–77.

224 'Why do you': 1 Samuel 17.8–10 (NEB)

225 'Shouted aggression': For the continuing emotional power of the battle shout, in attack or mourning, see the New Zealanders grieving the death of their companions in Afghanistan http://www.nzherald.co.nz/nz/news/article. cfm?c_id=1&objectid=10829992.

225 'Morning and evening': 1 Samuel 17.16 (NEB/KJB)

225 'I cannot go': 1 Samuel 17.39–40 (NEB/KJB/AN)

226 'And the Philistine came on': 1 Samuel 17.42–4 (NEB/KJB/AN)

226 'and all the world': 1 Samuel 17.46–7 (NEB)

226 'And David put': 1 Samuel 17.49 (KJB)

Chapter 12: Homer's Odyssey

228 'tossing backwards and forwards': *Odyssey* 20.25

229 'at which any': *Odyssey* 5.72–3

229 'but was called Thapsos': For Thapsos in the Bronze Age see Anthony Russell, *In the Middle of the Corrupting Sea: Cultural Encounters in Sicily and Sardinia Between 1450–900 BC,* 2011 PhD thesis, University of Glasgow, online at http://theses.gla.ac.uk/2670/; David Abulafia, *The Great Sea: A Human History of the Mediterranean,* Oxford University Press, 2011, pp.34–5

230 'at a loss': P. Leigh Fermor, Letters to D. Devonshire; Diodorus Siculus, *Library of History,* 5.3.2, online at http://penelope.uchicago.edu/Thayer/E/Roman/Texts/Diodorus_Siculus/5A*.html

231 'swooping down': Odyssey 5.50–3 (combination of Fagles, Lattimore and AN)

231 'Hermes does everything': Mary W. Helms, *Ulysses' Sail: An Ethnographic Odyssey of Power, Knowledge and Geographical Distance,* Princeton University Press, 1988, pp.111ff

232 'the axis always fixed': *Odyssey* 5.274

233 'reaching towards him': *Odyssey* 5.281

234 'death's decision': *Odyssey* 5.326

235 'Seabirds are too beautifully present': For birds in Homer see J. MacLair Boraston, 'The Birds of Homer', *Journal of Hellenic Studies,* Vol. 31 (1911), pp.216–50; Sylvia Benton, 'Note on Sea-Birds', *Journal of Hellenic Studies,* Vol. 92 (1972), pp.172–3; Paul Friedrich, 'An Avian and Aphrodisian Reading of Homer's *Odyssey*', *American Anthropologist,* New Series, Vol. 99, No. 2 (Jun. 1997), pp.306–20

236 'like a diving tern' *Odyssey* 5.353

236 'The earth-shaker': *Odyssey* 5.367

236 'Just like the kind': *Odyssey* 5.394–9

237 'Spent to all use': George Chapman's translation of *Odyssey* 5.454–5

238 'heartsick on the open sea': *Odyssey* 1.4

238 'her surpassingly beautiful': *Odyssey* 10.347

239 'His story held them': *Odyssey* 11.334, Fagles 11.379

240 'Many were the people': *Odyssey* 1.3

240 'for his return': *Odyssey* 1.13

240 'the fascinating imaginative realm': Quoted by Richard Rorty in 'Trotsky and the Wild Orchids' (1992), from *Philosophy and Social Hope,* 1999

241 'rocky Ithaca': *Odyssey* 21.346

241 'the kind of island': This point, in connection with the Iron Age, is made by Helen Waterhouse in 'From Ithaca to the *Odyssey*', *Annual of the British School at Athens*, Vol. 91 (1996), pp.301–17

241 'bends to kiss': *Odyssey* 13.354

241 'an Assyrian relief': See e.g. Julian Reade, *Assyrian Sculpture*, 1983, 1998, fig. 57, p.54

242 'there is nothing sweeter': *Odyssey* 9.28

242 'She withered': *Odyssey* 9.28

242 'Knossos, where Minos reigned': *Odyssey* 19.172–8

243 'When she appears': *Odyssey* 16.415 for Penelope standing by column; 20.42 for her shining among women

243 'Artemis and Aphrodite': *Odyssey* 17.37, 19.54

243 'the nightingale': *Odyssey* 19.518–24 (Murray/Dimock, adapted)

244 'Like all the great women in Homer': Penelope with well-balanced mind *Odyssey* 18.249; weeping 19.209; weaving 17.97, 19.128; with cloths 19.232, 255; and veil 20.65

244 'a queen regnant': Penelope as governor 19.106ff

244 'grow in goodness': *Odyssey* 19.114

244 'Just as a bitch': *Odyssey* 20.14–16 (Murray/Dimock, adapted)

245 'swimming in blood': *Odyssey* 22.307

245 'are repeated here': *Odyssey* 22.325

245 'like a lion': *Odyssey* 22.401–3 (Murray/Dimock, adapted)

245 'He found them': *Odyssey* 22.383–8 (Murray/Dimock, adapted)

245 'They led him out': *Odyssey* 22.474–7 (Murray/Dimock)

246 'the cable of': *Odyssey* 22.465

246 'Just as when': *Odyssey* 22.468–73 (Murray/Dimock, adapted)

247 'the well-built bridal chamber': *Odyssey* 23.178

247 'her knees were loosened': *Odyssey* 23.205–8 (Murray/Dimock)

247 'As when the land': *Odyssey* 23.233–40

Conclusion: The Bright Wake

249 'spirit of cruelty': Note to *Iliad* 4.75 in his translation; see, for this and the following valuable references to Blake and Barlow, Michael Ferber, 'Shelley and "The Disastrous Fame of Conquerors"', *Keats-Shelley Journal*, Vol. 51 (2002), pp.145–73

249 'Blake blamed Homer': David V. Erdman, ed., *The Complete Poetry and Prose of William Blake*, revised edn, Berkeley: University of California Press, 1982, p.270

249 'but he has given': From David B. Davis, ed., *Advice to the Privileged Orders in the Several States of Europe*, in a chapter on 'The Military System', Ithaca: Cornell University Press, 1956, p.39

250 'There are certain ages': Susan Sontag, 'Simone Weil, *Selected Essays*, translated by Richard Rees', *New York Review of Books* (1 Feb. 1963)

251 'Nietzsche, at his worst': Richard Rorty, 'Against Belatedness', *London Review of Books*, Vol. 5, No. 11 (Jun. 1983), pp.3–5, a review of *The Legitimacy of the Modern Age* by Hans Blumenberg, trans. Robert Wallace, 1983

251 'praised Homer's *enargeia*': Alice Oswald, *Memorial: An Excavation of the Iliad*, 2011, p.1

251 'a telling out': See Heinrich F. Plett, Enargeia in *Classical Antiquity and the Early Modern Age: The Aesthetics of Evidence*, 2012, p.27

Bibliography

Greek texts

The Iliad, with parallel translation by A.T. Murray, Loeb/Harvard University Press, 1925

The Iliad, with parallel translation by W.F. Wyatt, Loeb/Harvard University Press 1999

The Odyssey, with parallel translation by A.T. Murray, revised by G.E. Dimock, Loeb/Harvard University Press, 1999

Hesiod, Homeric Hymns, Epic Cycle, Homerica, with parallel translation by H.G. Evelyn-White, Loeb/Harvard University Press, 1914

Lives of Homer, in *Homeric Hymns etc.*, with parallel translation by M.L. West, Loeb/Harvard University Press, 2003

Translations

Chapman's Homer: The Iliad, ed. Allardyce Nicoll, Princeton University Press, 1956

Alexander Pope, *The Iliad*, 1715–20

Alexander Pope, with W. Broome and E. Fenton, *The Odyssey*, 1726

T.E. Shaw, *The Odyssey*, London, 1932

Homer, *The Odyssey*, translated by E.V. Rieu, revised by D.C.H. Rieu, London, 1946

Richmond Lattimore, *The Iliad of Homer*, Chicago, 1951

Richmond Lattimore, *The Odyssey*, New York, 1967

Homer, *The Iliad*, trans. Robert Fagles, New York, 1990

Homer, *The Odyssey*, trans. Robert Fagles, 1996

Adaptations

Christopher Logue, *War Music*, 2001

Alice Oswald, *Memorial: An Excavation of the* Iliad, 2011

On the date of Homer

Sir Moses Finley, *The World of Odysseus*, London, 1954

Ian Morris, 'The Use and Abuse of Homer', *Classical Antiquity*, Vol. 5, No. 1 (Apr. 1986), pp.81–138

Gregory Nagy, *Homeric Questions*, 1996

Susan Sherratt, 'Archaeological Contexts', in John Miles Foley, ed., *A Companion to Ancient Epic*, Blackwell, 2005, pp.119–42

John Miles Foley, ed., *A Companion to Ancient Epic*, Blackwell, 2005

The Pylos fresco

Carl W. Blegen, 'The Palace of Nestor Excavations of 1955', *American Journal of Archaeology*, Vol. 60, No. 2 (Apr. 1956), pp.95–101

Mabel L. Lang, in *The Palace of Nestor at Pylos in Western Messenia, Vol. II: The Frescoes*, Princeton University Press, 1969

Emily Vermeule's review of Lang in *The Art Bulletin*, Vol. 52, No. 4 (Dec. 1970), pp.428–30

Casey Dué, '*Epea Pteroenta*: How We Came to Have our *Iliad*', in Casey Dué, ed., *Recapturing a Homeric Legacy: Images and Insights From the Venetus A Manuscript of the* Iliad, Center for Hellenic Studies, Washington, 2009, pp.19–30

Seferis

George Seferis, *Complete Poems*, trans. and ed. E. Keeley and P. Sherrard, 1995 (2009)

Anthropology of Homer

Carol Dougherty, *The Raft of Odysseus: The Ethnographic Imagination of Homer's Odyssey*, Oxford, 2001

Mary W. Helms, *Ulysses' Sail: An Ethnographic Odyssey of Power, Knowledge and Geographical Distance*, Princeton University Press, 1988

Criticism and reception

Matthew Arnold, *On Translating Homer: Three Lectures Given at Oxford*, Longman, Green, Longman, Roberts, 1861, online at http://www.victorian-prose.org/

Kenneth Rexroth, *Classics Revisited*, 1968

Robert Baldick, ed. and trans., *The Goncourt Journals by Edmond and Jules de Goncourt*, New York Review of Books, 1962 (2007)

Nicholas Boyle, *Goethe: Revolution and Renunciation 1790–1803*, Oxford University Press, 2003, p.265

Matthew Reynolds, *The Poetry of Translation: From Chaucer and Petrarch to Homer and Logue*, 2011

Samuel Johnson, 'Life of Pope' (1779), in *The Works of the English Poets, from Chaucer to Cowper*, J. Johnson, 1810, Vol. 12, p.112

Penelope Murray and T. Dorsch, *Classical Literary Criticism: Plato:* Ion; Republic 2–3, 1; *Aristotle:* Poetics; *Horace:* The Art of Poetry; *Longinus:* On the Sublime, 2000, p.1

Rodelle Weintraub and Stanley Weintraub, 'Chapman's Homer', *The Classical World*, Vol. 67, No. 1 (Sep.–Oct. 1973), pp.16–24 [an article on T.E. Lawrence]

Keats

Andrew Motion, *Keats*, London, 1997

Charles Cowden Clarke, 'Recollections of Keats' (1861), in *Recollections of Writers*, 1878, pp.120–57

Andrew Laing, *The English Poets: Selections with Critical Introductions*, ed. Thomas Humphry Ward, 1880, Vol. 1, p.510

S.T. Coleridge, 'Notes on Chapman's Homer', in *Notes and Lectures Upon Shakespeare and Some of the Old Poets and Dramatists: With Other Literary Remains of S.T. Coleridge*, Vol. 2, p.231

J.P. Mallory and D.Q. Adams, *The Oxford Introduction to Proto-Indo-European and the Proto-Indo-European World* (Oxford Linguistics), 2006, p.136

J.G. Lockhart, 'On the Cockney School of Poetry, No. V', *Blackwood's Edinburgh Magazine* (Apr. 1819)

Transmission of the text

Joh. Baptista Caspar d'Ansse de Villoison, *Homeri Ilias ad Veteris Codicis Veneti Fidem Recensita*, 1788

Robert Southey, ed., *The Works of William Cowper*, 1836, Vol. VI, p.266

Nicholas Boyle, *Goethe: Revolution and Renunciation 1790–1803*, Oxford University Press, 2003, p.265

Thomas de Quincey, 'Homer and the Homeridae', *Blackwood's Edinburgh Magazine*, No. 312 (Oct. 1841), pp.411–27

Dante, *Inferno*

L. Labowsky, *Bessarion's Library and the Biblioteca Marciana – Six Early Inventories*, Rome, 1979

William M. Flinders Petrie, *Hawara, Biahmu, and Arsinoe*, London, 1889

Graeme Bird, 'Critical Signs – Drawing Attention to "Special" Lines of Homer's *Iliad* in the Manuscript Venetus A', in Casey Dué, ed, *Recapturing a Homeric Legacy: Images and Insights From the Venetus A Manuscript of the* Iliad, Center for Hellenic Studies, Harvard, 2009, pp.112–14

Richard P. Martin, 'Cretan Homers: Tradition, Politics, Fieldwork', *Classics@* 3, Center for Hellenic Studies, Washington, DC, 2012

Ideas of Homer

S. Butler, *The Authoress of the Odyssey*, 2nd edn, 1922, p.142

David Garnett, ed., *The Letters of T.E. Lawrence*, London, 1938

Felice Vinci, *Omero nel Baltico*, with introductions by R. Calzecchi Onesti and F. Cuomo, Rome, 1998

Florence and Kenneth Wood, *Homer's Secret* Iliad: *The Epic of the Night Skies Decoded*, 1999

Iman Wilkens, *Where Troy Once Stood*, 2nd edn, 2009

Théophile Cailleux, *Pays atlantiques décrits par Homère. Ibérie, Gaule, Bretagne, Archipels, Amérique*, Paris, 1878 and *Théorie nouvelle sur les origines humaines. Homère en Occident. Troie en Angleterre*, Bruxelles, 1883

Henriette Mertz, *The Wine Dark Sea: Homer's Heroic Epic of the North Atlantic*, 1964

M.L. West, ed. and trans., 'Lives of Homer', in *Homeric Hymns etc.*, Harvard University Press, 2003

M.L. West, *The East Face of Helicon*, Oxford, 1999

J. Black, 'Some Structural Features of Sumerian Narrative Poetry', in M.E. Vogelzang and H.L.J. Vanstiphout, eds, *Mesopotamian Epic Literature: Oral or Aural?*, Lampeter, 1992, pp.71–101

M.L. West, *The Making of the* Iliad: *Disquisition and Analytical Commentary*, Oxford, 2011

M. van der Valk, ed., *Commentarii AD Homeri Iliadem Pertinentes AD Fidem Codicis Laurentiani Editi*, 4 vols, 1971–87

Emporio and Pithekoussai

John Boardman, *Excavations in Chios 1952–1955: Greek Emporio*, The British School at Athens. Supplementary Volumes, No. 6 (1967), pp.iii–xiv

Giorgio Buchner, 'Recent Work at Pithekoussai (Ischia), 1965–71', *Archaeological Reports*, No. 17 (1970–71), pp.63–7

D. Ridgway, *The First Western Greeks*, Cambridge, 1992

G. Buchner and D. Ridgway, *Pithekoussai, La necropoli: Tombe 1–723. Scavate dal 1952 al 1961*, Rome: Accademia Nazionale dei Lincei, 1993

Catherine Connors, 'Monkey Business: Imitation, Authenticity, and Identity from Pithekoussai to Plautus', *Classical Antiquity*, Vol. 23, No. 2 (Oct. 2004), pp.179–207

John K. Papadopoulos and Deborah Ruscillo, 'A Ketos in Early Athens: An Archaeology of Whales and Sea Monsters in the Greek World', *American Journal of Archaeology*, Vol. 106, No. 2 (Apr. 2002), pp.187–227

Kate Monk, *Onomastikon*, 1997. http://tekeli.li/onomastikon/Ancient-World/Greece/Male.html

B. Powell, 'The Dipylon Oinochoe Inscription and the Spread of Literacy in 8th Century Athens', *Kadmos*, Vol. 27 (1988), pp.65–86

M.L. West, 'Grated Cheese Fit for Heroes', *Journal of Hellenic Studies*, Vol. 118 (1998), pp.190–1

D. Ridgway, 'Nestor's Cup and the Etruscans', *Oxford Journal of Archaeology*, Vol. 16 (1997), pp.325–44

Christopher A. Faraone, 'Taking the "Nestor's Cup Inscription" Seriously: Erotic Magic and Conditional Curses in the Earliest Inscribed Hexameters', *Classical Antiquity*, Vol. 15, No. 1 (Apr. 1996), pp.77–112

Milman Parry and the oral Homer

M.S. Edmondson, *Lore: An Introduction to the Science of Folklore and Literature*, New York, 1971, p.323

R. Bentley, *Remarks Upon a Late Discourse of Free Thinking*, London, 1713

William C. Greene, 'Milman Parry (1902–1935)', *Proceedings of the American Academy of Arts and Sciences*, Vol. 71, No. 10 (Mar. 1937), pp.535–6

Albert Lord, *The Singer of Tales*, Vol. 1, 2000

Harry Levin, 'Portrait of a Homeric Scholar', *Classical Journal*, Vol. 32, No. 5 (Feb. 1937), pp.259–66

Renan's essay on 'L'Avenir de Science', Paris, 1892, 292, quoted in Adam Parry, *The Making of Homeric Verse: The Collected Papers of Milman Parry*, Oxford University Press, 1987

Adam Parry, *The Making of Homeric Verse: The Collected Papers of Milman Parry*, Oxford University Press, 1987

James I. Porter, 'Homer: The Very Idea', *Arion*, 3rd Series, Vol. 10, No. 2 (Fall 2002), pp.57–86

Steve Reece, 'Some Homeric Etymologies in the Light of Oral-Formulaic Theory', *The Classical World*, Vol. 93, No. 2, Homer (Nov.–Dec. 1999), pp.185–99

M.M. Kumpf, *Four Indices of the Homeric Hapax Legomena*, Hildesheim, 1984

M.W. Edwards, *The Iliad: A Commentary*, Vol. 5, Cambridge, 1991

T.S. Eliot, *Selected Essays*, 3rd edn, 1999

Halil Bajgori, 'The Wedding of Mustajbey's Son Bećirbey', Parry no. 6699: www.oraltradition.org/static/zbm/zbm.pdf

Harry Levin, 'Portrait of a Homeric Scholar', *Classical Journal*, Vol. 32, No. 5 (Feb. 1937), pp.259–66

An eEdition of 'The Wedding of Mustajbey's Son Bećirbey', as performed by Halil Bajgorić, ed. and trans. John Miles Foley, on www.oraltradition.org

John Miles Foley, *Traditional Oral Epic: The Odyssey, Beowulf, and the Serbo-Croatian Return Song*, University of California Press, 1993

Richard Janko, 'The Homeric Poems as Oral Dictated Texts', *Classical Quarterly*, New Series, Vol. 48, No. 1 (1998), pp.1–13

Albert Lord, *The Singer of Tales*, Harvard, 1960

James A. Notopoulos, 'The Genesis of an Oral Heroic Poem', *Greek, Roman and Byzantine Studies*, Vol. 3 (1960), pp.135–44

Maartje Draak, 'Duncan MacDonald of South Uist', *Fabula*, Vol. 1 (1957), pp.47–58; William Lamb, 'The Storyteller, the Scribe, and a Missing Man: Hidden Influences from Printed Sources in the Gaelic Tales of Duncan and Neil MacDonald', *Oral Tradition*, Vol. 27, No. 1 (2012), pp.109–60

The Calum Maclean Project, Department of Celtic and Scottish Studies, University of Edinburgh, http://www.calum-maclean-project.celtscot.ed.ac.uk/home/;http://calumimaclean.blogspot.co.uk/2013_02_01_archive.html

Douglas Young, 'Never Blotted a Line? Formula and Premeditation in Homer and Hesiod', *Arion*, Vol. 6, No. 3 (Autumn 1967), pp.279–324

Epic and memory

E.R. Lowry, Jr., '*Glaucus*, the *Leaves*, and the Heroic Boast of *Iliad* 6.146–21 1', in J.B. Carter and S.P Morris, *The Ages of Homer: A Tribute to E. Townsend Vermeule*, University of Austin Press, 1995 (1998), p.193

J.B. Carter and S.P Morris, *The Ages of Homer: A Tribute to E. Townsend Vermeule*, University of Austin Press, 1995 (1998)

Jonas Grethlein, 'Memory and Material Objects in the *Iliad* and the *Odyssey*', *Journal of Hellenic Studies*, Vol. 128 (2008), pp.27–51

C.W. Blegen and M. Rawson, *The Palace of Nestor at Pylos in Western Messenia, Vol. I: The Buildings and Their Contents*, Princeton, 1966

C.W. Blegen and K. Kourouniotis, 'Excavations of Pylos, 1939', *American Journal of Archaeology*, Vol. 43 (1939), p.569

Ione Mylonas Shear, 'Bellerophon Tablets from the Mycenaean World? A Tale of Seven Bronze Hinges', *Journal of Hellenic Studies*, Vol. 118 (1998), pp.187–9

Christoph Bachhuber, 'Aegean Interest on the Uluburun Ship', *American Journal of Archaeology*, Vol. 110, No. 3 (Jul. 2006), pp.345–63

T.R. Bryce, 'The Nature of Mycenaean Involvement in Western Anatolia', *Historia*, Vol. 38 (1989), pp.13–14

Rufus Bellamy, 'Bellerophon's Tablet', *Classical Journal*, Vol. 84 (1989), pp.289–307

Byron Harries, ' "Strange Meeting": Diomedes and Glaucus in *Iliad* 6', *Greece and Rome*, Vol. 40 (1993), pp.133–47

T.R. Bryce, 'Anatolian Scribes in Mycenaean Greece, *Historia*, Vol. 48 (1999), pp.257–64

Emily Townsend Vermeule, 'Jefferson and Homer', *Proceedings of the American Philosophical Society*, Vol. 137, No. 4, 250th Anniversary Issue (Dec. 1993), pp.689–703

M.L. West, 'The Rise of the Greek Epic', *Journal of Hellenic Studies*, Vol. 108 (1988), pp.151–72

Cathy Gere, *The Tomb of Agamemnon: Mycenae and the Search for a Hero*, London, 2006

Emily Vermeule, *Aspects of Death in Early Greek Art and Pottery*, University of California Press, 1979

Bronze and the mine

Bryan D. Hope, *A Curious Place: The Industrial History of Amlwch (1550–1950)*, Wrexham, 1994

B.W. Roberts, C.P. Thornton and V.C. Piggott, 'Development of Metallurgy in Eurasia', *Antiquity*, Vol. 83 (2009), pp.1012–22

Evgenii N. Chernykh, *Ancient Metallurgy in the USSR: The Early Metal Age*, trans. Sarah Wright, Cambridge University Press, 1992

Kristian Kristiansen and Thomas B. Larsson, *The Rise of Bronze Age Society: Travels, Transmissions and Transformations*, Cambridge University Press, 2005

Richard J. Harrison, *Symbols and Warriors: Images of the European Bronze Age*, Bristol: Western Academic and Specialist Press, 2004

A.P. Fitzpatrick, *The Amesbury Archer and the Boscombe Bowmen*, Salisbury: Trust for Wessex Archaeology Ltd, 2011

Pippa Bradley, 'Death Pits at Cliff End', *British Archaeology*, Vol. 131 (Jul.–Aug. 2013)

Stephen Oppenheimer, 'A Reanalysis of Multiple Prehistoric Immigrations to Britain and Ireland Aimed at Identifying Celtic Contributions', in B. Cunliffe and J.T. Koch, *Celtic from the West*, Oxbow, Oxford, 2010

Philip L. Kohl, *The Making of Bronze Age Eurasia*, Cambridge University Press, 2007

Seamus Heaney, *Death of a Naturalist*, London, 1966

E. Vermeule, *Aspects of Death in Early Greek Art and Poetry*, University of California Press, 1979

A. Schulten, *Fontes Hispaniae Antiquae*, Vol. 1, 1922

B. Rothenberg and A. Blanco-Freijeiro, 'Ancient Copper Mining and Smelting at Chinflón (Huelva, SW Spain)', *British Museum Occasional Paper*, 20 (1980), pp.41–62

Ben Roberts, 'Metallurgical Networks and Technological Choice: Understanding Early Metal in Western Europe', *World Archaeology*, Vol. 40, No. 3 (2008), pp.354–72

Anthony F. Harding, *European Societies in the Bronze Age*, Cambridge University Press, 2000

M.A. Courtney, 'Cornish Folk-Lore', Part III, *Folk-Lore Journal*, Vol. 5, No. 3 (1887), pp.177–220

James C. Baker, 'Echoes of Tommy Knockers in Bohemia, Oregon, Mines', *Western Folklore*, Vol. 30, No. 2 (Apr. 1971), pp.119–22

Georgius Agricola, *De Animantibus Subterraneis*, 1548

Ronald Finucane, *Appearances of the Dead*, Junction, 1982

Gaston Bachelard, *The Poetics of Space*, Beacon Press, 1958 (1994)

M. Eleanor Irwin, 'Odysseus's "Hyacinthine Hair" in Odyssey 6.231', *Phoenix*, Vol. 44, No. 3 (Autumn 1990), pp.205–18

The background on the steppe

J.P. Mallory, *In Search of the Indo-Europeans: Language, Archaeology and Myth*, London, 1989

N.G.L. Hammond, 'Tumulus-Burial in Albania, the Grave Circles of Mycenae, and the Indo-Europeans', *Annual of the British School at Athens*, Vol. 62 (1967), pp.77–105

R. Scott Smith and Stephen M. Trzaskoma, trans., *Apollodorus' Library and Hyginus' Fabulae: Two Handbooks of Greek Mythology*, Indianapolis: Hackett, 2007, *Fabula*, 95

Adam Parry, 'The Language of Achilles', *Transactions and Proceedings of the American Philological Association*, Vol. 87 (1956), pp.1–7

M.D. Reeve, 'The Language of Achilles', *Classical Quarterly*, New Series, Vol. 23, No. 2 (Nov. 1973), pp.193–5

Steve Nimis, 'The Language of Achilles: Construction vs. Representation', *The Classical World*, Vol. 79, No. 4 (Mar.–Apr. 1986), pp.217–25

W. Donlan, 'Duelling with Gifts in the *Iliad*: As the Audience Saw It', *Colby Quarterly*, Vol. 24 (1993), p.171

Dean Hammer, 'Achilles as Vagabond: The Culture of Autonomy in the "Iliad"', *The Classical World*, Vol. 90, No. 5 (May–Jun. 1997), pp.341–66

J.P. Mallory and D.Q. Adams, *The Oxford Introduction to Proto-Indo-European and the Proto-Indo-European World*, Oxford, 2006

Benjamin W. Fortson IV, *Indo-European Language and Culture: An Introduction*, 2nd edn, Chichester, 2010

David W. Anthony, *The Horse, the Wheel, and Language: How Bronze-Age Riders from the Eurasian Steppes Shaped the Modern World*, Princeton University Press, 2007

David Miles and Simon Palmer, 'White Horse Hill', *Current Archaeology*, Vol. 142 (1995), pp.372–8

M. Detienne and A.B. Werth, 'Athena and the Mastery of the Horse', *History of Religions*, Vol. 11, No. 2 (Nov. 1971), pp.161–84

Grace H. Macurdy, 'The Horse-Taming Trojans', *Classical Quarterly*, Vol. 17, No. 1 (Jan. 1923), pp.50–2

Simone Weil, *L'Iliade ou le poème de la force*. See Simone Weil and Rachel

Bespaloff, *War and the Iliad*, trans. Mary McCarthy, *New York Review of Books* (2005)

Edwin Muir, *One Foot in Eden*, 1956

D.Ya. Telegin and David W. Anthony, 'On the Yamna Culture', *Current Anthropology*, Vol. 28, No. 3 (Jun. 1987), pp.357–8

Katarzyna Slusarska, 'Funeral Rites of the Catacomb Community: 2800–1900 BC: Ritual, Thanatology and Geographical Origins', *Baltic-Pontic Studies*, Vol. 13 (2006), Poznań

M.L. West, 'The Rise of the Greek Epic', *Journal of Hellenic Studies*, Vol. 108 (1988), pp.151–72

The impact of the sail

Thomas F. Strasser et al., 'Stone Age Seafaring in the Mediterranean, Plakias Region for Lower Palaeolithic and Mesolithic Habitation of Crete', *Hesperia*, Vol. 79 (2010), pp.145–90

Cyprian Broodbank, *An Island Archaeology of the Early Cyclades*, Cambridge University Press, 2000

The gang and the city

C.B. Armstrong, 'The Casualty Lists in the Trojan War', *Greece and Rome*, Vol. 16, pp.30–1

Bruce A. Jacobs and Richard Wright, *Street Justice: Retaliation in the Criminal Underworld*, Cambridge University Press, Cambridge Studies in Criminology, 2006

Colton Simpson with Ann Pearlman, *Inside the Crips*, St Martin's Press, 2005

Martín Sánchez-Jankowski, *Islands in the Street: Gangs and American Urban Society*, University of California Press, 1991

D.F. Easton, J.D. Hawkins, A.G. Sherratt and E.S. Sherratt, 'Troy in Recent Perspective', *Anatolian Studies*, Vol 52 (2002), pp.75–109

D.F. Easton, 'Priam's Gold: The Full Story', *Anatolian Studies*, Vol. 44 (1994), pp.221–43

Christoph Bachhuber, 'The Treasure Deposits of Troy: Rethinking Crisis and Agency on the Early Bronze Age Citadel', *Anatolian Studies*, Vol. 59 (2009), pp.1–18; Mikhail Treister, 'The Trojan Treasures: Description, Chronology, Historical Context', in Vladimir Tolstikov and Mikhail Treister, eds, *The Gold of Troy*, 1996, pp.225–9

Susan Heuck Allen, 'A Personal Sacrifice in the Interest of Science: Calvert, Schliemann, and the Troy Treasures', *The Classical World*, Vol. 91, No. 5, The World of Troy (May–Jun. 1998), pp.345–54

E. Meyer, 'Schliemann's Letters to Max Müller in Oxford', *Journal of Hellenic Studies*, Vol. 82 (1962), pp.75–105

D.F. Easton, 'Heinrich Schliemann: Hero or Fraud?', *The Classical World*, Vol. 91, No. 5, The World of Troy (May–Jun. 1998), pp.335–43

J.B. Carter and S.P. Morris, *The Ages of Homer: A Tribute to E. Townsend Vermeule*, University of Austin Press, 1995 (1998)

James C. Wright, 'The Place of Troy Among the Civilizations of the Bronze Age', *The Classical World*, Vol. 91, No. 5, The World of Troy (May–Jun. 1998), pp.356–68

Elizabeth Wayland Butler, *Women's Work: The First 20,000 Years: Women, Cloth and Society in Early Times*, Norton, 1994

Tamara Neal, 'Blood and Hunger in the *Iliad*', *Classical Philology*, Vol. 101, No. 1 (Jan. 2006), pp.15–33

The view in the mirror

R.B. Parkinson, ed. and trans., *The Tale of Sinuhe and Other Egyptian Poems 1940–1640 BC*, Oxford University Press, 1997 (2009)

A.H. Gardiner, *Historic Papyri in the British Museum, Third Series Chester Beatty Gift*, London, 1935, p.41

Barry Kemp, *Ancient Egypt: Anatomy of a Civilisation*, Routledge, 2007, p.62

Carleton T. Hodge, 'Indo-Europeans in the Near East', *Anthropological Linguistics*, Vol. 35, No. 1/4, *A Retrospective of the Journal* Anthropological Linguistics: *Selected Papers, 1959–1985* (1993), pp.90–108

Margalit Finkelberg, '*Timē* and *Aretē* in Homer', *The Classical Quarterly*, New Series, Vol. 48, No. 1 (1998), pp.14–28

J.M. Cook, 'Bath-Tubs in Ancient Greece', *Greece and Rome*, 2nd Series, Vol. 6, No. 1 (Mar. 1959), pp.31–41

Steve Reece, 'The Homeric *Asaminthos*: Stirring the Waters of the Mycenaean Bath', *Mnemosyne*, 4th Series, Vol. 55, Fasc. 6 (2002), pp.703–8

Gilgamesh Epic XI: 239–55, trans. A Heidel, *The Gilgamesh Epic and Old Testament Parallels*, Chicago: 1949

J.P. Mallory and D.Q. Adams, *The Oxford Introduction to Proto-Indo-European and the Proto-Indo-European World (Oxford Linguistics)*, 2006

Gary Beckman, ed., *Hittite Diplomatic Texts*, 2nd edn, SBL Writings from the Ancient World series, Society of Biblical Literature, 1999

Hans G. Güterbock, 'Hittites and Akhaeans: A New Look', *Proceedings of the American Philosophical Society*, Vol. 128, No. 2 (Jun. 1984), pp.114–22

Martin L. West, 'Atreus and Attarissiyas', *Glotta*, 77. Bd., 3./4. H. (2001), pp.262–6

Adrian Kelly, 'Homer and History: "Iliad" 9.381–4', *Mnemosyne*, 4th Series, Vol. 59, Fasc. 3 (2006), pp.321–33

T. Dothan, *The Philistines and Their Material Culture*, 1982

T. Dothan and M. Dothan, *People of the Sea: The Search for the Philistines*, 1992

L.E. Stager, 'The Impact of the Sea Peoples in Canaan (1185–1050 BCE)', in T.E. Levy, ed., *The Archaeology of Society in the Holy Land*, 1995, pp.332–48

Seymour Gitin, Amihai Mazar, and Ephraim Stern, eds, *Mediterranean Peoples in Transition, Thirteenth to Early Tenth Centuries B.C.E.*, Jerusalem: Israel Exploration Society, 1998

Azzan Yadin, 'Goliath's Armor and Israelite Collective Memory', *Vetus Testamentum*, Vol. 54, Fasc. 3 (Jul. 2004), pp.373–95

J. Daniel Hays, 'Reconsidering the Height of Goliath', *Journal of the Evangelical Theological Society*, Vol. 48, No. 4 (Dec. 2005) pp.701–14

A.J.N.W. Prag, Lena Papazoglou-Manioudaki, R.A.H. Neave, Denise Smith, J.H.Musgrave and A. Nafplioti, 'Mycenae Revisited: Part 1. The Human Remains from a Grave Circle', *Annual of the British School at Athens*, Vol. 104 (2009), pp.233–77

Odysseus's journeys

Anthony Russell, *In the Middle of the Corrupting Sea: Cultural Encounters in Sicily and Sardinia Between 1450–900 BC.* 2011 PhD thesis, University of Glasgow, online at http://theses.gla.ac.uk/2670/

David Abulafia, *The Great Sea: A Human History of the Mediterranean*, Oxford University Press, 2011

Diodorus Siculus, *Library of History*, 5.3.2, online at http://penelope.uchicago.edu/Thayer/E/Roman/Texts/Diodorus_Siculus/5A*.html

Mary W. Helms, *Ulysses' Sail: An Ethnographic Odyssey of Power, Knowledge and Geographical Distance*, Princeton University Press, 1988

J. MacLair Boraston, 'The Birds of Homer', *Journal of Hellenic Studies*, Vol. 31 (1911), pp.216–50

Sylvia Benton, 'Note on Sea-Birds', *Journal of Hellenic Studies*, Vol. 92 (1972), pp.172–3

Paul Friedrich, 'An Avian and Aphrodisian Reading of Homer's *Odyssey*', *American Anthropologist*, New Series, Vol. 99, No. 2 (Jun. 1997), pp.306–20

Richard Rorty, 'Trotsky and the Wild Orchids' (1992), in *Philosophy and Social Hope*, 1999

Helen Waterhouse, 'From Ithaca to the *Odyssey*', *Annual of the British School at Athens*, Vol. 91 (1996), pp.301–17

Julian Reade, *Assyrian Sculpture*, 1983, 1998

Homer's meaning

Michael Ferber, 'Shelley and "The Disastrous Fame of Conquerors"', *Keats-Shelley Journal*, Vol. 51 (2002), pp.145–73

David V. Erdman, ed., *The Complete Poetry and Prose of William Blake*, revised edn, Berkeley: University of California Press, 1982

David B. Davis, ed., *Advice to the Privileged Orders in the Several States of Europe*, Ithaca: Cornell University Press, 1956

Susan Sontag, 'Simone Weil, *Selected Essays*, translated by Richard Rees', *New York Review of Books* (1 Feb. 1963)

Richard Rorty, 'Against Belatedness', *London Review of Books*, Vol. 5, No. 11 (16 Jun. 1983), pp.3–5

Alice Oswald, *Memorial: An Excavation of the* Iliad, 2011

Heinrich F. Plett, Enargeia *in Classical Antiquity and the Early Modern Age: The Aesthetics of Evidence*, 2012, p.27

Index

Page numbers in *italic* refer to illustrations

Aphrodite 67, 198, 243
Apollinaire, Guillaume 70
Apulia 62
Aramaeans 62
Arcadia 52
Arceisius 228
Ares 149, 201, 218
Argolid 48
Argolis, Gulf of xxii
Argos 46
Aristarchus 44
Aristotle 41, 46
   On Poets 49
   Rhetoric 77
Armenia 157
Arnold, Matthew 6–7
Artemis 243
Arthurian legends 114
Aryans 157
Ashnan 51
Asinē xxii
Assyria 241
Astyanax 127
Atē 183
Athene 97, 198, 229, 237
   cloth offering to 197
   and the death of Hector 205
   encourages violence 182
   formulaic phrases 74
   and horses 160–1
   and Odysseus's homecoming 241, 242, 246
   protects Odysseus 21, 126, 136–7
   and Telemachus's search for Odysseus 32
   temple in Emporio 57
Athens 41, 46, 48, 54–5, 59, 76, 106, 118
Athos, Mount 37
Atlantic Ocean 48, 128
Atreus 222
Attarissiya 222, 224
Attica 64
Auk (boat) 1–6, 233
Austria 115
Autolycus 228
Azores 48

Baal 120–3
Babylon 41
Bachelard, Gaston, *The Poetics of Space* 133
Bactria 157
Badajoz 134
Baghdad 183
Bagot, Rev. Walter 36
Bahrain 99, 156
Bajgorić, Halil 82–5
Balboa, Vasco Núñez de 24
Balkans 80–7, 117, 145
Baltic 47, 115, 157, 168
bards, hereditary 93
Barlow, Joel 249
Barra 95
Bašić, Ibrahim (Ibro) 85, 88–9
baths 214–16
Bavaria 115
beauty, male 136–7
Bellerophon 103–5
Benbecula 95
Bentley, Richard 69
Beowulf 57
Berkeley, University of California 71, 72
Berlin 208
Bernstorf 115
Beslan 246–7
Bible 3, 12, 45, 223–7
Biblioteca Marciana, Venice 37–8
Biblioteca Nazionale, Rome 48, 49
Bibliothèque Nationale, Paris 37
Bijelo Polje 81
birds 234–6, 246
Black Sea 46, 59, 102, 145, 148, 157, 161, 168–70, 192
Blackwood's Magazine 25
Blake, William 249
Blegen, Carl xix–xx, 28, 84, 100–1, 192, 195–6
Boardman, John 57–8
Bodleian Library, Oxford 37, 39
Bodrum 103, 118
Bogaskale 216
Bohemia 115, 217
Bosnia 82–3

Boston 118
Boston Museum of Fine Arts 194
Briseis 149–50, 151, 189
British Council 93
British Museum, London 208
British School, Athens 57
bronze 102, 114–15
Bronze Age xviii, 115–20
　　burial mounds 29, 156, 165–8
　　copper mining 131–2, 133
　　iron 100
　　lyres 138–9
　　population mobility 115–16
　　ships 115, 127–8
　　stone stelae 134–43
　　trade 115, 116
　　Troy's importance in 194
　　Ulu Burun wreck 102–3
　　warriors 117–20, 135–43
　　weapons 117–20, *118*, 128
Broodbank, Cyprian 175, 177
Buchner, Giorgio 62
Bulgaria 102
burials
　　Bronze Age 29, 156, 165–8
　　burial mounds 98–9
　　early Greek 144
　　Ischia 65
　　kurgans 157–8, 160, 165–8
　　Mycenaean Shaft Graves 106–12, 117, 144, 165, 193
　　Pithekoussai 62–3
　　rock-cut tombs 231
　　Sintashta 159–60
　　stone stelae 135–43
　　tumuli 168–70
Butler, Samuel 47
Byblos 62
Byzantium 35–6, 37–8, 40, 41, 192, 194

Calabria 62
Calliope 49–50
Calvert, Frank 195
Calypso 2, 5, 29, 32, 48, 61, 229, 230, 232, 234, 236
Cambridge 37

Cambridgeshire 48
Campania 62
Canaan 102, 215, 224
canoes 175
Caravaggio 227
Caribbean 48
Carlyle, Thomas 251
Carpathians 157
Carthage 62, 63
Caspian Sea 63, 117, 145, 157
Cassiopeia (constellation) 232–3
Castelluccio 194
Caucasus 116, 157, 168, 192
Cebriones 184–5
Celtologists 93–4
Chalcondyles, Demetrius 37
Chania 100
Chapman, George 19–24, 84
chariots 159–60, 161, 172–5
Charybdis 48, 228, 240
China 116, 152–3, 156
Chinflón 131–3
Chios 46, 48, 54–9, *58*, 76
Cicones 218
Circe 2, 34, 127–8, 129, 215–16, 238–9, 241
cities 116, 180–1, 190, 191–8, 202–7
Clare, County 156
Clarke, Charles Cowden 15, 16, 19–24, 25, 84
clay tablets 100–1, 216, 217
Cliffsend, Thanet 116
Clutorix 170
Clytemnestra 75, 214, 231
Coleridge, Samuel Taylor 19–20
Collins, Lieutenant-Colonel Tim 44–5
Columbus, Christopher 128
composition-in-performance 77–86, 94–5
Congreve, William 17
Constant, Benjamin 9
Constantinople 38, 192, 194
copper 114, 116, 129, 131–3, 165
Cordoba 128, 140
Corinth 63, 103–4
Cornwall 115, 128, 129, 132–3
Cortez, Hernando 24, 25
Courbet, Gustave, *Origine du Monde* 229

Cowper, William 36, 46
Crete 46, 113, 136, 194, 228
  baths 215
  clay tablets 100–1
  kidnapping of General Kreipe
    89–93
  Minoan civilisation 106, 175, 214,
    242–3
  Mycenaeans 221
  songs 89–90
Crusaders 194
cummings, e.e. 70
Cyclades 48, 49, 52, 175
Cyclops 27, 218, 219, 228
Cyprus 46, 102, 175, 222, 224, 230
Czech Republic 115

dactyls 73
Daedalus 173
dance 49
Dante 37, 69, 77
Danube, river 145, 157, 169, 192
Dardanelles 192
Dark Ages xxi
David, King of Israel 225–7
De Quincey, Thomas 36
death, Hades 124–8
  see also violence
Deïphobus 162, 163
Delos 46, 49
Delphi 48
Demodocus 163–4
Denmark 115, 165, 168
Devon 115
Diodorus Siculus 230
Diomedes 43, 97–8, 103, 188–9, 211, 245
Dolon 188–9, 245
Dörpfeld, Wilhelm 192
Dover 168
Dué, Casey 47
Duntulm 93
Durham, County 132
Düsseldorf 112

Easton, Donald 193
Edinburgh 118

Egypt 48, 92, 103, 106, 113, 129, 192, 241
  jewellery 102, 194
  in the *Odyssey* 228
  papyrus rolls 38–40
  pottery 63
  The Tale of Sinuhe 208–14
  trade 59, 175
El Pozuelo 131
Elba 62
Eliot, T.S. 70, 77
Elpenor 125
Emporio 57–9, *58*, 100
England 115, 116, 168
Enlightenment 20, 249
epic xix–xxi, 72–6, 170–1
Epirus 168
Epomeo, Mount 61
Escorial, Madrid 37, 48, 51
Eteocles 222
Etruria 62
Euboea 62, 66
Euphorbus 200
Eurasia
  burial mounds 99
  metalwork 114–15
  steppe culture 144–75
  warrior culture xviii, 117
Euripides 28
Eurycleia 13–14
Eustathius 54
Evans, Sir Arthur 100, 101, 242
Examiner 18
Extremadura 124, 133–5

Fagles, Robert 1–6, 22, 176, 185, 218
Fairhurst, George 1, 3–4
Faroe Islands 48
Fates 182
fatherhood/fatherland 182
Fayum depression 38
Fermor, Patrick Leigh 90–1
Finucane, Ronald 132
fish 27 and n., 184, 185–6
Florence 37, 48
food 27 and n., 153–4
formulaic verse 74–5, 78–9, 82, 86, 95

Fundy, Bay of 48
funerals 160

Galicia 116
Gamarrillas 140
gang culture 179–80, 187–91, 208
Gauguin, Paul 76
Gautier, Théophile 8
Gaza 224
Genesis 215
genetics 116
Geometric pottery 65
Germany 89–93, 115, 117, 132, 157, 165
ghosts 132–3, 239–40
Gibraltar, Straits of 127, 128
Gilgamesh 215, 216
Glaucus 97–8, 103–4, 139, 140
gods 155–6, 181, 239–40, 250
Goethe, Johann Wolfgang von 12
Gog Magog hills 48
gold 106–8, 111, 194
Goliath 224–7
Goncourt, Jules and Edmond de 8–12,
    14
Gorgythion 42
grain, winnowing 145–7, *146*
graves *see* burials
Greece
    Greek Renaissance xvii
    Homeric poems as foundation myth
        xviii–xix
    omission from *Iliad* 181–2
    origins of the Greeks 144–5, 147–60
Greek language 152, 171
Guadalquivir 128
guslari (singers) 80–7, 88–9

Hades 3, 29, 34, 124–30, 133, 145, 238–9
Hadrian, Emperor 48
hair 136–7
hammer-axes 194–5
Harris 29
Harrison, Richard 115, 134, 141–2
Harvard Homer multitext project 47
Hatti 216
Hattusa 216, 217, 222

Hawara papyrus 38–40, *40*, 41
Hayasa 219, 221
Heaney, Seamus 119–20
Hebrides 29, 87–8, 93–5
Hecabe 204
Hecamede 66
Hector 33, 100, 127, 149, 152, 167, 226
    compared to a horse 161
    death 111–12, 128, 138, 186, 203–7
    funeral 160
    hair 137
    hands 138
    isolation 142
    kills Patroclus 17, 200, 201
    returns to Troy 180
    speech to Trojans 42–4, 45
Heidelberg 37
Helen 149, 162, 174, 181, 189, 196–7, 205,
    250
Hell 125
helmets 100
Hephaestus 136, 173, 183
Hera 74, 170, 197–8, 199
Heracles 170, 239
Herakleion 90, 92
Hermes 2, 231–2, 238
Herodotus 193
heroes
    beauty 136–7
    fame 170–1
    formulaic phrases 72, 74–5
    isolation 142–3
    see also warriors
Herzegovina 85
hexameters 72–6
High Pasture Cave, Skye 139
Hippothoos 200
Hissarlik 195
Hitler, Adolf 92
Hittites 103, 216–17, 219–23
Homer
    Alexandrian editors 40–4, 45–7
    and Athens 54–5
    biographies of 48–50, 51–3
    blindness 50, 52
    dates of 105–6, 107–8

3	4	5	6
	14	15	16
	24	25	26	2
	34	35	36	3